Vg + in sl cfu vg du

£40

f8219

GERMAN OPERA

From the Beginnings to Wagner

German opera from its primitive origins up to Wagner is the subject of this wide-ranging history, the only one of its kind in any language. It traces the growth of the humble Singspiel into a vehicle for the genius of Mozart and Beethoven, together with the persistent attempts at German grand opera. Seventeenth-century Hamburg opera, the role of the travelling companies and Viennese Singspiel are all examined. Discussions that from early days absorbed Germans concerned for the development of a national art are explored, together with the influence of new critical thought at the start of the nineteenth century. The many operas studied are placed in their historical, social and theatrical context, and attention is paid to the literary, artistic and philosophical ideas that made them part of the country's intellectual history.

JOHN WARRACK has been the music critic of *The Sunday Telegraph* and Lecturer in Music at the University of Oxford. He is the author of *Carl Maria von Weber* (1968, 2nd edn 1976), *Wagner: Die Meistersinger von Nürnberg* (Cambridge Opera Handbook, 1994), and editor of *Carl Maria von Weber: Writings on Music* (1981), as well as co-author of *The Oxford Dictionary of Opera* (1992). He has lectured and published widely on German Romantic opera.

CAMBRIDGE STUDIES IN OPERA

Series Editor: Arthur Groos

Volumes for *Cambridge Studies in Opera* explore the cultural, political
and social influences of the genre. As a cultural art form, opera is not
produced in a vacuum. Rather, it is influenced, whether directly or in
more subtle ways, by its social and political environment. In turn, opera
leaves its mark on society and contributes to shaping the cultural
climate. Studies to be included in the series will look at these various
relationships including the politics and economics of opera, the operatic
representation of women or the singers who portrayed them, the
history of opera as theatre, and the evolution of the opera house.

Published titles

Opera Buffa in Mozart's Vienna
EDITED BY MARY HUNTER AND JAMES WEBSTER

Johann Strauss and Vienna: Operetta and the Politics of Popular Culture
CAMILLE CRITTENDEN

Die Zauberflöte, Finale, Act I. Sarastro's entrance: in the background the Temples of Wisdom, Reason, and Nature (Reproduced by permission of the Bildarchiv of the Österreichische Nationalbibliothek, Vienna)

German Opera

From the Beginnings to Wagner

John Warrack

CAMBRIDGE
UNIVERSITY PRESS

PUBLISHED BY THE PRESS SYNDICATE OF THE UNIVERSITY OF CAMBRIDGE
The Pitt Building, Trumpington Street, Cambridge, United Kingdom

CAMBRIDGE UNIVERSITY PRESS
The Edinburgh Building, Cambridge CB2 2RU, UK
40 West 20th Street, New York NY10011–4211, USA
10 Stamford Road, Oakleigh, VIC 3166, Australia
Ruiz de Alarcón 13, 28014 Madrid, Spain
Dock House, The Waterfront, Cape Town 8001, South Africa

http://www.cambridge.org

First published 2001

Printed in the United Kingdom at the University Press, Cambridge

Typeface Dante 10.75/14 pt   *System* 3b2   [CE]

A catalogue record for this book is available from the British Library

Library of Congress Cataloguing in Publication data
Warrack, John Hamilton, 1928–
German opera: from the beginnings to Wagner / by John Warrack.
    p.   cm.
Includes bibliographical references and indexes.
ISBN 0 521 23532 4 (hardback)
1. Opera – Germany. I. Title.
ML1729.W37 2001
792.1´0943 – dc21   00-062127

ISBN 0 521 23532 4

To my sons and stepdaughters

Simon and Nigel

Teresa and Em

Ben and Christoph

with love and gratitude

CONTENTS

ACKNOWLEDGEMENTS

I should like, first, to thank the Arts Council of Great Britain for financial support at the start of this enterprise, later the Leverhulme Foundation for an Emeritus Fellowship that enabled me to undertake essential travel and research in Germany. I am also grateful to the Oxford Faculty of Music, and St Hugh's and Exeter Colleges, Oxford, for much practical support and for allowing me periods of leave.

Libraries who provided me with hospitality and help include: the Abbey Library, Ampleforth; the Barber Music and Fine Art Library, Birmingham University; the Staatsbibliothek zu Berlin, Preußischer Kulturbesitz, Musikabteilung mit Mendelssohn-Archiv (former Deutsche Staatsbibliothek), Berlin; the Bibliothek des Musikwissenschaftliches Seminars, Detmold-Paderborn; the Sächsische Landesbibliothek, Dresden; the University Library, Durham; the Niedersächsische Staats- und Universitätsbibliothek, Göttingen; the British Library; The London Library; the Music Library, London University; the Bayerische Staatsbibliothek, Munich; the Music Department Library, Nottingham University; the Bodleian Library, Oxford; the Faculty of Music Library, Oxford; the Taylor Institution Library, Oxford; the Národni Muzeum, Hudebni Oddělení, Prague; the Österreichische Nationalbibliothek, Musiksammlung, Vienna. To the many librarians and their assistants and staff who made working in their libraries a pleasure, and who, as well as answering my queries and showing patience with all my importunities, often drew my attention to valuable sources and material I might otherwise have overlooked, I am profoundly grateful.

For placing their expert knowledge unstintingly at my disposal, for reading drafts of chapters, making suggestions and dealing patiently with my questions, I am especially grateful to Peter Alexander, Gerhard Allroggen, Eveline Bartlitz, Margaret Bent,

Peter Branscombe, Matthias Brzoska, David Cairns, David Charlton, David Criddle, Winton Dean, Denis Dyer, Michael Fend, Ludwig Finscher, Wolfgang Goldhan, Alison Gordon, Hans John, Karl-Heinz Köhler, Carolyn Martin, Antoinette Rogers, Michael Rose, Philip Smiley, Brian Trowell, Joachim Veit, John Wagstaff, Peter Ward-Jones, Helen Watanabe, Hans-Jürgen von Weber, Philip Weller, Ewan West and W. E. Yates. At Cambridge University Press, I acknowledge with thanks the help of Penny Souster and Victoria Cooper, and for their work on copy-editing Lucy Carolan and on the music examples Kathryn Puffett. My thanks are also due to Pauline Del Mar for her help with the Index. To my wife Lucy the debt is incalculable and beyond expressing. It goes without saying that while all these learned and kindly friends and colleagues have rescued me from error and misjudgement, as well as substantially improving the text, they are in no way responsible for remaining lapses.

Unless otherwise credited, all translations are mine.

JOHN WARRACK
Rievaulx, 2000

ABBREVIATIONS

AcM	*Acta musicologica* (from 1928/9)
AMw	*Archiv für Musikwissenschaft* (Leipzig and elsewhere, from 1918/19)
AMZ	*Allgemeine musikalische Zeitung* (Leipzig, 1798–1882)
Aurora	*Aurora* (Munich, 1804–5)
BMZ	*Berlinische musikalische Zeitung* (Berlin, 1805–6)
COJ	*Cambridge Opera Journal* (Cambridge, from 1989)
DTB	Denkmäler der Tonkunst in Bayern
DTÖ	Denkmäler der Tonkunst in Österreich
EDM	Das Erbe deutscher Musik
FétisB	*Biographie universelle des musiciens* (Brussels, 2/1860–5, suppl. 1878–80)
GS	*Richard Wagner: Gesammelte Schriften und Dichtungen* (Leipzig, 1871–3, 4/1907)
JAMS	*Journal of the American Musicological Society* (Boston, 1948; Richmond, Virginia, from 1949)
JLM	*Journal des Luxus und der Moden* (Weimar, 1789–99)
MA	*Musikalischer Almanach für Deutschland* (Leipzig, 1782–4)
ML	*Music and Letters* (London and Oxford, from 1920)
MM	*Magazin der Musik* (Hamburg, 1783–6)
MQ	*The Musical Quarterly* (New York, from 1915)
MT	*The Musical Times* (London, from 1844)
MTJ	*Münchner Theater-Journal* (Munich, 1814–16)
NOHM	*The New Oxford History of Music* (London, 1954–90)
NZM	*Neue Zeitschrift für Musik* (Leipzig, from 1834)
OQ	*The Opera Quarterly* (Chapel Hill, later Durham, NC, from 1984/5)
PRMA	*Proceedings of the Royal Musical Association* (London, 1944/5–1984/5)

SIMG   *Sammelbände der Internationale Musik-Gesellschaft*
       (1899 / 1900–13 / 14)
SMw   *Studien zur Musikwissenschaft* (1913–16, 1918–34, 1955–6,
       1960–6, from 1977)
VMw   *Vierteljahrschrift für Musikwissenschaft* (Leipzig, 1885–94)
WNA   *Wöchentliche Nachrichten und Anmerkungen, die Musik*
       betreffend (Leipzig, 1766–70)
WTz   *Wiener Theaterzeitung* (Vienna, 1806–8, 1811–59, 1860)
ZMw   *Zeitschrift für Musikwissenschaft* (Leipzig, 1918 / 19–1935)

BALTIC SEA

NORTH
SEA

Königsberg

Danzig

Rostock

Lübeck

Schwerin

Stettin

Hamburg

R. Elbe

Oldenburg

Bremen

R. Weser

Hanover

Berlin

R. Oder

Brunswick

Wolfenbüttel

Magdeburg

Dessau

Kassel

Halle

Leipzig

Breslau

Düsseldorf

Dresden

Cologne

Erfurt

Weimar

Eisenach

Jena

Aachen

Gotha

Meiningen

Prague

Wiesbaden

Frankfurt

R. Main

Mainz

Bayreuth

Darmstadt

Bamberg

Kaiserslautern

Mannheim

Würzburg

Heidelberg

Nuremberg

Ansbach

Karlsruhe

Regensburg

R. Danube

Baden-Baden

Stuttgart

Strassburg

R. Rhine

Ulm

Augsburg

Vienna

Pressburg

Colmar

Freiburg

Munich

Budapest

Basel

Salzburg

Zürich

Innsbruck

Graz

R. Rhine

Sixteenth-century beginnings

For many years, the accepted view of the birth of opera as a distinctive art form was that it arose from the discussions of the so-called Camerata that first met in the house of Count Giovanni de' Bardi in Florence in the 1580s. There is a truth in this, in that a number of ideas were poured into an intellectual crucible and amalgamated in the heat of discussion and experiment into a new condition; and in that with this dramatic interaction of poetry and music, the late Renaissance found a new form of creative expression. The steady development of opera in Italy, impelled by Italian skills in singing and the performance arts, and by Italian delight in show and in the conviviality of the theatre, gave it a primacy which the rest of Europe was compelled to acknowledge. Italian opera long remained, not only Italians have felt, a tradition to which all others related, especially when in various times and countries it was paid the respect of ferocious resistance by those arguing and working for a nationally independent art.

Like all artistic truths, this can be over-simplified. Definitions of opera as an art form, however variously expressed, tend to agree on it as a staged drama sung in costume, with instrumental accompaniment, in which the leading expressive element is music. However, what constitutes the enactment of a drama through music, rather than with music, can never be clear-cut. In Italy itself there has been a variety of dramatic forms dependent to differing degrees on music, both before and after 1600. It is useful to classify some of these as lying outside opera, such as the intermedio (with continuous music but consisting of a series of tableaux with no properly developed plot) and the pastoral play (with a continuous plot but with music confined to a series of interludes); but in practice some lie close enough for classifications to begin to lose their meaning. The situation is still less clear-cut in Germany, where the role of music as contributing an important element to a play was established at the time when German drama began taking on an individual character in the Renaissance. In many different spellings and formulations, the loose term Singspiel soon begins to appear, meaning nothing more than a play with music; but the need for the description indicates that the condition of the drama would be different without the music. It is a term now most familiar when attached to eighteenth-century works (including some of Mozart's) but could still fairly describe operas by Beethoven and Weber in the early nineteenth century, by Lortzing in the mid-nineteenth century, and can even cover the music theatre of Weill (who allusively used the term 'Songspiel') and others in the twentieth. Singspiel is a vital part of German opera, and the early elements of moral instruction seldom wholly left it, despite the more familiar comic aspects: indeed, comedy was often found to be the liveliest form of instruction and moral lesson. Together with this went, in thoughtful German minds, an anxiety about the artistic possibilities of so limited a genre; and even in the centuries when German opera could not free itself from Italian example or build upon French models, and had little of real distinction of its own to show, theorists were arguing for a closer identification of its constituent parts into a unified whole greater than their sum. Though this was the ideal condition to which so much in German opera, and in the discussions of operatic theorists, aspired from early days right the way through to Wagner, it is wrong to undervalue the tradition from which it grew and with which, for much of its history, it coexisted.

It was only with the growth of German humanism in court, city and above all university in the fourteenth and fifteenth centuries that there could also develop a culture deriving from ideas and ideals that were based on a common language and a shared experience, and justified by intellectual enquiry. Though the universities proved the greatest agent for the introduction of humanism into Germany, they were initially conservative and, despite a sense of common purpose, parochial and lacking in wider influence. However, by the latter half of the fifteenth century the balance of importance between the constituent faculties within them was changing. The liberal arts were becoming less an introductory study to theology, the 'Queen of the Sciences', and beginning to assert their own values and hence their own methods of instruction, sometimes prompted by the wandering scholars who assisted the spread of humanism. The arts hence came to acquire a new intellectual standing, especially with the fashionable enthusiasm for classical texts, above all Seneca, Plautus and Terence. A significant event was the acquisition by the University of Heidelberg in 1450 of a collection of manuscripts of Seneca and Terence, which were keenly studied; and all Terence's plays and several of Plautus's were translated into German before 1500. The performance of classical plays became more frequent, generally with a German prologue so as to acquaint a wider audience with the plot, and Latin drama was to survive well into the eighteenth century.

When Johannes Reuchlin (whose scholarship led Erasmus to compare him to St Jerome) published his popular farce *Henno* (1497), the first attempt by a German humanist to reproduce the spirit of Roman comedy, it was immediately taken up in Heidelberg. The first four of the five acts end with a choral song, set to a single melodic line with mensural note-shapes by one of the students, Daniel Megel. This is the first use of chorus texts, but they play no part in the action and have no connexion with the plot except as commentary: for instance, at the end of Act I, Elsa laments the loss of some stolen money and the chorus sings of vacillating fortune and the blessings of the poor who can lose nothing. Another of Reuchlin's comedies, *Sergius* (1496, but not published until 1504), includes choruses with instrumental accompaniment. The final 'Chorus cum choraule' consists of seven verses, each of them repeating the opening couplet (which also appears in *Henno*):

Musis poetis et sacro	To the Muses of poetry and to divine
Phoebo referte gratias.	Apollo give thanks.
Vates honor decet suus	Honour also is due to the musicians
Quos musica proportio	whose harmony
Aequare vult caelestibus	strives to make them equal to the gods
Dulcissimo convivio.	in sweetest companionship.

Reuchlin's fellow-humanist and wandering scholar Conrad Celtis, Germany's first *poeta laureatus*, who declared that new truths could be revealed through study of the ancient texts, wrote poetry with Ovid and Horace as his models, but also stage pieces to be enhanced by dances with music. His *Ludus Dianae* (1501), in a prologue and five acts (a structure owing much to the Italian intermedio), has many links with the Italian intermedi and is not so much a drama as a series of dramatic tableaux, but one in which music plays a part. Act I ends with the whole troupe singing in four parts the praises of the Emperor Maximilian I and his (Sforza) Empress Bianca Maria, while nymphs dance; Act II with four voices accompanied by fife and zither; Act III with a three-part choral ode; the brief Act IV with drums and horns accompanying revelry; and Act V with Diana thanking the Emperor, echoed by a four-part chorus. The music was published in the Nuremberg edition of 1501. Celtis 'would have considered his odes and dramas incomplete without musical accompaniment' (Spitz, 1957, 80). It is possible that he himself, an expert musician, added polyphony to the melodies by Franciscus Niger, in which metres and quantities are strictly observed, though more probably it was the work of a court musician.

Other examples occur; and though the musical contribution is incidental rather than functional, it was generally regarded as essential support, and it has a significance. Rather than, as in Italy, suggesting a revival of past glories and drawing on music of great sophistication, such plays, written on classical models but German in temper, and lying outside the influence of the Church, stirred curiosity about Germans' own past history, and presented ethical ideas with a vernacular music assisting their performance to a popular audience.

With the growing humanist concern for the education of the young, interest turned to the use of such dramas in schools as a means of instruction; and the practice was sufficiently established by the early sixteenth century for there to be at hand a valuable instrument for the spread of the ideas of the Reformation. Luther himself, a trained musician, set an example with chorales and their attendant melodies (many of them originating in popular folksongs), and these proved ideally suitable for use in the school dramas to press home a message or celebrate a moral. In such famous hymns as 'Ein feste Burg', Luther put into practice his precept that everything in the melody should grow from the inflections of the German language, and its original form is fluent and irregular. Moreover, a good many of his chorale melodies derive from folksong, so that 'O Welt, ich muß dich lassen' began life as 'Innsbruck, ich muß dich lassen'. In his table talk he once declared that 'Musica est optima ars, qua notae vivere faciunt verba' (Luther, 1883, *Tischreden* 2545) ('Music is the finest art, one by which notes bring words to life'); and his insistence on a vernacular music setting German is recorded in, for instance, a letter to Nikolaus Hausmann, 'mihi prorsus non placet, notas Latinas super verba germanica seruari' (Luther, 1883, *Brief-wechsel*, 26 Mar. 1525) ('I am absolutely opposed to the use of Latin melodies setting German words'). The school dramas were an apt medium for attacks on the Roman Catholic Church, with vernacular hymns and choruses providing the musical content (even when some chorales were based on Gregorian chant), and the tradition of farce offered, ready to hand, a means of satire.

Among those who took up the popular theme of the Prodigal Son was the fabulist Burkard Waldis, a Franciscan who converted to Lutheranism in Rome in 1524, and the author of a famous collection of tales based on Aesop. His *Fastnachtspiel*, or Shrovetide play, *De Parabell vam vorlorn Szohn* (or *Der verlorene Sohn*, 1527) has the prodigal robbed in a Papist house of ill repute at the Devil's instigation. While his pious brother at home places all his trust in good works, the chastened prodigal repents and returns to the bosom of his family, his conversion to true religion being saluted in a final hymn celebrating the Lutheran message of justification not by works but by faith. The hymns which mark the act divisions were clearly well known, as only the first lines are cited; but more significantly, there is a Te Deum sung during the feast, which is also accompanied by instrumental music for trumpets, shawms and flutes. Before the end 'ward gesungen der cxxix Psalm "Uth deper noeth" etc met v stimmen'

('Psalm 129, "Out of the depths" etc., is sung in five parts'). A more elaborate involvement of music comes with Paul Rebhun's *Susanna* (*Ein Geystlich spiel von der Gottfürchtigen und Keuschen Frawen Susannen*, 1536). As part of his metrical and structural experiments, music is made to play a more functional role by having lyrics that are connected to the drama: for example, the first chorus consists of four ten-line strophes, the first two telling of the power of Venus, the latter two extolling chaste love.

The effect of music in the Reformation drama on audiences is now of course difficult to gauge. However, the hymns, familiar from their use in Lutheran church services, clearly played a vital part in concentrating the religious message into a moment of meditation on doctrinal truth; and they would have acquired something more than the affective power of music on an audience, serving as they did to draw idea as well as emotion into a common experience, when they were associated with the architect of the Reformation himself. The chorales – hymns sung *choraliter* by Luther's 'priesthood of all believers' – struck a resonance which never faded from the German consciousness, which was given new power by successive composers and especially by the genius of J. S. Bach, and which was still awakening strong echoes in the time of Mendelssohn and above all with Wagner's invocation of the length and strength of German history in *Die Meistersinger von Nürnberg*.

Tribute to the effectiveness of the Reformation drama, spreading rapidly as it did through Northern Europe and especially into Bohemia and Switzerland, was not long delayed. Founded in Paris in 1534 by Ignatius Loyola with six companions, the 'Clerks Regular of the Society of Jesus' had their status approved by the Pope with the Bull 'Regimini Militantis Ecclesiae' of 27 September 1540. From the start, the Jesuits formed the spearhead of the Counter-Reformation. As early as 1556 there were over a hundred Colleges in Europe, organized in twelve Provinces, by 1600 over four hundred in twenty-seven Provinces. By 1626 there were over a hundred Colleges in German-speaking lands, and later in the seventeenth century 38 in the Austrian Province (embracing what is now Moravia, Hungary and Slovenia), 29 in Bohemia, and altogether in the so-called German Assistancy no fewer than 167. With the establishment of Jesuit Colleges throughout the Empire came a response to the success of the Protestant school drama, conducted with all the intelligence, shrewdness and forcefulness that were to characterize the Order. From 1550 until the Order's suppression in 1773, thousands of plays were produced in hundreds of towns, and in some cities the Jesuit performances even took on the character of a minor court theatre. Though the Jesuits claimed that artistry in their school dramas was secondary to the instruction of schoolchildren in religion and the preparation for leading a Christian life, they drew upon music, dance, spectacle (including equestrian displays and flying machines), costumes, décor, ghosts, vanishing acts and much else in their appeal not only to schools but to the population of the surrounding area.

The Jesuit drama evolved originally from instructional rhetorical dialogues. Loyola himself, though he confessed to enjoying music, did not believe that God had willed it as part of the liturgy and refused to admit it to the first Colleges. Only later was this proscription relaxed when, observing the effectiveness of the Reformation drama in its use of Terence and Plautus, the Jesuits found ways of turning a popular idiom to their own ends. This quickly led to dramatic presentation of Bible stories, such as a Counter-Reformation version of the Prodigal Son, who now returns from wasting his substance and imperilling his soul to be received into the forgiving bosom of the Roman Catholic Church. Other dramas, generally written by a Jesuit father appointed *choragus*, drew on comedy, or on the personification of virtues and vices. They could be blunt in their onslaught, as with one of 1565 that ends by consigning Luther and Calvin to Hellfire. Forms might divide into *Revuestücke* (principally instructional) that could also be *Heiligenviten* (portraying the lives of Biblical figures or saints and martyrs), *Marienspiele, Bischofspiele, Mirakelspiele, Totentanzspiele*, didactic and confrontational pieces, and pieces with an exemplary hero such as Belisarius, Cyrus, Themistocles, Constantine the Great, Joseph, David, even Thomas à Becket and Mary Stuart, and with villains including Herod and Julian the

Apostate. Generally, such plays were not given in church but in College halls or other theatres, publicly at Shrovetide, in part so as to restrain pre-Lenten excesses; other occasions would be school prize days or visits by prominent persons. They might last from two to seven hours, sometimes more, and would culminate in a scene using all their resources to make the greatest impact on the audience.

Already there were signs of the division between the musical and dramatic styles of Northern and Southern Germany which were to be strongly marked until virtually the end of the eighteenth century. The most important centre for the Jesuit drama outside Vienna became the Collegium Gregorianum in Munich, which by 1631 could claim no fewer than 1,464 pupils. At least in part, its significance rested upon the strong Roman Catholic connexions of the court; and the Wittelsbachs' love of music assisted the import of Italian composers and Italian stage expertise. *Samson*, staged for the marriage of Duke William to Renata of Lorraine in 1569, had choruses by Lassus, who had accepted the invitation to join Duke Albrecht's court in 1556. One of the most celebrated of all presentations was that of *Hester* in 1577, when some 1,700 costumed performers took part in procession through the streets on foot, on horseback, on elephants and in triumphal cars, accompanied by giants, devils, men with lions' heads, dolphins, tigers, wolves, executioners, lictors, magicians and Janissaries. The epilogue to this stupefying entertainment points the moral. Whereas, in the Old Testament, Esther had used her influence with King Ahasuerus to save the Jews from extirpation at the hands of the Grand Vizier Haman, we are now taught by Ecclesia that Hester is the Virgin Mary, Assuerus is God the Father and Aman the 'immanis Daemon', that is to say the Turks. Ecclesia asks Mary to support her against the Turks and against a much more dangerous enemy, Heresy. In this way, the analogy runs, she can soften the wrath of God and liberate the Austrian and Bavarian ruling houses and hence all dependent Christians from such threats to the soul.

These dramas often follow classical example and early Italian models by including choruses at the ends of the acts, showing the importance of music to confirm the religious message; and there was also an important use of dance in a symbolic role. With later dramas, music moved closer to the centre of the expression. In *Philothea*, given seven times in Munich in 1643, the heroine at first refuses to obey and casts herself into worldly pleasures, before bowing submissively to divine mercy. Set out in recitative with ariosos and short arias, finally choruses, this has violins to accompany the songs of Christ and the angels, violas to accompany Misericordia, Clementia, Amor and the sorrowing Philothea, cornetts to sound when Mundus and Philothea rejoice, and solemn trombones when Justitia steps forward and Christ appears as Judge; there are also theorbos and lutes for the joyful chorus of the Daughters of Sion. One version records the use of fifteen instruments. A contemporary male equivalent, *Theophilus*, describes Man's journey to Christ in a sequence of Biblical quotations, and uses thirty-two musicians. The text is sung SATB, with recitatives, arias, duets and choruses. The high point is the Sanctus, and the work concludes with the damnation of unbelievers.

Such lavish dramas naturally made a more sensational impact, leaving the humbler Protestant versions far behind. The Jesuit drama's greatest German writer was a Swabian, Jakob Bidermann, whose most famous play was *Cenodoxus, sive Doctor Parisiensis* (1602). Cenodoxus is honoured as a model of Christian virtue, an apparently pious scholar; but he is ruled by pride in his heart. As he is being buried with great pomp, the Heavenly Court on high pronounces damnation. In a famous performance in Munich in 1609, before an influential audience, the effect proved overwhelming:

> The hall was packed with an audience which included important nobles of the Bavarian court and the foremost citizens of Munich. At first the audience rocked with laughter at the opening comic scenes; but as the play progressed the mood changed to one of shock and horror as the spectators realized the enormity of the sins portrayed and became aware of the power of hell; and by the end of the play the members of the audience, trembling at the sight of a soul eternally damned, were reflecting in stunned silence on the punishment their own sins merited. The impact of the play was immediate. Fourteen members of the

audience went into retreat to perform the Spiritual Exercises of St
Ignatius, just as in the play Bruno retreated into the wilderness to found
his monastery and lead a life of spiritual contemplation; and the actor
who played the part of Cenodoxus shortly afterwards entered the
Society of Jesus and after a life of piety and holiness died in the odour of
sanctity . . . In a few hours the play had accomplished what a hundred
sermons could hardly have done.   (Dyer, 1975, 1–2)

Much in the staging of these dramas was clearly left to the
resources and talents of the time and the place. The so-called
periochae, or *Periochen*, essentially synopses and guides to help
German speakers follow the Latin action, generally consist of no
more than title page, argument, résumé of individual scenes and list
of performers, occasionally summaries or selected lines of the actual
text; they leave a great deal to the modern imagination, though they
are often the only source of information for lost dramas (see Szarota,
1987). Often the music is also lost: a rare surviving example is Johann
Caspar Kerll's five-act *Pia et fortis mulier* (1677), the first extant
Viennese Jesuit drama, which draws close to the condition of Italian
Baroque opera in its use of recitative, da capo aria, ensemble and
chorus.

There is disagreement as to whether the Jesuit tradition at its peak
should be denied the status of musical drama (Valentin, 1978) or is
the true ancestor of the *Gesamtkunstwerk* (Szarota, 1978–87). By the
second half of the seventeenth century, the title *Drama musicum* is
found attached to some of them, though this should not be taken as
indicative of what was meant by later use of such a term. Study of
periochae and of accounts of performances does not really indicate a
condition among the earlier examples in which music takes a
functional lead in what may have approximated more closely, at best,
to the dramatic nature of the English masque or the French *ballet de
cour* (which both involved a degree of audience participation).
Nevertheless, the essential role of music in the enactment of drama
was confirmed at the earliest stage of the genre, and taken to a
degree of high sophistication as the techniques of Florentine, Roman
and Venetian opera began to infiltrate the Jesuit dramas in the

seventeenth century. The influence and so increasingly the nature of the works was Italian, in a religious movement designed to counter the effect of the Protestant drama on a battleground not of its own choosing and with superior weapons brought across the Alps.

An important new stimulus to the German song play had meanwhile begun to appear from an unexpected quarter. The first appearance of a troupe of so-called *Englische Komödianten* in Germany was probably at Leipzig in 1585, at a time when plague had closed the London theatres. The companies were also encouraged by visits to England of German nobles, such as that by Count Friedrich von Mömpelgard to Queen Elizabeth in 1597: the presence of his embassy is obliquely mentioned in the play said to have been requested by the Queen from Shakespeare, *The Merry Wives of Windsor* (Act IV, scenes 3 and 5). There can be no doubt that visiting Germans would have taken back a good account of the Elizabethan drama to a land starved of theatre. Already in 1586 a troupe of five English players, led by William Kempe, who later acted in plays by Shakespeare, had travelled to Germany from the court of Denmark. From 25 September to the following 17 July they were at Dresden, where the terms of their engagement obliged them,

> Do wir reisen, Uns uf unsern bevehlich Jedesmahls folgen, wan wir taffel halten, und sünsten so ofte ihnen solchs angemeldet wirdt, mit Ihrer Geygen und zugehörigen Instrumenten auffwarten und Musiciren, Uns auch mit ihrer *Springkunst* und *andern, was sie in Zirligkeit gelernet,* lust und ergetzlichkeit machen. (Herz, 1903, 5)

> (When we travel, to accompany us dutifully on every occasion, and while we are at table, and also as often as required, to attend with their fiddles and accompanying instruments and to perform, and also to give pleasure and delight with their *acrobatics* and *whatever else they have learnt of elegance.*)

Their success led to a visit in 1592 by a troupe under Robert Browne, which then divided into two for employment by the Landgraf Moritz von Hesse (under Browne) and Duke Heinrich Julius of Brunswick (under Thomas Sackville, later Browne again, then John Green). In 1604–5 Moritz von Hesse even constructed for the visitors the first permanent theatre in Germany, the Ottoneum (named after his favourite son); designs show a handsome ornamented front. Both rulers were also to write pieces for their visiting players. Another troupe to tour widely and with success between 1604 and 1623 was led by John Spencer. There was much interchange between the personnel of the troupes, which numbered at their most some two dozen actors with half a dozen musicians; and this natural process was no doubt encouraged by the different characters of the directors. Browne was a humble, honest artist; Green was only out for money; Sackville was more original, and began to develop a type of fool that was to become immensely popular; whereas Spencer was an unscrupulous showman who did not hesitate to become a Roman Catholic so as to assure himself of a successful Lenten season in Cologne, keeping quiet about this conversion when he moved on to Berlin. This did not prevent him from having to slip secretly out of Cologne in 1616, abandoning his scenery, so as to avoid his creditors. A number of other troupes also continued to tour Germany; the last one recorded was in 1694, by when the tradition of the native German *Wandertruppen* was well established.

For many years afterwards little notice was taken of the English players and their plays, and their contribution ignored. Ludwig Tieck was almost alone in collecting materials, and he commented on these in his *Deutsches Theater* (Berlin, 1817). It was not until debts obliged Tieck to sell his library to Albert Cohn in 1850 that they were given their first serious study (Cohn, 1865). However, two collections of the material had been published, Fridericus Menius's *Englische Comedien und Tragedien* (1620) and a second, anonymous collection, *Liebeskampf oder ander Theil der Englische Comoedien und Tragoedien* (1630), which contained six plays and two so-called 'Singspiele'. Musical interludes occur in many of the other plays. The wider repertory of the troupes comprised standard works from the English stage, including plays by Beaumont and Fletcher, Dekker, Kyd, Marlowe and at least a dozen by Shakespeare. However, the versions were, to say the least, corrupt. *The Merchant of Venice*, as *Der Jude von Venetien*, incorporates the German clown Pickelhäring in a piece that is deplorably feeble and anti-Semitic. *Der bestrafte Brudermord, oder Prinz Hamlet aus Dänemark* (text in Creizenach, 1888) is a lame version of the original, interesting among little else for Hamlet's much-modified advice to the players (who arrive declaring, 'Wir sind fremde hochteutsche Komödianten'): though warned not to exaggerate, they are praised for the example their stage gives as presenting the world in miniature (Creizenach, 1888, 163–5). It should, of course, be remembered that at the time *Hamlet* was still, and would be for many years to come, regarded as a crude revenge play. There is considerable emphasis on the importance of music, which helped the actors to make their mark when performing in a tongue foreign to their audience. Not only were there fanfares, sennets, tuckets and so forth, but musical interludes and especially the use, as in ballad opera, of old tunes to new words. *Der engelländische Roland* includes various versions of a song very popular in Germany to different words, 'The fifteenth day of July', and it occurs again in *Von drey bösen Weibern, denen weder Gott noch jhre Männer recht können thun* (described as 'Ein Singets Spil'). A version of *Der verlorene Sohn* marks places for interludes and entr'actes, and tells the musicians to strike up cheerfully or play softly during the feast so that the speeches can be heard ('Die Spielleute fangen wider an geigen gar submisse, also dass man dabey reden kan'). Elsewhere, there can be found instructions for a certain kind of music, perhaps for the entry of a king, or to suggest darkness and night, and so forth.

Hamlet's advice to the players was evidently necessary. The English players were the first professional actors to perform in Germany, and their popularity rested largely on the vivid contrast between the formal, inert style thought proper to German guild plays (such as those of Hans Sachs) and the melodramatic manner the Englishmen had learnt in the conditions of Elizabethan London's public theatres. Stage directions exhort the players to pull exaggerated grimaces, strike attitudes, tear their hair, and spit blood; and in the early days when the plays were given in English, the ability to convey drama with the aid of mime was all-important. The aim was to thrill, amuse and shock (including with coarseness). The costumes were generally elaborate, a heritage less of the Elizabethan theatre than of the *commedia dell'arte*, in which they played an important part in days before an actor could expect any support from scenery and lighting. This also compensated for the difficulty in transporting sets that would have to be put up in the guild halls, ballrooms, fencing schools and riding schools in which the players performed.

The pioneering Browne began by giving plays in English, but it was quickly found necessary to have a linking German explanation given by a narrator, generally the troupe leader, perhaps a Dutchman who had joined them on their way from England, later a German actor. This task soon took on a dramatic function, allowing him to comment and intervene, perhaps with satirical observations. In turn it naturally developed the role of the English clown, and there swiftly emerged various immensely popular German versions of clown, passive (Jan Bouset, Pickelhäring), active (Wursthänsel or later Hanswurst), and acrobatic (Der Springer). Not surprisingly, there does not seem to have been any tradition of Shakespeare's philosophical fools. An example of how a favourite play evolved into new form can be seen with *Singing Simpkin*, a version of the story also found in the *Decameron* (vii, 6) of the faithless wife playing off two visiting lovers by making one, the mild Simpkin, hide in a chest and then be chased off, on her gullible husband's return, with mock outrage by the furious Blusterer (who is in the ancient Plautine tradition of the *miles gloriosus*). This becomes *Pickelhering in der Kiste, Pekelharing in de Kist*, and *Der Courtisan in der Kiste*, with Fraw, Pickelhering and Soldat, and tunes including 'Blind Cupid hath made my heart for to bleed' (Bolte, 1893). Pickelhering's regular appearances soon became more than occasional clowning: 'Der Clown der E[nglischen] K[omödianten], Pickelhering, ist gleichsam die Verkörperung des Geistes des Komödiantenstücks. Er ist der Lebensnerv ihres Theaters, die Wurzel, aus dem es seine urwüchsige Lebendigkeit holt' (Baesecke, 1935, 68) ('The EK's clown, Pickelhering, is, so to speak, the embodiment of the spirit of the comedians' pieces. He is the vital nerve of their theatre, the root from which their rough liveliness sprouts').

These wretched pieces performed by itinerant hacks have little artistic importance. They do have historical importance, however, since they stimulated the emergence of the native German tradition of the song play, and provided it with some ingredients. Of the two nobles who had welcomed the English players in 1592 and written plays for them, nothing is known of the works of Moritz of Hesse, the more regrettably as he was known as 'the Learned'. Like him, Heinrich Julius, the Protestant Bishop of Halberstadt who succeeded to an uneasy reign as Duke of Brunswick in 1589, played an enlightened patron's role; for he organized complete cycles of performances and thus gave visiting companies something close to a permanent base at his castle at Wolfenbüttel. In the two years following the 1592 visit he also wrote ten plays exploiting the English style. His comedies and his tragedies both have a moral intent in showing vice corrected. Boasting is punctured, the cheat exposed, adultery pilloried, privilege mocked by comparison with simple piety; and especially in some of his quasi-historical plays, such as that on a Neronian figure, *Von einem ungeratenen Sohn*, there is much supping on horrors. The Duke was also partly responsible, stimulated by his familiarity with the *commedia dell'arte* and perhaps also with Plautus, for giving further prominence to the clown, who would move in and out of the action, solicit laughs by his mangling of the language, and make conversational contact between the audience and the actors' formal verse. Musical interludes occur in many of the Duke's plays, and music is even made more functional to the plot: in Act V, scene 3 of *Vincentio Ladislao*, for instance, musicians appear and are brought into the dramatic and comic action as their performance is critically discussed.

Another writer to perceive what the English players held for German art was Jakob Ayrer, a Nuremberg lawyer who had often seen the visiting troupes in his city. He now attempted to combine their stage effectiveness with the good-humoured but dramatically rather tame *Fastnachtspiele* of his fellow-citizen Hans Sachs. Ayrer wrote seventy or so pieces, of which sixty-six were published in 1618 under the title *Opus Theatricum*, which declared itself to comprise 'thirty remarkably fine comedies and tragedies . . . as well as 36 fine, lively and diverting *Fastnacht-* or *Possenspiele'*. The collection includes histories as well as comedies and tragedies, and Ayrer was in his turn impressed with the effect of the English clowns, making them characters in his plays as well as commentators or between-the-scenes jesters. From Sachs he drew his style of *Knittelvers* (the sixteenth-century popular verse form using rhyming couplets of lines with four main stresses), from the English players the sensationalism and the figure of the fool. He suffered from lack of stage experience, but his 'singets spiele' are attempts to propel a story with the help of songs set to popular melodies, much as some of the pieces given by the Englishmen had done but in a more integrated fashion.

The material and its execution were both still very primitive; and the success of the English players and their imitation by native *Wandertruppen* were symptomatic. Germany was still a loose confederation of some three hundred states, with unification lying centuries ahead. Despite the achievements of Middle High German literature, and the profoundly reverberant event of the Reformation and its consequences for German coherence of feeling, the cultural Renaissance of other Western countries had, with some striking exceptions, largely passed her by. There was a sense of inferiority to the England of Shakespeare, to Italy's great artistic awakening in the fifteenth and sixteenth centuries, to the glories of Netherlands polyphony, above all to a France that under Henri IV had no hesitation in presenting herself as the European exemplar of civilized values. The song play which English models encouraged was indeed a humble affair, but it touched a nerve. There was the chance, observed by one or two dramatists, for the use of a musical vernacular in the theatre, and – if sketchily – some examples of music playing a functional role. It is difficult to see in which direction if any, even given more favourable social and political circumstances, this might have developed; for not until secular instrumental music had evolved into a much more advanced condition was it able to engage fully with drama in a manner particularly German. In any case, the chances of such a development were first confused by the appearance in Germany of a new kind of dramatic music, Italian opera; and then shattered by the horror of the Thirty Years War.

The Thirty Years War and its aftermath

In 1612, the opening year of his reign as Prince-Archbishop of Salzburg, Marcus Sitticus von Hohenems welcomed to the city the poet, singer and composer Francesco Rasi. The Archbishop was half-Italian, and keen to maintain cultural ties with Italy, in particular with the Gonzagas of Mantua. Rasi served the Gonzaga Court; but he was also one of the original members of Count Giovanni de' Bardi's Camerata in Florence, and had sung both Amyntas in Peri's *Euridice* in 1600 and probably the title role of Monteverdi's *Orfeo* in 1607. On his arrival, he dedicated a collection of his monodic music to the Archbishop, who no doubt responded with enthusiasm to the novel style and to its implications for the new Italian genre of dramatic music; for on 27 January 1614 there was given, on a stage specially constructed in the palace, an Italian 'Hoftragicomoedia', then on 10 February a pastoral, *Orfeo*, probably with music by Monteverdi. This first performance of Italian opera outside Italy was soon to be followed by others. The new Emperor, Ferdinand II, came to Salzburg in 1619 and saw what was probably the same *Orfeo*; and his marriage to Vincenzo Gonzaga's daughter Eleonora in Vienna in 1622 led to an invitation to the Comici Fedeli, the troupe who had given the first performance of Monteverdi's *Arianna* in Mantua in 1608. But meanwhile, Ferdinand's determination to suppress Protestantism had come to a head in Bohemia in 1618, when in defiance of an Imperial law guaranteeing freedom of worship to the country of Jan Hus, the Emperor attempted to impose Roman Catholicism, and invading Flemish troops backed by money from Spain were confronted by Bohemian soldiers. It was the beginning of the war which devastated the country for thirty appalling years from 1618 until 1648.

Not only the horrors and destruction of the Thirty Years War, but the added divisiveness forced upon German-speaking lands, meant that any serious growth in the arts of peace was trampled underfoot by the march and counter-march of soldiers practising the arts of war. There could be no question of a sustained development of what little had been achieved in the field of the musical drama. Perhaps the arrival of Italian opera in the south would in any case have overwhelmed German attempts; perhaps it would have served to deepen the Catholic–Protestant divisions represented by the two genres of school drama. Since the war ebbed and flowed across the whole country, leaving at times periods of comparatively undisturbed local activity, it was possible for the *Englische Komödianten* to continue with carefully chosen tours, mostly around Northern and Central Germany and the Baltic states, and for German *Wandertruppen* to develop their own operations. There were only a few rulers who could make a claim to sustain civilized values in dreadful times with the establishment at their courts of Italian opera.

In one instance, more might have been achieved by a composer of genius had the times been favourable. The musical life of Dresden, where Heinrich Schütz had reorganized the *Kapelle* on Italian lines in 1617, was interrupted when the war reached it in 1631, though not before an historic event had taken place at Schloss Hartenfels, in nearby Torgau, on 13 April 1627. For the wedding of his daughter Sophie Eleonore to the Landgrave Georg II of Hesse-Darmstadt, the Elector Georg I had made use of his connexions with the Florentine Court to obtain a copy of Peri's *Dafne*. Schütz set Rinuccini's libretto in a translation by Martin Opitz; and in the words of the Court chronicler, 'Den 13 agirten die Musikanten *musicaliter* eine Pastoral Tragicomoedia von der Daphne' ('On the 13th the musicians acted with music a Pastoral Tragicomedy of Daphne'). The text has Ovid appearing as Prologue, and the singers are Daphne, Apollo and Venus, with three Shepherds (replacing the Messenger), and with the appropriate addition of Cupid.

Dafne is often cited as the first opera to be sung in German. However, the claim is in various ways questionable. In the first place, the text is laid out in the familiar form of a token narrative with strophic songs, dances and choruses, and, as opera, does not appear to represent a qualitative advance on previous German example. Secondly, the music is lost, and may even have consisted of an arrangement of Peri's music to suit the framework which Opitz confesses, in the brief preface to the score, he was obliged to devise:

> Günstiger Leser, wie dieses Drama aus dem Italienisch mehrentheils genommen, also ist es gleichfalls auff selbige Art, und heutigem Gebrauche sich zu bequemen, wiewol auch von der Hand weg, geschrieben worden. Welches der Auctor zu seiner Entschuldigung setzt, dem sonst nicht unbekandt ist, was die Alter wegen der Trawerspiele und Comedien zu befehlen pflegen.

> (Gracious reader, since this drama has been largely translated from the Italian, it has been written in the Italian manner and in accordance with modern usage, although done so very hurriedly. The author mentions this to exculpate himself, for he is not unmindful of what the Ancients have decreed with regard to tragedies and comedies.)

Furthermore, in the following year Schütz made the second of his two visits to Venice, where Monteverdi gave him some instruction (and had a distinct influence on the operatic nature of the recitative in some of his Passions). In 1633 he wrote to his friend Friederich Lepzelter, reporting that

> auf meiner jüngsten in Italien gethanen reise ich mich noch auf eine absonderliche Art der Composition begeben hette, nemblich wie eine Comedi von allerhandt Stimmen in redenden Stylo übersetzt vndt auf den Schaw gebracht vndt singende agiret werden könne, welche Dinge meines Wissens (auf solche Art, wie ich meine) in Teutschland noch ganz ohnbekandt, bishero auch wegen des schweren Zustandes bey uns weder practiciret noch befödert worden, vndt ich dafür halte, das es Schade sey, das solche recht Majestätische vndt fürstliche inuentionen (worunter zwar meine Music nicht zu rechnen sein würde vndt sonsten wegen mehere dazu gehörigen Sachen also von mir intitoliret werden) ersitzen bleiben, von andern vndt bessern ingeniis nicht auch gestehn und practiciret werden soll.   (Schütz, 1931, 125–6)

> (on my recent journey to Italy I concerned myself with composition of a special kind, namely how a comedy with many voices could be

translated into stile recitativo and how it could be staged and acted while sung, which things (of this kind, I mean) are to the best of my knowledge quite unknown in Germany and on account of the difficult times could neither be practised nor encouraged here, and I therefore consider that it is a pity that such truly majestic and princely inventions (among which my music could indeed not be counted and because of several other related matters is not so called by me) have been neglected; nor do I see why they should not be taken up and put into practice by better heads than mine.)

The implication is that Schütz did not regard his own *Dafne* as representing this new condition of musical drama; and the surviving texts of his other stage works do not suggest anything very different from *Dafne*. Moreover, the text indicates something much closer to a ceremonial masque than the drama of which Schütz's Passions show him to be more than capable. It opens, for instance, with a shepherds' echo chorus; shepherds' choruses end the first four acts; and at the close of the fifth, nymphs and shepherds sing and dance round the laurel into which Daphne has been metamorphosed. Opitz has also eliminated many of the lyrical elements in Rinuccini's text, and played down the drama: for instance, in the Italian the people are dismayed in the presence of the dragon and accompany Apollo's battle excitedly, whereas in the German they urge silence so as not to arouse the beast.

Whatever was intended for *Dafne*, and however it resulted, the choice of Opitz to write the text was an inspired one. With his *Buch von der deutschen Poeterey* (1624), Opitz had established new principles of versification, emphasizing the value of rhyme and especially of natural verbal accentuation over earlier conventions, and claiming High German as a normal literary language, purged of the quasi-learned use of too much Latin. In the *Dafne* Preface he makes excuse and aligns himself with other German dramatic writers claiming to derive their standards from antiquity, which sets him apart from the Camerata's belief that they were recreating the actual practices of ancient drama. In another preface, for a version he made of an Italian text as *Judith* (1635), he again invokes classical canons while regretting the need to diverge from them for didactic and patriotic reasons.

Opitz's spirit – classical in that it sought to establish a set of poetic canons, yet anticipating the Romantic appeal to individual national feeling – was well suited to the temper of the times. In imitation of the Italian humanistic academies, there grew up in various towns during the first half of the century a number of literary societies or *Sprachgesellschaften*, often bearing pretentious titles and with a membership assuming waggish pseudonyms in a manner that was to be enduringly popular in Germany. Behind the superficies of this movement lay the serious aim of upholding the quality of German poetry by promulgating Opitz's literary reforms, as well as of studying the implications these had for music. The most famous of the societies was the Nuremberg 'Blumenorden an der Pegnitz', founded in 1644 by Georg Philipp Harsdörffer and Johann Klaj. The so-called 'Pegnitz Shepherds' were by no means free of such societies' obsessive attempts to Germanize all foreign influences out of the language; and Harsdörffer was capable of taking matters to an extreme degree. In his *Frauenzimmer-Gesprächspiele* (8 vols., 1641–9), his concern to separate contemporary German theatre from the influence of the classical and especially the Latin world led him to urge upon playwrights the task of bringing German poetry, music, dance, painting and stage design into a unified theatrical whole.

Volume IV of the *Frauenzimmer Gesprächspiele* attempts to put precept into practice with a 'spiritual pastoral', *Seelewig* (1644), set to music by Sigmund Theophilus Staden. The conversations in which the precepts are set forth comment on the text as various theatrical problems present themselves; and Harsdörffer argues for opera as a unified art form, with music acting as the force that blends poetry and painting with it into a new whole. Stage techniques that will aid the realization of this idea are discussed in detail, as when Harsdörffer proposes assisting the frequent scene changes suggested by music, with its capacity for instantly setting a new atmosphere, by means of a stage revolve. These radical suggestions necessitate rejection of Italian opera as being affected, artificial and (worst of all) foreign: German opera should present heroic deeds and moral instruction. The anticipation of many such later discussions is completed by the

(Shelter me, hill and rocky crevice, threatened as I am, so that punishment does not find me out. All my words are too feeble, all the rocks too low. Ah! the world is too small for me to escape such punishment. Hark! the echo resounds my woe, ah, woe!)

Example 1   Staden: *Seelewig* (1644), Seelewig

participants' anxiety that there can never be a single artist capable of effecting this synthesis by his own unaided talents.

Seelewig is entitled, in full, *Das geistliche Waldgedicht, oder Freuden-spiel, genant Seelewig. Gesangweis auf italienischer Art gesetzt.* It is an allegory on the progress of the immortal soul (the *ewige Seele*). The satyr Trügewalt (the Deceiver) attempts to lure Seelewig from the path of virtue by the attractions of the senses, with the aid of the nymph Sinnigunda (Sensuousness) and three shepherds, Künsteling (Artifice), Reichimut (Riches) and Ehrelob (Power). But the good nymph Herzigilde (Wisdom) and the older Gwissulda (Conscience) come to her aid and prove strong defenders. The action is carried on in songs linked by dramatic recitative, and there is an attempt to pursue Opitzian principles in the use of rhyme and metre, as well as with metrical and tempo changes, to depict the characters. Trügewalt tends to sing in a blunt 4/4, while the devious Künsteling changes between 4/4 and 3/2 in the same number; Seelewig's first number is in a flowing 6/4 then assumed by Sinnigunda. The popular Renaissance device of an echo aria, which the Italians inherited from classical use, is turned to neat ends with exchanges such as Trügewalt's deceiving answer to Seelewig: 'Was soll ich wünschen mehr?' 'Ehr' ('What more should I desire?' 'Honour'); and the expressive range which Staden can achieve from simple means is shown as Seelewig cowers from a storm (Example 1).

However, the lack of a tradition of German musical declamation inhibits a composer of modest gifts, and the songs themselves tend to be simple strophic numbers, syllabically set, of no very striking character. There are several instrumental pieces, for an ensemble of three each of flutes, 'Schalmenen' (shawms) and violins, with 'ein großes Horn' (effectively associated with Trügewalt) and theorbo. There is also a symphony for 'drey Pomparten oder Fagotten': an instrumental symphony introduces each of the three acts, and the latter two end with the characters in chorus (as well as an Angel Chorus). Clearly there is a connexion with the earlier German school drama (it is based on a Jesuit example) and with Ayrer's song-plays, in the moralising approach and in the use of the description *Freudenspiel*; and there is also the implied claim that Italian operatic methods have been taken over (*auf italienischer Art*, meaning the *stile rappresentativo*) in the use of a pastoral convention for a religious struggle, and in the pattern of recitative linking strophic songs. It is not an effective synthesis, and though *Seelewig* is the first through-composed Singspiel whose music survives, this is its only claim to be regarded as the first German opera. It was certainly a pioneering work, if only in that it exemplified the degree to which intelligent theorizing lay far ahead of musical achievement in these years, and was to do so in Germany for many years to come.

Any serious, coherent musical progress had, in any case, been brought to a halt by the war. The Peace of Westphalia in 1648 found the states of the Empire battered and exhausted, numbed by the worst destruction in German history. Vast tracts of the countryside had been devastated, with forests burnt and fields abandoned to weeds and undergrowth; some cities, especially in the south and the north-west, had escaped the worst of the marauding armies, but others had been ransacked, put to the flames, or laid waste; in the countryside two-fifths of the entire population had been killed, and in some areas the survivors were reduced to living like brutes. The horrors cast a black, smoke-laden shadow down the length of German history. Though the Peace brought respite, it left much essentially unchanged. Ferdinand had come close to controlling the whole of Germany in 1627, when his armies reached the Baltic, but he had been turned back partly by the efforts of the princes of the German states and partly by the intervention of Sweden and France: no central authority had been imposed. The recognition of Protestantism alongside Catholicism preserved rather than healed divisions, while the Treaty gave strengthened power to individual princes and cities, offering token protection to the Emperor without imposing obligations upon his subject rulers.

Despite the wish to preserve their autonomy, there was still a centripetal feeling towards a German whole among the disparate states and cities, and their princes and religious groupings; but the myth of a Holy Roman Empire had gone. As Voltaire cynically observed, it was 'ni saint, ni romain, ni empire' (*Essai sur les Mœurs et l'Esprit des Nations*, 1769, lxx): no religious imperative now bound it, no longer could it be seen as an imaginative successor to Ancient Rome, and it had nothing resembling an imperial condition. There were those who began to prefer the term 'Deutschland'. Meanwhile, the 'Empire' continued to provide a loose confederation even when greatly added power and independence had passed to the rulers of the territorial states. Some, even outside Habsburg-ruled Austrian lands, survived the war without any weakening: such were Bavaria and Saxony. Others, including Württemberg, remained of little influence. The ecclesiastical principalities lost much of their independent standing. In all states the tendency was for the prince to become an absolute ruler in his own domain, whether it were one of the great cities and regions with broadly based wealth and traditions, or a tiny castle from whose ramparts a knightly family could view their entire possessions.

The war had impoverished not only the country but people's inner lives. Loyalty to churches on both sides of the ecclesiastical divide held remarkably firm; but materially, the German lands were in ruins, and in no condition to compete with the economic expansion and foreign colonization of European neighbours, while culturally there was little chance of recreation and the sustenance of the arts for those who had endured three decades of misery and now sought enrichment to their lives. It was almost exclusively among the courts that the opportunity occurred for any kind of organized entertainment, and with this went the need to assert the temporal power and civilized values of the ruler. Italian opera, easy to import across the Alps and coming complete with practitioners expert in their art and in setting it at the service of a ruler's glorification, seemed to reflect an idealized court life, in which noble sentiments and heroic stances prevailed, in which dramatic truth was less important than splendid display and a celebration of the existing order, in which the choice of classical subjects suggested the continuation of a golden age under the auspices of a benevolent ruler. Comic interludes and subjects were by no means excluded, and audiences were often drawn not only from the court but from nobles and important burghers, especially for royal weddings or birthdays or christenings or coronations or other events which the panoply of a grand performance could celebrate. But this was essentially an art to give reassurance of order to the major rulers in a shattered country; and furthermore, Germany's relegation to a weakened position in

European history was emphasized by the rapid rise of its western neighbour, France, embarking upon its *grand siècle* just as the Thirty Years War had ended, and offering an example of court life, patronage and entertainment towards which many minor German rulers were to look wistfully.

It was naturally in the southern areas of German-speaking lands least affected by the war, as well as in Vienna, that musical traditions were best maintained; and these were to all intents and purposes Italian. Singers and musicians, especially from Mantua, continued to visit the Viennese court during the war, performing works (some to texts by Cesare Gonzaga) in Carnival and for occasions such as imperial birthdays; and this tradition was developed under the Holy Roman Emperor Ferdinand III (r.1637–57), for whose coronation the Mantuan company also gave the first Italian opera in Prague in 1627 ('eine schöne Pastoral-Comoedia', possibly by G. B. Buonamente). The number of performances increased further in the aftermath of the war, under Ferdinand's son, the Emperor Leopold I (r.1658–1705). Encouraged by his stepmother Eleonora Gonzaga, Leopold became one of the most important patrons of Baroque opera, developing the court *Kapelle* and himself composing a number of operas in a Venetian manner. Leopold's active participation, and that of other members of the imperial family, his knowledge of Italian opera, and not least his generous patronage, led to a tradition of sumptuous performances of which the most notoriously lavish was that of Cesti's *Il pomo d'oro* for Leopold's first marriage in 1668. Hitherto the court operas had been composed principally by Antonio Bertali, probably one of the Emperor's teachers, and Pietro Andrea Ziani; and after Cesti left for Italy, the dominant figure for some thirty years was Antonio Draghi, who provided a steady stream of dramatic works designed to flatter and never disturb court conventions. Virtually all of them were to texts by the court poet Nicolò Minato, and on the standard classical subjects: the only gesture towards German history was Draghi's *Gundeberga* (1672), to which Leopold contributed. Not until the appointment of Johann Joseph Fux in 1698 did a native Austrian of any significance hold a major court appointment. Leopold, under Jesuit influence more than his father had been, on the whole resisted Italian works, resolving to foster an Austrian version of an art that may have been Italian by origin but was seen to be of wider, national application.

In Salzburg, opera pursued the course that had been begun at the start of the century, alongside that of the Jesuit school dramas. The tradition remained one of Italianate works by, among others, Georg Muffat and Heinrich Biber. With *Chi la dura la vince* (1687), Biber and his probable librettist, Francesco Maria Raffaelini, make a pioneering national gesture by taking the story in Tacitus of the first-century chieftain Arminius (Hermann) and his rivalry with Germanicus, as the basis for a plot of multiple love intrigues. Though not primarily concerned with the defeat of Varus and his legions in the Teutoburg Forest, it is the first opera to touch on an heroic episode in early German history that was to stir the national imagination of many composers, and of writers including Klopstock, Kleist, De la Motte Fouqué and Grabbe. In Innsbruck, too, the Archduke Ferdinand II's marriage encouraged performances of dramatic musical works, and Jesuit school dramas remained popular; but the first operatic performances came in the reign of the Archduke Ferdinand Karl (r.1646–62), who married Cosimo Medici II's daughter Anna in 1646. Following an Italian tour in which they saw some opera, they built in 1654 the Komödienhaus, the first free-standing opera house in German lands with a permanent company, and one well equipped to handle the elaborate scenic requirements of Baroque opera. It was inaugurated by Cesti's *Cesare amante*, reworked as *Cleopatra*. Cesti's *Argia* was given in 1655 to celebrate the visit of the newly abdicated Queen Christina of Sweden, on her way to Rome as a convert to Catholicism; and on a second visit in 1662 she was entertained with his *La magnanimità d'Alessandro*. Cesti's two terms of office – 1652–7 and 1661–5 – saw the establishment of the first company in German lands to include German artists alongside Italians.

Munich, with its well-established Jesuit tradition, was better placed than either city to foster the new Baroque opera which the sumptuous school drama stagings had foreshadowed. Opera was introduced to Bavaria by the talented Adelheid Henriette of Savoy, wife of the Elector Ferdinand Maria (r.1651–79), with a performance in 1653 of her harp teacher Giovanni Battista Maccioni's dramatic cantata *L'arpa festante* for the visit of the Emperor Ferdinand III. Then in 1656 the Italian-trained Johann Caspar Kerll was summoned to become Kapellmeister, and in honour of the new Emperor Leopold I his *Oronte* was staged in the following year in the new opera house in the Salvatorplatz (a splendid building modelled on the Teatro Olimpico in Vicenza, and the first of its kind in Germany). Kerll composed more operas for Munich, but friction between him and the Italian musicians, anticipating many a subsequent quarrel between Germans with ambitions for an autonomous art and Italians immovable in their traditions, led to his resignation in 1673. So, at any rate, it seems: none of Kerll's operas survives, but his other music, especially that for *Pia et fortis mulier*, bears witness to an original spirit; and indeed he was famous as one of the most progressive musicians of his day, with a strong if intransigent personality. On Kerll's withdrawal, the initiative passed to three Italians, the father and son Ercole and Giuseppe Bernabei, and Ercole's pupil and assistant Agostino Steffani, who had also studied with Kerll and was in Munich from 1674. However, it may have been Kerll's influence which was responsible for a new development under the Elector Maximilian II, when some German Singspiels were performed at court.

Steffani's first opera, *Marco Aurelio*, was given in 1681; and the others which he wrote for the Munich court are the first of any importance in Germany to respond to French influences (including that of Lully), to which he had been exposed during a visit to Paris. These include a strong preponderance of arias in dance rhythms and a fondness for ballet interludes; while the demands of *Niobe* (1688: they include earthquakes, dragons, clouds and the movement of the planets) reflect the theatre's elaborate equipment and in turn the enduring Munich taste for display. The subjects are normally drawn from classical mythology, as usual, though an exception of a kind is *Alarico il Baltha* (1687). However, *Alarico*, on the subject of the

Visigoth leader Alaric and his siege of Rome in 410, shows no German characteristics to distinguish it from Steffani's other operas. It is essentially a succession of arias, often elegantly composed with little in the way of coloratura, linked by recitatives that serve to prepare for the next aria rather than further the drama. There are no ensembles, no choruses (apart from an exordium), few instrumental movements, and only three short duets.

Steffani also worked in one of the most enlightened of all North German Courts, that of Hanover. Here opera was first given in the reigns of Duke Johann Friedrich (r.1665–79) and his brother Ernst August (r.1679–98), by composers including Antonio Sartorio (Kapell-meister from 1666 to 1675) and Nicolaus Strungk. Until 1678, opera was given in the Ballhaus; then a 'kleines Schlosstheater' was opened in the castle. Competition between the Hanover and Brunswick branches of the Guelphs, who were descended from the twelfth-century Henry the Lion, was narrowly won by Hanover; and Ernst August had, for the opening of this 'grosses Schlosstheater' in 1689, confidently commissioned Steffani for *Henrico Leone* celebrating the 500th anniversary of the Battle of Bardowieck. In Hanover from 1688, new operas by Steffani were given almost annually, the last two of them being on German subjects, *Arminio* (1707, actually a pasticcio, on Hermann's defeat of the Romans in AD 9) and *Tassilone* (1709, set at the time of Charlemagne). His librettist was the Italian poet Ortensio Mauro, the Duke's secretary from 1675; and here, at least, an opera composer and his librettist were treated as civilized, and civilizing, human beings, for the Duke gave them a welcome to an intellectual circle that included (though by now only on its fringes) the philosopher Leibniz.

Dresden's affiliations also continued to be Italian, and were long to remain so. In 1651 Giovanni Andrea Bontempi entered the service of the Elector Johann Georg I, becoming in 1656 under Johann Georg II joint Kapellmeister with Schütz and Vincenzo Albrici. His *Paride* (1662) was the first opera by an Italian to be given in North Germany; written for a royal wedding, this vast so-called 'erotopegno musicale', or musical pledge of love, detained the guests, not to mention the bridal pair, from nine in the evening until two in the morning. It is a celebratory and not a dramatic work, in similar vein to its successor *Il pomo d'oro*, and making no deviations whatsoever from Italian principles. Bontempi's *Dafne* (1671), on the other hand, is set in German, using Opitz's translation for Schütz's opera. Meanwhile, Johann Georg III consolidated Dresden's Italian tradition by opening in 1667 a Comödienhaus seating two thousand in which there was installed in 1685 a permanent Italian company. In neighbouring Leipzig, which lacked a resident court, he was welcomed in 1683 with a 'dramma per musica' by Johann Kuhnau; and in 1692 his successor, Johann Georg IV, gave permission to Nicolaus Strungk to present a German Singspiel at his own expense during the great annual fair. Strungk seized his opportunity well, opening a theatre on the Brühl in the following year, composing for it, recruiting his daughters as well as performers from neighbouring Courts as singers, and making such a success as to cause a serious rift with Kuhnau, now at the Thomasschule, who found his choristers being wooed away by the lure of the stage.

It was generally in courts with less grandeur to proclaim, and fewer resources with which to pretend to any grandeur, that interest turned towards German opera, especially where there was a ruler with a concern for the progressive post-war development of his state rather than a return to an older order. Some were fortunate enough to have a member of the ruling family with artistic and intellectual interests. Brunswick became an important centre of Baroque music, including opera, thanks to the enthusiasm of the reigning family. Duke Rudolf August's brother Anton Ulrich wrote librettos for the resident composer, Johann Jacob Loewe, including a Singspiel-like text *Amelinde*. He also wrote a so-called 'Singespiel zur Lust und Ergetzung vor gestellt', *Der Hofman Daniel*: it includes a lute song for Darius's daughter Cassandane, and Daniel is sustained in the lions' den by a chorus of angels. Brunswick's vigorous musical life included performances in theatres in Wolfenbüttel, and in the Rathaus converted in 1690 by a rich burgher with a loan from the Duke. Other composers who worked in Brunswick included Hasse, Graun, and

Sigismund Kusser, whose *Cleopatra* opened the city's first commercial theatre in 1690. Another city with a diverse operatic life was Ansbach. Here, the Margrave's inclinations were to French culture and music, but a journey to Italy led him to plan an Italian opera house in the Residence; nevertheless, Italian operas were given in German, and there were original works by Christian Boxberg and the more significant Johann Wolfgang Franck. Similarly, Halle was made a centre of opera by Duke August of Saxony while he was living in the city as administrator of the Archbishopric of Magdeburg. He built a Comödienhaus and opened a small theatre in his residence; he also invited to the town Philipp Stolle, whose Singspiels (a genre the Duke encouraged) *Die Hochzeit der Thetis* and *Charimunda* were given in 1654 and 1658. In Gotha, Friedrich I also built a Comödienhaus in the west tower of the castle, and here Singspiels were given from 1683. Weissenfels went so far as to reject Italian opera altogether, and gave encouragement to Johann Philipp Krieger and Johan Beer and their Singspiels. Such enterprises, in the half century following the Thirty Years War, sowed seeds and even began to tend new growth in the scorched earth.

More cannot be claimed, and the situation was confused and even contradictory. Some courts were given over to Italian opera, but would also welcome visits from German touring companies; a few courts made a stand for German opera, but would not refuse Italianate works. There were German composers who adopted an Italian manner, and Italian composers (of whom the outstanding was Steffani) who made some use of German subjects and admitted French elements to their style. Italian librettos were sometimes translated or paraphrased into German. There were frequent exchanges and consequent shifts of emphasis as composers moved from one court to another. To darken still further the fog pervading the scene, in which only a few landmarks can be glimpsed, most of the stage music of the period is lost. There is not the reliable evidence, from scores and fragments that do survive, to suggest an historical pattern, even if one existed in such chaotic times. Moreover, there was neither the Italian framework of a small number of city-states building steadily upon a Renaissance of past glories, nor a capital city with the magnetism of Paris to draw artists and intellectuals together so as to concentrate debate and stimulate creative enterprise.

Nevertheless, debate continued, even when creativity seemed to lag; and it was given an authoritative voice by the deeply respected Kiel professor of poetry and rhetoric, Daniel Georg Morhof. In his *Unterricht von der Teutschen Sprache und Poesie* (1682), Morhof (who had visited England and written about Shakespeare) joined in the discussion relating the modern theatrical arts to those of the ancient world. In the Greek and Roman theatre, he claimed with prelapsarian fervour, poetry, music, acting and dance had all been combined; but with the decline of that civilization, the ideal had been lost, and it was for modern artists to recover and renew that dramatic synthesis.

> Dieses ist zu mercken / dass die alten Griechen und Römer es so weit herinne gebracht haben / dass wir noch bey ihnen in die Schule gehen müssen. Was wir darinne / gethan / haben war alles aus ihrer Nachahmung. Man hat bey ihnen die Singspiele / Täntze und Thöne viel vollkommener gehabt / als wir jetzo ihnen nachkünstler . . . gehandelt. Die nach ihren *pedibus* abgemessene Verse / die darauff sich gründende Music / und mit derselben verknüpfte Täntze / und Bewegungen der Glieder / können von uns nicht begrieffen werden. Man hat die *Pantomimos* gehabt / welche durch ihre stumme Leibesbewegung auch alle Reden haben vorstellen können / welches alleine durch den *Rhythmen*, den man in der *pronunciation* der Sylben / und in der Music gebrauchet / hat geschehen können. (Morhof, 1682, Ch. xvi, 349)

(It must be borne in mind that the ancient Greeks and Romans developed so far that we are bound to study them. What we have done is entirely in imitation of them. With them sung plays, dances and music were more of a whole than is the case now with us, their artistic successors . . . Their verses measured in feet, the music based on it, and the connected dances and movements of the limbs cannot be comprehended by us. They had pantomime, which by means of its mute bodily movement could also express all speeches which could otherwise only be realized through rhythm employed in the articulation of syllables and music.)

Morhof had no solution to offer to the long-enduring problem of how to find librettos that might encourage such a synthesis. Though dramatists generally wrote in expectation of a musical contribution, no question seems to have arisen of a serious musical collaboration between writer and composer. The most important mid-century dramatist, Andreas Gryphius (1616–64), found room for musical opportunities in many of his plays, both serious and comic. His so-called 'Freudenspiel' *Majuma* (1653) includes among its arias a six-strophe song for a lamed soldier. His 'Schertzspiel' *Horribilicribrifax* (c. 1650), a *miles gloriosus* comedy satirizing pedantry rather pedanti-cally, has an unaccompanied song and a final dance and chorus. *Ermordete Majestät* (written in 1649, the year of the trial and execution of Charles I which it portrays) has a first act ending with a chorus of murdered English kings ('Weicht Geister! Britten ist kein ort vor stille seelen!'), a second with a chorus of sirens, and the finale with a double chorus in which Religion contends with Heresy. But there is little musical advance here upon previous example, and little sign that any composer saw the chance of developing a more thorough-going musical drama. Not until 1678 did Hamburg establish the first public opera house outside Venice; and it is with this venture that the history of German opera takes a significant step forward.

Separated from the main areas of battle, and able to maintain trading contacts with the outside world, Hamburg had been almost entirely spared the convulsions of the Thirty Years War. At the Peace of Westphalia it was one of the largest and most prosperous of all German cities, its population of 40,000 including a substantial proportion of foreigners, many of them aristocrats, merchants and intellectuals fleeing political and religious persecution, especially Flemings and Walloons, Huguenots, Southern Germans and a good sprinkling of Spanish and Portuguese Jews. Moreover, the city's independence was assured by its value to England, Holland and later France as a distributing centre for their exports, together with its ability to play off Sweden against Denmark (who controlled respectively the left and right banks of the lower Elbe). Yet its own trading security was by no means assured, in precarious times and with the old Hanseatic League in decline; and the city fathers showed prescience in welcoming immigrants as full citizens. Government was in the hands of a *Senat* consisting of a hereditary group of twenty men chosen from the city's principal families – not the only respect in which this free, cosmopolitan port-city resembled Venice – together with a less powerful *Rath* of sixty burghers elected by those possessing the most property. The Church was ruled over by a *Geistliches Ministerium* consisting of all the city's pastors except that of the Cathedral. Intellectual life and education, which included a strong emphasis on church music, were vigorously encouraged, within the atmosphere of a dominant religious idealism that continued to characterize German life despite the growing atmosphere of intellectual scepticism in France and England. Nevertheless, at a time when most German cities, exhausted and often in near-ruins, were trying to recover and to rebuild on old institutions, Hamburg was concerning itself with new ones.

Communal participation in civic affairs, and social mobility free from national or racial constraints, were civilized policies, but also sound economics for a major international trading city looking to the future; and the immigrations by those escaping from political turbulence elsewhere in Europe swelled the city to an active and energetic population of 70,000 by 1680. In practice, the groups controlling commerce, the Church and education could be as powerful and proscriptive as all oligarchies, and often came into mutual conflict; while the same was true of those who gave their time to the arts that were beginning to flourish in these fertile conditions. Nevertheless, the city was ideally placed to found what was to be the first public opera house outside Venice, and receptive to influences from various nations upon it. Surrounding it, there was a well established northern 'circuit' embracing Danzig, Copenhagen and Berlin, along which there travelled performers and composers, some of them among the earliest practitioners of the *stile rappresentativo*. There was a disposition towards the popular stage, and an experience of the English players with repertories that included versions of Shakespeare, together with a strong interest in English literature and philosophy. The immigrants included musicians from France bringing with them their own skills and traditions, and also capitalizing on the general European respect for French classical drama. Awareness of Italian opera came through the travels and training of a few Germans. The city had the wealth and the intellectual curiosity but also the opportunities to encourage patronage for new ideas; and not least, there was the strong interest in church music and the secular theatre, and a forum for the exchange of the ideas they stimulated.

The initiative for a civic opera seems to have come from the exiled Duke Christian Albrecht of Schleswig-Holstein, who had supported opera in his court at Gottorf, but the prime mover was a member of a distinguished Hamburg family, Gerhard Schott. Educated in the city and at universities including Heidelberg and Basel, he received from the latter a law degree in 1665. He then toured Europe, including England and Italy, and may have learnt something of the business of opera in Venice. Certainly there was a Venetian tinge to the opera which Schott founded in partnership with another successful lawyer, Peter Lütjen, and the organist of the Catharinenkirche, Johann Adam Reincken. Land was rented on the Gänsemarkt, next to the site of the modern Staatsoper, and a building was erected to the designs of Girolamo Sartorio (who had been architect to the court of Hanover), possibly on the Venetian model of the Teatro di SS Giovanni e Paolo. The most important of the first designers for the theatre, from 1695 to 1705, Oswald Harms, had also worked in Venice. As befitted the democratic nature of the enterprise, the theatre was remarkable less for the sumptuousness of its auditorium than for its capacity, with a parterre, four levels of boxes holding nine to twelve seats, and a gallery, in all seating 2,000. Its almost equally spacious stage was some 80 feet deep and 40 feet wide, and was equipped with sophisticated stage machinery. There were fifteen *Kulissen*, or wings, fitted not only with slides but with so-called *Thelaren*, the old prism-shaped *periaktoi* that could be revolved so as to produce a rapid, even 'magical' scene-change (such as a cave changing to a garden at the wave of a sorcerer's wand). There were also three acting areas, one behind the other, so that a new scene could be prepared during the previous one; and use could be made of perspective (after the much-admired model of Palladio's Teatro Olimpico in Vicenza). The stage could, further, make use of two storeys, for scenes, say, between earth and Heaven, and of lifts to raise heroes to Olympus or to bring down a *deus ex machina*; and there was sophisticated use of lighting effects, even fireworks (Wolff, 1957, I, 351ff.). The fluency, as well as the splendour and intricacy, of these devices naturally in turn affected composers' techniques in what was to become the high point of German Baroque opera.

From the start, the Hamburg opera seized the opportunity of its break with such previous tradition as had existed by introducing the most advanced ideas in opera and operatic staging to a wide public. Those who wrote for the theatre and worked in it were required to satisfy an audience of aristocrats, burghers, merchants and the equivalents of Shakespeare's groundlings. Their conflicting expectations were not only often irreconcilable; they could clash with the ideas of different librettists and composers, the need of successive directors to keep the enterprise financially viable, and the suspicions of the Church. The season was year-long, from January to December, with the usual breaks for Lent and other religious holidays and a short summer recess, and up to ten operas might be staged in the course of sixty-five to one hundred performances that included between two and ten premières. Performances were on Monday, Wednesday and Thursday afternoons. From 1685 Schott acted as sole director, withdrawing in 1693 on becoming a senator but being obliged to return in 1696 after the venture failed when its lessee Jacob Kremberg fled his creditors. Schott tried to withdraw again in 1699, and again was forced to return to the rescue in the following year, remaining in charge until his death in 1702. Other troubles beset the enterprise, as when insurrection brought the government low and closed the opera in 1685, and when attack by the King of Denmark forced closure again in the following year.

On 2 January 1678 the house opened with *Der erschaffene, gefallene und auffgerichtete Mensch*, or *Adam und Eva*, to a text by Christian Richter and with music by Johann Theile, the composer brought to Hamburg by Duke Christian Albrecht. Such Biblical operas were characteristic of the early stages of the Hamburg enterprise, and their subjects were chosen partly so as to pacify the ecclesiastical authorities in what was soon to become an intellectual and moral battleground. Others that followed included *Die Geburt Christi* (1681), with music by Theile, and *Cain und Abel* (1689), with music by Johann Philipp Förtsch, both to texts by Christian Heinrich Postel. One of Hamburg's most prolific and successful librettists, Postel belonged to a group of writers who were happy to place their talents at the service of the new enterprise, and to take part, often with lengthy prefaces to their operas, in the debate concerning the nature and practice of the emergent German opera. They included the pastor Hinrich Elmenhorst, Lucas von Bostel, Friedrich Christian Bressand, Barthold Feind, and Christian Hunold, who wrote under the pseudonym 'Menantes'. From the start they began also to introduce a number of secular subjects, as with Theile's setting of a translation from the Italian, *Orontes* (1678).

One of the most substantial works of the early years was *Cara Mustapha* (1686), a double opera in two parts each of three acts, to a text by Bostel, set by Johann Wolfgang Franck (who had arrived in Hamburg in 1679 as a fugitive from justice in Ansbach). The opera is entitled in full *Der glückliche Gross-Vezier Cara Mustapha, erster Teil, nebenst der grausigen Belagerung und Bestürmung der Kaiserlichen Residenzstadt Wien; anderer Teil, nebenst dem freulichen Entsatze der Kaiserlichen Residenzstadt Wien* ('The fortunate Grand Vizier Cara Mustapha, first part, including the grim Siege and Assault of the Imperial Court City of Vienna; second part, including the Happy Relief of the Imperial Court City of Vienna'). The action is thus set only three years previously during the 1683 Turkish siege. Though there is a religious element, in the confrontation of Christianity and Islam, the work is really the story of the disordered passions of the Turkish commander, as a consequence of which his divided army is routed and he himself formally strangled at the Sultan's command. While the Biblical operas were to a considerable extent shaped by the German school drama, the influence on secular works came more from Venice and from Paris. In the case of *Cara Mustapha*, there was the immediate example of a tyrant overthrown in Antonio Sartorio's double opera of 1667, *La Prosperità di Elio Sejano* and *La Caduta di Elio Sejano*, performed on alternate nights in Venice in 1667 and familiar to Hamburg audiences from a German translation of Minato's libretto in 1678. From Venice also, where, as in Hamburg, a public drawn from different strata of society looked for entertainment, came the free intermingling of popular elements with a more elevated, aristocratic style which was to characterize Hamburg opera. Bostel admitted to a French influence on his text, which shows most immediately in his quite skilful use of alexandrines in a number of scenes. Franck and other composers and their librettists also drew freely upon adaptations of foreign plots, from the French (Molière and Corneille), from the Spanish (Calderón and Lope de

Vega) and from the Italian (Minato), as well as from the examples of English drama brought into Germany by the English players and from Singspiels and their use of familiar local types.

Together with Theile, Förtsch and Nicolaus Adam Strungk, Franck is the most important of the composers of the first period of the Hamburg opera. However, it is impossible to form more than the most tentative judgement about their contribution since of all their operas, only Franck's *Die drey Töchter des Cecrops* (1680) has survived complete. A number of individual operatic arias exist, but much more music was destroyed during the 1939–45 war, to be preserved only in examples previously copied by Helmut Christian Wolff. His detailed investigation, the second volume of which consists of copious music examples, remains the most thorough account of the Hamburg repertory, its composers, librettists and background (Wolff, 1957). However, Wolff's thesis, resting on an enthusiasm for the independence of German art, is that German Baroque opera differed substantially enough from its Italian origins as to constitute an independent genre with a central position in the general history of German opera. This is clearly intended as a counter to the more tenable views of critics including, for example, Hermann Kretzschmar, who declared that, 'Vor dem 19. Jahrhundert giebt es keine allgemeine anerkannte deutsche Oper, man kann für das 17. und 18. Jahrhundert nur eine Geschichte der Oper in Deutschland aufstellen, und diese Geschichte ist im grossen Ganzen nichts als ein Anhang zur Geschichte der italienischen Oper' (Kretzschmar, 1901–2, 270–1) ('Before the nineteenth century there is no generally recognized German opera, and for the seventeenth and eighteenth centuries one can only refer to the history of opera in Germany, which history is as a whole no more than an appendix to the history of Italian opera').

Certainly there is a new amalgam of styles, such as might be expected in a city with an openness to international influences; and it could be said that this was in itself a characteristic of German opera in times when it was still at an early stage of trying to form a national identity. However, only a few of the ingredients are as yet specifically

German in character. Franck writes expressive, quite dramatic recitatives, fluent though still distinct from the arias. Some of the latter owe their style to Venetian example, as so much in Hamburg opera does, but many are influenced by the spirit of German song, of which Franck was a master; and though he also drew (in a more French manner) upon dance rhythms in his concern to make a popular appeal to a wide public, he could write arias of greater emotional substance that set a German example in their harmonic expressiveness and in the importance of their orchestral contribution. In some cases these make use of his sacred songs: Wolff quotes an example from *Cara Mustapha*, the last of Franck's seventeen Hamburg operas, in which a Passion song (Jesus on the Cross bowing His head and dying) is elaborated with melismata, more affective harmony and an expressive ritornello for violins, to become an aria for Ibrahim under the threat of death from Mustapha (Wolff, 1957, II, 36–7). Still more affective is the lament of Ibrahim's beloved Baschlari, an aria whose striking qualities include a long, wide-ranging melodic line, well-judged instrumental contributions, and especially an increasing harmonic intensity in which a da capo is avoided and the aria taken forward to its emotion-laden chromatic conclusion (Example 2).

Franck dominated the Hamburg repertory between the years 1679 and 1686 with at least seventeen operas. His sole surviving work is *Die drey Töchter des Cecrops, in einem Sing-Spiel vorgestellt* (ed. G. F. Schmidt, in DTB, year 37–8, vol. 38). The title thus declares German intent, for all the Italian influences that, characteristically of the Hamburg operas, survive into text and music. The author of the libretto was Maria Aurora von Königsmarck, one of the many mistresses of Augustus the Strong; and it is well designed to set out for music the story (from Book II of Ovid's *Metamorphoses*) of Mercury falling in love with Herse, the fairest of King Cecrops's three daughters, his frustration by Minerva, and the eventual marriage of Herse's other suitor, Pirante, to her sister Pandrosus. The Italian influences in the music are evident especially in the Venetian character of many of the recitatives and arias, and in expressive touches such as the repeated melismata on the word 'Freiheit' in

Example 2   Franck: *Cara Mustapha* (1686), Baschlari

Venus's first aria. But Franck handles the conventions with an individuality that suggests new directions. When Mercury, flying overheard, spies Herse, he descends and, overwhelmed by her beauty, sings of her in a graceful arioso melody; he tries to fly off, but cannot bring himself to do so, and his emotion drives him into E♭ for a lyrical aria in triple time. The light unevenness of the verse and of its rhyme scheme gives Franck the cue for music in which Mercury's amorous confusion is expressed in a melody which not only avoids regular eight- (or sixteen-) bar phrases but produces unexpected metrical shifts within these, as words are repeated and their emphases altered (Example 3).

Much of the arioso writing is also freely structured, in eloquent

(These secret snares are like fetters; we perceive them when they entangle us,
and when we can no longer escape them.)

Example 3   Franck: *Die drey Töchter des Cecrops* (1680), Mercury

declamatory style and drawing on strong and expressive harmonic
support. The choruses vary from some lively Cupids who take their
manner from chorale (though not parodistically), to a solemn choral
response to the stately entry of the three sisters to celebrate a
sacrifice; while the arias, often in duple form (thus helping to propel
the drama) rather than da capo form, can also include lighter
elements, such as the popular Hamburg feature of a stammering

strophic song for the servant Sylvander (allowing Franck once more to play with dislocated rhythms, this time for comic effect). The characters are given a distinct musical identity, within their broader musical separation into gods, nobles and servants; and though the idea of actual motive is a long way off, there is even the suggestion of recurring rhythmic or melodic figures to identify characters (such as that accompanying Envy).

Even less than of Franck is known of Förtsch, who wrote some twelve operas that in their turn dominated the repertory between 1684 and 1690: their music is lost, and the four excerpts published by Wolff, two of them eight-bar snatches of strophic song, reveal little (Wolff, 1957, II, 54–6). From 1679, Strungk was director of the city and cathedral music in Hamburg, and in 1680 his first three operas were given there; two more followed in 1683, though by then he had removed to Hanover. He later established the opera in Leipzig, opening it with one of his Hamburg works, *Alceste*. Wolff suggests that with his first opera, *Esther*, he introduced the repetition of words and extended coloratura into Hamburg opera for expressive purposes, and that this Italianate manner may have derived from his father's friendship with Schütz (Wolff, I, 203–8; II, 15–23). However, he moved beyond Italian example, and what little survives may suggest an interest in breaking free from the repetitions of German strophic song and in extending an expressive harmonic and contrapuntal range.

The fame of the Hamburg opera made it a focus not only for composers, writers and other artists, but for the attentions of the Church. The obvious Italian influence on Baroque opera may have initially aroused the suspicions of Lutheran pastors fearing a Roman Catholic infection at work, especially since Baroque opera had so much in common with the more sumptuous manifestations of the Jesuit drama, but within their concern also lay doubts going back at least to St Augustine about the morality of the theatre when it made such a powerful appeal to the senses. These anxieties were not stilled by an attempt to appeal to a controversy of the previous century, when a party in German Protestantism known as the Adiaphorists had declared that certain matters could be regarded as *adiaphora*, or points of indifference as far as the conscience was concerned. The controversy was revived in the latter part of the seventeenth century, especially by the Pietists. Under the leadership of Philipp Jacob Spener, their attempts to infuse a more devotional content into Lutheran dogmatic instruction included disapproval of worldly entertainments, among which the luxury of opera seemed a prime example. So far from being a mere *adiaphoron*, opera was punningly categorized as *opera diabolica*, or a work of the Devil, and the Hamburg Pietists found a vigorous advocate when Spener's friend Anton Reiser became Pastor of the Jacobikirche. From his pulpit he denounced opera as by no means an *adiaphoron* but a cause of evil amply attested by the Fathers of the early Church, and from his study he delivered in 1681 a broadside in the form of a work entitled *Theatromania*, quoting at length from the Fathers to lend authority to his arguments.

The first to return the attack was a Roman Catholic actor, Christoph Rauch, with a spirited 150-page pamphlet which, turning Reiser's title against itself, he entitled *Theatrophania* (or 'Theatrical Clarity'). Opening with a Preface declaring the world to be a dramatic creation of God, Rauch proceeds by way of five Arguments. He asks who condemns painters, engravers and sculptors because they represent fact and fiction, or the performers of Biblical scenes in Church or castle, or who reproaches Aesop's fables as profane or declares that historians are intrinsically wicked. How much more, then, is the unification of these arts in opera to be valued as a work of the Nine Muses and an enlightenment of the mind: 'wer ist / der nicht auffs höchst alle freye Künsten / nehmlich Pictoriam, Musicam, Statuariam, Historiam, Ethicam, Pöesin. Rhetoricam preiset / welche alle in den Operen gleischsam in einen Gymnasio sich einfinden . . ?' (Rauch, 1682, 17) ('who does not hold in the highest regard all the liberal arts, namely painting, music, sculpture, history, ethics and rhetorical poetry, all of which in opera are brought together in a school of study . . ?'). With his argument that opera represents neither the moralising instruction which lay in the old school drama, nor a frivolous diversion, but a form that by its very unity in diversity was capable, through its multiple appeal to the senses, of elevating the audience's minds and spirits, Rauch set the tone for much subsequent discussion. He went on to meet the objections of *Theatromania* by pointing out that, as the Pietists refrained on moral grounds from visiting the theatre, they were scarcely in a position to act as opera critics, nor did they go beyond mere allegation in declaring the works (and their performers) to be diabolical. Their reliance on the authority of patristic writings he deals with in a formidable muster of refutations (literally 'reproofs', *Vorwürfe*) of no fewer than sixteen Fathers of the Church, from the comparatively obscure Arnobius and Minucius Felix to the Saints Cyprian, Isidore, Ambrose, Jerome, Clement of Alexandria, John Chrysostom and Augustine himself (who, not surprisingly, needs as many as twelve refutations). Rauch presents his cases fairly, sometimes conceding points, his argument being (in part by selective quotation) that Reiser has refused to realize that the Fathers were contending with the debauched or frivolous practices of the theatre of Rome or Carthage, and that the modern theatre was something essentially different.

Support for this idea of opera as a unified work of art fell on fertile ground. Though the actual form that unification might take was not made clear, the argument was to remain at the centre of all significant discussions on the condition to which German opera should aspire. Theory, both aesthetic and philosophical, continued to precede by a long way musical practice which was not yet formed to embody it. One of the most important philosophical voices in support came from Leibniz. His experiences at the artistically busy court of Hanover had brought him into contact with opera through his friendship with Steffani, and he now wrote to an anxious enquirer agreeing that patristic writings on the theatre could concern only the abuses of Ancient Rome. In his view, opera, like any art form, had no intrinsic moral standing, but could certainly have moral application and therefore be used constructively. Further, he followed Rauch in arguing that the unification of the arts represented by opera made a particularly strong appeal because absorbed through both ear and eye, this strength offering the possibility of being used in a positive social context.

Cannonades continued to be exchanged between rival pulpits. Reiser returned Rauch's fire with a pamphlet addressing him as 'der gewissen-lose Advocat' ('the unscrupulous lawyer'); but the most damaging salvoes were discharged by the Pastor who, to the Pietists' particular irritation, was prominent in the circle of Hamburg librettists, and thus literally practised what he preached. Heinrich Elmenhorst had written a large number of sacred verses which were set by Franck, who also composed three sacred operas to his texts; and in 1688 he published his *Dramatologia Antiquo-Hodierna, Das ist: Bericht von denen Oper-Spielen*. Despite setting at the head of his book an epigraph from St Paul's Epistle to the Corinthians pacifically declaring that there was no place for contentiousness in the Church (1 Cor. xi, 16), Elmenhorst enthusiastically carried the war into the enemy camp. He first reaffirmed that 'Adiaphora aber / oder Mittel-Dinge heissen die jenige Dinge / worvon die H. Schrift keinen deutlichen Befehl giebet / welch Sie nicht gebeut / auch nicht verbeut' (Elmenhorst, 1688, Preface) ('Adiaphora or intermediate matters are the names given to those things about which Holy Writ gives no clear indication as to whether they are to be imposed or forbidden'). Agreeing with Rauch that the condemnation of the Roman theatre by the Early Fathers was for its assault on Christians, as well as for the moral squalor of the circuses, he turned Reiser's argument on its head by suggesting that the effectiveness of the association of the Roman theatre with a pagan religion proved how different an art associated with the true Christian faith must be, especially since it had gone on to develop its own specific genres. Among these was opera, whose evolution into an independent form bore witness that theatrical spectacle was indeed an *adiaphoron*:

> Was ist aber eine Opere, darvon allhie die Streitigkeit ist? Eine Opere ist ein Sing-Spiel / auf dem Schau-Platz vorgestellt / mit erbaren

Zurüstungen / und anständigen Sitten / zu geziemender Ergötzlichkeit
der Gemühter / Ausübung der Poesie und Fortsetzung der Music.

(Elmenhorst, 1688, 101)

(So what is an opera, about which there is all the controversy? An opera
is a sung play presented on the stage, with all the proper equipment and
the suitable conventions for the due delight of the feelings, the exercise
of poetry and the expression of music.)

Later, he asserts,

Was aus denen Patribus und anderen wider die Schau-Spiele wird
angeführet / nicht wider die Hamburgische Operen mit Wahrheit könne
geredet / oder geschrieben / das ist / auff diese Spiele nicht appliciret
werden. (Elmenhorst, 1688, 177–8)

(What is quoted from the Fathers and others against the theatre cannot
truthfully be uttered or written against the Hamburg operas, that is to
say, is not applicable to these pieces.)

Opera, he insisted, had a healthy secular life that need be no concern
of the clergy provided it caused no specific religious affront. This
established, he proceeded to argue that the opera house was well
equipped to present moral ideas in the context of secular as well as
sacred subjects, appealing as it did to men's minds through their
imagination with the theatrical arts of painting, poetry and music (in
a form of musical declamation) and of stage machinery. He devotes
several pages to the importance of the latter, not as a trumpery
pleasure but for its power to create a constructive illusion in
association with poetry and music. He specifically proposes that
opera could encourage the cultivation of a German poetry suitable
for musical setting, and of respect for German history and tradition.

Among the voices raised in support of Elmenhorst, one of the
most effective was that of Georg Bertuch, who joined battle with a
dissertation submitted to the University of Kiel in 1693. Bertuch is
careful to distinguish between the theatre of the Greeks and the
Romans, emphasizing the superiority of the Greek in its use of vocal
and instrumental music, machines and other dramatic devices in a
unified form. He even troubles to counter Reiser's philological

arguments about *opera diabolica* with a piece of etymology of his own with reference to one of Reiser's revered Fathers of the Church, Tertullian:

> Sed enim denotat ac alias *Opera* Wercke / quod nomen per eminentiam quandam ludis hisce musico-scenicis inditum est, pari modo ac Græci hos ludos generaliter appellant δράματα, ab antiquo vocabulo δράν, quod idem est πράττειν, operari, facere'. (Bertuch, 1693, 15)

> (But he used the description *Opera*, works, by which is meant above all staged musical plays, in the same way that the Greeks usually called these plays dramas, from the ancient word to act, which is the same as to do, to operate, to make.)

After a sustained refutation of Reiser's accusations of intrinsic evil in the theatre, Bertuch proposes that drama is on the contrary a potential agent for moral good, and opera the more so as the singing voice is a gift from God commended by the Bible; and he concludes that as the created world is a divine drama, so the theatre reflects creation (Bertuch, 1693, 23, 25).

Those who attacked the theatre's enemies from the secular flank included Lucas von Bostel, who spoke with civic authority as Mayor of Hamburg from 1709 but had already distinguished himself as one of the most important of the city's librettists. *Cara Mustapha* was influential not only by virtue of its success as a work of art, but for Bostel's well-argued Preface. Siding with Elmenhorst's position, he asserted that so far from there being evidence of opera's destructive influence, it was actually conducive to civic harmony; and his own text for *Cara Mustapha* was, he believed, entirely in accordance with Lutheran principles. He supported this by boldly rejecting the Aristotelian unities of classical French drama in favour of action, supported by music and staging, that would highlight aspects of the plot and its moral teaching; and he went so far as to reject the natural analogy with spoken drama in favour of one with painting, in which there had to be concentration on the most important elements of the subject within a given framework. This, he declared, so far from distorting the truth was to provide the most vivid representation of it.

In some important respects, Christian Heinrich Postel followed these ideas closely. Like the other leading Hamburg librettists, his prefaces are lengthy and not without reason have been criticized for their pomposity; but the portentous manner, and the larding of the text with passages in Latin and Greek as well as several modern languages, were common to much German critical writing asserting solid learning and appealing to classical authority. They also reject the French reliance on the unities, as well as a strictly narrative manner. Both represented for Postel a constriction on the imaginative presentation of the ideas lying within a narrative, which should be the function of an art form so well able to appeal to the imagination of the listener, and to do so by means of the senses. Opera had a higher reality than literalism, and was governed by poetic and musical realities. To this end, he made a bolder move away from naturalism, fictionalizing events so as to heighten their poetic significance (and coolly directing objectors back to history or the Bible if they wanted the originals), and not hesitating to introduce comic relief or other diversions as part of the whole entertainment. The poet's role, on behalf of the composer, was to select for expressive purposes.

The consequence was a much freer form of libretto, with musical implications that were to remain valid for many years to come. First, the ability of the stage to move characters across time and space was an essential part of its nature, opening up new expressive possibilities. Further, he abandoned the use of alexandrines (with their French associations and their implication of a constrictive regularity), introducing a wider variety of metre to reflect contrasting character and state of mind. His devotion to Greek example took a more imaginative form than the assumption that opera was a re-creation of the Attic drama, or that it had been superseded by the Christian development of opera: rather, he used his familiarity with Greek epic and drama to select stories or aspects of stories (such as *Venus and Adonis*) so as to present in dramatic form an inner meaning; and his respect took the intelligent librettist's form of being willing to shorten even great speeches so as to make them available for the composer's art. Though he has been criticized by later ages for the artificial and even bombastic nature of his complex style, it was one well adapted to the time and the place; and while his texts remain firmly within Baroque convention, and within the doctrine of the affections as seen in contrasting operatic roles, they do not exclude the development of character.

Support for Postel came from the other Hamburg librettists, especially in the general concern to resist French influence; indeed, the vigour of the French attacks on opera on the grounds of its irrationality, above all in the writings of Saint-Evremond, served to rally German responses. It was, however, characteristic that these should take the form not of a united front defending a particular case, since it was the idea of an imposed orthodoxy that was being resisted, but of a series of heterodox theses. One of the most vigorous and articulate of those who argued for opera, as the supreme theatrical form by virtue of its combination of several arts, was Christian Friedrich Hunold. A major part of his stance rested on an appeal for each work to be judged on its own merits, not in accordance with predetermined canons; though not disputing the importance of standards, he was appealing for empirical criticism from an intelligent audience experiencing the effect of each work in the theatre. In saying this, he was obviously inviting a response not only incidentally to each new opera, but to the whole art of opera as representing a mixture of the theatrical arts whose proportions might vary according to the individual demands of the work in question.

But the most thorough articulation of Hamburg views came from Barthold Feind. A lively and contentious character, Feind was a lawyer and satirist who managed to fall foul of the civic authorities. They would not have taken kindly to his scarcely veiled allusions to civic oppression in his libretto for *Masagniello*, and one of his operas was the object of an official raid on the theatre. Later, he was exiled from the city and hanged in effigy, then undergoing imprisonment by the Danes for taking Sweden's part too enthusiastically. Though in many ways close to Postel and Hunold, he abandoned the argument, originally designed to counter ecclesiastical objections, that opera was the latest manifestation of a constantly evolving theatrical art, in favour of the idea that each nation and age had produced its own valid art forms. This was, naturally, advanced in support of the idea of empirical criticism as opposed to abstract formulations of principle, as well as for new art forms rather than a supposed re-creation of the methods of the Attic drama. In turn, this led him in the direction of a drama arising from its characters (rather than as a demonstration of the possibilities of the arts contributing to one another through theatrical devices): greater importance should be given to the singer as actor, appealing directly to the audience rather than to scholars and theorists, and projecting the drama through his own art rather than merely uttering his lines and melodies within a given situation. The objection that the increased emphasis on communicating more immediately to listeners might mean pandering to the lowest in audience taste was met by reference to Greek practice in mingling comic with tragic scenes, and also to Shakespeare. Feind was one of the first writers to understand more of Shakespeare than could be found in the bastardized versions that had made his plots familiar by way of the English players, and (over a century before the Romantics) to recognize him as an antithesis to the French classical theatre. Though he deferred to the prevailing intellectual temper by seeking a scientific rationale for his arguments – in his case, an appeal of slender justification to the emotions as based on the Four Temperaments – he did the most among the group of Hamburg librettists to prepare the way for composers who could rise to these challenges.

From 1690, Schott was able to rely on the contribution of composers who not only wrote for his theatre but were prepared to act as Kapellmeisters. The first was Johann Georg Conradi. Arriving in Hamburg from posts in Ansbach (where he would have made the acquaintance of Lully's works) and Römhild, he took up his position in 1690, and between then and 1693 nine out of his ten recorded operas were performed there. All were to librettos by Postel, and all were believed lost until an astute piece of detective work established that the first of Conradi's Hamburg operas, *Die schöne und getreue Ariadne* (1691), had in fact survived, wrongly attributed to Keiser (Buelow, 1972). The identification is important not just because the work is only the third German opera to have survived (if *Seelewig* be accepted as an opera); it also sheds light on Conradi himself, as a composer of significance, and perhaps more importantly on the kind of opera being given in the early years of the Hamburg venture.

Ariadne 'is a cosmopolitan mixture of Venetian, German and French musical styles in which the French spirit totally dominates everything but the recitatives' (Buelow, 1972, 111). There is a stately Lullian overture, and a Lullian final scene consisting of a passacaglia based on a four-bar descending tetrachord over which a sequence of seventy-eight well-varied statements provides a no less stately cere-monial close. Much of the melodic style is also French-influenced, with short arias and duets and comparative simplicity and freedom from vocal display; and there are signs of a wish to loosen the da capo structure of arias. The Venetian influence shows chiefly in the recitatives, which gain a more characteristically German and indi-vidual nature through the richness of the orchestral contribution, and in particular through the dramatic involvement of that greater emotional richness with the progress of the plot. Conradi's methods are sometimes deceptively simple: he has a gift for keeping to plain but expressive recitative, with affective touches, until the dramatic consequence of what is being narrated will flower into expressive arioso. There is enough here for the loss of the rest of his work to be a frustration.

For reasons that are not clear, but which may be to do with the regime under the feckless Jacob Kremberg from 1693, Conradi left, to be replaced as Kapellmeister in 1695 by Johann Sigismund Kusser. A quarrelsome man, Kusser had left Brunswick-Wolfenbüttel after a row when he publicly criticized his librettist Bressand. He now lost no time in falling out with Kremberg. Denied access to the theatre for his opera *Porus*, he staged a performance with Schott's help in the refectory of the cathedral, with such success that he succeeded

Kremberg after the latter's precipitate flight. However, the post only lasted a matter of months, and Kusser set off on a number of tours, finishing his career, after further quarrels on the way, in Dublin. His operas are all lost: the little of his music to survive suggests that he, too, had come under the influence of Lully, with whom he had studied in Paris. His admiration for Lully's orchestral discipline was reflected in his own skill as a conductor, which raised standards, and he helped to introduce Hamburg audiences to a wider international repertory.

Kusser's departure brought into Hamburg the first major composer of German opera, Reinhard Keiser. From 1696 Keiser composed a stream of operas at the rate of two to four a year, collaborating especially with Postel, Hunold and Feind, and (as far as can be judged from the slender evidence of what went before) taking the achievements of his predecessors on to a new plane. Certainly his was a dramatic talent of the highest significance for the evolution of German opera, one whose importance rested not only on innate musical gifts but on a concern to integrate these with the kind of drama being advocated by the Hamburg librettists, in particular Feind. For all their different approaches, their ideal consciously rested upon the example of a Shakespearian mixed dramatic genre, with violent or tragic events taking place on the stage and comic scenes mingling with serious ones, rather than upon the French classical style, respecting the unities and only reporting the occurrence of tragic events off-stage. It was also a drama in which the actions of the characters were an expression of their psychological attitudes. Such a prescription demanded a major musical talent to give full operatic life to what too often remained, for all the solemn arguments of the prefaces, sprawling, diffuse concoctions. Keiser was a composer in whom intelligence and creativity were admirably balanced.

His response, greatly varied as this was in the course of some sixty-six operas (of which about a third survive), brought a closer integration of the conventions of Baroque opera with the demands of a dramatic text, whether it were opera on popular German subjects (the double opera *Störtebecker und Jödge Michaels*, 1701), Biblical opera (*Salomon*, 1703 and *Nebuchadnezar*, 1704), historical drama (*Masagniello*, 1706) or classical drama (*Croesus*, 1711, rev. 1730). With an increased proportion of action over reflection came the need for greater emphasis on recitative to move the action forward, and this in turn gave Keiser the opportunity for a closer attention to words and the actions and states of mind they represented. His verbal inflections can be highly expressive, following characteristically German contours and rhythms of speech, and, in contrast to Italian secco, suggest a move between parlando and the arioso manner of Bach's more intensely emotional Passion recitatives (on which, indeed, they had considerable influence). From this follows the need for effective harmonic support, which can be highly inflected and involve well-judged variation in the pace of harmonic movement. This expressive range enables him even to make use of recitative for more than one character at a time in tense situations, sustaining the dramatic flow here rather than in aria.

It also suggests the need for expressive orchestral support; and here it is that Keiser can be at his most original. Even when there is no more than a continuo, this can take the form of considerably more than token harmonic backing and make use of figures, motives almost, which identify the characters and their emotions, mirroring and even projecting the course of the drama. It can expressively contradict the declared emotion, for instance indicating an inner turbulence at odds with calm words. Instrumentally, there is an increased use of colour to set the atmosphere of an aria, not only graphically (as with pastoral flutes) but with violas replacing violins to reflect a dark state of mind. Keiser can even anticipate Romantic practice by characterizing an entire opera instrumentally, setting a tone as with the simple but arresting trumpet, piccolo and drum fanfares opening *Croesus*, or the gentle recorder trio interrupted by the sounds of war opening *Masagniello* (recorders that return with muted strings in a beautiful slumber sinfonia). He can follow this up with a richness of orchestral response characteristic of the Hamburg composers but which goes much further than the others. He was particularly sensitive to woodwind combinations to express a mood, as with the five recorders in *Orpheus*.

Although these qualities came into new domination, tilting the balance of the dramatic means, they did not dislodge the central importance of the aria. However, the melodic elegance that won Keiser a reputation lasting beyond his lifetime was generally attentive to drama as well as to *Affekt*, with metrical structures avoiding the expected and falling into uneven bar-lengths, and with some development of a characteristic motive within the aria. The interest in a genre mixing the serious with the popular and comic naturally led to the copious use of popular idioms and hence the manner of popular song, so as to vary and then renew the tension as well as to satisfy the groundlings. Particularly in the earlier works, and before a need to meet an Italian challenge on its own territory presented itself, there is no great reliance on the da capo aria, and many arias are binary, strophic or through-composed. He was less successful at characterization. His heroes and heroines move colourfully and often impressively through a series of dramatic situations; they hold the attention with many a graceful turn of phrase or lively delivery of an emotion; but they rarely achieve the depth that was to be won out of the Baroque conventions by his protégé from Halle, later to be known as George Frideric Handel.

Handel came to Hamburg as a second violinist, also playing continuo and becoming friendly with the composer, critic and singer Johann Mattheson (a friendship that easily survived the famous duel occasioned by Handel refusing to yield the continuo at the first performance of Mattheson's *Cleopatra* when the singer-composer entered the pit after he had concluded the role of Antony). The only one of Handel's Hamburg operas to survive is his first, *Almira*, to a libretto by Friedrich Feustking. This might well have confused even the mature Handel, had he been unwise enough to accept such a farrago of French, German and Italian elements in such a ramshackle plot. 'The confusion of genres – two languages, three national styles, elaborate ballet sequences, abrupt shifts between near-tragedy and satirical comedy – and the absence of any serious attempt to integrate them are not in themselves indications of Handel's immaturity; they were characteristic of the whole Hamburg school' (Dean and Knapp, 1989, 56). The work is interesting not so much as a contribution to the history of German opera, but as an example of how the young Handel did his best to respond to Hamburg conventions and, still more, was swift to absorb the beneficial influence of Keiser, especially in the nature of his vocal writing.

Mattheson himself wrote five operas for Hamburg, *Die Pleiades* (1699), *Porsenna* (1702), *Cleopatra* (1704), *Boris Goudenow* (1710) and *Henrico IV* (1711), but of these only *Cleopatra* has survived. This libretto was also by Feustking, and it follows the story as we know it from Shakespeare. The rationalism that was to make Mattheson one of the most influential writers of his generation on the nature of opera is reflected in aspects of the work, especially in his concern for the logical, expressive and reasonable setting of the text. More than half of the seventy-one arias and solo ensembles make use of a figured bass, the remainder having an orchestral accompaniment. Much stress is therefore laid upon the melody; but it is melody of a kind distinct from that of Keiser (or of the young Handel). As George Buelow, the work's editor (in EDM, lxix), has written, 'Mattheson's melodies are usually smoother, more step-wise in motion, and therefore less angular than Keiser's. . . He takes more care than Keiser in maintaining poetic metre, and generally he avoids long melismatic passages, which are particularly characteristic of Keiser's arias' (Buelow, 1970, 95). No single pair of examples can, of course, comprehensively support this point, but it can be indicative. Two lovelorn heroines react in contrasting melodic manners. Livia, in Keiser's *Octavia*, implores her lover to return, 'Kehre wieder', in a gentle Andante with long held notes, trills and octave leaps at 'meine Seele seufzt' (Example 4). This is characteristic of Keiser's expressive, but not emptily virtuosic, use of melismata to emphasize a key word. Mattheson's aria for Cleopatra, also mourning the loss of love, pays more attention to the sorrowful declamation in its sinking phrases (Example 5). This, in turn, is characteristic of Mattheson's response to words: even Antony, in 'Des Krieges Glück ist wankelbar', keeps his

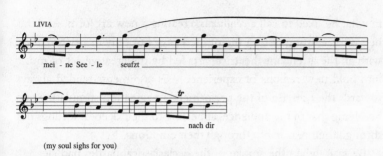

mei - ne See - le   seufzt

nach dir

(my soul sighs for you)

Example 4   Keiser: *Octavia* (1705), Livia

Ach,   wo blei - bet   lieb'____ und Treu - e,   ar - mes Herz__   ar - mes, ar - mes

Herz,   du gehst, du gehst zu   weit.

(Ah! where love and fidelity are no longer at your side, you, poor heart, venture too far!)

Example 5   Mattheson: *Cleopatra* (1704), Cleopatra

melismata expressing the uncertainty of war mostly to simple scales. Cleopatra's death scene consists of a restrained Adagio, an accompanied recitative and a Grave with unison strings and continuo, leading to her death over a curiously graphic effect of *pp* trilling strings.

These examples accord with a set of rules which Mattheson later drew up governing melodic invention, calling in particular for a sense of familiarity, avoidance of the exaggerated or obtrusively virtuosic, and conciseness – virtues, as he acknowledged, closer to those of the French than of the 'Welschen' (by which he here means the Italians) (Mattheson, 1739, 140). In turn, they reflect the ideas that run through all his voluminous, not to say prolix, writings concerning opera as a serious, creative and intellectual endeavour. In his first treatise, *Das neu-eröffnete Orchestre* (Hamburg, 1713), he declared these ideas to centre on opera as neither irrational nor frivolous, dangerous neither to society nor to the immortal soul, but transcending individual considerations of libretto or score and, by bringing the two together in what he liked to call a *confluxus*, creating a new art form. And this he saw as existing not on the printed page but only in performance, with all the attendant theatrical arts led by the creative act of music into bold new regions of experience. His arguments tended always towards the exercise of the performers' imagination stimulating and involving that of the audience, appealing to their deepest feelings not through their reason but through their emotions.

By 1728, when the smoke of the ecclesiastical battles had cleared, Mattheson was able to write, in *Der musicalische Patriot* (Hamburg, 1728), that all the human world was a stage, and that opera was by the very richness of its means an expression of that. With *Der vollkommene Capellmeister* (Hamburg, 1739), this experienced and thoughtful man of the theatre was setting out more detailed prescriptions for the practical implementation of his ideas, proposing among much else that, so as to bring the theatrical arts into a more expressive synthesis, singers should study the words of their parts carefully and even learn what was the dramatic meaning of the entire work – not something that most singers of the day (or many another day) felt was their business. Music must lead the drama, avoiding irrelevantly elaborate forms and aiming for what he called (anticipating Winckelmann) 'edler Einfalt', a noble simplicity. By *Die neueste Untersuchung der Singspiele* (Hamburg, 1744), he was emphasizing the full unification of the arts towards which all his arguments had been moving, claiming that opera was:

> eine hohe Schule vieler schönen Wissenschaften, worinn zusammen und auf einmal Architectur, Perspective, Mahlerey, Mechanik, Tanzkunst, Actio oratoria, Moral, Historie, Poesie und vornehmlich Musik, zur Vergnügung und Erbauung vornehmer und vernünftiger Zuschauer, sich aufs angenehmste vereinigen, und immer neue Proben geben.
>
> (Mattheson, 1744, 86–7)

> (a lofty school of many fine arts, in which together and at the same time architecture, scenic design, painting, machinery, dance, declamation, morality, history, poetry and above all music unite in the most agreeable manner and continually explore new ideas for the pleasure and edification of a distinguished and intelligent audience.)

With such ideas, he is already looking beyond not only the local need for the theoretical justification of opera, but past a strictly rationalistic approach and towards the Romantic unification of the arts and the ideal of the *Gesamtkunstwerk*.

Not with Mattheson, any more than with Keiser, did comic subjects play an important role in Hamburg, given the need first to still ecclesiastical suspicions of frivolity and later to establish opera as of major intellectual significance. Moreover, despite comic touches and the conventional use of popular song and local folk figures so as to satisfy the groundlings, there is little evidence of Keiser and still less the serious-minded Mattheson possessing much gift for comedy. The first composer to display a comic gift was also the last major composer to work at the Gänsemarkt, Georg Philipp Telemann; and too little of his operatic work survives for a thorough evaluation. He settled in the city in 1721, immediately producing a work that won an instant success with its mixture of the comic and the serious, *Der geduldige Socrates*. In the following year he became director of the Opera. Of the thirty-five operas he claimed to have written for the theatre, only seven survive. Some of the missing ones may have been arrangements or adaptations; certainly Telemann was active in the translation and revision of the operas of his friend Handel, giving them their first systematic hearing in Germany. His awareness of Italian opera buffa, as well as of French music, shows not only in the lightness of touch, but in some of the subject matter, which tends towards the comedy of manners and the amiable mockery of social conventions which mark the Singspiel of the latter part of the century. The resources of the Hamburg orchestra help him to give greater depth to some of the comic material, bringing it further into the centre of an opera rather than leaving such things on the periphery as occasional light relief. *Socrates* is skilfully composed so as to keep in balance the opera buffa element of the philosopher plagued by his two wives, parodistic arias allying the aristocratic characters and the absurdly affected Aristophanes with opera seria, and the young man Pitho to whom food and drink are more important than philosophy. Pitho delivers himself of a cheery macaronic drinking song, 'Corpus meum', and anticipates many later such comic numbers with 'Ein Mädchen und ein Gläschen Wein'. With *Adelheid*, Telemann also put into currency the figure of the bumbling, lovable village schoolmaster, Tumernix; and in *Pimpinone* he made another Italian import in the figure of the mild chambermaid turned shrewish mistress, though in the manner of the musical arguments there is more alternation than real altercation (he also anticipates Mozart's Papageno and Papagena with the stammering song, 'Pim-Pim-Pim-pina'). In all three works, Telemann makes some attempt to enliven the plain contours of German song with rhythmic interest by way of syncopations, distortions, hemiolae and other devices, also so as to reflect anxiety, tension or nervousness in the words. The variety is more apparent than real when the capacity for real human characterization is lacking.

Though Georg Caspar Schürmann cannot be accounted a Hamburg composer, since almost all his operas were performed during his long tenure as Kapellmeister at Brunswick from 1697 until his death, his early training and experience in the city seem to have coloured his operas (only three survive complete). Like the Hamburg composers, he was susceptible to Venetian influence, but his greater experience of working in Italy helped to lend his melodies much elegance, together with a coloratura that can engage expressively with the implications of the text. His arias include some attractive light dance numbers, and ballet plays a part; but he is also concerned for instrumental expressiveness and in particular for arioso recitatives in which his melodic gift is turned to strong dramatic effect. In *Ludovicus Pius* (1726) there is a striking passage in Act II, scene 10 when Adelheid finds herself alone and in confusion: a Cantabile with flutes and strings gives way to a warm accompanied recitative whose melody returns after the Cantabile is resumed, and this in turn leads to an Adagio moving into an Andante. Again, at the start of Act III, as Lotharius in the underworld comes to Acheron, tremolo strings and rushing scales surround him before he reaches calm and can sing a tranquil aria with bassoons and strings, 'Komm, sanfte Ruh'. There is in the opera's most striking passages a strong concern for dramatic movement expressed with a fluency that breaks free from set forms and also depends on a sure ear for instrumental colour.

Telemann's tenure of office was not easy, and the last decade of the Hamburg Opera from 1728 saw the enterprise beset with financial difficulties. Upon these has often been blamed the decline and eventual closure of the theatre; but they arose less from any failure in the city's prosperity than from a shift in taste. Attempts to retain audiences by introducing Italian opera, or by partly Italianizing the precariously established German tradition, were predictably unsuccessful, and the interests of the aristocracy and especially the merchant classes were moving more in the direction of the spoken theatre. This trend in turn reflected a problem endemic to the enterprise. A substantial part of the motive force that had generated the opera sprang from the wish, in the wake of national near-destruction in the war, to establish a form unifying the arts, and based on national ideas; and paradoxically these found their best encouragement in Germany's most international city. In the short term, the time and place were right; in the longer, the enterprise was premature. The Venetian example was excellent, and its significance for Germany was understood to a remarkable degree by writers and composers of considerable intelligence. Yet in too many ways they were insufficiently prepared. A vernacular music was not capable of absorbing much beyond gestures of local colour or comic relief. There was the long-enduring problem of training German singers, in turn made harder when there was so little precedent upon which they could build. Despite the resources of the Hamburg orchestra, which provided composers with the encouragement to move emphasis away from vocal display on to instrumental expression in a manner that was to be all-important for German opera, musical techniques were not yet at a point of development when the most could be made of this. Not least, there was the problem of the language itself. The strength and resonance of Luther's Bible did not mean that its style was suitable for every purpose, even in church; and for all the efforts of the humanistic academies, German was not yet independent of the influence of a Latin solemnity, nor immune to the allure of French infiltrations. The seventeenth century was not a great period for German literature, in which an example could be set for those hoping to bring it into the musical theatre.

Yet the Hamburg Opera was highly significant in the history of German opera. It can hardly be spoken of as influential, at any rate not in an immediate sense, for the traditions established and the arguments won did not affect the next generation of composers or opera houses to any important extent. Moreover, many of the Opera's features, such as the uncertain control of all the theatrical elements, which could lead to lengthy and ramshackle works trying to cram in too much, were not an example to be emulated. Such, at any rate, is the indication in the libretto texts and in the few complete works to have survived. Much in it, however, was characteristic of what lay ahead. This included the concern, typical of all artistic traditions feeling themselves to be historically belated (such as Russian opera in the nineteenth century), for discussion, argument and controversy to rage alongside creativity, indeed to anticipate it. This was to remain a feature of the opera of a nation so enduringly concerned with philosophical and intellectual enquiry. Most of all, the Hamburg Opera is significant for its demonstration, early in the history of an emergent German operatic style, that a prime concern was for the drawing together of all the theatrical means into a whole that transcended the sum of the parts.

Travelling troupes and changing attitudes

However striking the Hamburg achievements, they left little immediate mark upon opera in German-speaking lands. In the century between the end of the Thirty Years War in 1648 and the outbreak of the Seven Years War in 1756, musical theatre was almost entirely in the hands of the more prosperous courts, where Italian opera seria reigned, and the multifarious troupes of strolling players who crossed and recrossed Germany. Crude though the wares which the *Wandertruppen* purveyed often were, they served a purpose not simply in providing the only theatrical entertainment which most towns could expect, but in keeping alive a tradition in which German vernacular music played a part. Without them, it is doubtful if the emergence of a more mature Singspiel in the second half of the century would have been possible.

Though the troupes included players who found it adventurous, or for various reasons expedient, to keep on the move, they travelled more from necessity than from desire. With the Italians and other companies jealously guarding their own positions, the most a troupe anxious to establish itself could hope for would be occasional appearances, playing at a castle or in a town hall (through good luck or good management), at a fencing or riding school hired for the occasion, but perhaps only in the space above a covered market, in a barn, at an inn or even in a booth outside the town walls. Timing was important, and much sought after were the great annual fairs at Leipzig and Frankfurt. For engagements, a *Privilegium* from a nobleman or a town council would be solicited, and might enable a company to present itself as 'Court Theatre of . . .' The hope was that a successful season would lead to the promise of a repeat visit, perhaps an annual season to tide a company over the hard winter months, in rare cases establishment in a permanent site that could

63

come to mark the beginning of a town's operatic history. There were many obstacles to be overcome, including the long-enduring prejudice – not limited to Germany nor confined to the clergy – against 'theatricals' as being morally disreputable, little short of vagabonds. 'Komödianten? Ihm galt das für ein Schimpfname' (Benedix, 1847, 3) ('Actors? that's just a term of abuse'), wrote J. R. Benedix, himself a member of the Bethmann company, in his *Künstlerroman* on the life of the strolling players; and his picture of their ramshackle nature and sorry life is born out in the diaries and memoirs of other itinerant actors such as Carl Ludwig Costenoble (Costenoble, 1912) and Eduard Genast (Genast, 1862).

A troupe was usually formed by a *Prinzipal*, who would recruit from his family, including from the children who grew up playing among the stage props and the covered waggons, from friends, from actors and actresses migrating from other companies, from students seeking temporary employment, from misfits or those without any other craft who would take to the road when all else had failed or when creditors or the police were at their heels. The itinerant life was far from being a comfortable one. Only in exceptional cases could a company rely on sufficient takings to be able to stay in any one place for more than six or eight weeks; and in the larger towns, the necessity of playing a wide repertory bore heavily on the company and meant that standards suffered. Ticket prices varied, averaging two to three kreutzers (Creizenach, 1888, xvii–xviii), and costs could be high, when on top of the hire of premises it might be necessary to pay for police supervision or a sentry guard, to give Benefits for the poor, to dispense free tickets, to pay for posters and advertising and to hire someone to march about the town literally drumming up custom. Travelling expenses might swallow a third of the takings, so that there was competition for regions in which towns lay close together: however, the Schönemann troupe, which had a *Privilegium* for Prussia, followed others in visiting Königsberg, Danzig and Stettin, and like both Neuber and Ackermann (see pp. 69–71 below) made tours into Russia. Wages were low: the Neuber troupe was said to pay the best with five gulden per week (two gulden for beginners). The actors had to stay in orphanages, asylums, work-houses, only rarely in even the humblest of inns. F. C. Paldamus is but one historian of the *Wandertruppen* to inveigh passionately against the 'slavery' to which an ageing, broken-down player or even whole families were subjected by being unable to break away from the tyranny of a director because they could not find better work (Paldamus, 1857).

Few of the companies gave anything that could really be described as opera, though Singspiel of a kind was sometimes included in the assorted repertory, and those were mostly the companies who could manage to establish themselves for some length of time and to assemble a few instrumentalists. The average diet was the so-called *Haupt- und Staatsaktion*, a more or less serious play deriving its exaggerated drama of kings and queens and executions and conspiracies from the material of the *Englische Komödianten*, perhaps followed by a comic Nachspiel. The earliest surviving poster promises just such mixed fare:

> Zu wissen sey jedermann, daß allhier ankommen eine gantz newe
> Compagni Comoedianten, so niemals zuvor hier zu Land gesehen, mit
> einem sehr lustigen Pickelhering, welche täglich agiren werden, schöne
> Comoedien, Tragoedien, Pastorellen (Schäffereyen) und Historien,
> vermengt mit lieblichen und lustigen interludien, und zwar heut
> Mitwochs den 21. Aprilis werden sie praesentirn eine Comoedi, genant
>   Die Liebes Süssigkeit verändert sich in Todes Bitterkeit.
> Nach der Comoedi soll praesentirt werden ein schön Ballett, und
> lächerlichs Possenspiel. Die Liebhaber solche Schauspiele wollen sich
> nach Mittags Glock 2 einstellen vffm Fechthauß, allda umb die
> bestimmte Zeit praecise soll angefangen werden.
>
>   (facsimile in Creizenach, 1888, between xxiv and xxv)

> (Let everyone know that there has arrived a completely new Company
> of Players, never before seen in this country, with a very merry
> Pickelhering, who will daily perform fine Comedies, Tragedies, Pastorals
> and Histories, mixed with delightful and entertaining interludes, and will
> present this Wednesday, 21st April, a comedy entitled
>   Love's Sweetness turns to Death's Bitterness.

After the comedy, there will be a fine ballet, with a humorous farce.
Lovers of such shows should take their places at 2 o'clock in the
afternoon in the Fencing School, as the performance will begin
punctually at the announced time.)

From the English players also came the habit of mixing serious and
comic scenes. Sometimes well-known operas would be adapted for
such presentation; but very seldom could any more ambitious musical
piece be staged, and then the standards were chaotic. As late as 1810,
Carl Maria von Weber (himself the child of a travelling troupe directed
by his father, Franz Anton von Weber) was writing of the Dengler
Company mounting performances of Mozart, Winter and Cherubini
'bei ungefähr 3½ Mann im Orchester' ('with only about three and a half
orchestral players') (Weber, 1908, 418–19; Weber, 1981, 56); and his
own *Der Freischütz* was once given by the Obstfelder Company as a
spoken piece, the poster announcing, 'Da die Musik nur die Handlung
stört, so wird dieselbe weggelassen' (quoted in Goslich, 1975, 67) ('As
the music only disturbs the action, it will be omitted').

The efforts of the German touring companies to make their way
and improve their standards were not helped by the reputation of the
English players, by the presence of highly professional Italian troupes
such as the renowned Mingotti Company, and then by the numbers
of French companies who travelled across Germany, impressing
audiences with their sophisticated pieces and elegant presentation.
Goethe makes the Count indicate as much when Wilhelm Meister's
troupe arrives at his castle:

'Wenn es Franzosen wären', sagte er zu seiner Gemahlin, 'könnten wir
dem Prinzen eine unerwartete Freude machen, und ihm bei uns seine
Lieblingsunterhaltung verschaffen'. 'Es käme darauf an', versetzte die
Gräfin, 'ob wir nicht diese Leute, wenn sie schon unglücklicherweise nur
Deutsche sind, auf dem Schloß, so lange der Fürst bei uns bleibt, spielen
ließen. Sie haben doch wohl einige Geschicklichkeit'.

(Goethe, 1795–6, Bk. III, Ch. 1)

('Had they been but Frenchmen', said he to his lady, 'we might have
treated the Prince with an unexpected enjoyment, and entertained him
with his favourite pastime at our house'. 'And could we not', said the

Countess, 'get these people, though unluckily they are but Germans, to
exhibit with us at the Castle, while the Prince stays here? Without doubt,
they have some degree of skill'. Goethe, 1824, Bk. III, Ch. 1)

Aurelia comes to display a lively resentment of this superiority:

'Ich hasse die Französische Sprache von ganzer Seele'. 'Wie kann man
einer Sprache feind seyn', rief Wilhelm aus, 'der man den grössten Theil
seiner Bildung schuldig ist, und der wir noch viel schuldig werden
müssen, eh' unser Wesen eine Gestalt gewinnen kann?'

(Goethe, 1795–6, Bk. v, Ch. 16)

('I hate the French language from the bottom of my soul'. 'How can you
be hostile to a language', cried our friend, 'to which we Germans are
indebted for the greater part of our accomplishments; to which we must
become indebted still more, if our natural qualities are ever to assume
their proper form?' Goethe, 1824, Bk. v, Ch. 16)

Wilhelm Meister gives the most vivid of all fictional accounts of the
conditions under which a German travelling troupe worked, by a
great poet who was also a practical man of the theatre; and he is at
pains to emphasize the contrast between the ragged condition of the
players and Wilhelm's intelligence and idealistic longing for *Bildung*.
The sardonic note extends to the provision of music:

er componirte aus dem Reichthum seines lebendigen Bildervorraths
sogleich ein ganzes Schauspiel mit allen seinen Acten, Scenen,
Charakteren und Verwicklungen. Man fand für gut, einigen Arien und
Gesänge einzuflechten; man dichtete sie, und Philine, die in alles einging,
passte ihnen bekannte Melodien an, und sang sie aus dem Stegreife.

(Goethe, 1795–6, Bk. II, Ch. 10)

(from the wealth of his living imaginative store, he forthwith constructed
a complete play, with all its acts, scenes, characters and plots. It was
thought proper to insert a few catches and songs; they composed them;
and Philina, who entered into every part of it, immediately fitted them
with well-known tunes, and sang them on the spot. Goethe, 1824, Bk. II,
Ch. 10)

The Baroness manages to improve upon this.

Auf eine geschickte Weise wusste die Baronesse Wilhelmen wieder bei
Seite zu schaffen, und liess ihn bald darauf wissen, sie habe die übrigen

Sachen auch besorgt. Sie schickte ihm sogleich den Musicus, der des
Grafen Hauscapelle dirigirte, damit dieser theils die nothwendigen
Stücke componiren, theils schickliche Melodien aus dem Musikvorrathe
dazu aussuchen sollte. (Goethe, 1795–6, Bk. iii, Ch. 7)

(The Baroness, in her dextrous way, again contrived to lead Wilhelm
aside, and let him know that she had been providing all the other
necessaries. Shortly afterwards, she sent him the musician, who had
charge of the Count's private band; and this professor set about
composing what airs were wanted, or choosing from his actual stock
such tunes as appeared suitable. Goethe, 1824, Bk. iii, Ch. 7)

The first significant director of a German travelling troupe to
emerge after the Thirty Years War was Johannes Velten. He studied
theology in Wittenberg and Leipzig, also learning French, Italian and
Spanish, and graduated as Magister in 1661. Having then cast his lot in
with a company under Karl Andreas Paulsen, he made use of his
education to improve the repertory and with it the group's artistic
standing. He also married Paulsen's daughter Katharina. In 1678 he
assumed control of the company, which performed in Dresden as the
Chursächsische Comödienband; and thereafter he led it to many of
the most important cities of Germany, as well as into the Baltic lands
and Scandinavia with a repertory that included, among much inferior
material, works by Molière, Corneille and Calderón. Velten came to
be regarded by actors of succeeding generations working in the
Wandertruppen as the father of their profession. His reforms included
giving female parts to women for the first time; he also trained and
set an example to some of the actors who went on to form their own
companies. Four of the most important eighteenth-century travelling
troupes owed their origin to him, those of Neuber, Schönemann,
Koch and Ackermann. In different ways, they exemplify the myriad
companies who by the middle of the century were contributing
much to German theatrical life. Still despised by the authorities as
belonging to an outcast profession, he was refused the Sacrament on
his deathbed.

The widow of one of Velten's actors, Julius Elenson, married first
another actor named Haack, then Johann Ernst Hoffmann, who in

1656 was Principal of the so-called Hochdeutsche Komödiantenkompagnie and of the Innsbruck and Palatinate Hofkomödianten. It was this couple who trained Johann and Caroline Neuber. Of the pair, Caroline was the more enterprising, a vigorous and idealistic woman who was to have an important influence on the development of Singspiel, whereas Johann, with whom she eloped at the age of twenty, was more easy-going. Between them, however, they did much to raise standards with the company they formed in 1727 with a *Privilegium* from Augustus the Strong. They insisted on the moral role of the theatre and set a patriarchal example that was to be followed by other companies, making the actors work on scene-painting, the actresses on costume-making, and some of the students in the company on translating Corneille, Racine and Molière. However, their lot was no easier than that of any of their contemporaries. Their experiences in Leipzig included having to adapt a space above the meat market, then, when ousted by J. F. Müller on the lapse of their *Privilegium* with Augustus's death in 1733, being forced to build a temporary theatre in a garden outside the Grimmaisches Tor. They set up again in a riding school that only had gallery seats, and when in debt built a stage in a disused dyer's loft. After a long series of further misfortunes, the company finally collapsed in 1748 (Reden-Esbeck, 1881).

One of the Neubers' most important actors was Johann Friedrich Schönemann, who worked with them from 1730 to 1739, then in 1740 forming a company that included Conrad Ackermann and two artists later to achieve great distinction, Sophie Schröder and Konrad Ekhof. Although the company style was said to be precious and affected, Schönemann did make some effort to improve the repertory, by including more German drama, ballet, pantomime, French *comédie larmoyante*, and especially pastorals that employed songs and dances as important ingredients. These were popular as a cheap substitute for opera, and Schönemann found an audience for them in Hamburg in the 1740s in the wake of the collapse of the Opera. Among the pieces played here was a version of Charles Coffey's ballad opera *The Devil to Pay*, translated in 1743 as *Der Teufel ist los* by Caspar Wilhelm von Borck, who as chargé d'affaires in London had observed its popularity. It won a following in Hamburg and elsewhere, though its real success dates from the Weisse version with music by J. C. Standfuss nine years later. However, the quarrels endemic to the travelling life rent the company: Schröder and Ackermann left, and though Schönemann nearly managed to establish himself in Berlin, he had to settle for a licence to tour Prussia, and his company went into decline until taken over by Koch in 1758 (Devrient, 1895).

Conrad Ernst Ackermann, a man of varied gifts and wide culture who defected with Sophie Schröder in 1741, did not greatly prosper. Their first company, in her name, only lasted for a few months in Hamburg in 1742, failing to compete successfully with the rival attractions of the famous Italian troupe directed by Pietro and Angelo Mingotti; they tried again in 1746, without any greater success. On a visit to Moscow in 1749 they married, and then embarked on various enterprises, including the construction of Germany's first privately built public theatre in Königsberg, which they were forced to abandon in 1756 in the face of the Russian advance during the Seven Years War. Though Ackermann had rather more luck after the war in Hamburg, borrowing money in order to build a theatre, his company was taken over when the Hamburg National Theatre was set up three years later. He made less mark than Gottfried Heinrich Koch, another gifted and intelligent man, who spent 21 years with the Neubers before setting up in 1750 on his own in Leipzig, with a *Privilegium* for Saxony. Koch's was one of the most important and enterprising companies of the middle of the century, and it survived the war, as a near-permanent company in Hamburg, to enable him to build upon the tentative achievements of the others and see the growth of Singspiel into a new condition. He managed to attract some respectable singers to the company, which gave very varied programmes, with comic operas and musical intermezzos, ballets and farces as well as tragedies and comedies, and in Leipzig in 1752 he was the first to stage the controversial Weisse/Standfuss *Der Teufel ist los*. Koch was so popular in Leipzig in 1763 that an angry university professor whose five o'clock lectures coincided with the performances had him restricted to two per week.

Many other names crop up in passing references, in city and town records, and in contemporary accounts. By far the most important company to emerge after the war, one of the most significant for the development of German opera, was that of Abel Seyler. He could draw upon Anton Schweitzer and Christian Neefe as composers, and with actors including the great Konrad Ekhof recruited to his ranks he travelled in north west Germany (ousting Ackermann from Hanover) and also made wide summer tours, succeeding Koch in Weimar. Mozart was sufficiently impressed to agree to write a duodrama for the company in 1778, a plan that never came off. However, in the first half of the century high standards were rare, and achieved only in the face of almost impossible conditions. A pamphlet put out by J. F. Löwen with Ekhof's help deals scathingly with the defects of the contemporary German theatre, not sparing even the Neubers from reproach. Löwen, a Hamburg writer and critic, complains of uncultivated actors and actor-managers seeking only profit, unable to call upon proper authors, working without proper support from princes or municipalities and opposed by the clergy. He calls for properly organized non-profitmaking theatres, dramatic academies, improvement in the standing and behaviour of actors, and the encouragement of dramatists with prizes (Löwen, 1766). He was not alone, and more powerful voices came to join his. The war interrupted progress, but did not halt it.

Meanwhile, the decline in the fortunes of the Hamburg venture, and the apparently unassailable position of Italian opera, had not halted discussion about the nature and viability of German opera. As early as 1715 Barthold Brockes, the Hamburg senator and poet whose dramatic Passion text had drawn Hamburg composers including Keiser, Telemann, Handel and Mattheson, was sufficiently anxious about the city's artistic heritage to follow earlier precedent, and to form a society for mutual support. The concerns of his *Teutschübende Gesellschaft* included investigation of the history of German-language opera, taken up with enthusiasm especially by Johann Ulrich König.

However, König's preference was for greater lucidity and simplicity in librettos than was familiar in Hamburg, and his consequent distaste for Postel and Hunold, in particular, dismayed his colleagues. They cannot have been sorry to see him depart for Weissenfels in 1716, whence he later moved to Dresden in 1729 as Court Poet. Hamburg suspicions rested fundamentally on König's apparent espousal of French neoclassicism; and it is true that, in the introduction to his *Theatralische, geistliche / vermischte und galante Gedichte* (1713), he had argued for the unities and other apparently French ideals in opera. However, he regarded opera as the art form with the greatest potential of any, combining as it did poetry, drama, ballet, stage effect and elaborate machinery, with music serving this amalgamation of the arts; and he further insisted that it had a moral part to play in a social context.

It was this stance which brought him into conflict with the powerful figure of Johann Christoph Gottsched. Originally warm friends, the two fell into bitter polemic over the question of opera. Gottsched was able to find support in the writings of the French theorist who had epitomized for Germans the challenge to opera, Charles de Saint-Evremond. With relentless mockery, Saint-Evremond had followed up a satirical comedy, *Les Opéras*, with a *Lettre sur Les Opéras* (1677) addressed to his friend and patron the Duke of Buckingham. In this he attacked what he saw as the confusing and enervating sensuality of a medium that relied so much upon music and stage effect, and upon the absurdity of men, whether in battle or council or everyday matters, conducting their affairs in song. Music, he held, rather than having the potential for enriching drama, was at the most an incidental diversion and should never be allowed to intervene in the forms and disciplines of tragedy. The *Lettre* had a disproportionate impact on Germans feeling unsure of their theoretical ground and too readily disposed to defer to French authority in aesthetic matters; and it was easy for Gottsched to rest his own case upon this apparent authority. His most sustained attack came with his *Versuch einer critischen Dichtkunst* (1730), in which his opposition to opera was close to Saint-Evremond's and made its appeal to Aristotelian canons:

Dabey hub man alle Regeln der guten Trauer- und Lustspiele gänzlich auf. Es wurde nicht mehr auf die Erregung des Schreckens und Mitleidens, auch nicht auf die Verlachung menschlicher Thorheiten gesehen: sondern die phantastische Romanliebe behielte allein Platz. Die Einigkeit der Zeit und des Ortes wurde aus den Augen gesetzet; die Schreibart wurde hochtrabend und ausschweifend; die Charactere waren theils übel formiret, theils immer einerley, nämlich lauter untreue Seelen, seufzende Buhler, unerbittliche Schönen, verzweifelnde Liebhaber u.d.gl. Mit einem Worte, die Oper wurde ein ganz nagelneues Stück in der Poesie, davon sich bey den Alten wohl niemand hätte träumen lassen. So muss ich sagen: Die Oper sey das ungereimteste Werk, dass der menschliche Verstand jemals erfunden hat.

(Gottsched, 1730, 365–6)

(Thereby all rules of good tragedy and comedy are completely abolished. It is no longer a question of the arousal of pity and terror, or the mockery of human folly; rather, a fantastic novelettish passion alone holds sway. The unities of time and place are no more seen; style is grandiloquent and extravagant; characters are at once ill-formed and always the same, that is to say nothing but faithless souls, sighing paramours, heartless beauties, despairing lovers and the like. In a word, opera is a brand new kind of poetry which the ancients could never have dreamt of. So I have to state: opera is the most absurd creation the human mind has ever produced.)

Gottsched's distaste sprang, then, not from hostility to music in its own right, but from what he perceived to be its role as part of the irrationality of Baroque opera; and on this basis, it was easy for him to make mock of the castrati, of elaborate stage machinery, of arias that halted the action with demonstrations of virtuosity, and so forth, in a vein that was to become very familiar:

Sie sprechen nicht mehr, wie es die Natur ihrer Kehle, die Gewohnheit des Landes, die Art der Gemüthsbewegungen und der Sachen, davon gehandelt wird, erfordert: sondern sie dehnen, erheben, und vertiefen ihre Töne nach den Phantasien eines andern. Sie schelten und klagen nach dem Tacte; und wenn sie sich aus Verzweifelung das Leben nehmen, so verschieben sie ihre heldenmässige That so lange, bis sie ihre Triller ausgeschlagen haben. Wo ist doch das Vorbild dieser

Nachahmungen? Wo ist die Natur, mit der diese Fabeln eine
Aehnlichkeit haben? (Gottsched, 1730, 367)

(They no longer speak as demanded by the formation of their throats, by
national custom, by the nature of emotions and the matters these
express; but they drawl, they raise and lower their tones according to
another's fantasy. They bawl and wail on the beat; and when they take
their own lives in despair, they delay the heroic deed until they have
completed their trills. Where is the model for these imitations? Where is
the nature to which these fabrications relate?)

True art, Gottsched concluded, must be governed by intellect and
moral purpose, and must not result from a mysterious moment of
irrational inspiration; and it was this that led him towards the French
canons of tragedy, upholding the unities on the grounds that all other
options were too 'magical' in their claim on the audience. In turn, he
was led to set a new value on the writer as a moral instructor, and
hence upon the actor as the lucid purveyor of the writer's meaning.
In Leipzig, he had come into contact with the theatre through his
part in the *Deutschpoetische Gesellschaft* (successor to the *Teutschübende
Gesellschaft*), and was busily inveighing against the absurdities of the
Haupt- und Staatsaktionen which he had encountered when, in 1725,
he found himself much impressed with the Neuber troupe. Caroline
Neuber's determination to give actors a standing as artists rather
than mere mountebanks, her treatment of her company as one
purveying drama as well as casual entertainment, and her interest in
improving the repertory all appealed greatly to Gottsched. From 1727
to 1740 he acted as her consultant, among much else suggesting
Racine and Corneille to her and making translations himself. His
dislike of clownishness extended to a famous gesture in 1737 when, in
a piece given by the Neubers, Hanswurst was formally banished
from the stage: needless to say, he soon bounded back. However, for
all his intelligence and articulacy, and despite the reputation which
these qualities won him, Gottsched's writing became increasingly
strident; and the times were beginning to move against him. His
appeal to reason had a sound pedigree, but it rested on a fundamental
failure to appreciate what might be possible of opera; and so much

attention would not have been paid to his voice had some form of German opera been more securely established, and had the attempts not already endured such a history of controversy. Attacked by one wing of the church in the seventeenth century as an affront to God, opera now found itself under attack in the eighteenth century for its blasphemy of a newer God, Reason.

However, among the voices raised against Gottsched there were several prepared to view Baroque opera not as old-fashioned and 'illogical' but as capable of offering a way forward in changed times. Among them was the now little regarded Johann Friedrich Uffenbach, whose wide contacts with painters, singers, producers and composers gave him a particular interest in the relationship between the arts offered by opera. Without challenging the greatness of classical drama, he questioned whether it was necessarily an arbiter for modern times, and suggested that precedent could be a limiting factor rather than a standard for all ages. Opera, he suggested in *Von der Würde derer Singgedichte*, provided the opportunity for re-examining the relationship between the arts, with poetry and music meeting on equal terms.

> Ein Dichter soll und muss von Rechts wegen ein Kenner der Musik seyn, welche ihn eigentlich auf die Spur, Ohr und Gemüthe zu reizen, bringet. Doch will ich eben damit nicht sagen, dass er einen Sclaven der Componisten abgeben solle . . . Beyde Künste sind Schwestern, und müssen also schwesterlich und friedlich vereint seyn, und eine der andern was nachgeben.   (Uffenbach, 1733/1747, 381)

> (A poet should and must by rights be expert in music, which really puts him on the right path to stimulate his ear and his feelings. However, I am not saying that he must become a slave of the composer . . . The two arts are sisters, and must be united in peaceful and sisterly fashion and yield something to one another.)

This novel interaction of the arts, declared Uffenbach, meant that ancient aesthetic canons were no longer necessarily valid; and pointing out, as an example, that if classical precepts were to be strictly adhered to, there would be no place for rhyme in modern dramatic verse, he declared that rules should follow contemporary taste and invention rather than the other way round. In support, he quoted from *The Spectator*: 'Music, Architecture and Painting, as well as poetry and oratory are to deduce their Laws and Rules from the general Sense and Taste of Mankind, and not from the principles of those Arts themselves. Or, in other Words, the Taste is not to conform to the Art, but the Art to the Taste' (*Spectator*, 1/29 (London, 1726), III, quoted in Uffenbach, 1733/1747, 385). This was, of course, to challenge much Enlightenment teaching; and Uffenbach consequently found the so-called illogicality of opera a potential strength, in that it could release the imagination in novel directions.

> Wenn nun aus allem angeführten erhellet, dass der Vorzug der Comödien vor denen der Opern noch eben so gar ausgemacht nicht ist, so gereichet die öftere und kostbare Veränderung des Schauplatzes und des Maschinenwerkes denen letzteren ebenfalls nicht zum Nachteile. Sie erweisen vielmehr, dass die vornehmsten Künste, nämlich die Mahlerey, Mechanik, Bau- und Perspektivkunst, Musik, Tanz und Erfindungskunst in Kleidern, Feuerwerkerey, Poesie und Redner Vortheile ihr bestes mit gesammten Kräften anwenden und sich vereinbaren, um des Zuschauers Sinn und Gemüthe zu ergetzen und ihm **ein prächtiges Fabel oder Dichtwerk vorzubilden, wenn zu gleicher Zeit ihm eine löbliche Heldenthat nach hergebrachter oder hypothetischer Wahrscheinlichkeit zur Nachahmung tugendhafter und guter Sitten vorgestellt wird**.
>
> (Uffenbach, 1733/1747, 395: his bold letters)

> (If it is clear, from all that has been adduced, that the supremacy of a play over an opera is not entirely settled, then the latter's frequent and costly shifts of scene and stage machinery are likewise not to its disadvantage. They demonstrate, rather, that the finest arts, namely painting, machinery, building and perspective, music, dance and inventive skill with costumes, fireworks, poetry and declamation are employed to their best advantage when their powers are united and come together to delight the beholder's senses and feelings and **to fashion for him a magnificent fable or fiction, if at the same time there is set before him an admirable heroic tale according to a well-established or hypothetical probability introduced in exemplification of good and noble sentiments**.)

Uffenbach's final argument takes the form of an appeal to the intellect to respond to what he often refers to as a 'hypothetische Wahrscheinlichkeit' ('hypothetical probability'), by which he really means an effort of the imagination, the more valuable if it runs counter to reason; and he concludes that, in any case, reason does not in fact abdicate in the act of enjoying a statue, a garden, a picture or a masterpiece wrought in gold. It is an argument considerably ahead of its time.

Though the Seven Years War cannot be regarded as a watershed in German life to the extent that the Thirty Years War had been, like all wars it accelerated processes of change. While Frederick the Great himself remained so attached to French intellectual influences (and to Italian opera) as to remain virtually outside Germany's intellectual development, different ideas were growing in other areas. A new reading public was forming, one no longer confined largely to ecclesiastical and learned circles: whereas a quarter of the books published in the middle of the century appeared in Latin, only one twentieth did so by the end of the century. In the field of music, hardly any of the thirty-odd journals published before the successful and long-lived *Allgemeine musikalische Zeitung*, founded by Johann Rochlitz in 1798, appealed to the public enough to ensure survival for more than a few years or a few volumes, since in the first half of the century they all reflected the general tendency in other journals – devoted to history, geography, the law, politics, theology, or medicine and the natural sciences – towards matters of scholarly enquiry or moral uplift.

The first German musical periodical had been founded in Hamburg in 1722 by Johann Mattheson, with a portentous title over fifty words long and hence conveniently referred to as the *Critica musica*. Brimming with self-confidence, Mattheson declared that he would establish basic principles and expose weaknesses, and some of his attacks (for instance, on the musicians of Munich) are entertainingly vituperative. His anonymous *Der musicalische Patriot* (1728) was more moralizing in tone; and this quality was reflected not so much in two rather unsuccessful journals edited by the polymathic Lorenz Mizler as in Johann Scheibe's fortnightly (later weekly) *Critischer Musicus* (1737/8–1739/40). In conscious emulation of Gottsched, Scheibe felt called upon to bring the spirit of the Enlightenment into musical theory. He took an aggressively rationalist stand on 'die Rechte des Ohrs und der gesunden Vernunft gegen die Zahlenmusik' ('the rights of the ear and of healthy reason against the music of calculation'), also declaring that 'Das wahre Wesen der Musik besteht in einer vernünftigen Nachahmung der Natur' ('the true essence of music rests on a rational imitation of Nature') (60th *Stück*, 554). There is much else in this vein, with plenty of fun poked at the 'irrationality' of opera seria, and a good deal more assertion than clarification. After the war, *Der critische musicus an der Spree*, founded in 1749 by F. W. Marpurg, began to set a new tone which was developed in his longer-lasting and more substantial *Historisch-kritische Beyträge zur Aufnahme der Musik* (1754–78); now, essays and reviews and news columns reflected the interests of the new burgher audience, and so as to address this in his third periodical, his *Kritische Briefe über die Tonkunst* (1760–4), Marpurg turned to the popular form, familiar from *The Spectator*, of letters. His topics in these include opera, as when *Brief xlii* anticipates later writers (including Berlioz) by envisaging an ideal musical city in which opera will only have elevated subjects, with no trivial ballets and no absurdities of casting that go against dramatic verisimilitude. *Brief xliv* follows this up with a vision of co-operation between poet and composer:

> Der Poet und der Componist arbeiten beyde zu einem
> gemeinschaftlichen Endzwecke. Einer bequemt sich dem andern. Jener
> in Ansehung der Sylbenmasses, der Versarten, der leichtfliessenden und
> wohlschallenden Worte, der abwechselnden Affecten, u.s.w. Dieser im
> richtigen Ausdruck des Sinnes sowohl als der Leidenschaften.
>
> (Marpurg, 1760–4, I, 346)

(Poet and composer work together towards a united purpose. Each one accommodates the other. The one with regard to metre, versification, fluent and euphonious choice of words, variety of effect, etc. The other with true as well as passionate expression of feeling.)

A similar public to Marpurg's was envisaged by J. N. Forkel in his short-lived *Musikalisch-kritische Bibliothek* (1778–9) and by the energetic and versatile Johann Friedrich Reichardt in several periodicals. These and other journals reflected a decisive shift in the public response to the arts that was mirrored in the foundation of the first German theatrical journal, at Stuttgart in 1750, by Gotthold Ephraim Lessing and his cousin Christlob Mylius, the *Beyträge zur Historie und Aufnahme des Theaters*. The foreword to their first issue protested against the domination of French art and broke a lance for non-French theatre, while later issues carried translations of Plautus and Machiavelli, and criticism designed to help the interested playgoer.

Lessing's writings on the subject of opera here and subsequently are uneasy and somewhat inconsistent, and implicitly resist the hopes for a German opera unifying the arts. He recognized how, in Italian opera, poetry and music might serve one another, but only alternately (in recitative and aria) rather than in true expressive conjunction; the entire premise underlying his most important work, *Laokoon* (1766), is that each art has its own disciplines and systems of expression, and is autonomous, that, for instance, 'Ein poetisches Gemälde ist nicht notwendig das, was in ein materielles Gemälde zu verwandeln ist' (Lessing, 1965, xiv, 154) ('A poetic picture is not necessarily convertible into a physical picture'). The second half of the century was also marked by the appearance of more periodicals appealing to an intelligent general readership, and finding it. An example was Friedrich Nicolai's *Allgemeine deutsche Bibliothek*, a review of rationalist tendency founded in 1765 that included Herder among its writers, and that had in its first two decades over a thousand regular subscribers. The *Allgemeine Literaturzeitung*, founded in 1785, could claim Kant and Schiller, later Goethe, as contributors, and sought to include the young in its readership.

New movements in thought, which the journals reflected rather than formed, and which were also to give impetus and character to the still primitive art of Singspiel, came from other thinkers and writers; and the most important of them helped to give the second half of the century a distinctive character, and to stir moves in the direction of Romanticism. One, on the face of it paradoxically, was the great classical art historian Johann Joachim Winckelmann, who was to be the object of Lessing's attack in *Laokoon*. Like others of his day resisting the Baroque, which he associated with a Franco-Italian despotism ruling German taste, he turned back to Raphael and then to ancient Greece, first with a brilliant study that made his name, *Gedancken über die Nachahmung der griechischen Werke in der Malerei und Bildhauerkunst* (1755). In his *Geschichte der Kunst des Altertums* (1764), rather than give a technical account, or draw moral lessons, or even treat art as pleasant diversion, he interpreted Greek master-pieces as the expression of a higher existence, of a sublime serenity, an ideal he describes (in a phrase adapted from earlier criticism but which he then made his own) as 'eine edler Einfalt und eine stille Grösse' ('a noble simplicity and a silent grandeur'). In Greek sculp-ture of the fifth century BC he found this ideal, revealing, he declared, the expression of nature in its highest form and incarnating pure beauty. Such beauty could be appreciated not by exposition and reason, but only by the senses and the spirit. He held that the silent nobility of the Greek statue of the dying Laokoon was essentially superior to the cries of despair given him by Virgil. Attached to Winckelmann's approach was, certainly, a nostalgia for an ideal past, irrecoverable though with lessons for the present; and also connected was the concept of Greek art as the expression of a particular nation, a state in ideal social and political and artistic equilibrium. Italian art, for Winckelmann, was a secondary tradition, though one which also drew his admiration and praise, providing encouragement for the whole German *Sehnsucht nach Italien* that was to find its greatest exemplar with Goethe and his *Italienische Reise*.

Such ideas were to stir latent Romantic feelings about the arts among Germans. In this they were joined by those of Jean-Jacques Rousseau. Though he became one of the Romantics' most favoured philosophers, this was more for what were perceived to be his views than for his actual writings. His novel *La Nouvelle Héloïse* (1761), his educational treatise *Emile* (1762), his political treatise *Du Contrat Social* (1762), and his posthumously published *Confessions* all made a great impression on the younger generation, especially for their appeal to nature and natural man, and to loyalty to inner feelings, as being the best guide to living one's life, contrasting such feelings with the constrictions of convention and the corroding influence of modern civilization. Often invoked, Rousseau had a particular appeal to musicians for being himself the composer of the Singspiel *Le Devin du Village* (1752), in which, typically, rustic natural virtue triumphs over sophisticated aristocratic temptation.

However, as Isaiah Berlin has written, 'Rousseau shares more presuppositions with the Encyclopaedists than he denies, and in any case conceals his inconsistencies beneath a torrent of marvellous rhetoric' (Berlin, 1993, 23). The real voices in the new movement of feeling were bound to come from within Germany. An early voice, whose influence was considerable on his contemporaries but later became obscured, was that of the so-called 'Magus of the North', Johann Georg Hamann, a passionate opponent of both the scientific and the dogmatic approach to human experience and the first articulate and sustained enemy of the Enlightenment:

> Hamann rose in revolt against the entire structure of science, reason, analysis – its virtues even more than its vices. He thought the basis of it altogether false and its conclusions a blasphemy against the nature of man and his creator; and he looked for evidence not so much in theological or metaphysical axioms or dogmas or a priori argument, as in his own day-to-day experience, in the empirically – not intuitively – perceived facts themselves, in direct observation of men and their conduct, and in direct introspection of his own passions, feelings, thoughts, way of life. (Berlin, 1993, 23)

The beliefs in the principles of the *Aufklärung* (the name generally applied to the German version of the Enlightenment) were the more urgently resisted by Hamann for their very strength and idealism:

> These [beliefs] were, in effect, the conviction that the world, or nature, was a single whole, subject to a single set of laws, in principle discoverable by the intelligence of man; that the laws which governed inanimate nature were in principle the same as those which governed plants, animals and sentient beings; that man was capable of

improvement; that there existed certain objectively recognisable human goals which all men, rightly so described, sought after, namely happiness, knowledge, justice, liberty, and what was somewhat vaguely described but well understood as virtue; that these goals were common to all men as such, were not unattainable, not incompatible and that human misery, vice and folly were mainly due to ignorance either of what these goals consisted in or of the means of attaining them – ignorance due in turn to insufficient knowledge of the laws of nature. Moreover, and despite the doubts expressed by Montesquieu and his followers, it was by and large believed that human nature was fundamentally the same in all times and places; local and historical variations were unimportant compared with the permanent central core in terms of which human beings could be defined as a single species, as minerals or plants or animals could be. Consequently the discovery of general laws that govern human behaviour, their clear and logical integration into scientific systems – of psychology, sociology, economics, political science and the like (though they did not use these names) – and the determination of their proper place in the great corpus of knowledge that covered all discoverable facts, would, by replacing the chaotic amalgam of guesswork, tradition, superstition, prejudice, dogma, fantasy and 'interested error' that hitherto did service as human knowledge and human wisdom (and of which by far the chief protector and instigator was the Church), create a new, sane, rational, happy, just and self-perpetuating human society, which, having arrived at the peak of attainable perfection, would preserve itself against all hostile influences, save perhaps those of the forces of nature. (Berlin, 1993, 27–8)

Taking up Hamann's ideas, and vigorously opposing himself to Brockes and particularly to Gottsched, was Herder. From Hamann he secured his first post, as a teacher, and also acquired an early interest in the common roots of music and language, subjects that independently and in conjunction were to absorb his life. In these matters, he in turn profoundly influenced the young Goethe from the moment of their meeting in 1770. To *Von deutscher Art und Kunst* (1773) they contributed influential essays, in Herder's case on 'Ossian' (in whose genuineness he believed) and Shakespeare. In Weimar with Goethe from 1776, he developed his ideas, which had greatly

influenced the *Sturm und Drang* movement, notably on the appreciation of nature and art by the whole personality, rather than by the
isolated faculty of reason, and stressing the supremacy of those
writers closest to nature.

Among these he included the unknown authors of folksongs, of
which he published a collection in 1778–9. It was Herder who coined
the term *Volkslied*; and in his usage it taps a depth of feeling that does
not translate neatly into 'folksong'. For Herder, the *Volk* was finding
expression in songs that welled up instinctively and was not primarily
governed by reason. Many Singspiel composers were happy to make
use of a popular song, or to contrive something of their own close to
it; but Herder had identified something that gave this use a larger
value, and his stature and eloquence lent authority to songs and their
context that might otherwise have continued to be regarded as trivial.

At the centre of Herder's thought is the sense of communality,
especially a cultural communality, uniting and defining human
beings living and working in a society uniquely their own and
different from those of other cultures both in time and in place.
Nothing is more important in giving individual expression to this
than language:

> To be a German is to be part of a unique stream of which language is the
> dominant element, but still only one element among others. [Herder]
> conveys the notion that the ways in which a people – say, the Germans –
> speak or move, eat or drink, their handwriting, their laws, their music,
> their social outlook, their dance forms, their theology, have patterns and
> qualities in common which they do not share, or share to a notably lesser
> degree, with the similar activities of some other group – the French, the
> Icelanders, the Arabs, the ancient Greeks. Each of these activities belongs
> to a cluster which must be grasped as a whole: they illuminate each
> other. Anyone who studies the speech rhythms, or the history or the
> architecture, or the physical characteristics of the Germans, will thereby
> achieve a deeper understanding of German legislation, music, dress.
> There is a property, not capable of being abstracted and articulated – that
> which is German in the Germans – which all these diverse activities
> uniquely evince.   (Berlin, 1992, 195)

These ideas inform Herder's whole approach to music, to which he made contributions as a poet and librettist. Further, he helped to change his countrymen's attitudes towards their art by encouraging confidence in its quality and independent strength. In a powerful essay, 'Auch eine Philosophie der Geschichte zur Bildung der Menschheit', he deplored the fact that the Enlightenment had lost the capacity for wonder and an acknowledgement of the mysterious, thus weakening the *Kraft*, the energy for living, which he saw as complementary to order in achieving human equilibrium, and insisted that nothing could be effectively studied or understood except in the context in which it occurred. Accepting that the physical impact on the eye or ear was one thing, its conduct through the physiological nervous system another, its psychological interpretation a third, he declared that it was the working of all three purposefully together which constituted human creative energy (1774; Herder, 1877–1913, v, 475–594).

In Bückeburg from 1771 until his removal to Weimar, Herder worked closely with Johann Christoph Friedrich Bach, writing for him a libretto, *Brutus*, the only one of five operatic projects to have survived and been set to music. Herder also offered this to the composer he admired above all others, Gluck, accompanying his proposal with a letter explaining that the disjointed nature of his text was deliberate and intended to stimulate the operation of the music. However, Gluck declined, and Bach's score is lost. There are indications that Herder's dissatisfaction with the work – his text is one of high moral seriousness, distinctly static by nature and in fact suggesting something not far removed from opera seria – rested upon disappointed expectations. These were for a kind of opera that would transcend convention and make a music drama from the opportunities held out in a text whose quasi-Shakespearian elements included rejection of the unities. It was of a piece with Herder's belief in the very qualities which had been derided by Enlightenment thinkers as unruly and destructive, but which he saw as forming a wholeness of the human personality out of which a stronger truth would come. Nevertheless, his views changed during the course of his life, from regarding the music as of primary importance to placing greater emphasis on the text, though he always regarded the two as complementary. As part of his rejection of French values, in a short essay *Ueber die Oper* he rails furiously against French opera as empty, merely decorative, artificial and grandiose, something for the deaf who could see (Italian opera was for the blind who could hear), expressing what he saw as the guiding principle of the French nation, *Ehre* – which in this context should be translated as *la gloire*. Against this, he calls for a German opera in which everything, from décor and dance to music, must be drawn together, with no constituent part of the whole being irrelevant, and always to be based on human feeling. He saw this as lying, not in the hands of the aristocracy nor the *Pöbel*, the illiterate rabble, but in those of the Bürger with whom the formation and integration of a community rested (Herder, 1877–1913, IV, 483–6). In another important essay, 'Tanz und Melodrama', he refers to 'ein zusammenhängend lyrisches Gebäude in welchem Poesie, Musik, Action, Decoration Eins sind' (Herder, 1877–1913, XXIII, 335–46) ('a coherent lyrical edifice in which poetry, music, action and décor are unified'), joining his resonant voice to those who called for the *Gesamtkunstwerk*. There was no mistaking the urgency of his demands, even if they were sometimes rather incoherently put, or the passion in the famous cry that lies at the centre of the essay on French opera:

> O eine neu zu schaffende Deutsche Oper! Auf Menschlichem Grund und Boden; mit Menschlicher Musik und Deklamation und Verzierung, aber mit Empfindung, Empfindung; o grosser Zweck! grosses Werk!
>
> (Herder, 1877–1913, IV, 484)

> (Oh for a newly created German opera! On a human basis and foundation; with human music and declamation and décor, but with feeling, with feeling! Oh mighty purpose! mighty task!)

The Treaty of Hubertusburg in 1763 brought a period of thirty years of comparative peace to Germany, and gave to the arts of peace a time in which their cultivation seemed assured. However, little at first was to change. From Frederick the Great himself, with his rigid separation of culture and national aspirations, there was no chance of a new lead. His devotion to French ideals was founded on the belief that classical principles were valid for all times and peoples; and the friendship with Voltaire that underpinned his Enlightenment attitudes led him to deplore Rousseau (for Germans a far more influential philosopher) and, in *De la littérature allemande*, to attack the German language in general as 'à demi-barbare' (Frederick, 1780, 6) and Goethe in particular for imitations of the irrational model of 'les abominables piéces de Schakespear traduits en notre langue' [sic] (Frederick, 1780, 46). The King had no better respect for German opera, and his youthful experiences in Dresden led to him summoning Carl Heinrich Graun to Berlin in 1740 to install Italian opera; in this same year he took into his personal service Francesco Algarotti, whose influential *Saggio sopra l'opera in musica* (1755) holds Graun up as a model. Over Graun's work Frederick exercised a typically despotic rule until war diverted his attentions, when the opera promptly went into decline.

Dresden itself, where from 1731 Johann Adolf Hasse and his wife Faustina Bordoni had made the court the most lavish centre of Italian opera north of the Alps, suffered during the conflict, and the company was forced to close; such ventures as were later initiated remained almost entirely Italian. In other courts, Italian opera remained supreme as a demonstration of civilized taste, with the absence of any serious German competition. The most extreme example was in Stuttgart, where Duke Carl Eugen's expenditure on a sumptuous opera house in 1750, with a company under Niccolò Jommelli between 1753 and 1769, was by 1775 to ruin the entire Württemberg economy. However, the emergence everywhere after the war of a more literate and intelligent public, one with a growing interest in the burgeoning German drama, had the effect of providing new audiences for such German opera as existed, and before long also of encouraging attempts to turn the achievements of Italian opera to German effect.

The war compelled Heinrich Koch to suspend activities, but he managed to regroup and to arrange for a version of Coffey's sequel to *The Devil to Pay*, entitled *The Merry Cobler* (1735), as *Der lustige Schuster* (1759). Back in Leipzig on the cessation of hostilities, Koch was in 1766 able to perform *Der Teufel ist los* in its original form with Standfuss's music and, more significantly, in a revision as *Die verwandelten Weiber* by his friend Johann Adam Hiller (the full details of this famous occasion are to be found in a comprehensive survey of the whole history of eighteenth-century North German opera, Baumann, 1985).

Like many others before and after him, Hiller was greatly impressed by the example of Hasse, in particular by the melodic grace and rhythmic liveliness that lay within a Metastasian apparatus he had no wish to emulate. In C. F. Weisse, Koch found an ideal collaborator for Hiller; and Leipzig, with its busy intellectual and commercial activity, was fertile ground for this gifted triumvirate. Though constrained by the poverty of vocal resources that was long to dog the progress of German opera, the genre which they developed set an encouragingly popular example. Weisse turned for many of his opera texts to French models, familiar to him from his time in Paris during the war:

Diese suchten nicht, wie die meisten italienischen durch
Possenreißereyen und groteske Carrikaturen lautes Lachen zu erregen,
sondern stellten die Ausführung einer artigen Fabel, meistentheils auf
dem Lande lebende Personen auf, in deren Mund der Gesang eines
kleinen, leichten Liedchens der Natur ziemlich angemessen war. Diese
Chansons waren von so faßlicher und singbarer Melodie, daß sie von

dem Publico sehr geschwind behalten und nachgesungen wurden und
das gesellschaftliche Leben erheiterten.   (Weisse, 1806, 103)

(These did not seek, like most Italian examples, to raise loud laughs by
means of cheap theatrical thrills and grotesque caricatures, but unfolded
an agreeable tale, generally of people living in the country, in whose
mouths the singing of a light little song was quite appropriate. These
chansons had such catchy and singable tunes that they were quickly
memorized and repeated by the public and enlivened social life.)

In *Lottchen am Hofe* (1767) and *Die Liebe auf dem Lande* (1769) (both
after Favart), Weisse provided Hiller with just such Rousseau-
inspired texts, in which humble rustic innocence prevails over aristocratic urban corruption. There were those, among them the librettist
Johann Michaelis, who resisted French influence in favour of a
simple, jolly farce, sometimes in a mythological context; but others
provided encouragement for the sentimental and moral element
characteristic of French vaudeville, even if (as with the formerly
influential philosopher Friedrich Nicolai) they believed that they
were supporting Enlightenment values when they were actually
letting in touches of Romantic feeling. Hiller, meanwhile, who had
no love for French music, responded with melodies which derive as
much from German folk tunes as from anything in Hasse or in
French vaudeville. While he made no serious attempt to develop his
musical material in association with the movement of the drama,
which remained spoken, he was able to illustrate events with neat
graphic touches and to use his melodic gift to sketch character deftly.
In this vein, his gifts found their best outlet in the immensely popular
Die Jagd. Dedicated to the Duchess Anna Amalia of Weimar, it was
first performed there in 1770.

Based on the drama *La Partie de chasse de Henri IV* by Charles
Collé, Weisse's libretto tells of three rustic couples. The old village
judge Michel and his wife Marthe will not allow their daughter
Röschen to marry her lover Töffel until their son Christel has been
restored to his lover Hannchen; she has meanwhile disappeared with
Count Schmetterling. Hannchen confounds Christel's gloomy suspicions when she turns out to have been abducted, and her return is

(As in my loft I moistened a piece of thread, out of the bushes there came a breathless girl. She said, Oh! oh! have pity! come to my father! The poor man has fallen and broken his left leg!)

Example 6   Hiller: *Die Jagd* (1770), Röschen

observed by the King, separated from his hunting party in a storm and able, in disguise, to preside over this happily reunited family and to punish the wicked Count. There is a three-part overture, a vigorous storm sinfonia and a lively huntsmen's chorus, busy with cries of 'Tatrah-rah-rah', but the burden of the expression falls upon the melodic differentiation between the various groups. The light-hearted Röschen and Töffel tend to keep up an amiable 6/8 or a merry 2/4; the more sentimental Hannchen, in particular, prefers an expressive 3/4, as at her grateful return home, or 4/4, as with her six-verse narration of her abduction. The latter is an early example of the Romanze that was to be such a popular feature of German opera, generally simple and melodious in style, with a plain accompaniment, telling a story contingent to the plot. 'Als ich auf meinem Bleiche' was an early example of many that were close enough to folksong for them to pass into the vernacular, and even into folksong collections as genuine (Example 6).

The King is distinguished with more ambitious arias, including a Polacca which brought this lively instrumental dance into operatic popularity. The work's means are extremely simple, not to say plain, but Hiller had a very sure idea of what he was doing.

Freylich darf ein Bauermädchen nicht Arie di bravura einer italienischen Opernheldin singen; aber ein Astolph in *Lottchen am Hofe*, ein König in *Der Jagd*, kann auch nicht mit Gesängen eines Bauermädchens auftreten. Diesen Unterschied der Charaktere habe ich, nach der Zeit, in allen ländlichen Scenen, die unser Weisse mit so vielem Glücke bearbeitet hat, vor Augen gehabt; doch aber auch immer darauf gesehen, dass die Form der Arien sich nicht zu sehr von einander entfernte.   (Hiller, 1784, 312)

(Clearly a peasant girl cannot sing an Italian operatic heroine's Aria di bravura; but equally an Astolph in *Lottchen am Hofe* or a King in *Die Jagd* cannot take the stage with a peasant girl's songs. I have always kept my eye on this distinction between the characters in all the country scenes, which our friend Weisse has fashioned so successfully; but I have also always seen to it that the form of the arias is not too diverse.)

The work's enduring appeal – it was given forty times consecutively in Berlin in 1771, and frequently revived during the nineteenth and even twentieth centuries – rests largely upon music that was close to many people's experience, in the context of an agreeable Rousseau-ish moral tale of simple virtue among familiar rustic characters who triumph in the face of sophisticated wickedness, with a benign ruler to preside over restored order and bless the outcome.

No-one grasped the significance of *Die Jagd* more fully than Hiller's pupil Johann Friedrich Reichardt, whose book *Über die deutsche comische Oper* takes the work and an extended analytical description of it as text for a polemic on the laggard state of German opera. He opens with the ringing declaration, 'Es ist wohl keine Meynung allgemeiner, als diese, dass die Deutschen in den Künsten nur Nachahmer sind' (Reichardt, 1774, 3) ('There is no more generally accepted opinion than this, that in the arts the Germans are only imitators'); and he goes on to complain of the supremacy of Italian and French opera, with German opera a hesitant newcomer in this company, always looking over its shoulder. He puts his finger on an essential matter when he writes of Hiller, 'Schon an den Symphonien seiner Opern wird man gewahr, wie er den Charakter des ganzen Stücks vorhero aufs sorgfältigste überdenkt' (Reichardt, 1774, 12) ('One is well aware with the orchestral passages in his operas how carefully he considers the character of the entire piece'), going on to emphasize the vital importance of good instrumental writing.

However, Hiller was not the composer to develop instrumental music to the point at which it could assume a more functional role in a musical drama; and after about 1773 he turned away from opera in other directions. These included conducting, editing, and not least teaching. He was only too well aware that a factor holding back the development of German opera was the amateurish standard of singing. Of Koch's company, he wrote, 'Das Theater hatte keine eigentlichen Sänger und Sängerinnen, sondern wer von Natur eine leidliche Stimme und ein bischen Tactgefühl hatte, unternahm es in den Operetten zu singen' ('The theatre had no actual singers; however, anyone on whom Nature had conferred a tolerable voice, and a bit of ability to keep time, undertook to sing in the operettas'); and he goes on to admit that this led him to have over-ambitious ideas about what could be made of them (Hiller, 1784, 311). Reichardt gave Hiller much credit for what he achieved with such modest material:

> Er wusste es ja, und was ich an ihm bewundere, er hat es nie aus den Augen gelassen, dass er nicht für Sänger, sondern für Schauspieler schrieb, die es sonst kaum hatten einfallen lassen, beym Weine zu singen; und dass sie ihre Kehlen durch Kirchengesänge nicht ausgeschrien, dafür konnte er auch so ziemlich sicher seyn.
>
> (Reichardt, 1774, 14)
>
> (He knew well, and I admire him for never losing sight of the fact, that he was writing not for singers but for actors to whom it would hardly occur to sing even over a glass of wine; and he could also be pretty sure that they would not have lifted their voices bawling hymns in church.)

Frederick the Great declared still more robustly that he would rather listen to his horse than to a German soprano. Hiller consequently interested himself in the training of singers, and wrote with great pride of the notable successes he had with the launching of Gertrude Schmeling (later better known by her married name, Gertrude Mara) and Corona Schröter. An actress who greatly impressed Goethe and became his admired Iphigenia, Schröter was a stately and commanding figure, a pioneer as a singing actress, but 'marmorschön und marmorkalt' (Eisenberg, 1903, 928), as Reichardt discovered when he was unlucky enough to fall in love with her.

Hiller's most important composition pupils were Reichardt and Neefe. Reichardt's wandering career and varied interests included spells in Berlin, in Paris (where he failed in his attempt to capitalize on the successes of his admired Gluck) and in Weimar. Here he was to befriend Goethe and come under the great man's influence. Christian Gottlob Neefe, later to be Beethoven's first teacher, was gifted with a more expressive melodic manner than Reichardt, and like Reichardt his songs show anticipations of the Romantic Lied; but in his operas of the early 1770s his two most important librettists were Johann Michaelis and Johann Jakob Engel, both of whom argued for farce and low comedy as essentially German.

Within these constraints, Neefe wrote music of considerable expressive range. *Die Apotheke* (1771) includes an episode in which the old apothecary Enoch is being lathered by the barber Trist, who, with the satire on fashionable or pedantic devotion to the classics that long endured in German opera, drives his client to distraction. Neefe's witty handling of this includes a mock-serioso lamentation, in the minor-key dotted-note conventions of many a classical heroine of opera seria, that is also built into a skilful tripartite structure. However, the characterization remains by aria type, with Enoch's daughter Crönchen livelier than his more forceful niece Fieckchen, whose anger when she believes her lover Vincent unfaithful leads her to announce, with unsuitable violence, that in that case she will become a nun. Whatever Engel's German intentions, Vincent sings with an elegance (as in a minuet marked 'con discrezione') and Crönchen with a charm close to opéra-comique. There are similar suggestions in *Amors Guckkasten* (1772), as well as hints that Neefe is putting musical pressure upon the restraints imposed by the librettos of Engel and Michaelis. These become stronger in *Der Einspruch* (1772, rev. 1773), even though the work has recourse to such regular stand-bys as a Schoolmaster who prates macaronically in Latin and German. This convention returns in an amiable little comedy by

Joseph Schuster, *Der Alchymist* (1778). Though touched by Italian example, the piece departs no real distance from Hiller's model: its seventeen numbers are for characters who include a foolish father absorbed with alchemy, a shrewish wife, a pair of young lovers, and a pompous tutor who delivers himself of an aria beginning 'Otium est vitium, lautet das Proverbium' ('Idleness is a vice, so the proverb tells us').

The success of Abel Seyler's company in the post-war years was rooted in his business acumen, coupled with a flair for attracting talent, but he would not have flourished without the greater respect beginning to be accorded the travelling theatre companies in the new climate of interest in drama and hence in dramatic music. Seyler was not only able to recruit actors of the distinction of Konrad Ekhof; in 1769 he appointed Anton Schweitzer as music director, charged with adding opera to the spoken repertory. Frustrated by the low standards in singing, Schweitzer kept his eyes and ears open on his travels, and was able to recruit the excellent soprano and baritone couple Josepha and Friedrich Hellmuth and the brilliant young soprano Franziska Koch. By then, in 1771, Seyler's company had been able to put behind it the itinerant life, with its diet of occasional pieces in various genres, and accept a position such as all theatre directors must have dreamt of, permanent engagement in Weimar at the court of the art-loving Duchess Anna Amalia. With this came reasonable prosperity, decent working conditions, and respect for actors and musicians not as mountebanks but as artists welcome on equal terms in court intellectual circles. The turn from a casual, hand-to-mouth existence to secure establishment at a cultured court represented a new condition in German theatrical life; it also provided the circumstances for a new condition in German opera.

Already in position in Weimar since 1761 was Ernst Wilhelm Wolf, appointed by Anna Amalia to duties that included teaching her sons as well as herself. He had composed operas for the Seyler company, but was essentially a conservative figure with neither the talent nor the inclination to develop opera beyond the manner of Hiller. His occasional, rather uneasy attempts at a more elaborate style tend to fall flat partly through his limited technical range, but at least as much because of his insecure dramatic judgement. It is difficult to disagree with the view of these as 'disembodied musical niceties at best and inappropriate artifice at worst' (Baumann, 1985, 82). Not surprisingly, Wolf viewed the arrrival of the Seyler troupe and its composer Schweitzer with deep misgiving, and his jealousy was fuelled by the resentments of his singer wife, Maria Karoline Benda.

Schweitzer possessed the greater talent, with ambitious ideas to accompany it. He had also been frustrated by the limited opportunities afforded him by the Seyler company's circumstances. His earlier music included works with spoken dialogue, farces, ballets, and occasional pieces; settled in Weimar, he produced a comic opera, *Die Dorfgala*, and a setting of a German translation of Rousseau's melodrama *Pygmalion* (both in 1772). He also collaborated on a short piece with Christoph Martin Wieland, whose invitation to Weimar in 1772 to act as tutor to the young dukes was Anna Amalia's most important step, before Goethe's arrival in 1775, in establishing her little duchy as a centre of civilized values and artistic excellence.

Wieland harboured his own ambitions for a German national opera, which he proceeded to articulate in a set of essays in his journal *Der teutsche Merkur*, founded in 1773 on the model of the *Mercure de France*. The most significant of these was his 'Versuch über das teutsche Singspiel', testing theories, which he put into practice in his collaboration with Schweitzer on *Alceste*, against Francesco Algarotti's *Saggio*. Though the *Saggio* was written in the year after Algarotti's return to Italy in 1753, it was widely translated and reprinted, and Algarotti's years at the court of Frederick the Great gave his views particular weight in Germany. Calling Dr Burney as witness, Wieland argued that German was a sound language for singing, and the Germans' gift for music undeniable. He contested the argument that it was possible for the example of ancient Greek drama to be followed in modern Germany, declaring that social and political conditions were totally different, but also, rejecting Algarotti's idea that subjects must be in the realm of the marvellous or the exotic, he claimed that a Greek subject was another matter:

Denn wenn ich lieber *Griechische* Süjets zum Singspiele wählen möchte,
so wär' es mehr darum, weil sie uns nach unsrer bisherigen, hierin
lobenswürdigen, Erziehungsart ungleich bekannter, und also auch schon
darum interessanter sind, als *Hyperboreische, Indianische, Mexicanische* und
so weiter, als aus irgend einem andern Grunde; wiewohl auch der
Umstand, dass wir mit dem Begriffe von *Griechen* überhaupt die Idee eines
von allen Musen vorzüglich begünstigen Volkes zu verknüpfen pflegen,
hier nicht ganz ohne Gewicht seyn möchte.   (Wieland, 1928, 88–9)

(So if I prefer to choose *Greek* subjects for Singspiels, it is more because
they are incomparably better known to us by reason of our admirable
educational background – and are therefore more interesting than
Hyperborean, Indian, Mexican etc. subjects – than for any other reason,
although the fact that we are accustomed to connecting the concept of
the *Greeks* above all with the idea of a people especially favoured by all
the Muses is not altogether without weight.)

He goes on to argue that classical subjects are well suited to opera as,
though they suggest a higher state than ours, it is one in the same
tradition. The four precepts which he advances are first, to get rid of
all superfluous events; second, to choose characters and situations
suitable for music; third, to keep everything simple; finally and most
importantly, to ensure that inner expression takes precedence over
outer action. Having summarized Algarotti's objections to opera
seria, he makes an appeal based on recognition of Gluck's genius for
a new era in Germany. Whatever reservations he felt about Gluck,
he had no hesitation in claiming that more composers in his mould
were needed to bring about 'diese schöne Zusammenstimmung aller
Theile zur grossen Einheit des Ganzen, auf dem lyrischen Schau-
platze' (Wieland, 1928, 99) ('this beautiful unison of all parts for the
greater unity of the whole on the operatic stage'). Whatever the
shortcomings of his own *Alceste* with Schweitzer, or of his real
understanding of the nature of Greek tragedy, these were the ideals
governing him.

Alceste (1773) divides the classical legend into the standard tragic
five acts, with Alceste first confiding to her sister Parthenia that she is
resolved to die in place of her sick husband Admet, then duly parting

from him and her children when he returns to health. In Act III, Herkules offers to fetch her back from the shades, and sets off, leaving Admet (in the next act) to imagine Alceste wandering in the Underworld. Finally, Herkules returns with a mysterious woman whom he offers as a substitute for Alceste to the shocked Admet, but when she is revealed as Alceste all ends happily. Even so bald a summary does not simplify the plot unduly; for, according to his precepts, Wieland hoped to recapture what he believed was Greek simplicity. He was, moreover, constrained by there being only three able singers in the Seyler company. Franziska Koch was to sing Alceste, with the Hellmuths as Admet and Parthenia; the weakness of the part of Herkules reflects the lesser talent of a fourth member of the company, Friedrich Günther. What, however, turned out to be a reduction of the classical, tragic and Greek to something more nearly contemporary, domestic and German drew the fire of Goethe in a short farce, *Götter, Helden und Wieland* (1773). In this noisy little squib the unfortunate author is hauled out of bed by Mercury (already annoyed at having his name taken in vain for *Der teutsche Merkur*) and arraigned before Euripides and his characters. The satire, which Wieland took in good part, was misplaced, since for all its faults his text served his declared purpose of a librettist's task, to provide words for the opera a composer wishes to write.

This is built around solo numbers, with two duets and a single trio, together with a closing quartet (and a token role for a mourning chorus). Schweitzer is adept at characterizing the four participants. Alceste's lines in her arias are graceful, Parthenia's more subtle and chromatic, Admet's plainer and blunter, while Herkules first appears in an unsuitably enfeebled condition reflected in his weak melodies, and only gradually manages to assert something like heroic resolve in a coloratura-laden Allegro maestoso. This aspect of the work is not, however, its most remarkable, and indeed Mozart was scornful about Schweitzer's inability to write for the voice: 'ja, unglücklich der sänger oder die sängerin die in die hände des schweizers fallt; dann der wird sein lebelang das singbare nicht lernen!' (Letter to his father, 11 Sep. 1778) ('Unhappy the singer who falls into Schweitzer's hands, for in all his life he'll never learn to write singable music!'). The work's expressive strengths lie more in the richness of the contrapuntal writing (as in Admet's aria opening Act II), the control of harmonic tension, and above all in the ability to use the orchestra eloquently: a striking instance of the latter comes in Alceste's 'Ihr Götter der Hölle', when muted violins in the first part of the aria make a crescendo to an unmuted Allegro con spirito. Though some of the recitative can be plain, it is a characteristic for expressive orchestral phrases to intervene, as at Alceste's first appearance. In the duet when Parthenia is trying to dissuade Alceste from her sacrifice in a long, fluent accompanied recitative, eloquent lines in the orchestra move gradually into an arioso, with touching phrases when she begins to feel herself growing weaker as Admet's strength returns, and finally into an aria, 'O du mein zweytes, bessres Ich!'

The most powerful passages in the opera, in fact, are those in which Schweitzer breaks away from formal aria and recitative into a freer melodic and orchestral declamation. When Admet is unhappily contemplating Alceste wandering by the River Lethe, nursing his fears that the waters of forgetfulness will drown all memory of the love that has been their whole existence, the music passes restlessly between arioso passages in different tempos, recitative, an Allegro with recitative interjections from the orchestra, and so forth, forming a long expressive sequence in which such distinctions become meaningless. In many such passages, Schweitzer is beginning to move beyond the condition of German opera which he inherited. The recitative has acquired an expressive fluency and momentum of its own, rather than relying on simple affective touches, and the orchestra has assumed greater expressive responsibility, outside set aria forms, as phrases are developed in response to the voice or create a situation which the voice articulates (Example 7).

Alceste had a great success at its first performance on 28 May 1773, and was quickly taken up by many other stages. It was the first through-composed serious German opera, recognized as a landmark by Mozart when he saw it in Mannheim in 1777: 'freylich hat das viell

(They are offering her brimming beakers from the waters of Lethe. Oh, beloved, take care! Do not taste their magic draught!)

Example 7 Schweitzer: *Alceste* (1773), Admet

beytragen, weil es dass erste teütsche singspiell war' (letter to his father, 3 Dec. 1777) ('certainly it has been very successful, as it was the first German Singspiel').

However, Wieland had not had his say about the condition of German opera. In 1774 he began publishing in *Der Teutsche Merkur* a novel, *Die Abderiten*, in which he took the Thracian town of Abdera and its legendarily foolish people as model for a satire on German artistic provincialism. In 1778 this was reworked to include a chapter, 'Euripides unter die Abderiten', in which his targets are extended to opera. Nomofylax composes music for Euripides's *Andromeda* 'unbekümmert, ob seine Musik den Text, oder der Text seine Musik zu Unsinn mache' (Wieland, 1818, I, 262) ('unconcerned whether nonsense was made of the text by his music or of his music by the text'). Wieland proceeds to make merry at the expense of the audience applauding rapturously and demanding encores at dramatically inopportune moments, of singers losing their places and recovering themselves with difficulty, especially of a fat soprano whose physical and vocal abundance enraptures the men in the audience but irritates the ladies, and other absurdities. Not knowing any better, the Abderites are enthralled. The presence of a glum guest highly critical of the whole thing, especially of the feebleness of the music, enrages them until they are taken aback to discover that this is in fact Euripides himself. Wieland goes on in a later chapter to describe another performance by Euripides' own company, which he holds up as an example:

> Da nun überdiess die Musik vollkommen nach dem Sinne des Dichters, und also das alles war, was die Musik des Nomofylax Gryllus – nicht war; da sie immer gerad aufs Herz wirkte, und ungeachtet der grössten Einfalt und Singbarkeit doch immer neu und überraschend war: so brachte alles diess, mit der Lebhaftigkeit und Wahrheit der Deklamation und Pantomime und mit der Schönheit der Stimmen und des Vortrags vereinigt, einen Grad von Täuschung bey den guten Abderiten hervor, wie sie noch in keinem Singspiel erfahren hatten. Sie vergassen gänzlich, dass sie in ihrem Nationaltheater sassen, glaubten unvermerkt mitten in der wirklichen Scene der Handlung zu seyn, nahmen Antheil an dem

Glück und Unglück der handelnden Personen, als ob es ihre Blutsfreunde
gewesen wären.   (Wieland, 1818, I, 324–5)

(Since the music was now completely in accordance with the poet's
intention, and therefore was everything that the music of Nomofylax
Gryllus was not; since it always directly affected the heart, and in spite of
the greatest simplicity and singability was always new and amazing: so all
this, with the liveliness and truthfulness of the declamation and the acting,
and with the beauty of the voices and the execution, created a degree of
illusion among the good Abderites such as they had never before
experienced in any Singspiel. They completely forgot that they were
sitting in their National Theatre, believed that they were unobserved in
the middle of the real scene of the action, and took part in the fortune
and misfortune of the characters as if they had been their closest friends.)

Not surprisingly, *Die Abderiten* caused widespread offence, which gave
Wieland the opportunity to continue his argument that it was in the
musical theatre that the best hopes lay for the development of German
culture, only provided that the art, whether comic or tragic, were taken
with the true seriousness that Germans owed to it and to themselves.

At the same time as Wieland was publishing *Die Abderiten*, there
also appeared Johann Georg Sulzer's *Allgemeine Theorie der schönen
Künste* (the first volume in 1771, the second in 1774). Though regarded
as a fundamental work of German classicism, this extremely influential book contains some forward-looking views that draw Sulzer
surprisingly close to Wieland and to a more Romantic standpoint.
He begins his observations on opera in some bewilderment:

Bey dem ausserordentlichen Schauspiel, dem die Italiäner den Namen
Opera gegeben haben, herrscht eine so seltsame Vermischung des
Großen und Kleinen, des Schönen und Abgeschmakten, daß ich verlegen
bin, wie und was ich davon schreiben soll . . . Die Oper kann das Größte
und Wichtigste aller dramatischen Schauspiele seyn, weil darin alle
schönen Künste ihre Kräfte vereinigen . . . Poesie, Musik, Tanzkunst,
Mahlerey und Baukunst vereinigen sich zur Darstellung der Opera.

(Sulzer, 1771–4, 842 [misprinted as 642])

(In the extraordinary drama to which the Italians have given the name
opera there reigns such a strange mixture of the great and the small, the

beautiful and the tasteless, that I am at a loss to know how and what to write about it . . . Opera can be the greatest and most important of all dramatic presentations, since all the fine arts unite their powers . . . poetry, music, dance, painting and architecture unite in the production of opera.)

When Sulzer talks about the arts uniting (*vereinigen*), he is here really meaning 'coming into contact' rather than forming a new artistic unity, since he goes on to quote Algarotti and to complain that the various arts never really do combine. However, he continues by declaring that the most secure future for opera lies in it being bound up with the national ambitions, though he agrees with those who feel that the spirit of Greece and Rome has been lost. He anticipates Romantic interests by suggesting Ossian as authentically operatic material, proposing *Temora* for its bards, battles and the watching presence of Fingal, with its changes of pace and emphasis indicating recitative, arias and choruses, all bringing the arts together constructively: 'Ein solche Oper wär allerdings eine völlig neue Art des Dramas' (Sulzer, 1771–4, 847) ('Such an opera would indeed be a completely new kind of drama'). From here he goes on, after attacking singers' abuses, to lament the lack of arioso merging recitative and aria and to take a stand for expressive scenery:

> Eine feyerliche Stille; eine Scene, die finster und traurig, oder prächtig und herrlich ist; der Auftritt der Personen, deren Stellung, Anzug und alles was zum Aeußerlichen gehöret, mit jenem Charakter der Scene übereinkommt – diesen zusammengenommen, würket in den Gemüthern der Zuschauer eine so starke Spannung zur Leidenschaft, daß nur noch ein geringer Stoß hinzukommen darf, um ihren vollen Ausbruch zu bewürkten; die Gemüther sind schon zum voraus so sehr erhitzt, daß nun ein kleiner Funken alles darin in voller Flammen setzet.
>
> (Sulzer, 1771–4, 849)

(A solemn silence; a scene that is either dark and gloomy or grand and magnificent; the entrance of the characters, their posture, clothes and everything concerned with their appearance that matches the character of the scene – all this brought together produces in the audience's feelings such a strong emotional tension that it needs only a small impetus for them to burst out completely; emotions are so heated beforehand that only a small spark will set them ablaze.)

If not for these reasons, the Weimar court theatre did burn down in 1774, and Abel Seyler had to leave with his company, to be given shelter by a scarcely less enlightened ruler, Duke Ernst II of Saxe-Gotha. Here they found installed, as court composer, Georg (Jiří) Benda. Of Bohemian origin, Benda's family had settled in German lands and, during his time at Gotha from 1750, he had written an Italian opera, *Xindo riconosciuto* (1765). However, it was the arrival of the Seylers that brought both drama and opera to the town, with a success that was to lead to their establishment under court administration as a Hoftheater. Benda paved a new way by welcoming into the repertory works by Grétry and Monsigny as part of the wave of interest in a more serious vein of French opéra-comique that was sweeping Germany, and also saw how the new interest in drama, together with the Seylers' resources, might be put to good effect. In the space of a year, 1775, he wrote a comic opera, *Der Jahrmarkt*, and, in the wake of Schweitzer's *Pygmalion*, *Ariadne auf Naxos* and *Medea*. Though described as 'duodramas', since they are for two actors, the latter two works are melodramas in that they use the spoken word only, over music or separated by short musical passages. In 1776 there followed *Walder* and *Romeo und Julie*.

Der Jahrmarkt is a slight piece much in the manner of Hiller, who indeed contributed numbers to its revised version as *Der Dorfjahrmarkt*. Originally an adaptation of a play by Engel, it had to be rewritten when Ekhof angrily objected to what he saw as the trivialization of one of his favourite roles in it, and the result is a village farce concerning the efforts of a recruiting sergeant, Fickfack, to win Bärbchen away from her jealous lover Lukas by getting him drunk and enlisting him; the day is saved by the intervention of the regiment's kindly commanding officer acting as Colonel *ex machina*. Much of the piece falls into the usual conventions, with sturdy arias for the Colonel, comical-absurd ones for Fickfack, charming ones for Bärbchen's sister Süschen, and a virtuoso closing aria, flashing with

Un poco lento

Hier fleh' ich knie - end, ich fleh' knie - end um Er - bar - men

(Kneeling here I beg for mercy)

Andante

Ach, ich fühl's, es ist ver - schwun-den e - wig

hin der Lie - be Glück

(Ah, I feel it, love's happiness has vanished for ever)

Example 8
(a) Benda: *Der Jahrmarkt* (1775), Bärbchen
(b) Mozart: *Die Zauberflöte* (1791), Pamina

coloratura, designed to show off the skills of Josepha Hellmuth as Bärbchen herself. Only in the key scene when the angry Lukas thinks Bärbchen has betrayed him does the music take on greater expressiveness by adopting some of the pathetic conventions of opéra-comique: perhaps there is even the sly suggestion that Bärbchen is consciously using these well-tried wiles to put on a bit of an emotional act. She woos him in a brief moment of accompanied recitative before embarking on an Allegro impelled by jabbing accents as she declares that only death will part them, then delivering a touching Lento appeal before resuming her forceful Allegro. Lukas is no match for this emotional onslaught, and blithely gives in. The effect of the Lento, 'Hier fleh' ich kniend', may have caught Mozart's ear when he came to write Pamina's 'Ach, ich fühl's' as she, too, feels that love has fled (Example 8).

The presence in Gotha of the actresses Charlotte Brandes and Sophie Seyler clearly influenced Benda's two melodramas; but the works also reflect the general enthusiasm for drama and, further, the widespread concern about German as a language for singing which had long occupied composers and writers. It was one thing to link simple songs with dialogue, or to write elaborate arias as if the language could be treated in the same way as Italian (which must be one part of the reason for Mozart's complaint about Schweitzer); it was another to discover a good declamatory musical manner that was identifiably German. As Herder observed, in words that were to be much studied and reiterated,

> Das eine Volk spricht eherne Panzer von Worten; das andre mit feinern Sprachwerkzeugen tönet Silberwellen, die durch feinere Hörorgane zu silbernen Pfeilen geschmiedet, die Seele durch Töne, wie durch einfache Punkte treffen. Da sinds alsdenn nicht Metaphern, was wir von dem Sprachgesange der alten Griechen lesen, die gleichsam zween Abmessungen der Sprachtöne mehr hatten, als wir, Harmonik und Rhythmik – keine Metaphern, wenn sie auch im Grundgefühl eines Tons tiefer empfanden als wir. Noch ist die halbsingende Sprache der Italiener mit ihrer Natur zur *fühlbaren* Tonkunst vereinigt; wie die süsstönende Stimme des weiblichen Geschlechts mit einem seiner Gefühle der Musik. Die Natur selbst hat für solche Völker gearbeitet, und ihnen in einen seinern Himmelsluft feinere Sprach- und Hörwerkzeuge und gleichsam ein natürliches Saitenspiel der Empfindung gewebet. Sie sprechen und hören und fühlen Silbertöne; wo andere rauhere Völker, die nur Schälle reden, auch nur Schälle hören können.
>
> (Herder, 1877–1913, IV, 1078)

(The language of one race consists of words like the bronze of body armour, that of another, using more refined instruments of speech, of silver waves of sound, which more refined ears forge into arrows of silver that strike upon the spirit with the directness of sharpened points. Thus when we read of the musical speech of the ancient Greeks that they had as it were two degrees of tonal receptivity in speech more than we – harmony and rhythm – that is no metaphor, if their sensitivities were more profound than ours even in the basic impression made by a single sound. The language of the modern Italians – part speech, part song – is linked to their instinctive feeling for the musicality of speech, as the sweet sound of a woman's voice is to the sensitivity to music peculiar to her sex. Nature herself has worked to the advantage of such races, has created for them in their particular climates more sensitive organs of speech and hearing, and has strung for them, as it were, an inborn instrument of sensibility. They speak and hear and feel notes of silver, whereas other, coarser races, whose speech consists of mere sounds, hear only sounds as well.)

Benda's melodramas *Ariadne auf Naxos* and *Medea* (both 1775) may appear to confront the problem of German declamatory recitative only to evade it, but actually they invoke the sounds of the language itself, in contact with music but not subject to it. The problems which Benda thereby set himself as a composer are also confronted, and met in ways that were to have strong implications for German opera. In a medium where the music is essentially discontinuous, and ruled by the spoken word, there is at the same time the need for the orchestra to assume the expressive burden. This clearly encounters the difficulty of how to sustain and develop material, and in turn compels Benda to refine and concentrate the expression, with taut harmony and vivid modulations, and to induce continuity by exploring the possibilities of motive. The words sometimes accompany the music, but more often are spoken between musical entries; and the score is bound together chiefly by motivic devices or associative reprises. Occasion is found, however, for some more extended music. The overture is a powerful piece, in the middle of which the curtain rises to show Theseus approaching the sleeping Ariadne to take his agonized leave of her, and it includes a tense depiction of Ariadne's dream of this betrayal (a skilful Romantic reworking of the traditional Italian *sonno*, with an event passing immediately into the dreamer's unconscious). As she awakes, an Oreade, or mountain nymph, tells her of Theseus's treachery, to a touching bassoon solo which returns later; and Ariadne herself has an elaborate violin solo, winding around her words as she mourns her lost innocence and prepares for death. There is also occasion for the description of raging wild beasts and for some sea and storm music in the orchestra, which builds up momentum not by developmental melodic means but through the cumulative effect of heaving basses, whirling chromatic figures, stabbing arpeggios and rushing scales, material which was by no means new to operatic description but which brought

Nature in action to the centre of a musical drama. Far more than in the work of Rousseau the composer, music is made to articulate Nature and to illuminate its connexions with the inner world of the emotions in the manner of Rousseau the philosopher.

While *Ariadne* reflected the expressive tenderness of Charlotte Brandes, *Medea* was written for the dramatic vehemence of Sophie Seyler. There is a greater fluency of movement between words and music, and a subtler use of them in combination. Benda has devised a stronger, more cohesive tonal scheme, and further concentrated his use of motive, associating his main one, a rushing upward scale followed by a dotted-note figure, with the impetuous and obsessive nature of Medea herself. By being set throughout the work against melodic invention permeated by downward scale figures, this serves to isolate Medea from Jason and from her supplanter in his affections, Kreusa; and it returns with savage irony at the end of the work to impel the horrified Jason to fall upon his sword. It also separates Medea's infanticide from normal human emotions; and, after an elaborate violin solo as she reflects upon her children, Benda portrays the murders with a powerful storm which she generates as she rushes into the palace to slay them (off-stage, in Greek fashion), then emerging to slow, eerie string phrases.

The success of Benda's melodramas in reconciling German dramatic narrative to the art of music led to a string of imitations, including those by Neefe (*Sophonisbe*, 1776), Reichardt (*Cephalus und Prokris*), Vogler (*Lampedo*, 1779), Danzi (*Cleopatra*, 1780) and Zumsteeg (*Tamira*, 1788). Winter's first three dramatic works were melodramas, *Cora und Alonzo* (1778), a piece of exoticism set among the Incas, *Lenardo und Blandine* (1779), on a grisly Bürger ballad, and *Reinhold und Armida* (1780), deriving from Tasso. Danzi's *Cleopatra*, also much influenced by Benda and making some use of motive, is quite a complex handling of the tragedy, tending to alternate dialogue and music until the dramatic crisis of the Queen's suicide, when speech and music are united; and it reflects his Mannheimer's interest in vivid orchestration. One of the most successful works, before this brief phase of the genre spent itself, was by Christian Cannabich. The effects in *Elektra* (1781) include an off-stage march and an invisible female chorus of consolation, and the climax at the off-stage murder of Klytemnestra by Orestes effectively steps up tension by swift alternations of speech and music. It is a work of considerable resource and effective dramatic timing which also makes good use of thematic recall.

Among the greatest admirers of Benda's melodramas were Reichardt and Mozart. Reichardt described dragging himself reluctantly off to the theatre where *Ariadne* was playing, only to have his suspicions completely allayed:

> Bendas Genie hat einen solchen Zauber über das Ganze ausgegossen, daß die Wirkung seiner Musik bey jedem Menschen von Gefühl alles Raisonnement bey weitem überstimmt. Selbst Stellen, die mir hernach als tadelhaft erschienen, reißen mich noch oft beym Klavier so hin, daß ich mich aller vorhergegangen Kritiken darüber ärgere und schäme.
>
> (Reichardt, 1782/91, I, 86)

> (Benda's genius has cast such a spell over the whole work that the effect of his music on any man of sensibility far overtakes all reasoning. Even passages that had hitherto seemed to me faulty impress me so much at the keyboard that all previous criticisms of them vex and shame me.)

Reichardt's practical response to Benda's achievement, his own successful *Cephalus und Prokris* (1777), was in turn enthusiastically welcomed by Carl Friedrich Cramer (*MM*, 1783, 89). Mozart was no less impressed, as he wrote to his father from Mannheim in 1778):

> die seilerische trupe ist hier – die ihnen schon per Renomè bekant seyn wird; – H: v: Dallberg ist Director davon; – dieser läst mich nicht fort, bis ich ihm nicht ein Duodrama componirt habe, und in der that habe ich mich gar nicht lange besonnen; – denn, diese art Drama zu schreiben habe ich mir immer gewunschen; – ich weis nicht, habe ich ihnen, wie ich das erstemal hier war, etwas von dieser art stücke geschrieben? – ich habe damals hier ein solch stück 2 mahl mit den grösten vergnügenn aufführen gesehen! – in der that – mich hat noch niemal etwas so surprenirt! – denn, ich bildete mir immer ein so was würde keinen Effect machen! – sie wissen wohl, dass da nicht gesungen, sondern Declamirt wird – und die Musique wie ein obligirtes Recitativ ist – bisweilen wird

auch unter der Musique gesprochen, welches alsdann die herrlichste
wirckung thut; – was ich gesehen war Medea von *Benda* – er hat noch
eine gemacht, Ariadne auf Naxos, beyde wahrhaft – fürtreflich; sie
wissen, das *Benda* unter den lutherischen kapellmeistern immer mein
liebling war; ich liebe diese zwey wercke so, dass ich sie bey mir führe;
Nun stellen sie sich meine freüde vor, dass ich das, was ich mir
gewunschen zu machen habe! – wissen sie was meine Meynung wäre? –
man solle die Recitativ auf solche art in der opera tractiren – und nur
bisweilen, wenn die wörter *gut in der Musick auszudrücken sind*, das
Recitativ singen. (Letter to his father, 12 November 1778)

(The Seyler Company is here, whom you'll already know by reputation.
Herr von Dalberg is their Director. He won't let me go until I've
composed a duodrama for him, and in fact I didn't reflect for long, as I've
always wanted to write a drama of this kind. I don't know, did I tell you
anything about this kind of drama the first time I was here? I then saw
one such piece twice, with the utmost pleasure. In fact, nothing has ever
surprised me so much, as I'd always imagined that something like that
would have no effect. As you well know, it's not sung, only declaimed,
with the music like a kind of obbligato recitative, sometimes with speech
under the music, and this has a marvellous effect. The work I saw was
Benda's *Medea*. He's written another one, too, *Ariadne auf Naxos*, and
they're both really excellent. As you know, Benda has always been my
favourite of all the Lutheran Kapellmeisters. I like these two works so
much that I carry them about with me. Now, imagine my delight that
I've got to do just what I've always wanted to do! Do you know what I
think? One ought to treat operatic recitative in this way, and only have
sung recitative when the words *can be well expressed by the music*.)

Mozart later wrote to his father, on 3 December, that he was at
work on the first act of *Semiramis*, but nothing of this survives.
However, Benda's influence strongly marks the melodramas that
open each of the two surviving acts of *Zaide*, and traces of Mozart's
appreciation of the technique show in *Die Entführung aus dem Serail*.
He never seems to have solved to his complete satisfaction the
problem of how to write German-language recitative. Apart from
two passages for Constanze and one in duet with Belmonte, there is
none in *Die Entführung*. It is only in sections of *Die Zauberflöte*, above

all in Tamino's recitative confrontation with the Speaker before the gates of the temple, that one feels that another German-language opera, freed from the conventions of Viennese Singspiel, might have enabled him to find the eloquence in his own language that he had discovered in the freely composed passages of *Idomeneo*.

In the year following the two melodramas, 1776, Benda wrote *Walder* and *Romeo und Julie*, described respectively as *ernsthafte Operette* and *ernsthafte Oper*. *Walder* suffered from comparison with Grétry's *Silvain*, whose success in Paris in 1770 had been reflected in Germany; but it seems likely that in adapting Marmontel's libretto Gotter was trying to create opportunities for Benda to compose the subject along German lines. The plot concerns Walder, disinherited by his father Dolmon when he takes a humble wife, Sophie, and goes to live in a woodland village; here he finds himself defending the peasants' rights against his angry brother, Dolmon Sohn, and against his father, who is, however, won round by Sophie and his little granddaughters. There was much to appeal in this tale of a threatened pastoral idyll, with moral strands in a plot concerning the rights of peasants and the duty of parents to achieve reconciliation with their children. Although Benda cannot approach Grétry's charm of manner, the *ernsthaft* intention allows him to give the moral dimension greater depth in music of striking melodic fluency and instrumental resource. It was the heroine's rondo 'Selbst die glücklichste der Ehen' which captivated audiences and set other composers writing rondos; but the most remarkable number is the final quartet, 'Bricht ihr Herz', which leaves the audience with the moral question still being posed as Dolmon Sohn treats the others' sweetness towards one another as mere weakness and storms out of the opera. His powerful rejection of traditional virtue looks forward to later Romantic villains, and it is a pity that, having elevated him from Marmontel and Grétry's small spoken part to a central role in the drama, Gotter and Benda then felt obliged to tie up the ending with some conventional moralizing.

Benda's *ernsthafte Oper* can claim to be the first opera based on Shakespeare, even if the distinction is a hollow one. The work dismayed those who, fired with the enthusiasms of the *Sturm und Drang*, understood the Romantic elements in Shakespeare and found them suppressed, first by Weisse keeping strictly to the unities in his prose version and fashioning a happy ending, and then by Gotter satisfying the demands of conventional operatic usage. To all intents and purposes a vehicle for his young pupil Sophia Preysing, it gives scant opportunity to Romeo (who was sung by Johann Ernst Dauer, Mozart's first Pedrillo), reduces Capulet (Capellet) and Friar Laurence (Lorenzo) to little more than agents in the plot, replaces the Nurse with a confidante for Julie, Laura, and dispenses entirely with Mercutio, Tybalt and any opportunity for light relief. Julie grieves over her enforced parting from her banished husband Romeo, but he resists her suggestion of a double suicide. She deflects Capellet's proposal of another bridegroom, and Lorenzo suggests a potion simulating death so that she may escape to Romeo. Hearing of her death, Romeo arrives in her tomb and is about to stab himself when she calls his name and they join in a rapturous duet. Outside the vault, the despairing Capellet has been persuaded to promise her to the man of her choice if only she can be revived; and when Lorenzo reveals the lovers, all are reconciled.

Neither the conventionalization of the plot nor its detail gives Benda much opportunity for the writing of the serious opera he intended, despite his best efforts, among which is a splendid funeral chorus showing how much he was prepared to learn from Gluck. There are some incidental delights, such as Laura's pretty nightingale aria, 'Lasst ihr, Nachtigallen', a convention to which many composers turned so as to lend justification for indulging their sopranos with coloratura; and Capellet comes to life rather belatedly from his bufferish protestations when overcome by emotion at his daughter's apparent death. The duets between Romeo and Julie, even their Act I 'Ja, der Lerche frühe Kehle', are sadly routine, and left to himself Romeo lapses into empty flourishes. The best music comes with the passages in which Benda can further explore his gift for mixing recitative, arioso and aria in freely composed movements, as when the overture moves into the drama without pause, and in particular with Julie's 'Ihn wieder zu seh'n', when anxiety mingles with excitement at Lorenzo's plot and takes the form of a flexibly expressive passage which dissolves the current distinctions between kinds of word-setting.

Mannheim was the ideal city in which Mozart might absorb some of the many influences that went into his art. Ever since Carl Theodor's succession in 1742, and the opening of the new Hoftheater, the city had enthusiastically cultivated its opera scarcely less than its famous orchestra. From 1753 the Kapellmeister was Ignaz Holzbauer, who drew to Mannheim composers of the enterprise and stature of Jommelli, Traetta, Piccinni and J. C. Bach, all of them writing Italian opera but essaying more empirical forms that were to be associated above all with Gluck. French influences were still more keenly encouraged; and the 1775 performance of Gluck's *Alceste* led Holzbauer to attempt a major German opera, most unusually choosing a German subject, in *Günther von Schwarzburg* (1777).

Holzbauer had written operas for Italy, and Anton Klein, the librettist of *Günther*, was a Jesuit dilettante of Metastasian leanings with little sense of dramatic momentum and less of how to pay more than lip service to novel ideas. The intentions are impeccably nationalist, with a subject loosely taken from a fourteenth-century episode in German history. There is much setting of self-consciously German scenes, such as the opening palace hall 'mit Bildsäulen und Schildern aus der alten deutschen Geschichte geziert' ('decorated with statues and escutcheons from old German history'); and there are frequent reminders in text and stage directions of the Teutonic nature of the proceedings. The plot deals with the struggle for the Imperial throne between Günther and his rival Karl of Bohemia, son of the evil (and fictional) Asberta. Supported by the Count Palatine Rudolf, whose daughter Anna loves Karl, Günther is crowned. However, Asberta secures the throne for Karl by poisoning Günther. When her villainy is revealed, she foils the guards who rush to arrest her by stabbing herself. Holzbauer's awareness of the fluent structures to be found in Jommelli and Traetta means that some of the choruses and ensembles have become functional to the drama, but

Andante grazioso

(When the silver of your hair adorns your helmet and your brow)

Adagio

(O Isis and Osiris, confer the spirit of wisdom on this young couple)

Example 9
(a) Holzbauer: *Günther von Schwarzburg* (1777), Rudolf
(b) Mozart: *Die Zauberflöte* (1791), Sarastro

the work remains essentially a solo opera, with fourteen arias to set against one trio, one duet and four short choruses. There is ingenuity in the modifications of da capo structure to dramatic ends, but Holzbauer has difficulty in escaping wholly from Italian aria convention, and the opera's stylistic unity suffers badly. When in Act I, scene 3 Rudolf asserts, 'Ich bin ein Fürst, ein deutscher Mann', it is to a strong, simple phrase, which he then proceeds to ruin with tame repetition before taking off into some flighty Italianate coloratura and ending with a limp cadence; the offence is compounded in Act II with 'Wenn das Silber deiner Haare', the fine opening section of which, before it disintegrates into more coloratura, must certainly have been in Mozart's mind when he came to conceive Sarastro's dignified utterances (Example 9).

Holzbauer has not shaken off some of the weaker aspects of Jommelli and Traetta. A similar problem besets his characterization of Anna, whose Act I 'Der glänzende Himmel' suffers from another of the opera's weaknesses, the Mannheim convention of a protracted introduction with obbligatos for its famous instrumentalists (here for Franziska Danzi and her husband, the oboist Ludwig August

Lebrun). The respected Algarotti's words often went unheeded when it came to the crunch:

> Una delle più care usanze al dì oggi, sicura di levare del teatro il maggior plauso colla più strepitoso batter di mani, è il far provar in un aria di una voce e di un oboe, di una voce e di una tromba; e far tra loro seguire con varie botte e risposte una gara senza fine e quasi un duello sino all'ultimo fiato. Ma se tali schermaglie hanno potere di prendere gran parte della udienza, riescano pure alla più sana parte di essa rincrescevoli.
>
> (Algarotti, 1755, 448–9)

(One of today's favourite practices, certain to rouse the theatre to the loudest applause and the noisiest clapping, is to make a contest in an aria between a voice and an oboe, or a voice and a trumpet, and thereby to pursue an interminable struggle with various blows and counterblows, like a duel to the death. But if such skirmishes have the power to grip the larger part of the audience, they irritate the saner element.)

Mozart himself did not escape from this convention with 'Martern aller Arten' in *Die Entführung*, though his genius almost transcends it; and when he came to write his Queen of the Night, he may well have remembered Franziska Danzi's ability to soar up to f''' (and beyond: she and Lebrun were both famous for their use of the highest registers). Even Asberta's 'Dein Haupt wird heut', which begins with a graceful melodic idea, loses itself in fragmentary phrases and coloratura, though this sinister character, with her flashing phrases and glittering passagework, is the Queen's emotional ancestress. However, a well-disposed audience would doubtless have been willing to ignore, or even find acceptably familiar, such reversions to Italian practice. Günther himself is dully drawn, with too much of his 'greatness' asserted but not portrayed. He dies on a speech which, in its plea for German unity and its fear of foreign ways weakening the German spirit more than force of arms, is kin to Hans Sachs's final address in Wagner's *Meistersinger*. The work's success at its first performance was overwhelming, perhaps at least as much for the national fervour it aroused as for its genuine strengths and beauties.

Yet *Günther* has remarkable qualities. The depiction of the principal non-historical figure, Asberta, as a malign force, passionate in nature, glinting menace and with an undercurrent of the supernatural, lies closer to a sorceress of opera seria such as Handel's Alcina than to anything in previous German example. It put into new currency the dramatic villainess, a figure who was to reappear almost immediately with Mozart's Elettra as well as with the Queen of the Night, and later in German opera with Weber's Eglantine and Wagner's Ortrud. Asberta directly anticipates the last two in her shuddering invocation of the powers of darkness, 'Ihr schwarzen Mächte'. It is in moments such as this, when he can shake himself free from writing static aria introductions, that Holzbauer finds his strongest vein of instrumental originality. Partly this is because he could rely on the famous orchestra, writing some self-defeating virtuoso music for its solo players but, more successfully, entrusting it with the burden of the expression at moments of high dramatic tension. Taking Schweitzer as his model, he writes free arioso and recitative passages with the orchestra integrating narrative, reflection and action. Karl and Asberta each have some fine scenes in this vein, and one of the most striking comes immediately with Anna's first utterances as she broods on the absent Karl. Her opening scene picks up the music of the overture for her recitative, and after an Andantino aria embedded in this, 'Ihr Rosenstunden', turns to a troubled reflection in which it is the orchestra that portrays the anxiety in her heart (Example 10). The scene must have struck Mozart when he came to open *Idomeneo* with Ilia reflecting on the absent beloved, and with an aria, 'Padre, germani', contained within recitative consisting of expressive fragments exploring the anguish in her own heart.

The establishment of this technique so early in the opera allows Holzbauer to have recourse to it at crucial moments. None is more powerfully composed than the climax to the whole work. Asberta's revelation that she has poisoned Günther takes place in a protracted scena alternating a tense Allegro with edgy phrases marked, unusually, Andante vivace, and, as she sees the black path to the underworld opening before her and plunges the dagger into her breast, Andante tremolos recall her earlier invocation of the powers of darkness. Wieland, so much admired by Holzbauer's librettist Klein, wrote in his article 'Versuch über das deutsche Singspiel und einige Gegenstände' in *Der Teutsche Merkur* for 1775 that operatic characters should be drawn 'in Empfindung und innerer Gemütsbewegung' ('with feeling and inner emotion'); and even if much is incompletely realized, there is an emphasis on orchestral depiction, with the inner drama taking place in the orchestra, which was to prove significant for German opera. Mozart wrote admiringly of the performance he saw in 1777 that 'die Musick von Holzbauer is sehr schön. die Poesie is nicht werth einer solchen Musik, an meisten wundert mich, dass ein so alter Mann, wie holzbauer, noch so viel geist hat; denn das ist nicht zu glauben was in der Musick für feüer ist' (Letter to his father, 14 November 1777) ('Holzbauer's music is very beautiful. The words don't deserve such music. What surprises me most of all is that such an old man as Holzbauer should still have so much spirit, for you can't imagine what fire there is in the music').

Günther also affected Schweitzer's last opera, *Rosamunde*, in the use of obbligatos but more importantly in the emphasis on recitative and fluently composed orchestral narrative passages, as well as with the climactic scene of Rosamunde's stabbing, just as she has ascended the throne, by the villainous Elinor. Schweitzer was so keen to capitalize on the success of *Günther* that he hurried to Mannheim to rehearse *Rosamunde* in December 1777, then falling ill and leaving Mozart, who admired the work even more than *Alceste*, to take over a rehearsal. *Günther* struck audiences with particular force, coming as it did in the wake of Klopstock's *Hermanns Schlacht* of 1769, and only a year after *Götz von Berlichingen* had taken Germany by storm. Goethe's quasi-Shakespearean drama, disregarding classical precepts in the manner that had so irritated Voltaire and hence Frederick the Great, with its fluid scenes and its depiction of the German Middle Ages as a time of full-blooded life and high Romantic passions, was one of the first major works of the movement given its name in 1777 by Max Klinger's play *Sturm und Drang. Günther von Schwarzburg*, in the same year, seemed to offer a musical equivalent, and was incontestably the movement's strongest opera.

Example 10   Holzbauer: *Günther von Schwarzburg* (1777), Anna

By now, Reichardt's wanderings had taken him to Berlin, where in 1775 he became Frederick the Great's Kapellmeister at the Italian opera. However, German opera was in the ascendant with the arrival there of Heinrich Koch's company in 1771, despite the triviality of most of his offerings. At his death in the year of Reichardt's arrival, his company was taken over by Carl Theophil Döbbelin, who improved the repertory and engaged the distinguished Marie Sophie Niklas as his principal soprano and Johann André as his music director. André had already made a mark with Marchand's company in Frankfurt with his first opera, *Der Töpfer* (1773), written, as Goethe pointed out, in response to a fashion for popular vernacular works to set against French imports such as Grétry's *Zémire et Azor*:

> Dagegen hatte sich ein realistischer Dämon des Operntheaters bemächtigt; Zustands- und Handwerksopern thathen sich hervor. Die Jäger, der Faßbinder, und ich weiß nicht was alles, waren vorausgegangen. André wählte sich den Töpfer. Er hatte sich das Gedicht selbst geschrieben, und in den Text, der ihm angehörte, sein ganzes musicalisches Talent verwendet.
>
> (*Dichtung und Wahrheit*, Pt. iii, Bk. 17)

(On the other hand, a demon of realism had possessed the opera house; operas about classes and crafts appeared. *The Hunters*, *The Coopers* and I don't know what else were produced. André chose *The Potter*. He had written the libretto himself, and lavished his whole musical talent on his part of the text.)

Der Töpfer is a lively comedy about a lottery. It includes a sympathetic characterization of the good-hearted Jew, Amschel, who in a spirited quintet tries (with forlorn cries of 'Au wai') to resolve the argument about how the winnings should be distributed, in the face of forceful resistance from the work's most vivid character, the termagant Marthe. German and French elements are mixed, but though André does not wholly escape the influence of Grétry, in the circumstances it is natural that the German should predominate. However, Hannchen lacks the sentimental 'French' aria she seems to need, though she manages a nice love duet with Gürge. A more positive contribution is some expressive 'German' use of the orchestra. André found ways of strengthening one of the work's weaknesses, the characterization of the two lovers, when he came to write his next work, a collaboration with Goethe on *Erwin und Elmire*. Drawn from the ballad *Edwin and Angelina* which Oliver Goldsmith included in *The Vicar of Wakefield*, this is a sentimental pastoral comedy about the separation and reconciliation of Erwin and Elmire. It includes some more graceful love music than did its predecessor, which not only helped it to win wide popularity but led to his appointment to Döbbelin's company. For some years André's operas dominated its repertory, together with the French works which

Döbbelin increasingly began to import after the dismissal of the French dramatic company, which had been working in Weimar, in 1778. Reichardt's opportunity came, after more years of travel, on Frederick the Great's death in 1786 and the accession of Friedrich Wilhelm II. However, neither the success of *Andromeda* (1788), nor the more lasting one of *Brenno* (1789), sufficed to maintain his position in Berlin; and intrigue forced his dismissal in 1794.

Reichardt had meanwhile made friends with both Herder and Goethe in Weimar. Of these two great men, it was Herder who had the larger vision of what might be possible for German opera. His perceptions were sometimes distorted, and rhetoric could cloud practical considerations; but lying within the misjudgements of his Shakespearean libretto *Brutus* (1772) is an awareness that the words and their dramatic structure are of value only in so far as they encourage a composer's unifying imagination. Having failed to interest Gluck, Herder tried to engage Reichardt's attention, also unsuccessfully. It is, indeed, doubtful if Reichardt could have made much of Herder's text, which, apart from being technically far from ideal for opera, presupposed an aesthetic not yet formed and composing techniques still in their operatic infancy. His talents were far better suited to Goethe, and his songs eventually included all 140 of Goethe's poems available for setting; the best of these remain significant contributions to the early history of the German Lied. Goethe's approval of them was based largely on Reichardt's willingness to accept the role of music as serving poetry, at most heightening it into a more vivid lyric condition rather than creating a new art form; and this acceptance marks his comparatively modest contributions to the Singspiel. Goethe's taste here had been formed by the works he enjoyed as a young man in Frankfurt and Leipzig, in which French opéra-comique dominated the repertory, and in which music was an animating feature of the drama but did not transform the genre. *Erwin und Elmire* (written in 1773–5) attempts to go only a little beyond the conventional rustic idyll, and despite some original treatment does not fundamentally challenge its nature. It struck a chord with a number of composers, initially Johann André (1775), then, after Goethe's removal to Weimar, Anna Amalia herself (1776) and Carl David Stegmann (1776) (these settings are usefully compared in Baumann, 1985, 152–68, suggesting the respective influences of French, German and Italian opera). *Claudine von Villa Bella* (written in 1776) is very close to Goethe's *Sturm und Drang* manner. It goes a little way towards Romantic opera in its subject – which concerns a glamorous villain, at odds with society, who has cast his lot in with vagabonds and fails to frustrate the central lovers – and also in its structure, with the action carried on during the duets and in something approaching a continuous central finale. It was, indeed, to capitalize upon this limitation that Reichardt sought to inaugurate a German answer to French vaudeville, the so-called Liederspiel, in which existing poems were given new, more or less functional musical settings in a spoken drama.

The move in emphasis away from Italian towards German opera in the 1770s and still more the 1780s, even if it were an opera still strongly coloured by foreign influences, naturally assumed different forms in different places. Economic considerations played a part everywhere, as the expense of mounting opera seria took its toll, but the growing interest in a national opera also gave a lead, most decisively and effectively in Berlin and especially in Vienna.

Döbbelin's success in Berlin was based partly on good fortune. The dissolution of the French company on the outbreak of the War of the Bavarian Succession in 1778 conveniently served to strengthen his position. But he could also draw on his entrepreneurial skills, rather than on his actors' talents, to satisfy a Berlin public avid for opera. He leant heavily on his music director, Johann André, and his leading lady, Marie Sophie Niklas; and a further significant figure in the popularity of his troupe was Christoph Friedrich Bretzner, librettist of some of his most successful operas. Bretzner's strengths included a deft hand with a comic plot, taking as his model both opéra-comique and opera buffa; but he was also concerned to find ways of providing his composer with scenes which invited continuous music, and which were responsive to the Romantic ideas beginning to cross into opera from the drama. *Das wütende Heer*

(1780) wholeheartedly embraces the *Schauerromantik*, with its tale of Laura, imprisoned in a tower in a deep forest haunted by the ghostly hunt of the title, and her rescue by Albert through a shattering thunderstorm and mysterious howls, by the agency of a strange dove whose deceit he must also overcome. The libretto is awkwardly paced, but it gave André an opportunity which he seized with great address in the ghostly chorus calling the wild hunt into action. With its shrieking piccolos and blaring horns, its violent dynamic contrasts and shuddering string tremolos, its sinister calls on reiterated single notes, later, obsessive scales and half-scales surging to and fro, even its building of a whole scene around a diminished seventh chord, this looks forward forty years to another Berlin opera, *Der Freischütz* (Example 11, pp. 122–3).

Allegro

(Many offstage voices, singing with a fearsome, strong cavernous voice)

Her-aus! Her-aus! Her-aus!

(Out! out! out!)

Example 11

(a) André: *Das wütende Heer* (1780), Chorus

(b) Weber: *Der Freischütz* (1821), Chorus

By the 1780s, the domination of North German opera was beginning to weaken as it became increasingly difficult for managements in their repertories, and for composers in their works, to resist French and Italian blandishments. The seductions of Italian opera had always been particularly alluring in southern courts, while French ideas were affecting German opera as surely as French music influenced its forms.

In Stuttgart, the presence of Jommelli from 1754 to 1769 cast a long shadow, even after the collapse of Duke Carl Eugen's extravagant opera house and the construction of the Schauspielhaus auf der Planie in 1779. Christian Ludwig Dieter attempted in his operas, with some success, a reconciliation which he knew would please his patron between, on the one hand, a popular Swabian song manner and, on the other, larger-scale arias after the fashion of Jommelli; and he was able to use Italian example, Jommelli's in particular, to give his orchestration a more eloquent quality in the comic genre in which he excelled. His setting of Bretzner's text *Belmont und Constanze* (1784) proved sufficiently popular for the first local performance of Mozart's version, *Die Entführung aus dem Serail* (1782), to be delayed until 1795. The more gifted and wide-ranging Johann Rudolf Zumsteeg, active in the theatre from early days, embraced Mozart with enthusiasm, and though his own operas also combine local material with Jommellian arias and orchestral subtleties, his finest work, *Die Geisterinsel* (1798), was to come significantly later, after the influence of Mozart had been absorbed.

In Munich, a powerful Italian influence also stood in the way of significant progress, though an increasing number of operas by German composers began to enter the mixed repertories during the 1770s, together with opéra-comique and opera buffa in German translation. The succession of Carl Theodor in 1777 gave more encouragement to local works when he moved from Mannheim in the following year with his orchestra, one that had, famously, stimulated a whole group of composers (and left its mark on Mozart) through its virtuoso string ensemble and its brilliant, individual woodwind artistry. A characteristic Munich opera, in its mixture of local popular song styles with some neat depiction of Bavarian types, was *Die Dorfdeputierten* (1783), by Johann Lukas Schubaur, though the piece's expressive range is, to put it mildly, limited. The real influence brought in by Carl Theodor was French, and his theatre director Theobald Marchand had a considerable public success, with works by Grétry, Philidor, Monsigny and Dalayrac beginning to play a regular part in the repertories and to stimulate critical discussion. However, it was a full decade before Carl Theodor felt himself in a strong enough position actually to forbid Italian opera, in 1787. Not only did this decree open the way to operas by Mozart, Dittersdorf and other composers from Vienna; it gave crucial encouragement to Peter Winter, who had moved from Mannheim with Carl Theodor in 1778, and Franz Danzi, who joined Winter in 1784. Even so, their most important work was not to be done immediately.

The long Italian tradition in Vienna itself had roots going back to the very origins of opera and the arrival of artists associated with the original Florentine enterprise. But the city's theatrical life embraced many dramatic forms; and indeed it has always been of the essence of Vienna, stimulated by its position at the most significant European artistic cross-roads, to assimilate diverse influences and, with its devotion to its own traditions, to confer a local character upon them. Plays with music were given by the *Englische Komödianten* and the *commedia dell'arte*, each adding their own characteristics to the local parodies of Italian court opera, and even to the all-pervading Jesuit dramas that were witness to the powerful influence the Society had upon Viennese life until the 1770s.

A focus to this was provided when in 1710 or 1711 a company of German actors under Josef Anton Stranitzky established itself at the new Comödienhaus am Platze nächst dem Kärntnertor, or Kärntner-tortheater. Stranitzky set about adapting Italian librettos to his own purposes, cutting down the number of arias, and adding comic scenes for himself as Hanswurst with a handful of other carefully chosen players. Much of this was improvised material, whose un-predictable and sometimes outrageous nature disturbed, for different reasons, both Enlightenment critics and the Imperial family. Attempts at curbing this so-called *Stegreifkomödie* ('extemporized comedy') had, of course, little effect except to enhance its popularity. However, 'It is clear from external and internal evidence that . . . music was an important ingredient of Stranitzky's bill of fare', writes Peter Branscombe, going on to demonstrate that the incidence of songs and other musical interpolations gave these entertainments the character of Singspiel, even though no actual music survives until the 1750s (Branscombe, 1971, 102–3). After his death in 1726, Stranitzky was soon succeeded by the less efficient but more gifted Gottfried Prehauser; and when the company was joined by Joseph von Kurz, a versatile singer who took the name Bernardon from his own version of Hanswurst, and whose Italian wife Franziska was an excellent soprano, music became still more important. One of the composers to be identified as providing music for the surviving Bernardon plays was, for *Der neue krumme Teufel* (1752?), 'Herr Joseph Heyden'. This was Haydn's second opera and, as with its predecessor *Der krumme Teufel* (1751?), the music is lost. His further contributions to German opera were few, and in most cases are also lost, doubtful or survive in fragmentary form. The most striking is the marionette opera *Die Feuersbrunst* (comp. *c.* 1775–8), which includes some attractive arias but gives little indication of dramatic instinct. Haydn may well also have contributed music to some of the later Burgtheater plays. Meanwhile, in the 1780s after the opening of the Theater in der Leopoldstadt, Hanswurst and Bernardon were to take on a new character in Johann La Roche's Kasperl, an apparently stupid but actually sly servant, lecherous and greedy, who owed more than a little to the *commedia dell'arte*.

It was partly the indecencies in these pieces that gave the Empress

Maria Theresia the excuse to reassume control of the theatres in 1752 and to install at the Burgtheater a French company which brought into the city greater awareness of operas by Grétry, Duni, Philidor, Monsigny and others, as well as plays by Molière and Racine. The architect of the Burgtheater's success was the influential and indefatigable Count Giacomo Durazzo, *en poste* as Ambassador from Genoa, a city then subject to France and deeply under the influence of French culture. The Austrian Chancellor Wenzel von Kaunitz himself, as Ambassador to France from 1750 to 1752, had laboured successfully to bring about the alliance that led to the Seven Years War against Prussia. As 'directeur de spectacles' from 1754, Durazzo was able to invite Gluck to the city and to complement Kaunitz's Francophile policies with his importation of opéras-comiques and French ballet to the Burgtheater, while also encouraging German music in the dramatic repertory at the Kärntnertortheater. Moreover, it was through Durazzo's support that Gluck was enabled to develop the operatic reforms which had such a profound influence on Italian opera seria and left their indelible mark upon the course of French and of German opera, from Cherubini to Berlioz, from Mozart to Wagner. The content and much of the actual detail of Gluck's operatic prefaces, especially the famous one to *Alceste*, reflect not only Benedetto Marcello's brilliant satire on operatic excess *Il Teatro alla moda*, and in particular Algarotti's *Saggio*, but a great deal of the German writing on the subject that had for so long contested operatic abuses and pleaded for opera as a dramatic art. Both Traetta and Jommelli – with their turning away from the domination of the da capo aria in favour of fluent scenas, their accompanied recitatives, their comparative restraint of vocal display, their greater emphasis on the expressive role of the orchestra, their functional use of the chorus – had impressed audiences and composers who heard their works in Stuttgart, Mannheim and Vienna. For all their remarkable and still underestimated qualities, the difference was that in Gluck there was a great operatic dramatist, and one first proving in practice, with works of genius, theories which he could then expound.

Italian opera returned to the Burgtheater in the 1760s. The

influence of the Italians on Viennese operatic life and opera composers was also considerable, and between them the French and the Italian companies, and Gluck's achievements in particular, dominated Viennese musical life. But the German players were gradually taken more seriously, in times that were coming to question Enlightenment values and showing a greater interest in national identity. Gottlieb Stephanie was echoing a growing number of voices when he declared, 'Alle patriotische Freunde der Schaubühne würden zugleich in ein freudiges Jubelgeschrei ausbrechen, wenn einem Orte ihr Wunsch: das gute Nationaltheater einmal fest gegründet zu sehen, in Erfüllung gebracht würde – und welcher Ort verdiene diese Ehre mehr als Wien?' (Hadamovsky, 1966, ix) ('All patriotic theatre lovers would unite in a cry of joy at the realization of their wish, to see the firm establishment of a good National Theatre – and what place deserves this honour more than Vienna?').

These voices did not escape the ear of Joseph II, already determined to strengthen national unity by the promotion of the German language, and to use the stage as one means of achieving this end. The French company had left in 1765, times were increasingly against opera seria, and after a series of theatrical misfortunes and mismanagements led to a steep decline in standards during the 1770s, the Emperor took action. With his usual brusque confidence in his own decisions as enlightened despot, he issued a document in March 1776 bringing the Burgtheater under strict control and declaring that it would henceforth be known as the Deutsches National-Theater. The company set about staging German plays, and on free days the theatre admitted touring French or Italian companies, who also now had easier access to the Kärntnertortheater. In the following April, Joseph paid a visit incognito to his sister Marie Antoinette in Paris, where among much else he observed the flourishing operatic activity of Gluck and Piccinni. Back in Vienna, and encouraged by a successful year at the National-Theater, he now founded the Deutsches National-Singspiel.

Simultaneously with the opening of the National-Theater, Joseph declared a *Spektakelfreiheit*, which by removing the ban on new theatres opened the way for novel musical ventures. Three of these theatres were to provide homes for some of the most characteristic Viennese Singspiels of the latter part of the century. The Theater in der Leopoldstadt, which opened in 1781, acquired Wenzel Müller as its director of music in 1786; he was shortly joined by Ferdinand Kauer, who as director of the music school embarked on the training of singers. Its chief rival, from 1787, was the Theater auf der Wieden, of which Emanuel Schikaneder was appointed director in 1789. Less significant was the Theater in der Josefstadt, opened in 1788. Within the space of a few years, Vienna was furnished with five theatres in which native opera was not only permitted but given strong Imperial encouragement.

The entertainments which characterized these theatres took various forms – or rather, gave different emphases to popular forms generally marked by a musical contribution more significant than that of North German Singspiel. One of the most successful was the *Zauberstück*, which made copious use of stage machinery to create 'magical' effects, sometimes in comic contrast to everyday normality: this would naturally often include elements of the *Maschinenkomödie*, giving full opportunity to the theatre technicians to relish their skills and to test the composer's fantasy. The *Lokalstück* drew on local colour and familiar types and their habits of speech. In the *Besserungsstück*, which became popular in the nineteenth century, a character was led, generally by means of the magic of some benign spirit or of some charade practised by the others, to mend his ways and perhaps remove an obstacle to young love: the idea is of course much older than the definition. Other genres included the *Parodiestück*, making fun of an established work. These were, naturally, appellations that did not confine a piece very strictly; and in an artistically eclectic city, the subjects of the works ranged wide, though more in superficies than in substance. Following the French lead, plots often drew upon Rousseau's example by emphasizing the sincerity of the simple rustic life, with young love at first frustrated and eventually fulfilled; a natural disaster might form the climax and perhaps turning point of the plot; magic might play a part (rather too often helping the playwright out of a corner and so weakening the dramatic motivation). The local *Stegreifkomödie* left its mark, Italian opera buffa bequeathed much (especially in the characters of the *commedia dell'arte*), and most important of all was French opéra-comique; however, the complexity of the heritage reveals itself in, for instance, works that began life as a Latin or Italian comedy being transformed into opéra-comique and then reworked in a German setting.

Given these circumstances, it would seem unremarkable to a Viennese audience for different manners to coexist within a single work. Since the plots were frequently varying treatments of similar ideas, characters were often associated with a particular aria type, and (as in other operatic traditions) established conventions came in turn to play a role in defining the character for the audience, especially when associated with a vocal type or even a particular singer. An aria of buffo origin with rapid parlando passages might serve as the occasion for comic blustering, but also as the basis of a boasting, vengeance or rage number for the villain. The heroine would often be found an excuse by the plot for an ornate coloratura aria, perhaps with instrumental obbligato: this would normally provide an opportunity for a display of passionate or tragic emotion. A tenor, especially when lovelorn, might echo the tones of opéra-comique. Viennese song would certainly make an appearance – generally for servants or peasants – simple, tuneful, strophic and given a light accompaniment, all so as not to tax unduly one of the secondary singers in the company: such numbers were often distinguished as Lied, Cavatine, or Romanze. Place for a narrative song or a serenade might be found, and a drinking song was a popular standby. Sometimes folk-like material would be incorporated into a larger aria, or would provide the basis of the invention: there was clearly a direct appeal to what the audience found familiar here, but also a deeper suggestion that the familiar and popular were deserving of artistic treatment. Ensembles might bring some of these manners into dramatic conflict, for instance in a trio portraying two characters together at odds with a third. Choruses were less popular than in opéra-comique, and, when they did occur, tended to reflect fairly simple technical standards and not to be functional to the plot, though they might serve to set the scene at the rise of the curtain. The idea of an action finale was yet to come, and matters were often concluded with a *Rundgesang* or Vaudeville (the latter taken over from opéra-comique), expressing reconciliation and general moral satisfaction with the outcome of affairs, at least half addressed to the audience.

Joseph's thoroughness with the venture extended to the provision of a library, his own personal attendance at rehearsals as well as performances, and the insistence – of great importance in a city with long experience of Italians – on acquiring the best possible singers; he had no interest in accepting North German opera as a standard, especially its frequent unavoidable use of untrained singers. The actor and director Johann H. F. Müller was sent on a recruiting trip, and succeeded in forming the nucleus of a good ensemble. This included Caterina Cavalieri and Therese Teyber, both not quite eighteen, who had already made a mark in the city, but the even younger Wilhelmine Stierle was engaged in Frankfurt, and they were joined in the following year by Aloysia Lange. Though all still in their teens, they were trained and had acquired useful experience in mixed repertories. The characteristics of Cavalieri, Teyber and Lange are clearly reflected in the roles Mozart was to compose for them, which include Mme Silberklang in *Der Schauspieldirektor* and Constanze in *Die Entführung* for the powerful Cavalieri; Blonde was written for the livelier Teyber. The less steady-voiced Lange later also sang Constanze (unevenly, according to Leopold Mozart) as well as Donna Anna and Sextus. The men first engaged were less impressive, though Joseph Ruprecht, also a composer, was admired for his voice if not for his acting abilities. Matters improved in 1780 when they were joined by Valentin Adamberger and Ludwig Fischer, soon to be Mozart's first Belmonte and Osmin: Fischer's arrival allowed the much weaker bass Johann Adam Fuchs to withdraw to acting roles. With a chorus of thirty and an orchestra of thirty-six, under the direction of the violist and composer Ignaz Umlauf, there was the substance of a company with enough operatic experience and ability to make a success of the new enterprise.

Given the nature of Vienna and of its theatrical fare, together with Joseph's wish to distance himself, for different reasons, from both Italian opera and North German Singspiel, not to mention the presence of French troupes at various times, it is natural that the majority of the fifteen works given during the first season should have been opéras-comiques. Three were on versions of the standard Rousseau-inspired plot in which a simple pair of lovers must overcome difficulties and misunderstandings in order to wed: these were Monsigny's *Rose et Colas* (as *Röschen und Colas*), Gossec's *Toinon et Toinette* (as *Anton und Antoinette*) and Grétry's *Lucile*, each of them already familiar to Viennese audiences. Also familiar were Grétry's *L'Ami de la maison* (as *Der Hausfreund*) and *Silvain* (in a new translation, but not as *Walder* so as to avoid confusion with Benda's opera on the same plot); his *La Fausse Magie* was introduced to Vienna in a new translation by Stephanie, who also translated the French-domiciled (but German-born) composer Jean-Paul-Egide Martini's *L'Amoureux de quinze ans* as *Der Liebhaber von fünfzehn Jahren*. The only Italian work was Pietro Guglielmi's *La sposa fedele*, popular in Vienna from 1769 and revived as *Robert und Kalliste* in 1776. Benda's *Medea* was also included, together with a novelty by another Bohemian composer, Josef Barta, to a text by Stephanie, *Das ist nicht gut zu rathen*. Three new works by Viennese composers were Carlo d'Ordonez's *Diesmal hat der Mann den Willen* (a parody opera after Monsigny), Maximilian Ulbrich's *Frühling und Liebe* and Franz Asplmayr's *Die Kinder der Natur*. The latter was exceptional in keeping stylistically close to North German opera: it lasted only three performances. The remaining two operas were by Umlauf himself, *Die Apotheke* and – a work commissioned for the Burgtheater and inaugurating the whole enterprise – *Die Bergknappen*.

After various delays, the opening night took place before a large and appreciative audience on 17 February 1778. Paul Weidmann's text is scarcely subtle, but it was designed to make the audience feel at home with both the genre and its subject matter, and to give suitable opportunities to Umlauf and to the newly recruited singers. The young miner Fritz loves Sophie, ward of old Walcher, who wants to marry her himself. In punishment for a tryst the lovers have made, he ties her to a tree in his garden; but the gypsy Delda takes her place, making Walcher believe that a mysterious transformation has occurred. When Delda further reveals that Sophie is his own daughter, stolen by gypsies, he almost consents to her marriage; but, changing his mind on discovering how he has been deceived, he storms off with his miners to work, ignoring Fritz's apprehensive account of a dream about a new shaft's collapse. The shaft does indeed cave in, trapping Walcher, but after Fritz has heroically freed him he gives the lovers his blessing.

Umlauf was scarcely the composer to fashion a masterpiece out of this material, and it is easy to point to the work's shortcomings. However, it was important for the success of the enterprise that he should address the audience's expectations, and he understood the conventions well. The characters are in familiar mould. There is local colour in the depiction of mining life. There is a touch of the supernatural with the gypsy Delda. The resolution comes with a disaster averted by heroic action. Walcher is led to *Besserung* in gratitude for his salvation. So it is with the musical conventions. The opening duet for Sophie and Fritz is a simple Lied (one plain to the point of dullness), and this is followed by a drinking song for Walcher (even though it remains distinctly low-proof: Fuchs was not the singer to be entrusted with any virtuoso roistering). It is not until the ensuing Trio that matters liven up, with the lovers pouring out tender phrases against Walcher's staccato bluster. The presence of Cavalieri in the cast inspires Umlauf to some spirited coloratura when Sophie finds herself lashed to her tree, and again to a graceful aria with oboe obbligato as rescue seems to be at hand. But the attempt at pleasing a Viennese public with mixed fare results not so much in stylistic variety as in uncertainty, in a composer who could follow examples, ranging from opera seria show arias to homely folk-like jollities, but not confer upon them a distinctive personality. The music associated with the life of the miners is more individual, as when they sing their evening chorus, interrupted by Fritz's aria to Sophie, interrupted in turn by a shivering middle section; and there is again a more personal touch when they gather from afar before setting off to work. The most original scene comes at the climax, as Walcher sets off to excavate the new shaft. In a dramatic recitative, Fritz describes the sinister rumbling of the earth, to quivering tremolos and juddering chords: the miners shout that Walcher has been trapped by a fall, at which (permitting himself eight bars in which to reflect upon where his duty lies) Fritz brushes them aside and plunges into the mine, surrounded by crashing scales and dense clouds of tremolo. Rocks continue to fall during Sophie's freely composed scena, until, recovering from a faint, she sings her graceful aria of hope – justified, as Fritz now emerges having dug Walcher out from the hollow in which he was trapped. Matters then relapse with a plain *Rundgesang* for all, which Sophie and Fritz conclude in duet. At least one good opportunity has been missed, that of musically recalling Fritz's prophetic dream of a rock fall when the real disaster occurs; but Umlauf was not one to risk confusing the audience for a new venture by disturbing the conventions with such an innovation.

The following seasons offered audiences fare similar to the first; but standards did not improve, despite some successes which included the overwhelming triumph of Mozart's *Die Entführung aus dem Serail* in 1782; and the company was soon riven with the intrigues endemic to most theatres, especially Viennese ones. Not even nationalist feelings could overcome the realization that there were too few Singspiels which could compete seriously with French opera, or with the Italian opera which began returning to the repertory in translation, so that matters were left substantially as they had been before the opening of the National-Singspiel.

Umlauf himself did manage to capitalize upon the popularity of *Die Bergknappen* with a lively, more relaxed comedy, *Die schöne Schusterin* (1779) and still more with *Das Irrlicht* (1782), both to librettos by Gottlieb Stephanie. *Die schöne Schusterin* has a farcical plot of concealments, deludings and misunderstandings, and is entirely French in manner, with songs taken from a French comedy, *La Cordonnière allemande*, and set by Umlauf in popular style. Unable to call upon Cavalieri and Teyber, he was obliged to write the leading role, Lehne, for a contralto, Marianne Weiss, and others for two tenors and a baritone. Much more simply composed than *Die Bergknappen*, it is naturally also more lightly scored, though Umlauf shows some ingenuity in varying his resources with effects such as passages for solo horns and even solo timpani, unaccompanied violins to open two arias, and some deftly judged alternations of colour. Only Lehne's music is more fully scored, as befitted Weiss's quality of voice. There is an Act I finale in which Umlauf attempts some more extended music, but he tends to overwork a rhythmic figure before abandoning it for the next one or for a new tempo, so that some degree of musical liveliness remains unconnected to any real dramatic movement. The Act II finale reverts to the old *Rundgesang*, in quite an ingenious variation, for all seven characters. In *Das Irrlicht*, a prince who has abused his position to seduce the ladies of his court is placed under a curse which he can only expiate by wandering the swamps as a will-o'-the-wisp until he finds a girl who will love him for himself alone. The plot takes its nature not only from Rousseau-ish rustic purity overcoming aristocratic corruption but from the Viennese delight in the contact between the human and the spirit worlds. There is an element of the *Besserungsstück*; but there are also Romantic adumbrations in the Prince's assumption of spirit nature, not for comic effect but in the quest for a pure woman who can with her love redeem him from his curse.

Umlauf's success was such as to excite comments from Mozart, especially about a minor piece called *Welche ist die beste Nation?* (1782), which were so aggressive as to suggest anxiety about a rival in a strong position; he was also scornful about the length of time (almost a year) which Umlauf had taken to write *Die Bergknappen*, a piece he regarded as worth a fortnight's effort. Umlauf could not single-handedly maintain standards in the National-Singspiel, and in 1783 Joseph acted with typical peremptoriness and closed it down, engaging instead an opera buffa company. Here, following his triumph with *Die Entführung*, Mozart was to find in Joseph's newly engaged theatre poet, Lorenzo da Ponte, the ideal collaborator for his three greatest Italian operas, *Le nozze di Figaro* (1786), *Don Giovanni* (Prague, 1787), and *Così fan tutte* (1790). Even Joseph's endeavour to provide competition to the Italians by reviving a 'Deutsche Opéra Comique' in the Kärntnertortheater in 1785 did not last for long, and, despite the great popular success of Dittersdorf's *Doktor und Apotheker* in 1786, it was closed again in 1788.

One of the most influential figures in the whole enterprise had been Gottlieb Stephanie. A reluctant conscript to Frederick the Great's army during the Seven Years War, he was taken prisoner at the Battle of Landshut in 1760 and, after a period of undistinguished service as a sergeant in the Austrian army, arrived in Vienna. Here he quickly set about proving himself considerably more skilled in the arts of theatrical warfare. He took easily to Viennese life, letters and the stage, making a name as an actor and playwright, and in 1776 became an inspector of the National-Theater and in 1781 director of the National-Singspiel. In the process, he acquired a host of enemies. Mozart deplored Stephanie's reputation, while appreciating his experience and his offers of help:

> Nun muß ich ihnen erklären, warum wir auf dem Stephani argwohn hatten. dieser Mensch hat, welches mir sehr leid thut, in ganz Wienn das schlechteste Renomèe; als ein grober, falscher, verläumderischer Mann; der den leuten die grösten ungerechtigkeiten anthut. – da mische ich mich aber nicht darein. wahr kann es seyn, weil alles darüber schmält – übrigens gilt er alles beym kayser; und gegen mich war er gleich das Erstemal sehr freundschaflich; und sagte. wir sind schon alte freunde, und ist mir sehr lieb wenn ich werde im stande seyn können ihnen in etwas zu dienen. – ich glaube, und ich wünsche es auch, daß er selbst für mich eine oper schreiben wird. er mag nun seine komœdien allein oder mit hülfe gemacht haben; er mag nun stellen oder selbst erschafen – kurz, er versteht das theater, und seine komœdien gefallen immer.
>
> (Letter to his father, 16 June 1781)

> (Now I must explain why we were suspicious of Stephanie. I'm very sorry to say that this person has the worst reputation in all Vienna, for being a rude, deceitful and slanderous man who treats people with the greatest unfairness; but I don't get myself mixed up with all that. It may

well be true, as everyone complains about it. However, he's very much in with the Emperor; and he was very friendly to me from the first and said, 'We're already old friends, and I'd be very happy if I were in a position to help you in any way.' I think, and also I hope, that he himself will write a libretto for me. He may have written his plays alone or with help, he may be a thief or write his own stuff, in short, he understands the stage, and his plays are always popular.)

Stephanie's dexterity, then, extended to his librettos, which respond fluently to the needs of the various theatres for which he worked. His librettos include three for Umlauf (*Die schöne Schusterin* (1779), *Das Irrlicht* (1782) and *Die glücklichen Jäger* (1786)), three for Dittersdorf (*Der Apotheker und der Doktor* (1786), *Die Liebe im Narrenhaus* (1787) and *Hieronymus Knicker* (1789)) and two for Mozart (*Die Entführung aus dem Serail* (1782) and *Der Schauspieldirektor* (1786)). To have provided Mozart with the text for his first great success, and to have set Dittersdorf on a career which was to characterize Viennese opera in the next decade, were considerable achievements, ones which indeed reflect his shrewd understanding of the various Viennese stages of the day and also of the capabilities of his composers. When he published his collected Singspiel texts in 1792, he prefaced them with an introduction in which he discusses the conditions of Singspiel and the theatre of the day in Vienna. Most singers, he states bluntly, were unmusical, and reluctant to interest themselves in speaking or acting properly between their numbers; there was also the long-standing prejudice against German as a singing language, and the inclination of German singers to find more gainful employment in other countries or at least in operas in *welsch*, that is to say, French or Italian. Protesting that there were too few good original operas in German (a fine complaint from a notorious pillager of opéra-comique and opera buffa), and that composer and librettist could each place too much restraint on the other, or both fail to understand basic rules of structure, he proceeds to set out a framework for a good Singspiel:

Erstlich müssen nicht zu viel und nicht zu wenig musikalische Stücke vorkommen; 24 kann man bey einem ganzen Singspiel als die höchste, in

18 as die kleinste Zahl annehmen; diese müssen gehörig in Arien und koncertirte Stücke abgetheilt und dann wieder verhältnißmäßig eingetheilt werden, damit, besonders die Hauptstimmen weder überladen, noch weniger aber vernachläßigt werden. Das Singspiel muß sich mit einem koncertirten Stück anfangen, und jeder Akt mit einem handelden Finale, wobey die Hauptpersonen erscheinen, schließen. Mehr als zwey Arien müssen selten auf einander folgen, und diese nicht von einer Person gesungen werden; ein Duett, Terzet oder Quartet, muß dann gleichsam einen Abschnitt machen. Die ersten Stimmen müssen jede, wenigstens drey Arien, ein Duett oder Terzet haben, und hauptsächlich in den Finalen erscheinen. Ferner muß dem Kompositor Gelegenheit gegeben werden, daß er in der Art der Musik abwechseln kann. Weiter gebe man Acht, daß man nicht zu geschwind musikalische Stücke auf einander folgen lasse, auch nicht zu lang damit aussetze; was von der Intrigue zu wissen unumgänglich nöthig ist, vergesellschafte man ja nicht mit Musik, weil es dann leicht verloren gehen kann, und der Zuschauer deshalb in Ungewißheit bleibt. Auf je weniger Personen ein Singspiel zu beschränken ist, desto besser wird es ausfallen, weil die dritten und vierten Rollen meistens schwach in Stimme und Musik sind, und nicht selten die gute Laune der Zuschauer stören. Besonders hüte man sich so viel möglich vor Chören, denn sie verursachen nicht nur viel Kosten, sondern verderben auch, nicht selten, durch ihre Steifheit das Ganze, und bleiben immer, so wie die vielen Comparsen im Trauerspiele, nur ein ärmlicher Behelf des Dichters, um seiner Sache einen Glanz zu verschaffen. Das wären so im Allgemeinen einige Regeln, welche ich bey den vielen Opernübersetzungen, die ich geliefert, als auch aus dem Umgange und Anleitung der Kompositoren, für welche ich geschrieben, und endlich während der durch sechs Jahre geführten Operndirektion beym K.K.Nat. Hoftheater zu Wien gesammelt habe. So wenig ich diese Regeln als vollkommen angeben will, so gewiß bin ich andrerseits, daß ein Buch auf solche Art geordnet, jedem Kompositor willkommen seyn, und, wenn es hinlängliches Interesse und Laune enthält, auch überall gefallen wird.

(Stephanie, 1792, ix–xi; quoted in Schusky, 1980, 94)

(Firstly, there must be neither too many nor too few musical numbers. Twenty-four in an entire Singspiel is the acceptable maximum and eighteen the minimum; these must be suitably divided into arias and concerted pieces, and then again divided up proportionally so that the chief voices, in particular, are not overtaxed and especially not neglected. The Singspiel must begin with a concerted piece, and each act must end with an action finale in which the main characters appear. Seldom must more than two arias follow one another, and these must not be sung by the same person; a duet, trio, or quartet must then create a kind of paragraph. Each of the principal voices must have at least three arias and a duet or trio, and especially must appear in the finales. Furthermore, the composer must be given the opportunity to vary the manner of the music. Care must also be taken not to let the musical pieces follow one another too quickly, nor to set them too far apart; anything absolutely vital to the plot must not be accompanied by music, since it can then easily be lost, and the spectator remain perplexed. The fewer the characters to which a Singspiel is confined, the better it will turn out, since the third and fourth roles are usually weak vocally and musically, and quite often upset the audience's good humour. Avoid choruses as much as possible, as not only do they create great expense, but they also frequently spoil the whole effect with their stiffness and, like the minor roles in tragedies, are little help to the writer in giving his material quality. These are a few general rules which I have assembled during my six years as Opera Director at the Royal and Imperial National Hoftheater in Vienna, both with the many opera translations which I have made and also for the guidance and instruction of the composers for whom I have written. Little though I regard these rules as complete, I am on the other hand sure that a libretto formed on these lines will be welcomed by any composer, and, provided that it contains sufficient interest and wit, will also give general pleasure.)

These precepts were, of course, based on considerable practice, and might serve as an account of the operatic procedures of the most prolific and successful of Stephanie's composers in the 1780s, Dittersdorf. They accord easily with the blander principles which Dittersdorf himself allowed to be published near the end of his life in Friedrich Rochlitz's new *Allgemeine musikalische Zeitung* (Dittersdorf, 1798–9). However, it was one thing for a theatrical craftsman such as Stephanie to provide a list of recommendations as a sound basis for librettists and composers writing operas in a particular time and place and for a particular audience; it was another for a composer to admit to following a set of guide-lines, and places Dittersdorf as essentially a formulaic artist. No great composer has ever constrained himself by publishing an account of his creative intentions, a rule proved by the major exception of Wagner, who having done so found his creativity forthwith bursting the bounds of his arguments. It was Dittersdorf's skill in working within a carefully studied set of conventions that gave him his position as the most successful Viennese composer in his heyday, with his first and most popular German opera, *Doktor und Apotheker*, at its première on 11 July 1786 easily overtaking Mozart's *Le nozze di Figaro*, of 1 May.

Naturally this tells us more about the audience than about Dittersdorf. When Franz Niemetschek included in his pioneering biography of Mozart the anecdote about Joseph II reproaching the composer for making *Die Entführung* too beautiful and for containing too many notes, only to be told that it contained just as many as were necessary, he added that the Emperor was merely repeating popular opinion. It was the immediate appeal of Dittersdorf's operas that conquered an audience seeking uncomplicated gratification, and in *Doktor und Apotheker* he hit upon a brilliantly successful formula. With almost a dozen Italian comic operas to his credit by the time he arrived in Vienna, he had already mastered buffo style, and it was his ability to use this skill to enliven the French-influenced and Italian-influenced German conventions as he encountered them, as well as his own musical quickwittedness, that ensured his popularity.

Der Apotheker und der Doktor (as the opera was entitled when it was first given at the Burgtheater) has the village apothecary Stössel and his wife Claudia attempting to marry off their daughter Leonore, who is in love with his enemy Dr Krautmann's son Gotthold, to the coarse invalid officer Sturmwald. Gotthold and his friend Sichel, who is in love with Stössel's niece Rosalie, manage to contrive a secret meeting with their girls, but they are interrupted by Claudia and then by Stössel and Sturmwald. Sichel and Gotthold now disguise themselves as Sturmwald and a notary, deluding Leonore's parents into preparing a wedding contract uniting the young lovers. The ruse

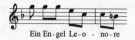

Example 12

(a) Dittersdorf: *Doktor und Apotheker* (1786), Gotthold
(b) Beethoven: *Fidelio* (1805), Florestan

threatens to miscarry when the real Sturmwald appears, at which point the lovers' invention fails. So does that of the librettist, who can only solve the situation by making Claudia have a change of heart and bless the young pair.

This plot, it can be seen, conforms easily to previous example, with a pair of sentimental village lovers, abetted by a livelier secondary pair and pitted against their crabbed elders, who favour a disagreeable rival for the heroine's affections. Dittersdorf's melodic fluency, together with his shrewd theatrical judgement, are among the qualities that enliven the plot and give the piece what has proved to be enduring appeal. The characters are endowed with unprecedented vivacity, if not with new psychological depth. Leonore's first aria, 'Wie kann wohl Freude', has genuine highspiritedness in the coloratura, together with a gravity in the Adagio section as she reflects on how delightful a happy marriage can be, how grim a bad one: she earns Gotthold's warm apostrophe (with its reflective chromatic postlude) as he lavishes his devotion on her in lyrical lines. These include a phrase which must have caught somewhere in the mind of the young Beethoven, playing in the orchestra in the 1789 season that brought the work to Bonn (Example 12).

The livelier patter of Sichel is animated by wit as well as mere pace, and with irony when he slily addresses Stössel, 'Excellentissime! et super docte, excellentissime Pharmacopaee!' ('most excellent! and moreover learned, most excellent apothecary!'). Stössel returns the pompous reply 'Galenus und Hippocrates sind gegen mich nur Stümper' ('Galen and Hippocrates are mere bunglers beside me'). He adds that Paracelsus is the one for him, a piece of braggadocio well matched to Krautmann's 'Ein Doktor ist, bei meiner Ehr', der grösste

Mann im Staate' so as to set these two titular figures of the opera in a novel central role. The arias embrace North German elements, in strophic song forms linked by spoken dialogue, as well as Italian opera seria vocal virtuosity (sometimes parodistically) and opera buffa wit, together with lyrical duets for the lovers and some ensembles that include well-contrasted part-writing. Such aria types appear in almost all his operas, most of which include examples of them all. Dittersdorf's most ambitious contribution to this new approach to the conventions is the long Act I finale. There can be little doubt that the immediate example of the *Figaro* Act II finale was not lost on this sharply observant composer, though his buffo experience would have made him ready for it, but its long sequence of linked tempos really owes more to Umlauf's in *Die schöne Schusterin* than to Mozart's genius in furthering drama through symphonic development.

The success of *Doktor und Apotheker* confirmed Dittersdorf in the belief that he had found a winning formula which he could variously animate, and three more operas swiftly followed, *Betrug durch Aberglauben* at the Kärntnertortheater (1786), *Democrito corretto* at the Burgtheater (1787, dropped forever after two performances), and *Die Liebe im Narrenhaus* again at the Kärntnertortheater (1787). *Betrug durch Aberglauben* has a superstitious father persuaded by mock apparitions to give his daughter his consent to marry: it was given twenty-three performances until November 1794, including three in the Burgtheater. *Die Liebe im Narrenhaus* has the longest finale yet, and draws upon a wide variety of styles. It must have employed some excellent singers, to judge from vocal lines whose demanding coloratura soars up to g''' for the soprano. The mockery of the inhabitants of an asylum includes an old-fashioned Baroque parody for the mad Poet, and a glissando ending which eerily dispels into vacuity the mourning of the singer who believes herself to be the violated Lucretia. Not even at the time did everyone find the pastime of jesting at madness to be acceptable, but the wide variety of styles which the work embraces gave Dittersdorf his opportunities and secured it a popular appeal.

Given the nature of Dittersdorf's talent, it is not surprising that he should have expressed himself as he did to the Emperor on the subject of Mozart, generous though the words are from a composer who, soon after dictating them, died embittered and neglected.

Er ist unstreitig eins der grössten Originalgenies, und ich habe bisher noch keinen Komponisten gekannt, der so einen erstaunlichen Reichtum von Gedanken besitzt. Ich wünschte, er wäre nicht so verschwenderisch damit. Er lässt den Zuhörer nicht zum Athem kommen; denn, kaum will man einem schönen Gedanken nachsinnen, so steht schon wieder ein anderer herrlicher da, der den vorigen verdrängt, und das geht immer in einem so fort, so dass man am Ende keine dieser Schönheiten im Gedächtnis aufbewahren kann.

(Dittersdorf, 1801, 237)

(He is incontestably one of the greatest of original geniuses, and I have never yet encountered a composer who possesses such an astonishing wealth of ideas. I could wish that he weren't so prodigal with them. He doesn't let the listener get his breath; for hardly has one grasped one beautiful idea when another marvellous one comes along and dispels the first, and this goes on the whole time so that in the end it's impossible to hold these beauties in the memory.)

Mozart arrived in Vienna from Salzburg on the morning of 16 March 1781, no longer the child prodigy who had astonished the city in 1762, nor the brilliant young composer whose fifteen months there in 1767 to 1768 had introduced him to, among much else, Gluck, but a mature genius, with no post in mind yet possessed by a determination to take the operatic world by storm. Like other artists of genius, he had a firm belief in himself, and with this went a certain ruthlessness and sometimes a scorn for rivals, characteristics that can be seen as arrogance but better as determined custodianship of great gifts. Like other composers of genius, too, he possessed in his early years an astonishing capacity for assimilating musical influences; and, more than a facility in assuming various manners, this was the power to sense what was valuable to him and to absorb it into a voice of rapidly growing individuality. In London at the age of nine, he was already improvising what were said to be impressive imitations of various operatic styles. Wherever his travels as a Wunderkind took him, he drank in thirstily the music he heard and unerringly found the nourishment he needed in it. From a very early stage he was able to write music that went beyond the bounds of the skilfully imitative.

Mozart's first dramatic work (apart from isolated arias) was Act I of a German sacred music drama, *Die Schuldigkeit des ersten Gebotes*, performed in Salzburg in 1767 (the other, lost, acts were by Michael Haydn and Anton Adlgasser). The action, such as it is, concerns the obligation upon a Christian to obey the First Commandment ('I am the Lord thy God . . . Thou shalt have none other gods before me'), and the contest for his soul between Der Christgeist (the Christian Spirit) and Der Weltgeist (the Worldly Spirit); it is couched in terms no different from many a Jesuit or Protestant music drama of the previous century. Nor does the eleven-year-old Mozart depart far from convention. A good deal of the work shows chiefly his immensely quick ear for established manners, and, as an aspect of this, his life-long capacity to satisfy singers' needs. However, there is instinctive good judgement, and the invention to support it, in his ability to confer dramatic meaning through an unexpected harmonic progression, a figuration expressively varied, or a vivid stroke of instrumental colour. The aria for Göttliche Barmherzigkeit (Divine Mercy), 'Ein ergrimmter Löwe brüllet', gives the fearful lion, roaring in the depths of the forest, music with a snarling violin figure and woodland horns which many a more experienced composer would be pleased to own. Long stretches of recitativo secco are no worse, if no better, than most composers could have managed, but there is another quality in some of the instrumental recitatives. Mozart had already encountered both Gluck and Jommelli, and the mark of their freely composed recitative shows in certain passages, such as those approaching and in particular succeeding the aria 'Erwache, fauler Knecht' for Göttliche Gerechtigkeit (Divine Justice). The howls of the damned are introduced by a furious burst of activity and answered by a wailing chromatic passage for bassoons and strings before calmer string chords accompany the search for salvation. After the aria, the rapidity of movement between instrumental illustration and recitative utterance is still more fluent and dramatic. There is nothing novel in the technique, and its implications for Mozart lie far in the future, but it is grasped with an instinct that betokens real creative interest. Only when he turns to plain secco recitative does he lapse into flatness, for there was no example before his ears of how to set German interestingly in such a manner.

Mozart's next dramatic work, after his Latin intermezzo *Apollo et Hyacinthus* and his first opera buffa, *La finta semplice*, was *Bastien und Bastienne*, written in Vienna in 1768. The diversity of the influences he had encountered, at the age of still only twelve, shows in a piece of very varied provenance but in turn of greater creative complexity than at first appears. Beginning life as *Le Devin du village*, the work which, through Rousseau's influential authorship, achieved vast popularity on its appearance in 1752, this tale of rustic innocence

prevailing over urban aristocratic allure set an example for dozens of
opéras-comiques and had entered the plots of many more works by
the time it came Mozart's way. Colin and Colette, sundered by
Colin's attraction to the lady of the manor and reunited by a
combination of Colette's pretence at similar behaviour and the
benign skills of a village soothsayer, are in Rousseau's handling no
more than sentimental Arcadians. But the work's appearance when
Paris was in the throes of the Querelle des Bouffons hastened a new
version by Charles Favart and Harny de Guerville as *Les Amours de
Bastien et Bastienne*. Generally described as a parody, this is a significantly new approach to the subject in which the characters are now
closer to real peasants. Mme Favart herself caused a sensation by
taking the stage in woollen dress and clogs. The work was given in
Vienna from 1755, and translated by Friedrich Wilhelm Weiskern in
1764. With various other contributions, it was then set by Mozart. It
had thus passed from its origin as a French intermezzo, by way of a
parody in popular French style, to being a Viennese comedy and
finally a Singspiel. Mozart, drawing on his already varied experience,
contributed Italian and German features to the French and Viennese
elements in, especially, the depiction of Bastienne herself.

In the course of these transformations, *Bastien und Bastienne* under-
went structural alterations as well as changes in tone. While sharpen-
ing the pace, Favart also more than trebled the number of Rousseau's
arias and provided irregular poetic forms; Weiskern returned to the
original fourteen, and increased the concentration on ensemble
while retaining Favart's metrical irregularity. A distinctive feature of
Mozart's treatment is his response to this, and with it his sense of the
musically irregular or unpredictable to create dramatic momentum.
Though the capacity for symphonic development that was to reach
greatness in *Figaro* is of course not yet at his command, he avoids
repetitive aria structures and maintains forward movement by skilful
changes in harmony, in melodic manner, in figuration and rhythm,
sometimes all within one tempo and guided by the words, so that
there is, at this comparatively simple level, dramatic motivation
shaping the course of music. Even in the recitatives, which were

composed later and are somewhat wider in harmonic range than those in *Die Schuldigkeit*, there is a feeling for musical direction. It is the manner of opera buffa applied with precocious dramatic instinct to Singspiel.

Six Italian stage pieces followed – *Mitridate, Re di Ponto* (1770), *Ascanio in Alba* (1771), *Il sogno di Scipione* (1772), *Lucio Silla* (1772), *La finta giardiniera* (1775) and *Il re pastore* (1775) – before Mozart turned again to German opera. From them, especially from the three Milan operas *Mitridate, Ascanio* and *Lucio Silla*, he brought a mastery of the vocal style of Italian opera seria, and an ability to turn it to new account. From *Lucio Silla* in particular, constrained though it still is by the conventions of opera seria, came adumbrations of the genius revealed in the fluent structures and the instrumental mastery of *Idomeneo*.

The unfinished Singspiel subsequently known as *Zaide* was written in Salzburg in 1779–80, probably for Johannes Böhm's company to take to Vienna in an attempt to establish an artistic bridgehead at the National-Singspiel. It would seem likely that this influenced the choice of one of the 'Turkish' subjects that had become so popular throughout Germany and especially in Vienna, in this case reworked by the court trumpeter, Andreas Schachtner, from an earlier play. The dialogue is lost, but from the words for the music the plot is clear, up to the dénouement. Zaide, captive and favourite of the Sultan, leaves her portrait beside a sleeping fellow-captive Gomatz, who wakes and promptly falls in love with its subject. The kindly Allazim aids their escape, but they are recaptured, to the glee of the overseer Osmin. Neither argument nor defiance can persuade the Sultan to relent; at which point the work breaks off. It seems likely that there would have been at least one more number before a final ensemble celebrated his clemency (in the original play, the pair are brother and sister, children of the Allazim figure who once saved the Sultan's life). When Stephanie rejected the work as too serious for Vienna, Mozart did not demur, and lost interest.

Even if he had not set the much superior libretto on a similar plot in *Die Entführung aus dem Serail* in the following year, it is unthinkable that he would have returned to *Zaide*. The reason has less to do with musical quality than with his rapidly growing dramatic powers in the wake of the achievement of *Idomeneo*, the opera which comes between them. At their best, the individual numbers of *Zaide* have a quality far transcending their conventions. Zaide's 'Ruhe sanft' over the sleeping Gomatz is a slumber aria whose beauty has given it life as a concert excerpt; and her pleading metaphor aria likening herself to a captive nightingale, 'Trostlos schluchzet Philomele', with its contrasting rage aria 'Tiger!', enliven a character of touching emotional impulsiveness. The others inhabit convention more readily, Gomatz an elegant tenor, especially in his 'portrait' aria, Allazim a morally irreproachable father figure whose pronouncements have not yet acquired the solemn dignity of Sarastro's, Osmin a comic blusterer, the Sultan a standard Turkish tyrant insisting on his leonine ferocity as well as his inclination to mercy. Yet they are clearly characterized, in particular through means that Mozart had not so thoroughly explored before in his operas, the use of different aria forms. The old da capo structure is abandoned in favour of ternary and especially binary arias as witness of a stronger interest in forward dramatic movement, together with a more inventive distribution of the texts; and within this the Sultan, with his aria, and Osmin, in strophic variations, are separated from the heroic trio of Allazim, Gomatz and Zaide herself, anticipating methods to be more richly explored in *Idomeneo*. The music is of a high standard, but remains within bounds that Mozart seems already to be seeking to burst with an assertion of music's dramatic supremacy. It is Zaide herself who gives the strongest suggestion of this when, in a beautiful Trio as they await embarkation and hail a rainbow unfolding while a storm dies down, her shuddering premonitions (as a few remaining lightning flashes stab the clouds) throw the music off course. Here and in the final quartet, poised as the opera breaks off, rather than in even the finest of the arias, or in the two melodramas which take up the manner of Benda which still interested Mozart, the music adumbrates a new dramatic condition in its relationship with words. From *Idomeneo*, return would have been impossible.

If Stephanie, with his sharp eye to the main chance, intended to make life easy for himself by simply handing Mozart one of the better examples of the Turkish librettos that were much in vogue, Christoph Friedrich Bretzner's *Belmont und Constanze* written for Johann André, he failed to realize the change from the Mozart of 1779–80 to the Mozart of July 1781. The passage of so few months in Stephanie's terms makes this understandable; awareness of *Idomeneo* and of the swift passage of time in Mozart's terms might have alerted this shrewd man of the theatre to what was to transpire. His past history with such projects suggests that he expected little revision to a lively, well-characterized plot for Viennese taste and resources: how wrong he was can be seen by studying parallel synopses (Baumann, 1987, 36–61). Mozart's comments to his father during what turned into a collaboration of a completely novel kind are perhaps the most quoted of all his writings, but their importance cannot be overestimated.

> die oper hatte mit einem Monologue angefangen, und da bat ich H: Stephani eine kleine ariette daraus zu machen – und daß anstatt nach dem liedchen des osmin die zwey zusammen schwätzen, ein Duo daraus würde. – da wir die Rolle des osmin H: fischer zugedacht, welcher eine gewis fortrefliche Bass-stimme hat . . . so muß man so einen Mann Nutzen, besonders da er das hiesige Publikum ganz für sich hat. – dieser osmin hat aber im original büchel das einzige liedchen zum singen, und sonst nichts, außer dem Terzett und final. dieser hat also im Ersten Ackt eine aria bekommen, und wird auch im 2:^ten noch eine haben. – die aria hab ich dem H: Stephani ganz angegeben; – und die hauptsache der Musick davon war schon fertig, ehe Stephani ein Wort davon wuste. – sie haben nur den anfang davon, und das Ende, welches von guter Wirkung seyn muss – der zorn des osmin wird dadurch in das kommische gebracht, weil die türkische Musick dabey angebracht ist. – in der ausführung der aria habe ich seine schöne tiefe töne . . . schimmern lassen. – das, *drum beym Barte des Propheten* etc: ist zwar im nemlichen tempo, aber mit geschwinden Noten – und da sein zorn immer wächst, so muß – da man glaubt die aria seye schon zu Ende – das allegro aßai – ganz in einem andern zeitmaas, und in andern Ton – eben den besten Effect zu machen; denn, ein Mensch der sich in einem so heftigen zorn

befindet, überschreitet alle ordnung, Maas und Ziel, er kennt sich nicht –
so muß sich auch die Musick nicht mehr kennen – weil aber die
leidenschaften, heftig oder nicht, niemal bis zum Eckel ausgedrücket
seyn müssen, und die Musick, auch in der schaudervollsten lage, das Ohr
niemalen beleidigen, sondern doch dabey vergnügen muß, folglich
allzeit Musick bleiben Muß, so habe ich keinen fremden ton zum f | :
zum ton der aria : | sondern einen befreundten dazu, aber nicht den
Nächsten, D minor, sondern den weitern, A minor, gewählt. – Nun die
aria von Bellmont in ADur. O wie ängstlich, o wie feurig, wissen sie wie
es ausgedrückt ist – auch ist das klopfende liebevolle herz schon
angezeiget – die 2 violinen in oktaven – dies ist die favorit aria von allen
die sie gehört haben – auch von mir. – und ist ganz für die stimme des
Adamberger geschrieben. man sieht das zittern – wanken – man sieht
wie sich die schwellende brust hebt – welches durch ein crescendo
exprimirt ist – man hört das lispeln und seufzen – welches durch die
ersten violinen mit Sordinen und einer flaute mit in unisono ausgedrückt
ist. –
der Janitscharen Chor ist für einen Janitscharen Chor alles was man
verlangen kann. – kurz und lustig; – und ganz für die Wiener
geschrieben. – die aria von der konstanze habe ich ein wenig der
geläüfigen gurgel der Mad:^selle Cavallieri aufgeopfert. – *Trennung war
mein banges loos. und nun schwimmt mein aug in Thränen* – habe ich, so viel
es eine wälsche Bravour aria zulässt, auszudrücken gesucht. – das *hui* –
habe ich in *schnell* verändert also: *doch wie schnell schwand meine freude* etc:
ich weis nicht was sich unsere teutsche dichter denken; – wenn sie schon
das theater nicht verstehen, was die opern anbelangt – so sollen sie doch
wenigstens die leute nicht reden lassen, als wenn schweine vor ihnen
stünden. – hui Sau; –
Nun das Terzett, nemlich der schluß vom Ersten Ackt. – Pedrillo hat
seinen Herrn für einen Baumeister ausgegeben, damit er gelegenheit hat
mit seiner konstanze im garten zusamm zu kommen. der Bassa hat ihn in
diensten genommen; – osmin als aufseher, und der darum nichts weis, ist
als ein grober flegel, und Erzfeind von allen fremden impertinent und
will sie nicht in dem garten lassen. das erste was angezeigt, ist sehr kurz –
und weil der Text dazu anlaß gegeben, so habe ich es so ziemlich gut
3stimmig geschrieben. dann fängt aber gleich das major pianißimo an –
welches sehr geschwind gehen muß – und der schluß wird recht viel

lärmen machen – und das ist Ja alles was zu einem schluß von einem
Ackt gehört – Je mehr lärmen, Je besser; – Je kürzer, Je besser – damit die
leute zum klatschen nicht kalt werden. –
. . . Nun sitze ich wie der Haaß im Pfeffer – über 3 wochen ist schon der
Erste Ackt fertig – eine aria im 2:^ten Ackt, und das Saufduett |: per li Sig:^ri
vieneri :| welches in nichts als in *meinem* türkischen Zapfenstreich
besteht :| ist schon fertig; – mehr kann ich aber nicht davon machen –
weil izt die ganze geschichte umgestürzt wird – und zwar auf mein
verlangen. – zu anfang des dritten Ackts ist ein charmantes quintett oder
vielmehr final – dieses möchte ich aber lieber zum schluß des 2:^t Ackts
haben.- um das bewerksteligen zu können, muß eine grosse
veränderung, Ja eine ganz Neue intrigue vorgenommen werden – und
Stephanie hat über hals und kopf arbeit da muß man halt ein wenig
gedult haben. alles schmelt über den Stephanie – es kann seyn daß er
auch mit mir nur ins gesicht so freundschaftlich ist – aber er arrangirt mir
halt doch das buch – und zwar so wie ich es will – auf ein haar – und
mehr verlange ich bey gott nicht von ihm!

(Letter to his father, 26 September 1781)

(The opera had begun with a monologue, and I asked Herr Stephani to
make a little arietta of it, and then to put in a duet instead of making the
two chatter together after Osmin's little song. As we have intended the
role of Osmin for Herr Fischer, who certainly has an excellent bass . . .
we must make use of such a man, especially as he has the public here
completely on his side. But in the original libretto this Osmin has only
one little song to sing, and nothing else apart from the Terzett and the
finale. So he's been given an aria in the first act, and will get another in
the second. I've indicated the whole aria for Herr Stephanie, and the
greater part of the music for it was ready before Stephanie knew a word
about it. What you have is only the beginning and the end, which is
bound to be effective. Osmin's rage is made comic because that's where
the Turkish music is brought in. In the working out of the aria I've
allowed his beautiful deep tones to gleam. The 'Drum beym Barte des
Propheten' etc. is in the same tempo, but with rapid notes, and as his
anger increases, then – just when one thinks the aria is over – the Allegro
assai, in a completely different tempo and in another key, is sure to
create the finest effect; for as a man who finds himself in such a towering
rage oversteps all order, measure and purpose and does not know

himself, so must the music not know itself, but since the passions, powerful or not, must never be expressed to the point of disgust, and music, even in the most horrifying situation, must never offend the ear but give pleasure and so always remain music, I've chosen not a key foreign to F (the key of the aria) but one related to it, though not the closest, D minor, but a more distant one, A minor. Now to Belmonte's aria in A major. You know how I've expressed 'O wie ängstlich, o wie feurig'; also, his tender loving heart is already depicted, with the two violins in octaves. This is the favourite aria of everyone who's heard it, mine too, and it was written entirely for Adamberger's voice. You see the trembling, the faltering, you see how his swelling breast heaves, which is expressed by a crescendo, you hear the whispering and sighing which is expressed by muted first violins and flute in unison.

The Janissary Chorus is all that one can wish for from a Janissary Chorus, short and lively, and entirely written for the Viennese. I've sacrificed Constanze's aria a little to Mlle Cavalieri's nimble throat, 'Trennung war mein banges Loos, und nun schwimmt mein Aug' in Thränen', I've tried to express as far as an Italian bravura aria allows. I've changed the 'hui' to 'schnell': 'doch wie schnell schwand meine Freude' etc. I don't know what our German poets are thinking of. If they don't understand the stage, as far as opera is concerned, at least they shouldn't make people talk as if they were facing pigs. Hui, sow!

Now for the Terzett, that's to say the end of Act I. Pedrillo has passed his master off as an architect so as to give him the opportunity of meeting his Constanze in the garden. The Pasha has taken him into his service. His steward Osmin, who knows nothing of this, being a coarse lout and the arch-enemy of all strangers, is insolent and won't let them into the garden. This first part is suitably very short, and because the words lend themselves to it I've made it quite a good piece of three-part writing. Then the major section begins pianissimo, and must go very fast, and the end will make a real lot of noise, which is just how the end of an act ought to be. The more noise, the better; the shorter, the better; so that people won't have time for their applause to cool down.

. . . Now I'm like a cat on hot bricks. The First Act was finished over three weeks ago; an aria in Act II and the drunken duet (for the Viennese gentlemen) (which consists entirely of *my* Turkish tattoo) is also finished. But I can't do any more because the whole plot's being altered, and what's more at my request. At the beginning of the Third Act there's a charming quintet, or rather finale, but I'd rather have this at the end of Act II. In order to make this practicable there has to be a big change, in fact an entirely new twist to the plot must be introduced, and as Stephanie is up to his ears in work one must have a bit of patience. Everyone reviles Stephanie, and it may be that with me too he's friendly only to my face, but he's organizing the libretto for me, and just as I want it down to the last detail, and by God I can't ask any more of him!)

Leopold's reply to this letter is unfortunately lost, but clearly it contained reservations about the text which Mozart felt obliged to answer:

Nun wegen dem text von der opera. – was des Stephani seine arbeit anbelangt, so haben sie freylich recht. – doch ist die Poesie dem karackter des dummen, groben und boshaften osmin ganz angemessen. – und ich weis wohl daß die verseart darinn nicht von den besten ist – doch ist sie so Passend, mit meinen Musikalischen gedanken |: die schon vorher in meinem kopf herumspatzierten :| übereins gekommen, daß sie mir nothwendig gefallen musste; – und ich wollte wetten daß man bey dessen aufführung – nichts vermissen wird . . . bey einer opera muß schlechterdings die Poesie der Musick gehorsame Tochter seyn. – warum gefallen denn die Welschen kommischen opern überall? – mit allem dem Elend was das buch anbelangt! – so gar in Paris – wovon ich selbst ein Zeuge war. – weil da ganz die Musick herscht – und man darüber alles vergisst. – um so mehr muß Ja eine opera gefallen wo der Plan des Stücks gut ausgearbeitet; die Wörter aber nur blos für die Musick geschrieben sind, und nicht hier und dort einem Elenden Reime zu gefallen . . . worte setzen – oder ganze strophen die des komponisten seine ganze idèe verderben. – verse sind wohl für die Musick das unentbehrlichste – aber Reime – des reimens wegen das schädlichste; – die herrn, die so Pedantisch zu werke gehen, werden immermit sammt der Musick zu grunde gehen. –

da ist es am besten wenn ein guter komponist der das Theater versteht, und selbst etwas anzugeben im stande ist, und ein gescheider Poet, als ein wahrer Phönix, zusammen kommen.

(Letter to his father, 13 October 1781)

(Now about the text of the opera. As far as Stephanie's work is concerned, you're undoubtedly right. But the poetry is wholly in keeping with the character of the stupid, coarse and malevolent Osmin. And I know well that the versification isn't of the best, but it's so suitable and fits so well with my musical ideas (which were already wandering about in my head) that I had to be pleased with it; and I bet that in performance nothing would be missed . . . In an opera the poetry absolutely must be the obedient daughter of the music. Why else are Italian comic operas popular everywhere – and with all their wretched texts – even in Paris, as I've witnessed myself? Because in them the music rules completely, and then everything else is forgotten. Certainly an opera must please all the more when the piece's plan is well worked out; but the words are written solely for the music and not put in for the sake of some wretched rhyme . . . nor for whole strophes which wreck the composer's entire concept. Verses are of course the most indispensable thing for music, but rhyme for rhyme's sake is the most damaging; the gentlemen who set to work so pedantically will always come to grief, together with the music.

So it's best when a good composer who understands the theatre and has something of his own to offer gets together with an intelligent poet, that true phoenix.)

The value of these celebrated passages is two-fold, first for the insight, matched only in Mozart's correspondence with his father over *Idomeneo*, which they give us into his compositional processes in opera, but also for the significance of the resulting work for German opera. His powers of assimilating a wide variety of influences, stimuli, practical necessities and popular opportunities had never been so taxed, nor his ability to make an original masterpiece out of such variety so breathtakingly demonstrated. Anxious to succeed in Vienna, he was clearly confident of this ability, and more than happy to make accommodations, indeed to let them stimulate his invention. Only with Caterina Cavalieri does he admit to compromise, for she was a fine singer whose 'geläufige Gurgel' would need some indulgence, especially since she was a poor actress. This makes it the more surprising that he should have bequeathed to singers and producers a problem in the need for her to enact some response during the long instrumental introduction to 'Martern aller Arten', a convention with which he had become familiar in Mannheim, especially in the person of Franziska Danzi in Holzbauer's *Günther von Schwarzburg*. He would have been unlikely to pass up the opportunity of beating Umlauf and Dittersdorf at their own game with the popular tenor Valentin Adamberger; and the detail of the writing for Adamberger's voice in 'O wie ängstlich' alone, on which he prided himself, suggests a vivid portrait of its style and nature (apart from its actual tone quality, said to have been nasal). He was also not going to let slip the chance of delighting the Viennese with the glowing tone of the well-loved Ludwig Fischer, and flattering their taste with a drinking song and a Janissary Chorus and even with their habits of applause.

More significantly, the use of such conventions is made functional to the opera. 'Vivat Bacchus' is a drinking song in a vein with which the Viennese would be comfortable, but (quite apart from the brilliance of its invention with the 'Turkish' music) unlike most such it plays a crucial role in the plot, and the same is true of Pedrillo's Act III Romanze. Over and over again, Mozart takes an aria form familiar to the audience he was wooing, and not only makes it an essential part in the furtherance of the drama but subtly transforms its inner nature by unexpected textual disposition, by harmonic and melodic gestures that transcend the ordinary into the unforgettable, by tonal drama that reflects character and situation. The most famous examples come with Osmin, as Mozart himself describes. He had not yet composed the final Vaudeville, in which again a simple convention is transformed by the subtle alterations to the repeated melody made by the pairs of lovers and then furiously shattered by Osmin. The presence of the highly intelligent Fischer, and his popularity with the public, encouraged a musical portrait unprecedented in German opera, one whose vividness and strength were to colour all subsequent example, and set this nominally secondary character threateningly near the centre of the opera.

Governing all the construction of the opera – a process unusually protracted for Mozart – is his determination that, in his famous phrase, poetry must be 'the obedient daughter of the music'. His insistence on the composer's primacy shows throughout: in the casually revealed detail that he already had much of the music of one aria in his head and in appreciation of another as 'well written for music', in his disdain of wilful rhymes and other verbal devices, in his ideal of a really good practical layout, and in his gratitude to Stephanie and unusual patience with him for being willing to oblige so constructively. Stephanie was indeed Mozart's phoenix.

With Stephanie's talent supporting his own genius, Mozart was able to take the drama into his musical inspiration as no previous composer of German opera had even remotely done. The genre is transformed by his ability to lead the drama musically, not only by his brilliant appreciation of what was practical, popular and effective with the voices, but by musical strategies that include the tonal planning (both long term and for immediate dramatic sensation), and so especially by a new significance conferred on the orchestra. It becomes meaningless to describe as accompaniment what has now taken on a leading role, even in an opera with a substantial contribution from the spoken word (and it may be noted that the obvious opportunities for melodrama have been virtually ignored, and that by February 1783 Mozart was writing to his father claiming that German was just as singable as French or Italian). The nature of Singspiel, even when brought to this new condition, obviously precluded the structures which arise from symphonic mastery and which are a central part of Mozart's great Italian operas, deriving as those structures do from the drama but expressing them with the disciplines of instrumental music. But the achievement of *Entführung* is one of the most acute of the causes for regret at the shortness of Mozart's life, regret in this instance that he did not live to turn his powers on the German grand opera that must have lain ahead of him.

Two unfinished Italian operas, *L'oca del Cairo* (1783) and *Lo sposo deluso* (1783), preceded *Der Schauspieldirektor* (1786). This is a largely spoken skit (a fine overture and four numbers) on singer rivalries in the troublesome assemblage of a theatrical company, and is notable chiefly for mildly entertaining in-jokes and for impressive show arias as the rival prima donnas manoeuvre for position. There followed the three Italian masterpieces, *Le nozze di Figaro* (1786), *Don Giovanni*

(1787) and *Così fan tutte* (1790). By now Mozart had had occasion to become familiar with the life of Josephine Vienna. The complexities and contradictions that mark *Die Zauberflöte* (1791) have their tangled roots in various literary origins but also in the city's intellectual and theatrical life, as well as in the mark set upon the city by the Emperor's individual manner of ruling; but, 'more important than any one source of *Die Zauberflöte* is the whole tradition of the Viennese Popular Theatre, of which this opera is the supreme product' (Branscombe, 1991, 4). In tracing the multiple literary sources of the work, Branscombe emphasizes how familiar Mozart was with the popular theatres of Vienna, having sketched the start of a couple of spoken comedies as well as written arias for members of the company of his collaborator on *Die Zauberflöte*, Emanuel Schikaneder.

The heterogeneous mixture of characters and genres and of elements of comedy and quasi-Freemasonic idealism in *Die Zauber-flöte* would have caused much less confusion to contemporary Viennese audiences than it has done subsequently, especially to those bent on finding solutions where much of the point is that in a fantasy world none exists. As a spoken drama, or one with lighter musical involvement than Mozart's, it would scarcely have been remembered beyond its day. At the same time, it would not have taken the form it did without Schikaneder's close collaboration with Mozart, whose contribution to the drama was based on his own intimate knowledge of the Viennese stage and its characters and conventions. A great deal in the work's success rested on the appeal to familiar expectations, which would have tended to override inconsistencies, especially in the actual theatre. The eighteenth-century theatre had plenty of bird-men and bird-catchers to show, some with names close to 'Papa-geno', and the cheerful rogue who gets away with everything has an obvious attraction, especially when set in contrast with the hero's moral rectitude. Details such as food and drink appearing by magic, prisoners escaping by enchanting their captors with music, and a pathos-laden appeal to the audience for absolution from suicide, were all popular devices; their recurrence has the reassuring ritual element that underlies much comedy. The presence of Monostatos in Sarastro's realm would not have disturbed a Viennese audience; and his sentence to the bastinado for his attempted rape of Pamina, imposed if later repealed by this upholder of humane values over retribution, would have caused even less surprise to those who had lived as subjects of the levelling and rationalizing, talented but capricious ruler who had supported the abolition of torture in 1776 but was capable of intervening in court cases to impose cruel punishments.

Mozart's ability to lift it all into a different dimension with music was probably (we lack supporting correspondence) no less carefully worked out with Schikaneder than it had been with Stephanie for *Die Entführung*. Comparison of the printed text and the score shows myriad alterations that prepare for music in details of prosody and in dramatic impact, even before the creative tensions which Mozart devised by going inventively against metrical expectations (Branscombe 1966, 45–63 and 1991, 101–6). Mozart was also, as always throughout his life, able to capitalize on a singer's success with the public and turn his or her characteristics to creative advantage, as with Sarastro and Franz Xaver Gerl's sonorous tones (descending to a well-exposed low F) or with the Queen of the Night and Josepha Hofer's scintillating coloratura and top Fs, now used to piercingly memorable effect.

The achievement of *Die Zauberflöte* in elevating the genre of Viennese magic opera to greatness rests no less upon the expansion of musical means. There is nothing of the day that is comparable, even in two works which have, with little reason, been held to have influenced Mozart. Paul Wranitzky's *Oberon, König der Elfen* went on to achieve immense popularity throughout Germany after its first staging in Vienna, by Schikaneder, in 1789. There are some obvious coincidences of plot and of character in its tale of Sir Hüon, with his child of nature squire Scherasmin, and the Sultan's abducted daughter Amande being tested in a number of trials that include shipwreck and attempted seduction by the Pasha of Tunis and his wife, with the lovers' rescue being effected through the use of a magic horn bestowed on them by Oberon (whose reconciliation with Titania depends upon their fidelity). Carl Ludwig Gieseke recognized an opportunity here when he adapted Sophie Seyler's libretto for Karl Hanke's *Hüon und Amande* (based on Christoph Wieland's epic poem *Oberon*), and capitalized on the Viennese love of magic theatre and the exotic, to which the opera's popularity in turn gave extra impetus. Though there are Singspiel conventions in common, little if anything influenced Mozart in Wranitzky's well-turned and tuneful score, one which invites lavish staging rather than deepening the text into an engagement with the mysterious fairy world, let alone into a substantial work of art.

About Wenzel Müller's *Kaspar der Fagottist*, Mozart was, not for the first time, being too dismissive concerning a rival attraction when he wrote to his wife saying, 'ich gieng dann um mich aufzuheitern zum Kasperl in die neue Oper der "Fagottist", die so viel Lärm macht – aber gar nichts daran ist' (letter of 12 June 1791) ('to cheer myself up, I went to the new opera in the Kasperl Theatre, the *Fagottist*, which has made such a stir – but there's absolutely nothing to it'). *Kaspar* is a tale of Prince Armidoro with his comic servant Kaspar taking a balloon flight so as to rescue a magic tinder-box from an evil but bumbling magician who is holding prisoner the fairy Perifirime's daughter Sidi and her companion Palmire, and derives from the story *Lulu, oder Die Zauberflöte* by J. A. Liebeskind in Wieland's collection of stories *Dschinnistan*. It includes some catchy numbers, and there are again details of plot and some incidents which resemble those in Mozart's opera. One of the most striking is the moment when Kaspar's music spellbinds the harem-keeper Zumio and his slaves, allowing him and Palmire to escape. Nevertheless, Kaspar's bassoon is a crude comic device beside Papageno's glockenspiel music, whose pretty tinkle so enchants Monostatos and his dancing slaves that it seems as if all the vileness in the world has been wafted away on a tune played by a simple soul.

Moreover, Mozart's Act I finale is a musical structure completely beyond the range of Wranitzky or Müller. Without breaking the convention, it expands the musical means of Viennese Singspiel to a new condition, in particular by giving recitative and the role of the orchestra new importance. Tamino's melodic declamation, as he approaches the temples, moves easily between quasi parlando recitative, expressive recitative, melodic phrases, and the Andante aria 'Wie stark ist nicht dein Zauberton', as he plays the magic flute which brings forth Papageno with Pamina, before the attempted recapture by Monostatos and eventually the stately arrival of Sarastro. The orchestra's role is comparably flexible, from supportive chords that serve to impel the recitative, by way of expressive accompaniment, with graphic figures indicating Tamino's impetuous advance upon the temples and his emotional uncertainty in his dialogue with the Priest to, eventually, the pomp of Sarastro's appearance. Especially in the early part of the scene, there is a fluency which Mozart would have admired in Gluck – for this scene, in particular the latter part of the opening scene of *Iphigénie en Tauride* – and had already put into practice with *Idomeneo*. Here, it acquires a dramatic momentum entirely its own, something new to German opera and affecting it profoundly.

The influence of three of Mozart's greatest operas, *Idomeneo*, *Don Giovanni* and *Die Zauberflöte*, on German opera is crucial, even though two of them were Italian operas, the first little noticed in Germany and the second initially making its way in all manner of unworthy versions and travesties. *Idomeneo* was only once performed in Mozart's lifetime after its 1781 Munich première. But the experience of writing it, and the care his letters show he lavished on its construction, deepened his operatic powers incomparably. The creativity with which he handles the conventions of opera seria has been more readily appreciated by twentieth-century audiences distanced from such conventions and so less confused by the music's originality. Among the qualities of this, his first masterpiece, several may be suggested as ingredients of Mozart's developing Romantic awareness. The use of some of the most chromatically advanced harmony he was ever to write indicates a new range and depth of feeling in the emotions of his characters. The melodic expansion which complements this bursts the bounds of the arias into a fluency in recitative which looks far beyond the manner of his immediate successors, is only touched upon in *Euryanthe*, and sets an example for Wagner. The functional use of the chorus has no real precedent in opera, not even that of Gluck, to whom the work is so deeply indebted, though from *Iphigénie en Tauride* certainly comes the idea of an emotional storm dramatically linked to a physical storm, a device familiar from Baroque opera in metaphor but now achieving a deeper Romantic function as Nature and Mind draw together. The storm, contrasting with the chorus reflecting the calm of the sea, 'Placido è il mar', brings Nature, in the form of the frighteningly unpredictable force of Poseidon, into the heart of the drama as Mozart never did again. He had not before made such expressive use of orchestral colour as an aspect of his invention and hence placed the orchestra as a leading element in what remains outwardly an old-fashioned opera seria. This opens up to him suggestions of motive, but more significantly develops a continuity of dramatic composition, especially in Act II, far ahead of his time. For all its Italian forms, *Idomeneo* is deeply marked by German ideas.

There is no evidence that E. T. A. Hoffmann knew *Idomeneo*. Had he done so, he would surely have fastened upon its Romantic elements, as he was to do with *Don Giovanni* when he came to write his epoch-making story, a full quarter of a century after the work's première. Despite the music's popularity and the praise of Goethe (who wished Mozart had composed for his *Faust*), not until then was the Romanticism of *Don Giovanni* fully appreciated. It is doubtful if the orchestral range and eloquence of *Don Giovanni* would have been possible without *Idomeneo*, nor the capacity to make use of these qualities and the use of searching chromatic harmony to speak directly to the darker side of an audience's sensibilities. In the characterization of the central figure – or, rather, the constructive non-characterization that gives him mythic quality – there is created a mysteriousness which has no operatic precedent, something the Romantics were to recognize with admiration and awe.

With *Die Zauberflöte*, popularity was immediate. The work's impact on its successors reflects this, with thinly disguised imitations of Papageno's entrance song, of Tamino and Pamina in their loving exchange before the ordeals, of Sarastro's grave pronouncements all entering operatic currency. Not only were there sequels, among them Schikaneder's *Das Labyrinth*, set by Winter in 1798 much in Mozart's style. There are also instances (as with Himmel's *Die Sylphen*) of the characters themselves actually invading later operas. In his concern to expand magic opera towards grand opera, following *Die Zauberflöte* Schikaneder provided texts for 'heroic-comic' operas of varying quality, among them Süssmayr's *Der Spiegel von Arkadien* (1794), Hoffmeister's *Der Königssohn von Ithaka* (1795), Wölfl's *Der Höllenberg* (1795) and, a collaboration by Mederitsch and Winter, *Babylons Pyramiden* (1797). More potent influences on Romanticism are also to be felt. The exoticism of the Egyptian setting had its appeal, and it is typical of this that early editions did not bother very much whether Tamino was Japanese or Javanese; he certainly has no characteristics of either nation, or even of the Orient, and we need only know that he is from a faraway land. The mysterious role of musical instruments themselves in the plot was an original one: Papageno's panpipes speaking as part of his voice, the chimes beguiling Monostatos's slaves, the Priests giving their assent to Tamino's candidature by intoning their horns in the three-fold chords which suffuse the opera, above all the magic flute guiding Tamino and Pamina through the ordeals, and chosen to give the opera its title.

The use of the magical for serious as well as for comic ends, serving a quest theme, spoke deeply to Romantics – composers, but also writers – as not simply providing material for music but actually needing the text's realization in music. Moreover, this new dimension enables the opera to find deeper resonances when a crucial part of Mozart's genius is to enter so fully into the nature of each character. Perhaps the greatest paradox of this most paradoxical of masterpieces is that the responsive listener, compelled to take music of such genius seriously, is lifted above confusion into a realm of understanding which leaves confusion behind. Indeed, it is actually from the conjunction of so many different operatic and theatrical elements, and from the inconsistencies and contradictions in the plot, that the work's liberating effect on Romantic opera flowed, undamming so much in the German imagination. For Wagner, it was the first great German opera. When bound by music of such evident greatness, all the inconsistencies compel not the exercise of reason invoked in the plot, but a flight of the imagination, borne upon the music, into a completely new realm of fantasy and beauty.

At the outbreak of the French Revolution in 1789, Germany was still some eight decades from unification, a widespread area of disparate territories held together by only the loosest of bonds. Politically decrepit, administratively in a state of advanced senility, the Holy Roman Empire was divided into some three hundred units that included states of the size and significance of Prussia and Bavaria, Free Cities either inert or with the vitality of Lübeck, Cologne, Frankfurt and especially Hamburg, regions governed idealistically or corruptly at the caprice of Archbishop, Bishop, Abbot, Duke, Landgrave or Margrave, and diminutive estates consisting of a castle and a few fields ruled by the Imperial Knights, or Reichsritter. Set against this was the intellectual and creative energy of Germany's philosophers, critics and authors in an age that saw the writings of Kant, Lessing, Moses Mendelssohn, Hamann and Herder, of Goethe, Schiller, Wieland, Klopstock and a host of other poets and dramatists whose work formed audiences who were bound by a common language and whose more intelligent members were also joined by a common enthusiasm for new ideas and ideals. In 1789 there were some 114 German periodicals of a political, philosophical or literary nature. Most towns of any size had a club or society which subscribed to a selection of these, maintained a library, and provided a meeting place for the exchange of views. When word of revolution in France crossed the Rhine, excitement was unbounded. A young writer, Friedrich Schulz, was the first to return from Paris and set the tone with his *Geschichte der grossen Revolution in Frankreich*:

> Vier und zwanzig Millionen Menschen waren von einem despotischen Bündnisse ihres Königs beraubt und wechselsweise der Kabale, der Ungerechtigkeit, der Armuth, dem Hunger und dem Kriege preisgegeben worden. Die Minister hielten mit ihren Helfershelfern alle

Kanäle zum Blute der Nation offen, unterdrückten den unschuldigen
Armen durch ungerechte Richter und zitterten vor dem strafbaren
Reichen mit ihnen; sie raubten Millionen ihre Freiheit und mußten
diesen Raub durch Kerker und oft durch Mord behaupten.

(Schulz, 1790, 5–6)

(Through a conspiracy with the king at its head twenty-four million
people had been plundered and left at the mercy, turn and turn about, of
intrigue, injustice, poverty, hunger and war. The ministers and their
accomplices kept open all the veins out of which the blood of the nation
might flow, they oppressed the poor and the innocent through
iniquitous judges, and trembled themselves, together with their victims,
before the rich and the guilty; they robbed millions of their liberty and
were compelled to make use of imprisonment, and often murder, to
maintain that robbery.)

Schulz goes on in this manner to give a report as vivid as a war
despatch of the fall of the Bastille and of all the events of that
momentous summer. Copies of his book were fought over in the
shops. Other writers followed in his path, while those who hailed the
events as a realization of the ideals of the Enlightenment included
Klopstock and Schiller (both made honorary French citizens), Höl-
derlin, Herder and Wieland, to whose voices were joined the
resonant pronouncements of Kant. Though French example did not
lead to more than sporadic and short-lived attempts at actual imitation in Germany, the inspiration was overwhelming, and – in the
radiance of the dawn in which Wordsworth found it bliss to be alive
– not all voices were silenced by news of the Terror. Many did recoil
in horror; there were also those who, not uncommonly in time of
revolution, found it possible to excuse extremes of means for the
good of the end (particularly when speaking from a safe distance).
Herder was the most significant of those few whose sober, consistent
view held that support for the ideals of liberty, equality and fraternity
did not mean that what was taking place in France could be
transferred to Germany, indeed that the German temper was
unsuited to French example.

However, French taste and ideas, French writing and French

music all acquired a new immediacy; and the French operas that had been making their way in German repertories starved of good native material took a further step forward in popularity. To some extent, this was a product of Germany's fragmented condition. With the opera houses almost entirely controlled by scattered courts, individual prestige had long counted for much and had encouraged imports of opera seria as the most impressive form, while, in the theatres that did give German opera, French opéra-comique provided attractive lighter fare alongside opera buffa. There existed no capital city, no intellectual centre which could give a lead in supporting a national opera. French opera increasingly dominated repertories in the century's last decade, which was for German opera one of confusion and uncertainty, of dead wood which soon crumbled into dusty obscurity, of fresh growth whose vitality was not always recognized, of decay and re-fertilization.

On the face of it, there seems a paradox in the contrast between the shattering European events of the quarter century following the Revolution and the enthusiastic support for the spread of French art and ideas. The tide of French opera flooding into German repertories in the 1790s was not stemmed by the outbreak of war in 1792, or by subsequent setbacks and the withdrawal of Prussia and the ceding of her possessions on the left bank of the Rhine to France in 1795. Austria's ceding, in turn, of the Low Countries to France at the Peace of Campio Formio in 1797 was not only the continuation of these humiliations but the opening of the great three-act drama, with Napoleon increasingly taking the centre of the stage, that was to lead to the long-due collapse of the Holy Roman Empire. The second act opened with the Peace of Lunéville in 1801, when the entire left bank of the Rhine became French and when, despite the so-called Princes' Revolution against its terms, the Empire lost its old constitution and became no more than an ever looser federation of secular states. Further setbacks confirming Napoleon's power, including his occupation of Hanover in 1803 and his defeat of the Austrians at Austerlitz in 1805, initiated the final act at the Peace of Pressburg in 1805. Napoleon's command of German lands meant direct intervention in their rule, sometimes with personal dynastic connexions by marriage, and included his installation of the Elector of Bavaria and the Duke of Württemberg as kings. The final curtain fell on the Empire on 6 August 1806 when Franz II renounced his Holy Roman title to become Franz I, Emperor of Austria. Napoleon's further triumphal progress was marked by the defeat at Jena in 1806 that led to the disarray of the army and government of Prussia, left with only half her territories, and the no less calamitous defeat of Austria at Wagram in 1809. In 1810 Napoleon annexed the whole of the northern coast as far as Hamburg and the Elbe. Not until 1812 was he to embark upon his doomed Russian adventure, though the real turning point of his power came not with the calamitous retreat from Moscow, but with his defeat at the hands of the Russians, Prussians and Austrians at the so-called Battle of the Nations outside Leipzig in 1813.

Such landmarks, charting a whole refashioning of the European landscape, give no indication of the tenor of life in the disparate German lands during these years. With mistrust everywhere – Prussia and Austria set against one another, the smaller German states suspicious of both – there were in the years up to 1813 the temptation and sometimes the necessity to find accommodation with France. In the French-governed lands along the Rhine and in the states of South Germany – Bavaria, Württemberg and Baden – French example in administration was taken up with an appreciation of its liberality and efficiency, if sometimes (as in the case of the absurd King of Württemberg) with confused perceptions. There was also a good deal of German admiration for Napoleon the military hero and for Napoleon the liberator. Even in Prussia, reforms in the wake of withdrawal from the war in 1795 reflected the French influence well established in the time of Frederick the Great; and the period before Prussia's unwise resumption of hostilities in 1806 saw a renewed intellectual fertility in Berlin and in the creativity represented by the Weimar of Goethe and Schiller.

In many of the most popular German operas that claimed audiences in the 1790s, the French content continued to lie chiefly in the influence of opéra-comique on plot, and hence with conventional character types. Many of these had little to do with nationality and hence were readily transferable. Sentimental lovers, crusty old buffers (perhaps the heroine's father or guardian), braggart soldiers, pompous doctors, crabby lawyers, wily servants: these tried and tested figures, already familiar from many a Singspiel, went back by way of opéra-comique and opera buffa to the *commedia dell'arte* and to a remoter ancestry in the comedies of Plautus, and even behind him to Menander. It needed only the introduction of a familiar popular figure – Kasperl, Hanswurst, or some instantly recognizable Bavarian or Tyrolean or Swabian type – speaking in dialect, cracking local jokes and singing a folksong, to win the piece a regional following. Later Singspiel continued to draw on such formulae, but there was no future here for a more mature German opera. It was to take at least a decade for the developments in French opera brought about by new times and new ideas to exert their crucial influence. More significantly, Romantic elements released by *Die Zauberflöte*, deeply felt if as yet not fully perceived, inspired the re-fashioning of other plots in its terms (or close to them), with magic, idealism, quest, exoticism and fantasy acquiring a new depth and significance. Meanwhile, the lighter type of French- or Italian-influenced opera continued to hold sway, and proved more enduringly successful in Vienna, and to an extent in Munich, than in the North.

As a young man in Mannheim, Franz Danzi had studied with Vogler, some of whose influence shows in his operas – that is, those of them that remain, for most of them are lost. One survivor is the early melodrama *Cleopatra* (1780), though it gives little indication of his mature language. His greatest success came with *Die Mitternacht-stunde* (1789), performed in 1798 in Munich, where he was established from 1784. It is a highly artificial light comedy (Spanish, via French, by origin), turning on a family convention that General Don Guzmann's niece Julie, in love with Captain Don Fernando, must marry a rich sea captain at midnight on a certain day. Fernando wagers Guzmann that if he can abduct Julie in time, he can marry her. Secondary characters involved in the plot are, on the lovers' side, their servants Bastian and

Laure, on Guzmann's side the duenna Cecilia, abetted by idiotic Niklas, lame Ambros and deaf Matthias, all of whom give rise to comic misunderstandings. Only at her third attempt does Julie manage to disguise herself and escape, in the nick of time.

Danzi's success rests largely on his skill in reanimating some of the conventional figures of earlier Singspiel. Guzmann is, on the face of it, the standard old buffer who must be outwitted for the sake of young love, but Danzi's touch with chromatic harmony gives him an amusing slyness as well. Irritated that this whipper-snapper should try to outwit him, he sets off pompously in his first aria, 'Ein Hauptmann sollte klüger seyn als ein erfahrner General?', trumpeting away with military rhythms, but an expressive descending chromatic figure gives him a subtler character as he resolves that his niece will never escape, a conjunction that Danzi may have learnt from Vogler and with harmony that may well have impressed his own protégé Weber (Example 13). Possibly from Vogler, too, came a passage in Fernando's first aria, 'Ich lieb' und hoffe', when he drops from a confident A major down a third into F as the castle of dreams he has built seems to be collapsing ('Wonnetrunken bau' ich ein Lustschloss . . . ein Donner rollt, es ist versunken') before he recovers his A major spirits (Example 14). Fernando sets another kind of example with lyrical lines that owe virtually nothing to Italian example and respond to the cadences of German speech. Julie has the by now almost inevitable Polacca, but a very good example of it, to make the second part of an Andantino aria ('Sonst war mit ihrer Liebe'). This is set against a fine expressive aria, harmonically rich, expressing love for Fernando and no enthusiasm for the sea captain, and also against another aria opening Act II, 'Ich will scherzen, lachen, singen', which has a drop from C to A♭ as she admits, 'doch ich fühl ein heimlich Beben'. She is an attractive character, with something of both Agathe and Aennchen in her. Danzi also has an excellent touch with the ensembles, which include a striking Sestetto pitting Laure against five male voices, Don Fernando, Don Guzmann and his three retainers; and his finales owe more to a constructive understanding of Mozart than to the example of Hiller. Perhaps from

Allegro maestoso

Example 13   Danzi: *Die Mitternachtstunde* (1789)

Andante con moto

(The thunder rolls! All is lost!)

Example 14   Danzi: *Die Mitternachtstunde* (1789), Don Fernando

the closing pages of *Le nozze di Figaro* Danzi drew the affecting stroke
on the last page of the whole opera, when eleven bars of pianissimo
music reflect on the danger that has threatened the lovers – 'Liebe
hat den Sieg vollbracht in der tiefsten Mitternacht' – before eight
final bars of merriment.

Danzi's next six operas are all lost, with the exception of a few numbers. *Der Triumph der Treue* (1789) is based on Wieland's *Oberon*, and can be seen from the surviving libretto to be a Singspiel; it was unlucky to encounter the success of Wranitzky's *Oberon* in the same year. Also to this year belongs Danzi's *Der Quasimann*, of which only an amiable rondo survives, and from 1799 a Viennese-type magic opera, *Der Kuss*, and from 1802 *El Bondocani*: all three had an exotic setting.

One of the genre's most popular practitioners in Vienna was Dittersdorf's pupil Wenzel Müller. Appointed to the Theater in der Leopoldstadt at the age of nineteen in 1786, he remained there almost continuously until 1830. His first success was *Das Sonnenfest der Brahminen* in 1790, but he really made his name in 1793 with *Das Neusonntagskind*, a piece which, to his great satisfaction, was performed in half a dozen foreign countries as well as throughout German-speaking lands (and which, Hummel told Ferdinand Hiller, Haydn regarded as a classic of its kind: Hiller, 1880, 21). It is a comedy of superstition, built upon the fear of ghosts exhibited by the otherwise favoured 'Sunday's child' of the title. This is the formidable Hausmeister who can collapse into a nervous wreck as well as deliver himself of cheerful songs, at least one of which, 'Wer niemals einen Rausch hat g'habt', became immediately popular; he can also indulge in an amiable duet with the heroine Lisette, 'Wenn d'Liserl nur wollt'. Somewhat awkwardly (and doubtless under singer pressure) the old Father is given an opening song that breaks free from a robust tune into highly unsuitable coloratura.

However, the influence of the times was shown in the following year when the same librettist, Joachim Perinet, provided Müller with the text for a much superior work, *Die Schwestern von Prag* (1794). The plot turns on the pursuit of Brummer's daughter Wilhelmine by the feeble poet Sperlinghausen, the French dandy Chemise and the good-hearted Gerstenfeld. When Brummer refuses to bestow his daughter's hand without the agreement of his sister, due to arrive from Prague, Sperlinghausen's foolish servant Krispin and Gerstenfeld's crafty servant Johann in turn disguise themselves as the sister. They are exposed, but meanwhile Brummer decides to accept Gerstenfeld as husband for Wilhelmine, whose servant Lorchen enthusiastically takes Johann. Though Müller writes some lively comic songs, there is a higher proportion of more serious arias, together with duets, trios and other ensembles. Some numbers derive in manner from opera buffa, some from Singspiel; others are more original, such as a virtuoso Rondo-Polacca for Wilhelmine and a parody number for Gerstenfeld ('Ich bin des Doktor Sassafras geschikter Substitut'), not to mention some up-to-the-minute mockery of Chemise's French accent ('Ick sehne nur mick nack Marie'). There is also, crucially, a considerable advance in orchestral subtlety, not only with varied accompaniments for the strophic songs but in the ingenious and sophisticated use of instrumental colour. The most remarkable number is the Act I finale, the so-called *Ständchenszene*, a feature of which is the manner in which Müller develops his emphasis on the orchestra as a functional part of the drama and advances it to the centre of events by developing the action with the use of a short motive. This scene opens with Wilhelmine and Lorchen at their window, praising the starless night as friendly to lovers. One by one the serenaders appear, each accompanying himself with a different instrument, only to be interrupted by the next: Gerstenfeld bearing a violin, Chemise a flute, Johann a trombone, Krispin a hurdy-gurdy and finally the waiter Kaspar a cimbalom. Predictably, chaos develops, curbed by the distant sound of the nightwatchman; but by now the neighbours have been aroused, and it is not until the nightwatchman actually arrives, together with the lamplighter, that quiet is restored. It seems likely that Perinet and Müller took the idea for this from Dittersdorf's *Hieronymus Knicker* (1789), in which the Act I finale has a set of amorous confusions by night in a village square that also leads to a scuffle interrupted by a nightwatchman, whose lantern exposes the characters' disguises. The traditional nightwatchman's cry, familiar to generations of German city-dwellers in various forms, makes an early appearance in opera here, to return in other shapes and guises, always with different music, until its most familiar occurrence in Wagner's *Die Meistersinger von Nürnberg* (Example 15).

(a)

Ihr Herrn laßt euch sa-gen wenn ihr euch

hier wollt schlagen so werd't ihr Prü-gel krie-gen

daß sich die Len-den bie-gen! be -

ge-bet euch ja bald zur Ruh! zur Ruh!

(Masters, let me tell you, if you want a fight you'll get a thrashing
that will bend your backs! Get you quickly to bed.)

(b)

Hö-ret mei-ne Herrn, und laßt euch sa-gen:

Die Glock hat elf ge-schla-gen

(Hearken, my masters, and let me tell you: the clock has struck eleven.)

(c)

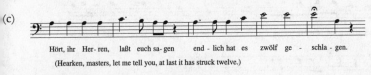

Hört, ihr Her-ren, laßt euch sa-gen end-lich hat es zwölf ge-schla-gen.

(Hearken, masters, let me tell you, at last it has struck twelve.)

Example 15
(a) Dittersdorf: *Hieronymus Knicker* (1789)
(b) Müller: *Die Schwestern von Prag* (1794)
(c) Hoffmann: *Die lustigen Musikanten* (1805)

Entertaining as the scene is, and witty in some of its touches,
Müller does not really possess the combination of musical resources
and dramatic flair to sustain its momentum. It is as if this highly
intelligent and experienced man of the theatre has glimpsed the value
of motive and understood the effect of Mozart's finales, and of his

(d)

(begins)

(Horn) (KAUZ) Hört ihr Herrn, und laßt euch

sa - gen mein Her - zens-stünd-lein hat ge - schla - gen

(ends)

(KAUZ) be - wahrt mein Feu - er und eu - er Licht (Horn)

(KAUZ) daß hier im Ort kein

(Horn **ff**)

Scha - den ge - schieht! (Horn **pp**)

(Hearken, masters, and let me tell you, my favourite hour has struck.
Conserve my fire and your light so that no harm befall this place.)

(e)

Hört, ihr leut, und laßt euch sa - gen, die Glock hat el - fe ge - schlagen: be -

wahrt euch vor Ge - spen-stern und Spuck daß kein bö - ser Geist eur' Seel' be -

rück'! Lo-bet Gott, den Herrn! **ff** (Horn)

(Hearken, people, and let me tell you, the clock has struck eleven: protect yourselves
from spectres and spooks so that no evil spirit enthralls your soul. Praise God the Lord!)

Example 15

(d) Mendelssohn: *Die Heimkehr aus der Fremde* (1829)

(e) Wagner: *Die Meistersinger von Nürnberg* (1868)

capacity to make the drama guide the music and yet be expressed in
it, without himself possessing the necessary symphonic resources.
Perhaps he recognized this, as the scene is an exception in his output.
More characteristic of the Viennese operas of the mid-decade were

two works, both dating from 1796, that reinterpreted a formula with such success that they also retained their popularity well into the next century.

Der Tyroler Wastel benefited from Schikaneder's sure touch with the *Lokalstück* in its plot, in which an innocent countryman satisfies Rousseau-ish impulses when his good-heartedness proves a match for shallow city values, while at the same time familiar Viennese characters are treated with more affectionate amusement than satire. Johann Jakob Haibel, a small-part tenor in Schikaneder's company, provided a score sufficiently catchy to make an appeal to audiences in cities as far flung as Paris and St Petersburg. Wastel, the honest Tyrolean, is cast not for a sophisticated, trained singer but for a 'Gesangskomiker', and his songs (such as the popular duet with Liesel, 'Tyroler sind often so lustig, so froh') rely on the simple, open-air arpeggiated Ländler melodies with which the overture sets the tone. Wastel is placed in contrast to his scheming, socially ambitious sister-in-law Frau von Tiefsinn. It is her lovelorn step-daughter Luise who has the most distinctive aria of the opera, a pretty nightingale song that gives her the chance to exchange trills and flourishes with a flute. Frau von Tiefsinn's fury, in her own main aria, is unfortunately muted by Haibel's inability to get away from three basic chords, so that she does not seem essentially more devious or threatening a character than anybody else. Local colour is provided by a Prater hotelier, with a lively buffo Catalogue Aria at accelerating speed recommending his menu and wine list, and by competing choruses of waiters and Fiaker drivers when a storm catches the cast unawares. In the end, natural goodness and simple values prevail as Wastel brings about Luise's union with the young baker Joseph, and after their simple love duet the piece ends with a *Schlussgesang* reprising the 'Tyroler sind often so lustig' melody.

A still more widespread and enduring success was the one-act *Der Dorfbarbier* (1796), which began life as a spoken comedy by Paul Weidmann and was set as a Singspiel at the suggestion of his actor-singer brother Josef. For this, Johann Baptist Schenk, already an experienced and successful theatre composer, provided a score that

contains the usual mixture of familiar ingredients – Singspiel couplets, buffo arias, a lyrical Cavatina, a polacca, folk-like melodies –
but does so with melodic verve and colour and with a gift for
characterization that lends the piece greater depth than most of its
kind possess. Though the basic idea of the plot is also familiar, and
concerns the outwitting of the barber Lux in his designs on his ward
Suschen and her eventual union with her beloved Joseph, it contains
a number of unusual twists. The final one has Joseph apparently
dying, a plot devised by the schoolmaster Rund so that a deathbed
marriage can be celebrated; once it is, up he jumps, hale and hearty
(given the popularity of Cervantes in German-speaking lands, it may
well be that this was lifted from the Camacho episode of *Don
Quixote*). However, Lux is more than appeased when told that this
miracle has been achieved by his secret cure for all ills, the
application of bacon, and seeing fame and especially fortune apparently calling, he quickly forgets Suschen. The hoax is accompanied
by a Viennese *Grablied* for Rund, 'Gedenk, O Mensch', solemnly
scored for clarinets and muted horns and trumpets, though the
game is given away by a chuckling bassoon. Both Hoffmann and
Weber, who conducted this immensely popular work respectively
in 1813 and 1816, would surely have appreciated the ironic orchestration. Moreover, Suschen's lively polacca may have given each of
them the idea of how this popular form could take on an extra
skittishness, for Mandane in *Der Trank der Unsterblichkeit* and for
Aennchen in *Der Freischütz* (Example 16). Schenk's ready ear also
enables him to open the proceedings for Lux with a very creditable
Vengeance Aria, interrupted when it strikes the frustrated barber
that a better way than fury to a woman's heart is through gentle-
ness, whereat he switches to a smarmy Andante. Best of all the
numbers is a septet during which the fuming Lux is obliged to
watch Joseph and Suschen whispering together in a corner while a
couple of customers insist on him carrying on with their shaves,
with dramatic interruptions from Rund and his apprentice Adam
reporting gory disasters. This occupies the position of a central
finale, and like the long opening *Introduzione* of linked numbers, it

(Girls are easily beguiled: you need only praise them to their face)

(Trust is the duty of virtue)

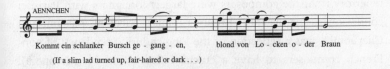

(If a slim lad turned up, fair-haired or dark . . .)

Example 16

(a) Schenk: *Der Dorfbarbier* (1796), Suschen
(b) Hoffmann: *Der Trank der Unsterblichkeit* (1808), Mandane
(c) Weber: *Der Freischütz* (1821), Aennchen

reveals a sure hand with the orchestra and a good sense of dramatic timing in moving the action forward.

The enduring claim of these and other works on German repertories is witness to the vitality of the Singspiel tradition and its capacity to bear a weight of meaning beyond its apparent expressive range, as was repeatedly to be shown. Matters are different in the case of *Die Zauberflöte*. Though it is clearly in the tradition of Viennese magic opera, and though Schikaneder and Mozart drew much from what they saw and heard around them, it has no real ancestor, and its true influence on the future does not lie with the various attempts at sequels or imitations. Already at the first performances it was a triumphant success, as Mozart delightedly reported to his wife in some of the last letters he was ever to write. Within weeks separate numbers and then arrangements began to appear, followed within a few years by a dozen vocal scores published in as many different cities; and by 1793 the opera was well on its triumphant progress through the opera houses of German-speaking lands. Together with his Italian works in translation, it headed the popularity of all Mozart's operas from *Die Entführung*, conquering repertories that in a thin decade for North German opera lay open not only to his genius but to the new taste for Viennese and Italian opera.

The pattern was indicative in Berlin, where at the start of the decade the National Theatre concentrated on Viennese and Italian opera, then from 1792 bringing in a succession of French operas that set Paris only a little way behind Vienna as the main provider of repertory (that the composers were largely foreigners with Parisian connexions – for instance, Kreutzer, Gluck, Sacchini, Piccinni and Cherubini – was a reflection of the long-enduring tendency of non-French composers to have a crucial influence on French opera). Goethe himself, directing the theatre at Weimar from 1791, turned the emphasis towards Viennese and Italian opera, with only four French works appearing between 1791 and 1799 (Baumann, 1985, 262–6); but he was one of the first Germans, and certainly the most influential of the time, to sense the significance of *Die Zauberflöte*. The opera reached Weimar at the beginning of 1794, and was to remain easily the most popular there for the rest of the decade, even in the mutilations which Goethe inexplicably allowed to be inflicted on the text by his brother-in-law Christian Vulpius. Within a year, admiration for Schikaneder's stagecraft, as well as for Mozart's music, led Goethe to begin work on a sequel, *Die Zauberflöte, zweiter Teil*, retaining the original characters and even settings. Collaboration was offered to Paul Wranitzky, who despite the success of his *Oberon* had the discretion to back away from valorous competition with Mozart.

Other composers were less hesitant. The most successful was Franz Xaver Süssmayr, whose experience as Mozart's pupil and assistant, and as harpsichordist and conductor in Vienna, made him an obvious choice when Schikaneder was seeking to capitalize on the success of *Die Zauberflöte* at his Theater auf der Wieden. Without imitating the plot of its predecessor, *Der Spiegel von Arkadien* (1794) draws upon some of its ingredients. There is a noble hero, Ballamo, seeking Philanie, whom Tarkeleon, the evil sorcerer brooding from his tower over the country he rules, recognizes as the daughter of his enemy, the King of Thessaly. A pair of comic lovers, Metallio and Giganie, are employed as viper-catchers; and among the confusions of a tangled plot is the use of the magic mirror of the opera's title, provided by Tarkeleon, which leads a woman to believe its possessor to be the man she loves. When Ballamo overhears Philanie's loving words to Metallio and the mirror, he angrily rejects her and she finds herself in Tarkeleon's thrall, from which she is only rescued through the agency of Jupiter and Juno, assisted by the genies Agathos and Kallos.

There are Mozartian echoes in the music. One is virtually parody: in Act II, Metallio's 'Seid ich so viele Weiber sah' is a close imitation of 'Der Vogelfänger bin ich ja', a calculated invocation of so popular a number since both Papageno and Metallio were sung by Schikaneder himself. A good many of the numbers keep to this Lied-like condition, among them Giganie's rondo 'Zu tändeln und zu scherzen', a lively piece that is superficially Mozartian but lacks the originality to add any real brilliance to the sparkle. Juno's Act II aria 'Juno wird stets um dich schweben' has something of Sarastro's dignity, but weakness of invention in the simple lines is shown by an attempted distraction with inappropriate coloratura. Other echoes include a pretty, childlike duet for the Genies, lightly scored, 'Die Milch ist gesunden'. It is often when Süssmayr departs furthest from the *Magic Flute* model that he is most successful. Though it has roots in Mozartian practice, Philanie's desperate rondo, 'Weh mir, ich bin vergessen und verlassen', has a power of its own, a tense opening recitative leading to a rondo with expressive contrasts between wind and strings, and with an effective Mozartian modulation as the horns hold the tonic, G, to make it the third of the new key as Philanie comes in strongly on the new tonic, E♭. Most remarkable of all is Tarkeleon's superb Vengeance Aria at his recognition of Philanie,

'Der Tag der Rache ist erschienen'. Taking as his model the Queen of the Night's vengeful fury, Süssmayr's Tarkeleon is a match for Cherubini's Dourlinski and many another vengeful villain, and directly anticipates in manner the vehemence of Beethoven's Pizarro and Weber's Caspar, rage and envy manifesting themselves in a D minor Allegro marked by furious arpeggiated melodies that include tense augmented intervals, much of the expression passing to an orchestra given over to restless syncopations, surging chromatic scales, jagged accents and violent dynamic alternations, with swirling wind, stabbing brass and a background of seething strings (Example 17).

Schikaneder got his success: the opera achieved 113 performances in Vienna by 1804. His other attempt to cash in – and he was in increasingly difficult financial straits – on the triumph of *Die Zauberflöte* and the proliferation of 'sequels' by writing his own was less of a success. *Das Labyrinth* was produced at the Theater auf der Wieden in 1798, to music by Peter Winter, and takes the story up with the marriage of Tamino and Pamina. The Queen of the Night is not done with them, however, nor with Sarastro. He sends the lovers for a final trial into a labyrinth, where the Queen abducts them; and only after a protracted battle are they reunited. Monostatos, in the guise of a bird, has meanwhile tried to woo Pamina, but she is rescued by a whole army of Papageno's relations, advancing to a glockenspiel march.

Some of the characteristics of the original work are reproduced, such as Papageno's pan-pipe scale (taken over for deceitful reasons by Monostatos) and his married duet with Papagena. They serenade each other in a charming number – it is of course with the lighter music that Winter approaches Mozart most closely – reiterating cries of 'La-la-le-ra, la-la-le-ra': the original 'Pa-pa-pa-pa-pa-pa-geno' calls are saved for his family in rather a protracted drinking song (it was an effect that had captivated audiences' imagination, and was still vivid in 1806 when Friedrich Himmel made use of it in *Die Sylphen*). There are references such as the thrice-three chords that open the overture, and these are later associated with Sarastro; but by taking part in the

Example 17
(a) Mozart: *Die Zauberflöte* (1791), The Queen of the Night
(b) Süssmayr: *Der Spiegel von Arkadien* (1794), Tarkeleon

action, Sarastro forfeits some of his aloof authority, recovering it
most fully as he sends the lovers into the labyrinth, 'Nun wandelt
muthig ihre Strasse'. Comparisons with Mozart become odious
when Winter attempts hieratic solemnity with a chorus in the Act I
finale, 'Heil! heil! o Isis und Osiris'. Tamino's rediscovery of Pamina
begins promisingly, but is too long and lacks the radiance of the

(Ha! What a moment! I shall slake my vengeance, your fate beckons:
to run him through the heart, O bliss, O great joy!)

(Hell's net has ensnared you! Nothing can save you from the abyss.)

Example 17
(c) Beethoven: *Leonore* (1805), Pizarro
(d) Weber: *Der Freischütz* (1821), Caspar

original. It is the Queen of the Night who opens the whole work
with a Vengeance Aria, 'Hier bald nahet sich die Stunde'; but lacking
as it does the sinister glitter of her original incarnation, the coloratura
remains mere virtuoso display. This ambitious scena sets the tone for
what is the opera's main weakness, a lack of dramatic timing, so that
repeatedly Mozart's swiftness, and his capacity to respond to a new
turn in the action with new invention, are replaced by inert scenes
that merely work themselves out musically.

To the influence of *Die Zauberflöte* can also be attributed the incidence of no fewer than seven German operas on Shakespeare's *The Tempest* in the closing years of the century. They are by Friedrich Fleischmann (Regensburg, 1796), Reichardt (Berlin, 1798), Winter (1798), Johann Rudolf Zumsteeg (Leipzig, 1798), Müller (Vienna, 1798), Friedrich Wilhelm Haack (Stettin, 1798) and Johann Daniel Hensel (Hirschberg, 1799) (an Italian eighth, by Luigi Caruso, Naples, 1798, can be no more than coincidence). As Winton Dean has pointed out,

> It is easy see why the plot's double intrigue of courtly conspiracy and low comedy, crossed with the spectacular elements of storm, shipwreck, and supernatural manifestations and the allegory of good and evil, appealed to the German temperament . . . There is an obvious correspondence between Prospero, Miranda, Ferdinand, and Caliban on the one hand and Sarastro, Pamina, Tamino, and Monostatos on the other, and no great ingenuity is needed to work Ariel into the posture of the three genii and Trinculo or Stephano into that of Papageno; Shakespeare even has a Queen of Night in the wings in the person of Sycorax.   (Dean, 1982, 457)

Neither Winter's opera (to a text by Franz Xaver Caspar) nor Müller's (text by Karl Friedrich Hensler) pursues these analogies: Müller's more or less slips into Viennese routine with extended and exaggerated comic roles, copious transformation scenes, magic instruments and other tricks of the Leopoldstädtertheater trade. But *Die Geisterinsel*, the text by Friedrich Wilhelm Gotter, after a version by his friend Friedrich von Einsiedel, reluctantly published in *Die Horen* by Schiller and hailed by Goethe as a masterpiece, was carefully structured to invite an operatic response to Shakespeare's drama. Viennese magic elements are not lacking, neither are sensational storm and transformation effects, but the lessons of *Die Zauberflöte* have been learnt in the manner in which a story of love and idealism threads its way through events both comic and threatening in a mysterious realm. An approach was made to Mozart, whose untimely death prevented discussions from getting anywhere, and several other composers were considered. Dittersdorf's response seems to have irritated Gotter for its attempts to reduce the text to his own kind of cliché. Fleischmann's setting was a failure, even when promoted by Goethe in Weimar in 1798, and those by Hensel (who adapted it considerably) and by Haack made no serious way.

Gotter's libretto brings on to the stage Caliban's mother Sycorax and invents a good spirit, Maja, respectively played by an actor and an actress. Sycorax is about to return to the island and, together with Caliban (busy making advances to Miranda), to attempt to overthrow Prospero, who must spend that night in a deep sleep. Ariel draws a ship through a storm towards the shore. Fernando is discovered, but Prospero decides to test the depth of the love that springs up between him and Miranda. Caliban persuades some of the shipwrecked crew to enlist with him against Prospero, who enjoins the lovers to keep watch that night separately counting corals. They are sent fleeing by a thunderstorm that conjures up Sycorax, but Maja intervenes to save Prospero. He wakes to find Miranda safe. An attempt by Caliban to kill Prospero is frustrated when Ariel substitutes a vision, and Caliban hurls himself into the sea to join Sycorax. Another ship brings news that the tyrant of Milan has been overthrown, and, breaking his magic staff, Prospero leaves the island to resume his rightful rule. These incidents, and the highly unShakespearean alterations, serve Gotter's purpose in disposing the play for a suitable balance of male and female singers (five and three respectively), with comic interest subordinated to the main dramatic elements. This he reinforced in his instructions to the composer for specific vocal forms and even in suggestions for musical treatment and for particular orchestration. Even though it is easier to share Schiller's doubts than Goethe's admiration, it is also possible to understand that Gotter's intention was not to follow the action of the play literally or to copy its speeches, but to make its characters and the atmosphere of magic and romance amenable to music.

Gotter did not live to see Reichardt's success with *Die Geisterinsel*: he died in 1797, in his work for Benda and with this text having contributed much to German opera. Reichardt follows many of his ideas and suggestions, and is drawn some way from his natural manner into more ambitious musical structures. Though Gotter saves the storm for the end of Act I, Reichardt takes the opportunity to compose it in his overture. This is quite an impressive affair, with plentiful use of atmospheric timpani and (a later addition) booming trombones: this was becoming a fashionable mannerism, so that only a few years later an irritated correspondent to the *AMZ* was complaining, 'Posaunen, Posaunen – dies sind für unsere neuesten Komponisten das Herrlichste, gerade wie die Trommeln für die Kinder' (*AMZ* 5 (1803), 817) ('Trombones, trombones – these are the finest thing for our latest composers, just like drums for children'). The overture anticipates later German practice by using themes from the main opera to make an instrumental drama: Reichardt, an outspoken admirer of the Revolution, had had the opportunity to observe French example when he visited Paris in 1794. What he heard there may well also have influenced him in his attempts to confer some sense of unity on the opening scenes by use of a simple motivic figure. The storm finale is another structure suggesting French example in its extended and linked series of numbers; here, too, the French enhanced reliance on instrumental colour for effect that marks the work, especially in its inventive use of wind and brass, is at its most striking. Nevertheless, Reichardt's reach is greater than his grasp, and he is less convincingly himself here, or in the transformation scenes, than when he is writing simple numbers, in at least one of them, Miranda's coral-counting song which opens Act III, achieving something approaching sublimity (Example 18). Zumsteeg's setting, produced only four months after Reichardt's, is in some ways a superior response to the libretto. Though characterization was not Zumsteeg's strong point, he does make Miranda a more passionate and sensitive character than Reichardt's child of nature (Example 19). The duet between her and Prospero, 'Vernimm die Schrecken', has considerable dramatic momentum as their relationship (some of the music suggests their actual kinship) unfolds in a sequence of aria, arioso and recitative. Ariel is a more conventional figure, marked only by flying coloratura, and the comic figures lack real individuality, though the banquet scene is saved by Zumsteeg's gift for the dramatic scena in another sequence of contrasted tempos (something which he had learnt in Stuttgart under the influence of

Un poco Adagio

Trau-ri-ge Ko-ral-len, zä-len soll ich euch! Doch wer zält die Thrä-nen

die ver-mischt mit euch in den Schoss mir fal-len? Trau-ri-ge Ko-ral-len,

zä-len soll ich euch! zä-len soll ich euch.

(Unhappy corals, I must count you! But who counts the tears that, mingled with you, fall into my lap?)

Example 18   Reichardt: *Die Geisterinsel* (1798), Miranda

MIRANDA

von der Weh-muth hin-ge-streut, von der

Weh-muth, von Weh-muth hin-ge-streut.

(. . . strewn with sadness.)

Example 19   Zumsteeg: *Die Geisterinsel* (1798), Miranda

Jommelli, and which in his songs greatly impressed the young Schubert). The storm builds up splendidly with threatening rhythms and a 'pathetic' oboe solo by way of scurrying violins and vehement woodwind interjections. Zumsteeg's greater mastery of harmonic drama and his more vigorous rhythmic sense give his extended structures direction and potency where Reichardt's are sometimes little more than a series, and his orchestration is in no way inferior. Following Miranda's sorrowful aria at Maja's tomb accompanied by flute and strings, a chorus of spirits scored for only clarinets and bassoons strikes with sombre effect; Caliban's evil nature is underlined with his heavy, relentless scoring; and the farewell sends Prospero on his way back to Milan with a lucidly scored Adagio serenade for clarinets, horns and bassoons. The work made a great impression: it was given an extended review over three issues of the newly founded *Allgemeine Musikalische Zeitung* (AMZ 1 (1799), 657–75, 689–711, 785–813), and had various revivals during the nineteenth century. But for his early death in 1802 at the age of forty-two, Zumsteeg might have made a considerable contribution to Romantic opera. He was one of those who had followed in Benda's footsteps with a duodrama (*Tamira*, 1788). But only two works came after *Die Geisterinsel*. *Das Pfauenfest* (1801) is an Arthurian opera, with a prominent part for Fee Morgana, reflecting Méhul's *Ariodant* of 1799 and also anticipating *Euryanthe* and *Genoveva* with the false accusation and eventual justification of an innocent girl in a courtly setting. The posthumous one-act *Elbondocani* (1803), set in Baghdad, is another well-scored piece with some good songs, suffering chiefly from a banal libretto.

The *Tempest* settings are among the most effective of those operas which make use of the growing interest in magic, in the exotic, in the quest theme, and in other elements, including the expressive connexion between serious and comic, given new weight and resonance by *Die Zauberflöte*, and now moving into territory that was being claimed for Romanticism. It was in a large part the subject matter that led to the wide-spread triumphs of what were in their different ways the two most successful operas between *Die Zauberflöte* and *Fidelio*.

Peter Winter's *Das unterbrochene Opferfest* (1796) adds, to a Viennese mixture of German song, solemn choruses, opera buffa and opera seria, a dénouement derived from the increasingly influential French rescue opera. In prehistoric Peru, Elvira and Villacuma take vengeance on the Englishman Murney by arranging for him to be sacrificed to the Sun God. He faces death bravely, despite his love for Myrha, but is saved at the last minute when the deception is exposed. The serious arias are generally plain to the point of a dullness that is not enlivened by coloratura of formidable difficulty, which also serves to halt any kind of dramatic movement. Some of the lighter songs for the servants are nicely turned, though their lack of dramatic relevance was fastened upon by one of the opera's admirers, Carl Maria von Weber, who commented approvingly on their omission from a performance he was reviewing. The most powerful scene is that of the interrupted sacrifice itself, together with that in which Murney confronts his end. A sombre C minor Adagio leads to an Allegro showing him resolute in the face of death, with a strong, confident melody over an accompaniment turbulent with jarring tremolos, rushing scales, urgent syncopations and sudden alternations of *ff* and *pp*. A contemplative A♭ interlude, with Murney reflecting upon death in somewhat Hamlet-like vein, leads to a strongly confident C major conclusion. The scene is well developed and well varied, not least by the skilful use of modulation. Nevertheless, the opera's successful career, contrasted with its real artistic quality, suggests that a potential for German opera had been glimpsed, rather than a true achievement reached.

It was, on the face of it, more extraordinary that the second work to have won European popularity, and retained it for decades, *Das Donauweibchen*, should have been a simple fairy-tale piece consisting of a string of short songs and duets by one of Müller's assistants. Ferdinand Kauer, violinist and trumpeter at the Theater in der Leopoldstadt from 1782 and director from about 1789, was no more than a capable theatre musician, competent enough at providing pleasant but unremarkable music for a given text. This one, described as 'Ein romantisch-komisch Volksmärchen mit Gesang in drei Aufzügen, nach einer Sage der Vorzeit' ('A Romantic-comic folk tale with song in three acts, after a legend of olden times'), was by the theatre's director from 1786, Karl Friedrich Hensler; more immediately, it was after a novel by 'B—g' (Thomas Berling), which was in turn a near-copy of the story *Die Saalnixe* by Christian Vulpius. Albrecht, with Käsperle in attendance, is intercepted on his way to his wedding to Bertha by the Danube water-spirit Hulda, upon whom he once fathered a daughter, Lilli. Hulda and Lilli try to regain his love with all manner of tricks, disguises and apparitions, and with farcical humiliations for Käsperle. Albrecht insists on going through with the marriage, even rejecting Hulda's plea for just three nights of love a year. However, she has the last word, using her magic to carry him off; and a final tableau shows him at her feet in her watery realm. Hensler seems to have been chiefly concerned to outdo his rivals in providing his audience with theatrical sensation, for he divided the three-act libretto into fifty-five different entrances in fifteen scenes, linking and filling them with an almost impossible number of transformations, magical happenings and bewildering illusions. Hulda's transformations include an old mother, a gardener's girl, a veiled lady, a young knight, the ancestress of a noble family, a female hermit, a coal-girl, a pilgrim, a miller girl, a Swabian zither-player and finally the water-spirit queen.

For this tale, Kauer provided an untroubling succession of songs, some two-thirds of them folk-like and simply harmonized, beginning with a cheerful Huntsmen's Chorus, 'Das Riedhorn erschallt im rauschenden Wald'. There are few through-composed scenes, though the music has a little more complexity in the introduction and the act finales. Most of the numbers are for Hulda, a soprano who is required to rise to d'''; she was sung at the first performance by Anna Gottlieb, Mozart's first Pamina. Hulda's four-year-old child Lilli is also a soprano, and was sung by Müller's six-year-old daughter Rösi, later famous as Therese Grünbaum. There is another soprano role for the water-spirit Erlinde, modest baritone roles for Käsperle (essentially a comic actor) and the mastersinger Minnewart, and a bass role for Albrecht's squire Fuchs. Albrecht and Bertha, as well as eight other roles, are all spoken. However, the score does manage to include a number of touching pieces such as Lilli's 'Es wechseln die Männer so schnell wie der Wind' and Hulda's 'In meinem Schlösschen ist's gar fein', and these won instant popularity. Within five weeks of the first performance, on 11 January 1798, a second part was performed, on 13 February 1798. There is a similar disposition of roles, with Hulda undergoing a further dozen transformations; and in 1803 popular demand led to a sequel, *Die Nymphe der Donau*, with music 'in Kauer's manner' by Gottlieb Bierey. By then, the piece had begun to spawn imitations, rewritings, further sequels, translations, parodies, all the apparatus of instant theatrical success. It was seized upon by the humblest stages looking for a quick financial return; it was taken up at Weimar by Goethe (as *Die Saalnixe*, and provided him with something in the beguiling Luciane in his novel *Die*

Wahlverwandtschaften); and E. T. A. Hoffmann staged it in Bamberg (also referring to it in *Der goldne Topf*), then persuading Friedrich de la Motte Fouqué to turn the *Undine* story on the subject into the libretto of his most famous opera. It crossed Europe in all directions and rooted itself in Russia in a new setting on the banks of the Dnieper, with a new text and new music in further different versions and sequels. The piece inspired the unfinished dramatic poem by Pushkin (who also quotes 'In meinem Schlösschen' in *Eugene Onegin*), and thence Dargomyzhsky's opera *Rusalka* of 1856, helping to keep alive a myth that was still potent by the time of Dvořák's *Rusalka* of 1901.

Das Donauweibchen touched on a nerve in the European imagination. The piece seems to be no more than an opportunistic combination of *Ritterdrama*, *Schauerroman*, *Kasperliade* and *Feenmärchen*, in the context of the Viennese magic theatre. Yet this novel heroine and her plight fascinated the new Romantic generation. Whether seductive or vengeful Slav *rusalka*, alluring Donauweibchen or betrayed Undine, the water-spirit had an appeal across national styles and transcended musical and theatrical conventions. Her bewitching power has obvious connexions with that of the Loreley and of Keats's Belle Dame Sans Merci, other figures of feminine beauty and terror who rose from the waters of the male subconscious at this exact time. The wild, instinctive creature and the rational, calculating man are drawn irresistibly together, yet are unable to find a true marriage. Each is liable to forfeit life and soul in the attempt. Even if the music was shallow, the tale spoke deep. Nature and Reason, too far sundered in the Enlightenment, are, in a post-Rousseau age, vainly seeking a new union.

With Germany remaining a loose association of states, each in a different and changing position towards France and presenting no united front, neither revolution nor war stemmed the tide of operas from Paris. It was a tide that ebbed and flowed with political events, channelled into different operatic centres and reaching different heights at different times. Repertories also changed. The shifting popularity of various genres and composers reflected the tastes of ordinary audiences, but there was increasingly an awareness among a more educated public, and especially among musicians and writers, of those composers who held a particular significance for German opera. In the years following the Revolution, there certainly remained an undiminished appetite for the light pieces that translated easily and enlivened German theatrical fare, as Weber was still to reflect in 1816:

> Seit einigen Jahren fangen die Erzeugnisse der französischen Muse an,
> hauptsächlich das Repertoire der deutschen Bühnen zu füllen, und der
> Geschmack an diesen leicht dahinspielenden Weisen, die mit einer
> liebenswürdigen Oberflächligkeit angenehm zu unterhalten wissen,
> nimmt mehr und mehr überhand.   (Weber, 1908, 267)

> (It is some years since productions of the French muse began to
> dominate the repertories of German theatres, and there is a growing
> taste for these pieces, light, easily staged here, whose delightful
> superficiality provides a pleasant form of entertainment. Weber, 1981,
> 156)

Weber was writing about Isouard's *Joconde* (1814), the most successful work of a composer he held in low regard, finding little to praise even in another highly popular piece, *Cendrillon* (1810). He was essentially making a distinction between what have often been described as *Konversationsopern* and more serious works, even though it is not always a very real one, especially since in translating the former for German stages there could often be a lightening, a localization, or otherwise a shift in emphasis (see Schneider, 1997). The composers with greater influence were often also popular, but, more importantly, they caught the eyes of writers and the ears of composers who were arguing and working for German opera.

Almost every German operatic centre of any importance found room for French opera, but certain composers may be singled out, and were singled out by critics, for their appeal to German taste. Some were of little renown. At least one work by Adrien Quaisain, the melodrama *Le Jugement de Salomon* (1802), was to be found in German repertories. E. T. A. Hoffmann gave it an appreciative but much-qualified review (Hoffmann, 1967–8, 238–42; 1989, 217–21), and there was even a plan for it to open the new house in Königsberg in 1810. Dominique Della-Maria also had successes in Germany with his *Le Prisonnier*, to a scarcely lesser extent with his *L'Opéra-comique* and *L'Oncle valet* (all 1798, in one act). *Le secret* (1796), a light, witty one-act comedy of misunderstandings by Jean-Pierre Solié, crossed and recrossed Germany for over half a century (it was the second piece which Weber conducted during his Dresden intendancy, though he avoided writing about it). Henri-Montan Berton's operas, including minor pieces such as *Le Grand Deuil* (1801), were performed and even published in Germany: as well as a certain melodic enterprise, his music shows a feeling for instruments and he makes some use of motive. However, his greatest success came with a more ambitious work, *Aline, reine de Golconde* (1803), popular throughout Germany and chosen by Hoffmann for his conducting début in Bamberg in 1808. Charles-Simon Catel's lighter operas, above all his first, *Sémiramis* (1802), remained popular, as did those of Pierre Gaveaux, especially *Le Petit Matelot* (1796), though his *Léonore* (1798) seems not to have crossed the Rhine. Even such minor works were regularly reviewed in the columns of the *AMZ*, and the publication of selections and indeed of whole operas was announced in the journal's regular *Intelligenz-Blatt*.

Isouard's great Paris rival Boieldieu was still more widely performed in Germany, and had greater significance. Only four months
after its première, the most successful of his operas of this period,
Jean de Paris (1812), began its conquest of German stages with two
productions in different translations in Vienna at the end of August
1812. Weber, who conducted several of Boieldieu's operas in Prague
and Dresden, set him well above Isouard. In an article introducing
Jean de Paris he put his finger on some essential national differences
when he claimed that while a single idea could stimulate a German
composer's imagination, and a single word the Italian's (presumably
a backhanded compliment to do with coloratura), the French composer made his best effect through intelligent use of words for music;
and he admired Boieldieu for effecting a rapprochement between the
three styles. He went on to praise Boieldieu for his superiority over
his rivals:

> durch seinen fließenden, schön geführten Gesang, durch die planmäßige
> Haltung der einzelnen Stücke wie des Ganzen, durch die treffliche,
> sorgsame Instrumentierung und die Korrektheit, die, den Meister
> bezeichnend, allein Anspruch auf Dauer und klassisches Leben in der
> Kunstwelt gibt. (Weber, 1908, 288)
>
> (by the freedom and elegance of his vocal line, the skilful construction of
> both individual numbers and the work as a whole, by his careful and
> excellent use of the orchestra and that masterly correctness which alone
> confirms a composer's claim to durability as a classic. Weber, 1981, 220)

Ten of the seventeen operas which Boieldieu wrote between 1798 and
1812 had careers in Germany, but it was not really until *Jean de Paris*
that he found the qualities which earned him Weber's admiration as a
composer from whom much could be learnt. However, there was
appreciation for his gently Romantic manner, as well as his harmless
mockery of contemporary fashions that included Italian opera. Boieldieu can poke light fun at provincialism, turn the fashion for rescue
opera (a term of much later coinage: see Charlton, 1992) to his own
ends in *Béniowski* (1800) by having the entire cast rescued from Siberia,
and amuse himself at the expense of exoticism by making Késie in *Le
Calife de Bagdad* (1800) seek a lover in the styles of France, Italy, Spain,

Scotland, Germany and England. Later in his career he achieved a minor masterpiece with *La Dame blanche* (1825), a work whose Romantic charm captivated Weber when he saw it in Paris.

There was much more for German composers in some of the operas of Nicolas Dalayrac. Some twenty of his lightest works, such as the enduringly popular *Nina, ou La Folle par amour* (1786), were staple repertory pieces in Germany in the 1780s and 1790s; but other rather more substantial pre-Revolutionary works widely taken up in several translations or in the original included *Azémia, ou Le Nouveau Robinson* (1786) (one of the many so-called *Robinsonaden* that built upon the European popularity of Daniel Defoe's *Robinson Crusoe*, but a work that also holds echoes of *The Tempest*), *Renaud d'Ast* (1787), *Raoul, Sire de Créqui* (1789) and *Les Deux Petits Savoyards* (1789). Beethoven owned a score of the latter, and Weber staged both this and *Adolphe et Clara* (1799); but for German composers in general the two most influential operas were *Léon, ou Le Château de Monténéro* (1798) and *Léhéman, ou La Tour de Neustadt* (1801). They possess a number of the most significant elements of the French operas of the Revolutionary period. Weber praised them as Dalayrac's most accomplished works, singling out two characteristics in his review of the 1811 Munich performance of *Léhéman* (which Max Heigel's translation as *Makdonald* relocates in 'Tudor Castle' in Scotland, metamorphosing the Hungarian rebel Ragotzi into Bonnie Prince Charlie). One was the functional use of the overture, which 'versetzt uns sogleich mitten in das Leben des Stücks durch ihr herzlichen, spannenden und kräftig auflodernden Stellen' ('transports us at once into the excitement of the drama by its delightful alternation of charm, excitement and sudden exhibitions of forcefulness') (Weber, 1908, 114; Weber, 1981, 83). Even more important was Dalayrac's emphasis on the use of reminiscence motive, the recall of music with a previous dramatic association, skilfully used here so as to express a new twist in the drama, and even to communicate between characters over the heads of their captors:

> Die Romanze 'Ein Pilger irrt' wird besonders durch ihre innige
> Verwebung mit dem Gange der ganzen Handlung interessant. Bei den

gespanntesten, entscheidendsten Szenen erscheint die freundliche
Melodie wie ein tröstender Stern und verheißt den erwartungsvollen
Zuhörern Rettung seiner Lieben. Solche Stücke sind die zarten Fäden im
Gewebe einer Oper, die von einem wahren dramatischen Komponisten,
so gesponnen wie hier, unwiderstehlich die Herzen der Zuhörer fesseln
müssen.   (Weber, 1908, 114)

(The Romanze 'Un voyageur s'est égaré' holds the attention by its close
connexion with the drama, at whose most exciting and critical moments
the amiable melody of the Romance appears, like a comforting star, to
reassure the anxious listener of his loved ones' rescue. Such passages
form the delicate threads in the fabric of an opera, which, spun, as here,
by a composer with a genuine dramatic gift, must irresistibly enmesh the
hearts of the listeners. Weber, 1981, 83)

As a German composer inspired, he said, more by an idea than by a
word, Weber clearly appreciated the associative use of the melody in
its various transformations, and he was to repeat the metaphor of the
threads in his review of Spohr's *Faust* in 1816 (Weber, 1908, 273–5;
Weber, 1981, 190–3). Dalayrac's melody is no mere identifying tag but
a living theme expressing an emotion that fills the characters
throughout this rescue opera, that of hope aroused, sustained,
frustrated, almost lost and finally realized. In *Léon* Weber could
scarcely have missed other uses of this motivic technique, or the
impressive overture whose 'symphonic power and musical originality set the emotional as well as the tonal world of the opera very
firmly in place' (Charlton, 1978, 44). Dalayrac is by no means unique
for his time in his ability to use keys and key patterns to make
dramatic associations and provide a plot structure, speaking with
music directly to the listener's sensibilities. However, in their use of
these characteristics his operas hold particular suggestions that
Weber was to develop in his own mature operas.

The roots go rather deeper. Much in Dalayrac can already be
found in at least one of Monsigny's operas. *Le Déserteur* (1769) had a
long and successful career on German stages. It was influential for its
powerful dramatic momentum (interrupting or actually breaking
conventional forms when the plot demanded), for its efforts, albeit

tentative, to make a key structure dramatically expressive, and not least for its overture. This pioneering piece epitomizes the plot by making the music of the chorus which celebrates its successful outcome surround the music of the central episode of the petition to the king on behalf of the deserter. Monsigny's remarkable work drew a lot of attention and admiration. However, if only by virtue of his immense popularity – almost thirty of his operas had been in circulation in German repertories by the end of the century – Grétry's mastery of the overture was still more influential. Over the course of his operatic output he sought to find ways of binding the instrumental introduction to the drama, whether by incorporating melodies which were to have dramatic importance, by subtly fore-shadowing them, or – as in the case of the popular *Zémire et Azor* – by actually uniting the overture with a storm to the main opera. The increasingly absorbing question of motive and its use was also given great stimulus by Grétry, in several of his operas of the 1770s which were widely performed in Germany but nowhere more than in one of his greatest successes of all, *Richard Cœur-de-Lion* (1784).

There was much here for the German composer. The opera set an early example of an historical subject from the period of high chivalry, with local colour on stage and in the score (including by means of functional use of the chorus) and a strong moral content in the plot. The most celebrated feature of the opera is the nine-fold repetition of Richard's song with which, following legend, the squire Blondel seeks out and identifies his master languishing in prison. Like much in Grétry, even in this opera, the music can appear slender for the expressive burden placed upon it; but with the Romance 'Une fièvre brûlante' limitations are turned to subtle advantage. The melody is first heard unaccompanied, and by its very anachronisms – the use of a modern violin, a modern interpretation of trouvère melody – makes its appeal to the imagination rather than to an antiquarian sense. Hence, its closeness to Grétry's idiom and method allows it to be more than simple citation and to enter the score in manifold ways and to play a developing role in the musical drama. The act of recognition between Blondel and Richard's beloved

Marguerite, when he first plays the tune, makes music an actual means of communication, a dramatic device but one with emotions exchanged between the characters and at the same time speaking directly to the audience. It enables Grétry to play with great art upon the possibility of re-presenting the tune in different contexts and with different settings and accompaniments so that it becomes the agent of the successful rescue of the king, but (again) the expression of the emotions that join him, Marguerite and the faithful Blondel. Past association, present tension and hopes for the future can all be brought together in the melody, sometimes played simply, sometimes given new expression by the orchestra, sometimes secreted in a vocal line. There is much in the work to justify Weber's observation, 'Vielleicht ist Grétry der einzige der in Frankreich erblühten Komponisten, der bedeutend lyrischen, ja sogar oft romantischen Sinn hatte' ('Grétry may well be the only French composer to have displayed in his music an unmistakably lyrical, indeed often even a Romantic, sense') (Weber, 1908, 292; Weber, 1981, 224).

Nevertheless, the two Parisian composers of the quarter century between the Revolution and the War of Liberation who most powerfully affected German composers, including Weber himself, and indeed the whole course of German Romantic opera, were Méhul and Cherubini. Méhul's use of motive owes more to Dalayrac than to Grétry. The duet 'Gardez-vous de la jalousie', in Act II of Méhul's second opera, *Euphrosine* (1790), quickly became famous as an example of how a simple figure could come to stand for an emotion motivating the drama, in this case (and as often with Méhul) jealousy. It consists of no more than alternating thirds, introduced as the villainous Countess sets out to implant jealousy in the heart of her rival by warning her against it. There is nothing representational in the motive itself; it is the insidious working of the figure across sixty-three of the first seventy bars of the duet, in bare octaves without accompaniment, that creates its sinister effect, so that rather than being superficially expressive of pain, the music dramatizes the burrowing destructiveness of the emotion. The responsibility for the quasi-symphonic development of this (a very different matter from

Grétry's reminiscence motive in *Richard*) is in turn cast upon harmony and orchestration. Hence 'Méhul's motif and its treatment, in so far as their effects may be tabulated at all, symbolise: (*a*) the abstract emotion of jealousy; (*b*) the dynamic force by which jealousy operates; (*c*) the objects causing the jealousy; (*d*) the ability of the countess to infect another with jealousy; (*e*) the countess's own jealousy' (Charlton, 1976, 369).

Berlioz, for whom *Euphrosine* was Méhul's masterpiece, regarded this duet as 'le plus terrible exemple de ce que peut l'art musical uni à l'action dramatique, pour exprimer la passion' ('the most tremendous example possible of the art of music unified with dramatic action to express passion'), and compared the effect to Iago's 'O! beware, my lord, of jealousy; / It is the green-ey'd monster which doth mock / The meat it feeds on' (Berlioz, 1852, 394). The consequence was to advance the orchestra further to the centre of the drama; and Méhul's mastery of instruments, his interest in harmonic and tonal experiment (with sensational use of dominant minor ninths, Neapolitan sixths and diminished sevenths), and the greatly extended fluency which resulted from his symphonic use of motive aroused the keenest interest in Germany. Building upon *Euphrosine* in *Stratonice* (1792; an opera not widely performed in Germany), he developed his ideas still further in *Mélidore et Phrosine* (1794). The theme of jealousy is again central, here in the context of the incestuous passion of a brother for his sister, a subject which curtailed the opera's career in Paris and abroad. It is unlikely that its remarkable innovatory features would have become known in Germany at the time, however much they anticipate later Romantic practice. They include striking modulations (some tritonal, as from D to A♭ and back again), experimental orchestration (including a famous passage for four stopped horns in three different crooks making a chord of A♭), and especially an astonishing sequence of numbers in different genres (song, melodrama, orchestral description) as the heroine plunges into the sea and manages to swim to safety through a storm, pursued by her jealous brother in a boat. From the first notes of the overture, the sea plays a large part in the orchestral fabric of the opera, not only lending the score a distinctive colour (which was increasingly to be a feature of Romantic opera) but in this case even looking forward to Wagner and *Der fliegende Holländer*. This, together with the sustained use of motive, symbolic key associations and a continuity across numbers even when separated by dialogue, all more immediately anticipate Hoffmann's techniques in *Undine* and still more Weber's in *Der Freischütz*.

Ariodant (1799) suffered in Paris from comparison with Berton's *Montano et Stéphanie* (1799) on the same subject, but won respect in Germany and was highly influential, though it did not escape the criticism frequently levelled at Méhul that he could be self-defeatingly learned.

> Ueberall hört man große Intentionen, oft auch recht glücklich ausgeführt; oft aber auch leider durch Ueberladung, und durch das unselige Bestreben harmonisch gelehrt zu seyn, und mehr noch zu scheinen, entstellt und verunglückt.　　　　　(Reichardt, 1804, 114)

> (Throughout one discerns great intentions, often very successfully realized; but also often regrettably from over-emphasis, and from the unfortunate urge to be harmonically learned, even more to seem so, disfigured and ineffective.)

The chivalric plot (taken, like that of Handel's opera, from Ariosto's *Orlando furioso*) is set in a Romantic Scotland, and turns on Ariodant being tricked into believing his beloved Ina unfaithful through a device of Othon, until all is finally revealed. The idea of jealousy that obsessed Méhul is here presented as furious descending discords associated with Othon's passion. These open no fewer than five of the opera's numbers, but they also permeate the entire score, suffusing it with the corrupting atmosphere of jealousy. No less striking is the orchestration, upon which Méhul, like Cherubini, was increasingly depending for his expressive and atmospheric effects. Much of the opera is set by night or in underground rooms and labyrinthine passages or a thick forest, and Méhul responds with some of the swarthiest orchestration he can contrive, setting the tone at once with an overture (brief, irregular in form, and ending in harmonic mid-air) beginning on three solo cellos and unison double basses. He may well have noted the striking effect of an opera with a dark subject taking place largely in the dark in other works of these dark times: Berton's *Les Rigueurs du cloître* (1790), a topical Parisian piece involving nuns freed from their corruptly run convent; Dalayrac's *Camille, ou Le Souterrain* (1791), in which the heroine is kept imprisoned in the vault of an abandoned convent filled with murky corridors and sinister cellars; Le Sueur's *La Caverne* (1793; widely popular in Germany), a robber opera with the heroine imprisoned in a cave and sought out by a blind minstrel who turns out to be her husband in disguise. However, there is a crucial difference in that, with Méhul's expressive orchestration, instrumental colour advances to the position of a functional element of the music rather than an expression of it, and becomes as much of a pervasive motive as the actual thematic material. The idea exercised a profound influence on Weber's *Euryanthe*, to a similar plot (in particular, the scene opening Weber's Act II, when Lysiart's jealous rage is expressed largely through the dark orchestral turmoil), and through him on Wagner's *Lohengrin*.

Though none of Méhul's operas was more influential musically than *Euphrosine*, *Mélidore et Phrosine* and *Ariodant*, much attention centred on several others. *Héléna* (1803) is an attractive work, in which the wife of the Duke of Arles disguises herself as 'Petit-Jacques' so as to rescue him from prison, with a trumpet signalling the happy dénouement, matters which probably caught Beethoven's eye. *Uthal* (1806) became famous for its 'Ossianic' subject, and for its banishing of violins (and trumpets) from the score so as to suggest a Romantic Scotland, permanently wreathed in mist and harbouring mysterious Romantic passions. A swirling, themeless overture, viola-led, with a disembodied voice calling through the murk, sets the mood impressively; but the ensuing opera is less remarkable, and Méhul was unwise to persist with the orchestration throughout a work which, even in its single act, can exhaust the listener's patience (as it did that of Grétry, an admirer of Méhul, who is said to have offered in exasperation 'un louis pour une chanterelle' – 'a louis for an E string'). Even Cherubini, to whom Méhul owed much, was taken aback by some of his wilder modulations, often through a series of barely related minor keys. *Joseph* (1807), written when Méhul's originality had begun to wane, nevertheless won huge popularity in Germany, and impressed Weber so much that (not only because of problems with singers) he opened his intendancy in Dresden with it in 1817. He prefaced his performance with a shrewd assessment of Méhul's achievement:

> Méhul behauptet unstreitig nächst Cherubini den ersten Rang unter den Komponisten, die auf ihrer künstlerischen Laufbahn in Frankreich sich vorzugsweise entwickelten und bildeten und durch die Wahrheit ihrer Leistungen endlich ein Eigentum aller Nationen wurden. Wenn vielleicht Cherubini noch für genialer zu halten ist, so tritt dagegen bei Méhul mehr Besonnenheit, die weiseste Berechnung und Anwendung seiner Mittel und eine gewisse gediegene Klarheit hervor, die deutlich das angelegentliche Studium der ältesten italienischen Meister und vorzugsweise der Gluckschen dramatischen Schöpfungen beurkundet.
>
> Große dramatische Wahrheit und lebendiges Fortschreiten ohne zweckwidrige Wiederholungen, die Erreichung großer Effekte mit den oft einfachsten Mitteln und eine Ökonomie der Instrumentation, die gerade nur das gibt, was durchaus notwendig ist, sind ihn vorzüglich bezeichnende Eigenschaften. (Weber, 1908, 278–9)

(After Cherubini, Méhul is undoubtably the finest of the composers who have formed and developed their art chiefly in France and eventually, by their unfailing truth to nature, become the property of the whole world. Cherubini may perhaps have more genius, but Méhul is more thoughtful, and his music shows the best-judged calculation and employment of the means at his disposal and a certain solidity and purity evidently achieved by a thorough study of the oldest Italian masters and more particularly of Gluck's dramatic works. The chief hallmarks of his music are great dramatic truth and a vivid forward movement with no irrelevant repetitions, the achievement of great effects often with the simplest means and an economy in his use of the orchestra which leads him to confine himself to what is strictly necessary. Weber, 1981, 208–9)

For Beethoven, Cherubini was the greatest of living opera composers, and he is known to have kept the score of *Les Deux Journées* on his desk. Arriving in Paris in 1788, Cherubini was set to conquer the Opéra with *Démophon*, a version of Metastasio by Marmontel, with various name changes and new characters in an added sub-plot. He found himself mocked for his repetitive handling of the text by a French public for whom language was, as Weber pointed out, a priority. In adapting himself to these demands, as he thought, he moved away from the convention of recitative and aria in the direction of more fluent forms, with long accompanied orchestral recitative merging into arioso and thence fluently into aria; but *Démophon* is a work easier to respect for its pioneering melodic declamation and its forceful use of the orchestra than to admire for its actual artistic success. Spoken dialogue was to remain an essential ingredient of what often continued to be designated as opéra-comique, despite the seriousness of some of the plots; in part, at least, this was an indication that the genre was separating itself in a new way from the aristocratic associations of 'serious' opera while appealing, as a no less serious genre, to an increasingly educated audience. Ever more importance is thus immediately placed upon the orchestra, with which Cherubini's greatest inventive talents lay, especially in the depiction of natural surroundings or cataclysmic events and in the articulation of the characters' emotions. In *Lodoiska* (1791) he had a success that, like his next two operas, *Elisa* (1794) and *Médée* (1797), and also like *Les Deux Journées* (1800), was even greater in Germany than in France.

There was much in *Lodoiska*, the finest rescue opera of the 1790s, to arouse the admiration of German composers and to inspire emulation. The action takes place in Poland, then regarded as a remote, mysterious, tragic country (the third of the devastating Partitions had just been completed by the time of the opera's first German performance, in Berlin in 1797). With all Cherubini's mastery of tone-painting, the overture sets the scene in the thick forest surrounding the castle in which the villainous Dourlinski has imprisoned Lodoiska, Nature at her most sinister, projecting dark emotions and evil intent. Seeking Lodoiska, Count Floreski has arrived beneath the battlements, where he encounters a Tartar band, their leader Titzikan preaching Rousseau-esque noble sentiments. As Floreski tricks his way into the castle, Act I dies away to a nocturnal march (this was a popular idea which perhaps originated in the one ending Act I of Grétry's *Les Deux Avares*: another occurs in the Entr'acte before Act II of Méhul's *Joseph,* and both may have influenced Weber for the end of Act I of *Oberon*). Dourlinski, frustrated in his attempts upon Lodoiska's virtue, delivers himself of a Vengeance Aria that, in its range and its orchestral energy, contributed much to Beethoven's Pizarro and Weber's Caspar. Other striking features of the work include the effect of the stifling prison vaults and the final rescue abetted by the besieged castle catching fire, not only an anticipation of the devices of later Parisian grand opera but (even if it is deliberately caused) a further instance of a violent natural force turning the course of a drama. There is, moreover, the powerful example for rescue opera, and beyond that for Romanticism, of the heroes (Count and Noble Savage side by side) triumphing not with supernatural or royal aid but by human effort. Grétry was among many to admire *Lodoiska*; for Beethoven there was not only the moral example of innocence delivered from tyranny but the flowing dramatic movement and the driving orchestral energy, whole ensembles moving towards symphonic proportions with restless, ferocious string writing punctuated by stabbing woodwind interjections. Cherubini's symphonic finales are anticipated only by Mozart; his chromatic harmony looks forward to Spohr.

In *Elisa,* Cherubini builds upon this greatly enlarged fluency of form and on his sure feeling for instrumental colour. Refused permission to marry Elisa by her father, the painter Florindo flees to Switzerland. The Alps are spread at once before the audience's ears in the singing of a group of monks, a piece of scene-setting that brought a new pictorialism into the use of a chorus in opera. Florindo arrives, and immediately sets up his easel, exclaiming, 'Ces rochers, ces glaciers, quels objets pour les arts!', an interaction between Nature and Art which his servant Germain has no difficulty in identifying as Romantic: 'Vous verrai-je toujours romanesque, exalté?' Florindo seems to be trying to correct this impression with the invocation, 'Poussin, viens m'inspirer!', a surprising choice of muse unless he meant Nicolas's more Romantically inclined brother-in-law Gaspard. False news of Elisa drives Florindo out into the mountains, where he hopes for death but is brought back to the monks' hospice. Elisa arrives with news of the misunderstanding and of her father's death, but before he learns of this Florindo sets off again and is trapped by an avalanche (a harmonically complex scene involving thunderous orchestral cascades that culminate in a diminished seventh C♯-E-G-B♭ over a bass D, with ferocious melodic figures sounding *sforzando* through the murk): it is another instance of Nature intervening in the plot, for he is found beneath the snow and hauled to safety and Elisa's arms. The score is filled with original effects, including eerie strings *sul ponticello*, and there is an emphasis on single instruments and especially clarinet and horn in a manner that was to impress Weber (and, when Cherubini's unaccompanied clarinets call pastorally across echoing distances, Berlioz in the *Symphonie fantastique*). Much in it helped to set Romantic standards, for German composers perhaps above all its example of the move away from singer-melody towards a primarily orchestral drama articulated through a combination of pictorial effect and motivic tension. *Médée* (still technically an opéra-comique and, in its original form, making use of spoken dialogue) is, despite its classical subject, another powerful Romantic opera, sombre in orchestral texture and making ever more enterprising use of wind, and – for all the sudden interruptions, pauses, dynamic extremes and abrupt changes of tempo that place great demands on the central role – continuing to move the burden of the expression away from the vocal line on to the orchestra.

So high had Cherubini's European reputation risen that *Les Deux Journées* reached Germany in 1801, only eighteen months after its Paris première. Though another rescue opera, it was written not in a time of revolutionary ferment but one of social reconciliation, to a text by one of the genuine liberals of these years, Jean-Nicolas Bouilly. For reasons of tact, if not censorship, the action was moved back to the seventeenth century and the time of the Fronde. But it was based, Bouilly claimed, upon a true event of the Revolution, when an heroic water carrier helped some aristocrats to escape the fury of the mob. Both Beethoven and Goethe praised the libretto as among the best known to them, Beethoven perhaps especially because the message it preached was that all men without exception are equal and stand in need of fair treatment. Reichardt was but one composer who admired the elegance and originality of the music and the richness of the orchestration when he saw the work in Paris (Reichardt, 1804, 330–1). But though there is use of motivic recall, this is plain beside what had been achieved by Dalayrac and Méhul, and even Grétry's aria repetitions in *Richard Cœur-de-Lion* have subtler dramatic involvement. Nor are the passages of melodrama more advanced than much that had become common practice a generation before; all the same, their skilful application, as danger deepens, was certainly one feature of the score that impressed Beethoven. The second melodrama, as Armand conceals himself up a tree ('Il fait une chaleur dans le creux de cet arbre') is an immediate model for the Dungeon Scene in *Fidelio*.

The opera's popularity even prompted a German sequel, *Mischelli und sein Sohn* (1806), by Johann Heinrich Clasing, which had some success in his native Hamburg. It is another rescue opera, in which Mischelli's son Anton allows himself to be pressed into the army so as to become one of the imprisoned Armand's guards and bring about his escape. Mischelli has a version of the original Mikéli's motivic aria 'Guidez mes pas' in a similar situation, and the accompaniment to Mikéli's 'Il est sauvé' is used for an instrumental movement; but the music is not otherwise close to Cherubini, except in some enterprising orchestration that includes an Act III Prayer for quintet over a solo double bass. It is, however, marked by some distinctive chromatic harmony, at its most effective when Armand is discovered at the start of Act II languishing in prison. The work's chief weakness is a certain dramatic slackness, but the characters are not without colour nor the music without life.

Weber had nothing but praise for *Les Deux Journées*, making it the subject of an account by a fictional traveller who excitedly chances upon it (Weber, 1908, 106–8; Weber, 1981, 76–9). He was less impressed by *Faniska*, whose plot has a good deal in common with that of *Héléna* and *Fidelio*, as the lovers are rescued from tyrannical imprisonment by an heroic girl disguising herself and a last-minute outside intervention. He conducted it in Prague in 1813, but felt that Cherubini 'habe sich doch zuweilen etwas Zwang angetan, um auf den weichlich gewöhnten Wiener Geschmack einige Rücksicht zu nehmen' ('did some violence to his own inspiration in order to conform with the somewhat effete taste of the Viennese public') (Weber, 1908, 299; Weber, 1981, 235). By the Viennese, the music was found, 'wo sie nicht gar zu künstlich ist, vollkommen ihres grossen Meisters würdig' (*AMZ* 8 (1806), 376) ('when not too arty, wholly worthy of the great master'). However, Weber's most thoughtful assessment of Cherubini came in the introduction he wrote to *Lodoiska* for the performance he conducted in Dresden on 24 July 1817:

> Einer der wenigen Kunstheroen unserer Zeit, der, als klassischer Meister und Schöpfer neuer, eigener Bahnen, ewig in der Geschichte der Kunst hell erglänzen wird. Die Tendenz seiner Geisteskraft gehört, gleich der Mozarts und Beethovens – obwohl jeder auf seine ihm rein eigentümliche Weise – dem in unserer Zeit Vorherrschenden, dem Romantischen an. Ernst, oft bis zum düstern Brüten – stets die schärfestbezeichnendsten Mittel wählend, daher glühendes Kolorit – gigantisch groß im Auffassen des Ganzen und der einzelnen Situation – kurz und energisch – manchmal scheinbar abgerissen, die Ideen hingeworfen, die aber, in dem tiefgedachtesten innern Zusammenhange stehend, mit dem üppig gewürztesten harmonischen Reichtume geschmückt, recht das wahrhaft Bezeichnende dieses Tonschöpfers ausmachen, und die Tiefe seines Gemütes – das, bei den großgedachten Konturen und Massen, die reichlichst ausgestattete Ausführung jedes scheinbaren Nebenzweiges sorgfältig berücksichtigt beurkunden: das ist seine Weise . . .
>
> Ein Anflug von Schwermut ist allen Arbeiten Cherubinis beigemischt, und seine humorreichsten und heitersten Melodien werden immer etwas Rührendes in ihrem Innern tragen. Bei seiner Art zu arbeiten läßt sich am allerwenigsten die ohnedies so einseitig bezeichnende und das

Kunstwerk so elend in zwei Hälften teilen wollende Redensart: dies oder jenes Musikstück sei besonders schön instrumentiert, anwenden. Ein wahrer Meister hat im Augenblicke des Empfindens auch alle ihm zu Gebote stehenden Mittel als Farben vor Augen. Er denkt sich so wenig als der Maler eine nackte Gestalt, die er erst später mit glänzenden Lappen und Steinchen aufputzen möchte. Ja! unter dem reichen Faltenwurfe entdecke man allerdings die innere Ursache desselben in der ihn erzeugenden Muskel usw.; aber das Ganze muß ganz gedacht sein, sonst bringt es auch nur Halbheit vor das Auge oder Ohr des Genießenden, ist ein angeputzter Gliedermann und keine lebende Gestalt. (Weber, 1908, 296–8)

(One of the few really great artistic figures today, a classical master and discoverer of new and individual paths, whose reputation in musical history will never be dimmed. The inclination of his temperament, like that of Mozart and Beethoven – though each in a wholly individual way – coincides with that most common at the present time, namely the Romantic. A serious composer, often to the point of gloomy brooding; always choosing the most sharply defined means, hence his glowing palette; laconic and lively; sometimes apparently brusque; throwing out ideas which in fact have a close inner connexion and when presented with their full harmonic flavour are the distinguishing feature of this composer and explain the depth of his musical character, which, in the vast contours and masses conjured up by his imagination, still takes full account of every apparent detail: that is Cherubini . . .

All Cherubini's music has a dash of melancholy; and even his most humorous and light-hearted melodies always conceal something touching. His method of working makes it impossible to say that this or that work is 'well orchestrated' – an expression that is in any case very one-sided and appears to make a quite unwarrantable division of an idea the moment it occurs to him. No more than a painter does he envisage a naked body that he then decks out with clothes and jewels. Not that beneath the heavy folds of a garment he is not aware of the anatomical details that cause those folds; but the whole picture must be seen *as a whole*, or the public will be aware of no more than a half-creature – a dummy or lay-figure in costume, and not a living human being. Weber, 1981, 233–4)

For German composers, the most significant elements in the

French operas of these years were the growth in the use of motive and the increased reliance on the orchestra. These were of course intimately related. Once the orchestra had assumed greater importance, there was the opportunity to sustain dramatic development by the use of musical ideas related to the drama; conversely, the advance of motive from simple reference to an expression of essential aspects of the drama, and to the development of emotional relationships within it, demanded not only descriptive passages but orchestral writing in something near a symphonic manner. The multifarious opportunities for orchestral description which Romanticism came to offer were presented to audiences by much in these operas; and it was with them that the orchestral interlude began to assume greater significance, and especially that the overture came to be regarded as not merely something to settle audiences into their seats but an essential element in preparing them for the experience of the opera. This had long been advocated by theorists, especially Algarotti:

> Suo principal fine è di annunziare in certo modo l'azione, di preparare l'uditore a ricevere quelle impressioni di affetto che risultano dal totale del dramma. E però da esso ha da prendere atteggiamento e viso, come appunto dalla orazione l'esordio. (Algarotti, 1755, 445)

> (Its principal aim is to announce the action in a conclusive manner, to prepare the listener to receive some of the emotional impressions produced by the whole piece; and therefore to form from it an attitude and a point of view just as is done of an oration from the exordium.)

But as so often in the emergence of Romanticism, practice lagged far behind theory, and it was the example of French composers in the handling of the overture that was repeatedly singled out for praise by composer-critics of the stature of Hoffmann and Weber. Hoffmann's choice of the obscure Quaisain's *Le Jugement de Salomon* as the subject of an article can be explained by the echoes of Algarotti in his fastening upon the overture for its qualities:

> Das Stück fängt mit einer Ouverture an die feyerlich gehalten sein soll, und nach Endigung derselben mahlt eine leichte frohe Musik der Gärtner lustiges Leben. Die Idee ist gut; jedes wichtige Stück sollte mit einer dazu geschriebenen Overture, die den Zuhörer in die dem Stück zusagende

Stimmung versetzt, anfangen, und auch eine Introduzzione würde in so
fern von Wirkung seyn, als diese nun den ersten Szenen näher tritt und
so den Uebergang von der Ouvertüre, die die Tendenz des Stücks im
Allgemeinen aussprach, zu den ersten Szenen, deren Charackter sie trägt,
machen kann. (Hoffmann, 1967–9, I, 238–9)

(The piece begins with a solemnly sustained overture, after which some
light-hearted music depicts the cheerful life of the gardeners. The idea is
a good one. Every serious play should begin with an overture designed
for it, to put the listener into an appropriate frame of mind. The effect of
an *introduzzione* would be in proportion as it approximates to the
opening character of the play in general, to the opening scenes, whose
particular mood it reflects. Hoffmann, 1989, 218.)

The significance of the overture became an important element in
discussions about opera. It did not go unremarked how far the
overtures to Mozart's three greatest Italian operas had creatively
overtaken theoretical ideas, providing Germans with a stick with
which to beat Rossini for cheerfully swapping overtures between
serious and comic works. The opportunity to weave motive into a
symphonic web was also something to appeal to the German
symphonic genius, to speak to the audience but also to indicate
where the weight of the expression was to lie. Over and over again, it
is the building of scene complexes, especially in act finales, which
impressed Germans both in their critical accounts of French operas
and in their attempts to develop and unify such scenes themselves.
Sometimes these are scarcely more than sequences of numbers,
loosely connected though without intervening dialogue, but even
the attempt indicates where creative interest lay, and in a good many
cases the growth becomes more organic, and dynamic, through well-
judged dramatic contrast guided not by musical forms but by the
demands of the action. From the increased reliance on the orchestra
also came an emphasis on colour not so much for its own sake as for
its expression of a dramatic situation, with the actual invention
coming to reside in the choice of instruments and instrumental
combinations. Even if many years were still to pass before the full

import of all this was perceived, the French operas of these years opened up vast horizons.

With Germany remaining divided, operatic confidence was erratic in development, and the busy intellectual leaven had yet to work its fermentation throughout the country as a whole. Surveying Germany with her sharp Parisian eye, Mme de Staël was to put her finger on part of the problem in 1810.

> Comme il n'existe point de capitale où se rassemble la bonne compagnie de toute l'Allemagne, l'esprit de société y exerce peu de pouvoir; l'empire du goût et l'arme de ridicule y sont sans influence. La plupart des écrivains et des penseurs travaillent dans la solitude, ou seulement entourés d'un petit cercle qu'ils dominent . . . La fierté des Anglais sert puissament à leur existence politique; la bonne opinion que les Français ont d'eux-même a toujours beaucoup contribué à leur ascendant sur l'Europe; le noble orgueil des Espagnols les a rendus jadis les souverains d'une portion du monde. Les Allemands sont Saxons, Prussiens, Bavarois, Autrichiens; mais le caractère germanique, sur lequel devroit se fonder la force de tous, est morcelé comme la terre même qui a tant de differents maîtres. (De Staël, 1958, 38–40)

> (As there is no capital where the élite of Germany gathers, the spirit of society has little power; the empire of taste and the force of ridicule have no influence. Most writers and intellectuals work in solitude, or surrounded only by a small circle which they dominate . . . The pride of the English has a powerful effect on their political life; the good opinion which the French have of themselves has always contributed much to their supremacy in Europe; the noble disdain of the Spaniards once made them rulers of part of the world. The Germans are Saxons, Prussians, Bavarians, Austrians; but the German character, on which the strength of them all must be based, is as fragmented as the land itself which has so many different rulers.)

To some extent, this applies to the different conditions obtaining in opera houses, where the numbers of French operas performed between 1780 and 1820 reveal some surprising statistics (see Schneider, 1997, 612–16). Hamburg was a special case, since from around the turn of the century the city, a prosperous international trading centre true to its old traditions, remained a magnet for emigrants fleeing the Revolution and, until the Battle of Jena in 1806, preserved a kind of neutrality, or at any rate a certain distance from German nationalism. Alone in Germany, it could support a French opera and ballet company, giving performances in the original language as well as others in translation. In every other operatic centre, operas were given in German, sometimes with several translations circulating for use.

In Berlin the succession of Friedrich Wilhelm III in 1797 gave Reichardt, never slow to trim his sails to the prevailing wind, the opportunity to advance his own cause and that of German as well as Italian opera. He had made significant contributions to both genres with *Die Geisterinsel* and *Brenno*. The King cared little for either, and did nothing to prevent the collapse and eventual closure of the long-established Italian company that had been in decline since the Seven Years War. When the French army arrived in 1806, they found the Italian opera house deserted, and stored their bread in it. Later that year, a French troupe gave works by Boieldieu, and in 1807 more by Berton, Cherubini, Paer and Le Sueur. But Reichardt, keen to establish the Liederspiel (including his own examples of it) partly as an attempt to naturalize the French vaudeville, was more resistant to original French music. His *Berlinische musikalische Zeitung* treated French opera dismissively. Reviewing Le Sueur's *Ossian* from Paris, it deplored the portrayal of the hero and the music as 'gallisch und mild', in a column and a half (*BMZ* 22 (1805)); the *AMZ* gave the work five columns, with a full synopsis and background information, praising its originality, characterization and theatrical skill (*AMZ* 6 (1804), 786–91). The advance of French opera in Berlin slowed, though it did not come to a halt.

A report from Vienna in 1803 declared that, 'Seit zwanzig Jahren, wo Grétry, Monsigny, Philidor u.a. auf unsern Bühnen glänzten und endlich verloschen, beginnt für die franzözische Musik nun die zweyte Epoche durch Cherubini, Méhul, Dalayrac. u.a.' (*AMZ* 5 (1803), 818) ('Twenty years after Grétry, Monsigny, Philidor etc. shone on our stage and were eventually extinguished, there now begins a second epoch for French music with Cherubini, Méhul, Dalayrac etc.'). These were prescient words. The first three composers were among those who had helped to form audiences and interest musicians; the latter three were now exerting a profound influence on a new generation of German composers, bringing emancipation from the dominance of Italian opera but above all fertilizing the native growth. The years between the Revolution in 1789 and the beginning of the War of Liberation against Napoleon in 1813 saw German opera increasingly shaping for itself a national identity that had learnt from the earlier 'epoch' of French composers but now began to take on its own strength.

Grétry had in fact retained his Viennese popularity, and his influential *Richard Cœur-de-Lion* (1784; Vienna 1788, much repeated) helped to set the fashion for other French rescue operas in Vienna, including Le Sueur's *La Caverne* (1793; Vienna, 1803), Paer's *Camilla* (Vienna, 1799) and *Leonora* (1804; Vienna, trans. Rochlitz, 1809) and Cherubini's *Lodoïska* (1791; Vienna, 1802, much repeated). Cherubini's huge popularity brought him to Vienna in person, where he conducted *Les Deux Journées* (with alterations and additions), and even led to a commission for another rescue opera, *Faniska* (Vienna, 1806), probably written in Italian to a text on a French original and then translated into German. Other Parisian composers who had Viennese successes in these years included Dalayrac, Devienne, Della-Maria, Catel, Berton, Isouard, Monsigny, Boieldieu, Spontini and in particular Méhul; their works were given alongside a surviving German Singspiel repertory and, especially in 1809 with the presence of the French army in the city, much Italian opera.

After Hamburg, Berlin and Vienna, it was Frankfurt that gave most French opera over these years, to a lesser extent Lübeck, Breslau and Königsberg (the latter, sharing seasons with Danzig, and despite many vicissitudes with inadequate theatres and managements, placing a strong emphasis on French rather than Italian opera). In Munich, the lifting of the Elector Carl Theodor's 1787 ban on Italian opera in 1805 readmitted works including Cimarosa's *Gli Orazi ed i Curiazi* (with additions by Danzi, a work smartly dismissed as 'mehr ein Wettstreit im Gesang, als ein dramatisches Werk' (*AMZ* 9 (1806), 42) ('more of a singing competition than a dramatic work')). But French music held its own. Méhul's *Joseph* and *Héléna* were popular, and *Une folie* was even performed in French (with a duet in Swabian added), and a French company gave a season in 1810 (though popular interest was muted); Dalayrac had a good following; and Spontini's *La Vestale* was welcomed in 1812.

In the repertories of many of the less prominent centres, French opera remained a central part of the theatrical fare alongside German Singspiel, while Italian opera continued supreme mainly in courts which could afford it (such as that of the King of Saxony in Dresden). Brunswick, for example, was receptive to visiting French companies, who brought the familiar repertory of Cherubini, Boieldieu, Méhul, Dalayrac, Le Sueur, Isouard and Berton. Dessau, with an impressive new 1,000-seat theatre built in 1798, welcomed similar companies, and even dedicated a new church with a production of *Joseph*. With the French occupying Kassel from 1806–13, and the installation of Napoleon's younger brother Jérôme as King of Westphalia, a substantial French operatic repertory was only to be expected, though no-one could have foreseen, in the six months from January to June 1812 alone, as many as sixty-nine performances of forty-eight operas by seventeen French composers, and in the following six months a hundred performances of fifty-one operas by eighteen French composers. These observations, concerning both French opera translated and staged locally and French operas performed by visiting companies, can do no more than give an indication of the diversity of the scene, but also of the extent to which the French influence came to have such an effect in Germany's operatic centres.

When Christoph Gottlieb Härtel took over the old Leipzig publishing firm of Breitkopf in 1796 and set about developing it commercially and artistically, one of his first enterprises was the foundation of a music magazine. Of the thirty-odd journals that had preceded it – much depends upon the definition of a journal, and in any case most of them failed to last more than a few issues even when they resurfaced under another name – the earliest was Johann Mattheson's *Critica Musica* (Hamburg, twenty-four issues between 1722 and 1725), and one of the most enduring was F. W. Marpurg's *Historisch-kritische Beyträge zur Aufnahme der Musik* (Berlin, 1754–78). Most of the early journals followed Mattheson's example in centring on the editor himself and his attitudes, as with Lorenz Mizler and his *Musikalische Bibliothek* (Leipzig, 1736–54) and with Johann Adolf Scheibe, a sturdy battler against foreign influence, in his *Critischer Musikus* (1737–40). Johann Adam Hiller's *Wöchentliche Nachrichten und Anmerkungen die Musik betreffend* (Leipzig, 1766–70) concentrated more on reports of musical events and composers, announcements of events and writings, and comments on theoretical and practical matters. The first real critic was J. F. Reichardt, with his *Musikalisches Wochenblatt* (Berlin, 1791–2), followed by J. G. K. Spazier and the first *Berlinische musikalische Zeitung* (Berlin, 1793–4). The general eighteenth-century tendency was a movement from the earnestly professional learned articles of the first journals towards reports and reviews, widening the coverage and the appeal to professional musicians so as to include the gradually emerging audience of amateurs. In the wake of the French Revolution, it was the growth of bourgeois interest and participation in music, together with the development of concert and operatic life, publishing, singing and concert societies and Liedertafeln, conservatories and domestic music-making, and not least much greater access to opera, which provided the conditions for the appearance of another of the 'general' or *allgemein* journals, this time devoted to music.

The intentions of the intelligent, farsighted Härtel were a characteristic blend of idealism and business sense. He set out to provide his readership with a journal that would stimulate the dissemination of music through informed reviews, broaden interest with reports of activities, encourage the discussion of ideas, bring news of the latest composers, performers and works, and provide musical supplements to support arguments or whet appetites. In this, his example was to some extent Hiller's successful *Wöchentliche Nachrichten*, his more immediate model the short-lived *Musikalische Realzeitung* (Speyer, 1788–90) of his fellow-publisher Heinrich Bossler; but his ambitions were set much higher, and though the purpose was to strengthen the position of the house of Breitkopf and Härtel, the new publication's title also declared it to be a general musical journal, the *Allgemeine musikalische Zeitung*.

In appointing Friedrich Rochlitz as editor, Härtel made an inspired choice. Born in Leipzig in 1769, Rochlitz had studied composition at the Thomasschule under Bach's pupil and successor Johann Friedrich Doles but, dazzled by Mozart's genius on their meeting in 1789, he abandoned the idea of a career in composition and turned to theology. However, he remained busy as a writer, publishing essays, stories, Novellen, Lustspiele and contributions to almanacs as well articles on science and theology, texts for songs and for other musical works, and translations (including of Sophocles' *Antigone* and a long-enduring German version of *Don Giovanni*). It was Rochlitz's intellectual range that attracted Härtel, hoping as he did to appeal to a wide musical audience. Each eight-page quarto weekly number began with an essay or biographical study, followed by reviews, reports, correspondence and miscellaneous items, with news in an *Intelligenz-Blatt* and copious music examples with sometimes complete pieces in supplements. Forming a good network of impartial writers did not prove easy, but by the end of the first decade he could call upon some 130 contributors; and his readership included the very interested Haydn, who was sent free copies, and Beethoven. Among the most important writers Rochlitz recruited were Carl Zelter, the lexicographer Ernst Ludwig Gerber, the theorist Justin Heinrich Knecht, the former editor of the *Berlinische musikalische Zeitung* Spazier, the acoustician Ernst Chladni, the publisher and educationalist Hans Georg Nägeli, and the aesthetician Christian Friedrich Michaelis, as well as a host of amateurs; composers included Franz Danzi and, in the earliest issues, Dittersdorf. Gracious interest, but no practical help, was offered by Goethe. With such support, and with many others rallying to the cause, Rochlitz succeeded in giving his journal a good intellectual basis and a solid reputation.

By upbringing a figure of the Enlightenment – his breeches and stockings, his buckled shoes, his powdered hair all reflected eighteenth-century manners and his own intellectual disposition – Rochlitz embarked upon the *AMZ* in a spirit of Kantian rationalism. However, he was also one of the first critics to appreciate Beethoven, whose development he followed warily but with thorough and perceptive articles. Beethoven, despite moments of irritation with the 'Leipziger Ochs', was in turn mostly respectful, and intended Rochlitz to be his biographer. Rochlitz also took up the cause of the emergent Romantic generation, discerning talent in some plain fugues by the boy Carl Maria von Weber in his second issue (*AMZ* 1 (1798), 32) and later championing Spohr as well as Weber. He also wrote texts which they set: he had a good conceit of his own gifts, and neither composer was in a hurry to offend so influential a supporter. Weber and E. T. A. Hoffmann were the most important Romantic writers whom Rochlitz brought in as reviewers of scores and performances; and anticipating later practice, he also encouraged them to follow the example of his own correspondence between 'Ferdinand' and 'Anton' (in *AMZ* 5 (1802), 1–18, 41–52, 57–70, 73–85, 89–100) and use fiction as a tool of criticism. Hoffmann's most influential writings on music first appeared from 1809 in the *AMZ*, among them his stories *Ritter Gluck* (*AMZ* 11 (Feb 1809), 305–19) and *Don Juan* (*AMZ* 15 (1813), 213–25) and his review of Beethoven's Fifth Symphony (*AMZ* 12 (1810), 630–42, 652–9). At least twenty-five of

Weber's critical articles were published in its pages, including the important review of Hoffmann's *Undine* (AMZ 19 (1817), 201–8). They were two among Rochlitz's writers privileged in being allowed to sign their articles. Gerber and Johann August Apel were almost the only others, together with Rochlitz himself, though pseudonyms were sometimes allowed. A rare exception was made for G. L. P. Sievers, a critic of modest attainments but one whose copious reports from 1807, on what Rochlitz regarded as the important topic of music in France, were given prominence. Rochlitz built up a network of writers in some hundred cities as far afield as London and St Petersburg, Lisbon and Naples, Kiev and Stockholm. Some half of these were within German lands, and it was Berlin, Breslau, Dresden, Frankfurt, Kassel, Königsberg and Munich, as well as Leipzig itself, which proved the sources of the best and fullest reports. However, the standard was very uneven, not surprisingly given the difficulty of control over local enthusiasms and rivalries. In some cities, notably Hamburg, Rochlitz never found a regular correspondent of real quality. Aware of the problem of critical standards, he printed a pair of articles by Nägeli, attempting to establish norms and standards of reviewing (AMZ 5 (1802), 225–37 and 265–74). If somewhat self-important, Rochlitz was a fair editor as well as a campaigning one. The journal was a commercial success, at any rate until the war brought a drop in circulation, and also a critical success until, after Rochlitz's resignation in 1818, it began to lag behind the times, eventually yielding pride of place to Schumann's *Neue Zeitschrift für Musik* in 1834. The pages of the *AMZ* give the fullest single account of German musical life throughout the twenty years of Rochlitz's editorship.

From the outset, Rochlitz made the *AMZ* a platform for the cause of German opera. His first issue opened with an essay, 'Gedanken über die Oper' ('Thoughts on opera': AMZ 1 (1798), 1–9), defining opera as 'ein Schauspiel, worin alles, was in andern gesprochen, gesungen wird' ('a drama in which everything, elsewhere spoken, is to be sung'). With this emphasis on a continuous sung drama, he begins to clear the ground for German opera with the now familiar complaints about the vocal and melodic exaggerations of the Italians, the confusion of the French in the wake of the Guerre des Bouffons, and the feebleness of the English in supporting only the great of other nations (such as Handel). He returned to the attack in the following year in the fifth of a series of his 'Bruchstücke aus Briefen an einen jungen Tonkünstler' ('Fragments from Letters to a Young Composer': *AMZ* 2 (1799), 161–70), in which he takes up the call (spacing the letters for emphasis), 'Die Oper ist das, was aus der Vereinigung aller Künste zu Einem, resultiert' ('Opera is that which results from the unification of all arts into one'). He appeals to his young composer to cultivate opera as a serious art, with more realistic heroes and heroines, stronger dramatic situations and greater musical originality, and to librettists to make more functional use of scenery and transformations: 'dann haben wir nicht ein blosses Singspiel, sondern eine wahre, wenn auch etwas verjüngte Oper' (166) ('then we shall have not just a Singspiel but a true if also somewhat rejuvenated opera'). In 'Über Oper und Opernwesen' ('On Opera and the Nature of Opera': *AMZ* 2 (1799), 197–201) he observes that in opera the events are but the means for the poet to portray feeling: the main point is not, say, the detail of Ariadne's tragic fate but the emotion of love's betrayal, and the composer's responsibility is to express this so that the appeal is more to the ear than to the eye. He goes on to defend German against the old criticisms of the language as one unsuitable for singing by going over to the attack: 'Uns Deutschen scheint es vorbehalten zu seyn, den süssen Gesang der Italiäner mit der declamatorischen Behandlungsart der Franzosen zu verbinden' (*AMZ* 2 (1799), 243) ('It appears to be reserved to us Germans to unite the sweet song of the Italians with the declamatory treatment of the French').

Especially in the first half dozen years of the *AMZ*, Rochlitz pursued a vigorous campaign with both precept and practical help. An article in 1803 (*AMZ* 6 (1803, 165–74, 181–7: 'Was soll man von dem Musikdirektor eines Operntheaters erlangen?') complained of the poor quality of most German music directors, suggesting how low standards were by demanding as basic requirements such skills as maintaining tempo without tapping or stamping (in Berlin, Righini used to whack the music stand with his roll of paper throughout numbers), being able to play the keyboard properly, having a practical knowledge of voices and instruments, and being able to master figured bass and the theory of music. Ideas looking forward to the unified work of art for which he was arguing included thoughts on the placing of the orchestra for maximum effect, on the handling of the chorus, and on skill in producing the singers so as to achieve the greatest dramatic reality. The feebleness of so much opera performance in provincial Germany was underlined by a satire, 'Das Operntheater und sein Publikum zu Krähwinkel' ('The Opera House and its Public in Krähwinkel': *AMZ* 7 (1804), 97–111). Modelling itself on Wieland's *Die Abderiten* of 1774 (see Ch. 5, pp. 99–100), this took the name 'Krähwinkel' from Jean Paul's *Das heimliche Klaglied der jetzigen Männer* (1801), popularized by Kotzebue in a comedy *Die deutschen Kleinstädter* (1802). 'Krähwinkel' immediately passed into common parlance as the epitome of an inert, backward provincial town of ludicrous complacency, narrowness, obscurantism and snobbery. The Krähwinklers go to the opera. The hero is applauded so much that he loses his place, the heroine has to repeat a dramatic scene, making nonsense of the plot, the tragic hero has just about the talent for Pickelhäring, the Priest booms in tones more suitable for sailor's songs, and the enormous leading soprano, of whose figure a sculptor could have made two sopranos from the material provided by nature for one, offers so much for the eye to feast upon that the ear is starved. Rapturous enthusiasm greets the performance, and, as in *Die Abderiten*, a solitary glum dissident, goaded into protesting that the music fails to express the feeling and spirit of the text, turns out to be the composer. The intention is not only to bring opera into the target area, but to suggest that nothing has changed in thirty years.

Nor was change in the offing. The Krähwinkel satire fired some accurate shafts. Orchestral standards in opera in the first decade of the century were wildly erratic, both from one town to another and from one year to the next. Frankfurt at the turn of the century, with its Nationaltheater under the direction of Christian Cannabich's son

Carl and supporting a strong Mozart tradition, benefited from the dissolution of the Kapellen in various Rhineland towns, chiefly Cologne, Mainz, Trier, Zweibrücken and Saarbrücken. Together with the splendid scenery of Giorgio Fuentes, its orchestra was said to be the best part of the opera, and (though Cannabich had by then left) in 1804 it was awarded the unusual privilege of a Benefit, the proceeds going to an orchestral player's widow; standards were still reported as being high in 1810. Cities under a strong royal or ducal protection could maintain a good orchestra: the Italian opera in Dresden had thirty string players and a large wind section in 1805. Kassel, enjoying a brilliant period under French occupation, possessed an excellent orchestra of forty-eight in 1811. Munich was in theory well endowed orchestrally, with a roll call of some eighty players under Carl Cannabich in 1806; but this included twelve trumpeters and four drummers, suggesting reinforcements from the local garrison, and in any case the orchestra was (as elsewhere) shared with the Italian opera. However, the uncertainty of standards even in major cities is shown by conditions in Stuttgart in 1806 under Johann Friedrich Kranz, typical of the company's general state: in an orchestra of twenty-nine, two of the violins, one of the double basses and a bass singer from the chorus had to double oboe, two of the contraltos doubled as dancers, and the chorus recruited half a dozen young school teachers to augment whatever could be assembled from the theatre personnel. Other towns and cities were still more precariously placed; and economic constraints compelled many smaller theatres to reduce their orchestras to a handful of players, even to dismiss the wind and resort to a positive organ to play their parts.

Sometimes reviews indicated, explicitly or implicitly, that it was better to draw a veil over orchestral quality; and even more was this so with standards of singing. Ferdinand von Biedenfeld, a cultured dilettante whose many subjects included opera, was but one writer to point out that the growth in the numbers of German theatres in the first years of the century was not matched by a comparable increase in singing schools (Biedenfeld, 1848). Rochlitz again took an initiative in trying to solve an old problem. In the first volume of the *AMZ* he published an article, 'Vorschläge zur Verbesserung der gewöhnlichen Singschulen in Deutschland' (*AMZ* 1 (1799), 465–71) ('Proposals for the improvement of the ordinary singing schools of Germany') , though this is aimed more at the general level of singing than at opera. Given the arguments about German as an operatic language, and above all with the lack of a convincing lead from German composers, the objections tended to centre on the poor quality of training in general and in particular on the tendency of singers to ape Italian manners. Over and over again reviews attack unsuitable trills, flourishes and roulades being inserted into arias, though it should be remembered that while singers were used to looking up to the Italians, they would also have found in most German serious operas passages that provided such Italianate decorations. A review from Hamburg in 1799 bewails the poor standard of singing and beseeches readers not to believe reports to the contrary, interspersing quotations with tart comments (*AMZ* 1 (1799), 711–15). Another from Hanover in 1804 concedes that there was a number of sweet and pleasant voices to be heard in the reorganized German theatre, but no true German school of singing (*AMZ* 6 (1804), 356–8). 'Dass man blos über den Alpen gut singen können, ist wahrlich nur ein Vorurtheil, das wahrscheinlich von den Deutschen selbst, die sich überall zu wenig kennen, herstammt', reproved a Munich critic in 1806 (*AMZ* 9 (1806), 43) ('The view that there is good singing only beyond the Alps is a prejudice that appears to stem from Germans themselves, who generally know too little').

The Italians working in Germany naturally made easy targets. Luigia Sandrini, who sang Paer's Dido in Dresden and later attempted some German roles, was only one of many who attracted disapproving comment. 'Zuweilen lässt sich jedoch diese Künstlerin von der falschen Ansicht hinreisen, dass nur Bravour die bessere Methode sey und dem Zuhörer gefallen könne. Sie irret; denn durch Bravour kann man nur das Staunen des Publicums erregen, statt dass im Gegentheil durch das Tragen und Binden der Stimme die Herzen aller Zuhörer gewonnen werden' (*AMZ* 14 (1812), 766) ('This artist seems to be of the false opinion that bravura alone is the best method, and alone can please the listener. She is wrong: for with bravura one can only astonish the public, whereas with a legato line the hearts of all listeners are won'). But German singers committing these sins got off no more lightly, from a reprimand for two minor figures who made so bold as to add Italianate flourishes to *Die Zauberflöte* in 1799, to a ferocious attack in Danzig in 1810 on Fischer (probably the great Ludwig's son Joseph) for his notoriously inept alterations and additions to Mozart, his disdain of acting, his failure to use his gifts in the service of opera as a dramatic art. In now familiar vein, the review declares, 'Die Oper ist das zusammengesetzteste aller Kunstwerke: vornämlich Vereinigung der dramatischen und musikalischen Kunst' (*AMZ* 12 (1810), 1018) ('Opera is the most unified of the arts: that is to say, a unification of dramatic and musical art'). Though the most forceful, the voice of the *AMZ* was by no means alone: for instance, a Munich report on Simon Mayr's *Amor non ha ritegno* (Milan, 1804) attacked the dislocation between the excellent music, the pointlessly sumptuous staging, and the feeble text (*Aurora* 102 (1804), 407). There were few to praise for living up to a still elusive ideal. Even Anna Milder (1785–1838: after her marriage in 1809, Milder-Hauptmann) did not escape criticism. Though she was the dominant dramatic soprano of these years – a great Gluck singer, Beethoven's admired Leonore in all three versions of his opera, an artist for whom Cherubini and Schubert both composed – and one whose beauty and clarity of voice and depth of dramatic feeling were widely admired, she was reproached for her insecure technique, and for a somewhat heavy 'declamation' rather than true singing. It was over this that she eventually fell out with another of her great admirers, Spontini, who was not alone in complaining about her difficulties with learning roles (which she was capable of getting embarrassingly wrong in performance).

However, it was during this decade, when abuses were still rife, that singers of a new nature and quality first began coming to prominence. Three women singers of the same age as Milder, in particular, set examples which stimulated German composers. Charlotte Häser (1784–1871) was one of the few German sopranos of the day to win praise both in Italy and in Germany, where she was admired for the absence of unnecessary ornamentation and for the clarity and simplicity of her singing. Helene Harlas (1785–1818) proved too German for the Italians, but was admired by Weber and by Poissl (who wrote several of his operas for her) and earned from the *AMZ* praise similar to that meted out to Häser for her expression and declamation rather than her ornamentation (e.g. *AMZ* 20 (1818), 597 and *AMZ* 21 (1819), 3–6). Marianne Schönberger (1785–1882), of mixed German and Italian birth, possessed a powerful contralto much admired by Cherubini. Her acting abilities, coupled with the lack of suitable roles, led to her being successfully encouraged by her husband to fill a notorious gap on the German stage by taking on tenor parts (*Rheinische Correspondenz* 56 (25 Feb. 1810)). The precocious Therese Grünbaum (1797–1876) was a poetic singer, if guilty of excessive coloratura, but one who as a mature artist was compared to Catalani and for whom Weber wrote Eglantine. These were the most important women singers to pave the way for the appearance of Wilhelmine Schröder-Devrient in the 1820s. The emergence of Franz Wild (1792–1860), upheld as the model of what a German tenor might be, was the more widely welcomed on his 1811 Vienna début as the general standard was so low. Wild had praise heaped on him not only for the sweetness and warmth of his tone and the strength and fullness of his voice but for acting abilities that made him excel especially in tragic opera (Eisenberg, 1903, 1124). In his last year as editor of the *AMZ*, Rochlitz bewailed in a long article the lack of tenors due to poor training, low expectations and singers being given too many easy options, a tendency to play to the gallery and (less convincingly) the unsettled times (*AMZ* 20 (1818), 301–12).

It may be added that the problem was a long way off resolution. J. A. Hiller's *Anweisung zur Singekunst in der deutschen und italienischen Sprache* (Frankfurt and Leipzig, 1773) was a pioneering eighteenth-century work in addressing itself to German problems, and almost the next with any authority in opera was Peter Winter's *Vollständige Singschule* (Mainz, 1824 – reprinted in 1874), though the emphasis here is still very Italian. Not until the middle of the century was there a more systematic approach to the problem, with Friedrich Schmitt's *Große Gesangschule für Deutschland* (Munich, 1854). Schmitt set out to repudiate Italian methods. Regarding vocal music as elevated speech, he abandoned solfeggi and insisted that exercises should start with speech instruction, and thence proceed to singing syllables and German phrases, with vocal training beginning on short notes since long ones did not occur in natural speech. Admired by Wagner, who sought his help (Hey, 1911), Schmitt was a controversial figure, in part through his abrasive character. However, Julius Hey won a success with *Deutsche Gesangs-Unterricht* (Mainz, 1886), a book which also led to the movement towards *Bühnen-Deutsch*, an agreed system of pronunciation free from dialect which was codified in Theodor Siebs's *Deutsche Bühnenaussprache* (Berlin, 1898). Singers and especially composers at the beginning of the century were already very well aware of the problems, and there remained (as critical comments reveal) an almost obsessive need to set a distance between Germans and Italians, with repeated emphases on the Italians' concern with the voice as a medium for bel canto as opposed to the Germans' insistence on vocal drama and meaning. The consciousness of linguistic differences – with greater vowel shading in German, more diphthongs, and heavier consonants than in Italian – were to seem less significant with time and achievement; but the day was yet to come when Wagner could claim to have learnt from Bellini, and when one of his greatest twentieth-century interpreters, Friedrich Schorr, could write that he built his phrases in Wagner just as he did in Verdi. In the early days of the formation of a national style, there was among singers still a strong sense of independence to be fought for and won.

Rochlitz was not content to criticize from the sidelines. In 1803 he published an article (*AMZ* 6 (1803), 365–77) in which the complaints about German operatic conditions focus on the difficulty which others had observed, namely that England and France had an advantage over Germany by possessing capitals which served to concentrate the best minds and the most original artists (the situation of Italy is conveniently ignored). Of some forty German theatres, only about half could be counted on to stage new works. Clearly some other form of organization was needed; and there follows a proposal for an agency, run from Leipzig and the *AMZ*. Each member theatre should put on two new works a season, one big Romantic opera (for which the examples are *Don Giovanni* and *Das unterbrochene Opferfest*) and one lighter piece (such as *Das Donauweib-chen*). Each theatre would suggest to the agency which composer and librettist it would like: the agency would arrange the collaboration, and each participant in the scheme would buy a copy of the two scores at the rate of 30 and 20 thalers. The librettist's fees would be 200 and 100 thalers, the composer's 400 and 300 thalers. Conditions were set out in some detail. However, this depended on twenty-four copies being taken, by Altona, Bamberg, Berlin, Brunswick, Breslau, Dessau, Dresden, Frankfurt, Hamburg, Hanover, Kassel, Königsberg, Leipzig, Ludwigslust, Magdeburg, Mannheim, Munich, Prague, Regensburg, Riga, Stuttgart, Weimar and two by Vienna. Of the cities approached, every one welcomed the idea. Breitkopf and Härtel's support was praised even in other journals, for instance in the Munich *Aurora*: 'Eine so lobenswürdige und uneigennützige Unter-nehmung verdient allerdings die Aufmerksamkeit des deutschen Publikums, welches von jeher eben so sehr durch den Mangel an National-Opern, als durch den Ueberfluß an Uebersetzungen gelitten hat' (*Aurora* 38 (1804), 152) ('Such a praiseworthy and disinterested enterprise certainly deserves the attention of the German public, which has suffered as much from the lack of national operas as from the superfluity of translated works'). Practical support was more cautious. Rochlitz's idea was an ambitious one – too ambitious for a Germany so strongly marked by division into cities and states guarding their independence. The major operatic centres held back, and the only cities to show purpose were Bamberg, Breslau, Dessau, Mannheim and Regensburg, to which were later added Linz, Lübeck and Nuremberg, with Weimar uncertain. By July 1804 Rochlitz was obliged to call the whole thing off.

Rochlitz was over-optimistic, at the very least premature, in hoping that the German unity of feeling he wished to encourage could be translated into practical terms across disunited territories. Nevertheless, the volume of operas being written and staged during the years between the turn of the century and the beginning of the War of Liberation in 1813 continued to increase, and new composers to come to prominence. Even if this were often a brief fame, attached to a single work that momentarily caught public taste, there were signs of Romantic ideas burgeoning, sometimes on plants that were not really deeply enough rooted or sufficiently robust to sustain their growth.

Patriotic enthusiasms, and the continuing ambitions for German grand opera, were sometimes reflected in the choice of fashionable subjects by composers who did not possess the inventive range to handle them. Among these was Johann Evangelist Brandl, who based his *Germania* (1800) on the enduringly popular subject of the Hermannsschlacht, the first-century battle in which Varus's legions were defeated by Hermann (Arminius). But despite a plethora of historically imposing roles and a dozen strenuously patriotic choruses, there is little musical distinction underlying Brandl's enterprise. Others who followed suit in this vein included Carl Leopold Reinecke, with *Adelheit von Scharfeneck* (1806) and Ignaz von Seyfried with *Bertha von Werdenberg* (1809), well-meaning in their attempts to construct German serious opera on the model of Holzbauer and *Günther von Schwarzburg*.

Among those less ambitious composers who sought to reconcile the simpler forms of Singspiel to mildly Romantic ideas was August Bergt, who had a success with his first opera, a one-act farce *List gegen List* (1801). Composed for only four characters, it dispenses with spoken dialogue and ends on a variegated finale that includes arias, romances and duets. He also won praise for *Das Ständchen* (1802), written for a single singer. However, though Bergt associated with Romantic circles in Dresden, he was content to remain essentially in the Singspiel tradition of Hiller; and in this he was far from alone. Peter Ritter's works include one of the first Falstaff operas in *Die lustigen Weiber* (1792). Shakespeare's *Merry Wives* plot is quite closely followed, and the score anticipates more famous works by giving Ford (here, Wallauf) a big jealousy aria, but the action is transferred to a very German setting, and moved forward more than two centuries. We find Hans Falstaff bragging in the Wirtshaus zum blauen Hasenbande of his exploits in the Thirty Years War, and the dénouement takes place in a rustic *Lustwäldchen*.

Ritter's most successful work, however, was *Der Zitherschläger* (1810), a pleasant little sentimental comedy in one act about the guitar-playing Raimund whose falling-out with Röschen is extended for long enough to make their reconciliation satisfactory when she reveals that he has really always been her choice of lover. The work caught Weber's ear, perhaps partly because Ritter and he had shared a teacher in Vogler, and was praised by him as a German work that could stand comparison with any French opera, and for its 'vortref-fliche, innige Musik':

> Sie ist wahr und echt dramatisch, die Situationen sind mit einer solchen Wärme und Herzlichkeit ergriffen und gehalten, daß Ref. sich seit langer Zeit nicht erinnert, so sehr von Musik angesprochen worden zu sein.
>
> (Weber, 1908, 101)

> (This is admirably, deeply felt music, true to life and genuinely dramatic, and the various situations are grasped and developed with such a warmth of feeling that the present writer can hardly remember any work that has made so strong an impression on him. Weber, 1981, 41)

Weber singled out Raimund's ballad 'Ritter Arno', which achieved much popularity; but he may well also have been impressed by some enterprising harmony and especially by word-setting that responds to the cadences of the German language. In an angry duet with

Allegro agitato

RAIMUND

Je - de Stel-le hällt mich hier ge - fan - gen,

die - ses Gärt - chen wo sie Blu - men hegt,

je - ner Baum der meinen Na - men trägt,

die - ser Pfad wo sie ein - her ge - gan - gen

(Every place keeps me captive here, this little garden where she tends
the flowers, that tree that has my name upon it, this path she takes . . .)

Example 20 Ritter: *Der Zitherschläger* (1810), Raimund

Röschen, Raimund's furious, irregularly barred phrases are set against her calming four-bar answers. Earlier, his agitation finds expression in a melody whose irregularity does not contradict his essentially lyrical nature (Example 20).

However, Ritter was an example of the 'one-work' composers of these years upon whom Weber commented:

> Wie ein gelungenes Werk, das die Aufmerksamkeit der Welt auf sich zog, nicht nur Nachahmer und Nachäffer von allen Seiten entstehen macht, sondern wie es auch den Schöpfer desselben bestimmt, auf dem einmal mit Erfolg betretenen Wege fortzuwandeln und sich lieber den sicher den Effekt bewirkenden Mitteln zu vertrauen und sie beizubehalten, als durch neue Versuche den schön lockenden Beifall des Augenblicks und der Zeitgenossen aufs Spiel zu setzen. Daher kommt es wohl, daß selbst bei bedeutenden Meistern, z. B. Winter usw., immer nur eines ihrer Werke den Kulminationspunkt macht. (Weber, 1908, 295)

> (A single successful, widely appreciated work will not only spawn imitators and mere copies; it also inclines the author himself to continue in the vein which has brought him success, and to prefer the means

which have once proved effective to the risk involved in new attempts to
win the elusive applause of his contemporaries. This explains the fact
that even in the case of exceptional masters such as Winter it is always a
single work that makes their reputation. Weber, 1981, 232)

Weber was here writing about Joseph Weigl; and he felt strongly
enough on the subject to repeat these comments from an essay on
Weigl's *Die Jugend Peters des Grossen* (1814) when in 1817 he came to
introduce the same composer's *Das Waisenhaus* (1808).

G. F. Treitschke's mawkish libretto for this immensely popular
two-act work concerns Gustav, placed in an orphanage because his
mother Therese's marriage has enraged her father. Therese has been
secretly working in the orphanage so as to care for the boy, when her
husband returns from exile and, believing them both dead, un-
wittingly chooses Gustav for adoption; simultaneously, her father
arrives, stricken with remorse, to rescue Gustav. The music is simple
and tuneful, and consists of an overture and thirteen numbers that
reflect all too well the blamelessly pious utterances which are a
feature of the text. Weber, introducing the work to his Dresden
audience, put matters generously when he wrote of the work's
'weichliche, fleißige und kenntnisreiche Samtmalerei' ('tender, scru-
pulous and skilful gift of depiction') and of Weigl's 'Streben, jedes
Musikstück möglichst melodisch abgerundet zu geben und mehr
dadurch, als durch die höchste Richtigkeit und Wahrheit des Dekla-
matorischen, die szenische Forderung zu erfüllen' ('concern with
making each musical number as self-sufficient as possible melodically, so as to fulfil the scenic demands of a work in this way rather
than by rigid adherence to dramatic truth in the declamation')
(Weber, 1908, 295–6; Weber, 1981, 232). Weber was himself, moreover, by no means exempt from the influence of Weigl, whose pre-
Biedermeier sentimentality was to have a debilitating effect on a
greater composer with a less assured dramatic instinct than either of
them, Schubert. Hoffmann, with a critical intelligence more robustly
developed than his creative musical invention, was a great deal
sharper when he reviewed the vocal score for the *AMZ*, though he
gave credit where he thought it was due:

Die Musik hat durchaus angenehme, sangbare Melodien, die freylich hin und wieder, wie weiter unten gezeigt werden soll, etwas verbracht sind; die Instrumentierung ist brillant, mit grosser Kenntniss der Instrumente angelegt; die harmonisch reichen Ensembles gehen kräftig und klar in das Ohr.   (*AMZ* 12 (1810), 809–19)

(The music certainly contains pleasant, singable melodies even if here and there, as will be shown below, they are admittedly somewhat stale; the orchestration is brilliant, conceived from a deep knowledge of the instruments; the harmonic richness of the ensembles resounds strongly and clearly in the ear. Hoffmann, 1989, 255)

However, his essay is really a sustained and witty attack on the piece's lachrymose complacency, and takes it as text for a discussion of the importance of a strong central idea being essential to stir a composer's imagination. Details of versification, Hoffmann insists, are of much less importance, an argument which was to find fuller realization in his essay *Der Dichter und der Komponist*.

Weigl had an even greater success with the work he produced in the following year, *Die Schweitzerfamilie* (1809). This is partly because Ignaz Castelli's three-act libretto furnishes him with a rather more varied plot in the sentimental-pastoral manner that suited him only too glibly. It turns on the predicament of an exiled Swiss family, headed by Richard and Gertrud, who are protected by a local Count but who fear for the well-being of their daughter Emmeline since she has had to abandon her lover Jakob. Though restrained by his friend Durmann, Paul falls in love with her, and believes she returns his love; but Jakob's timely arrival puts matters right. The range is in every way greater than in *Das Waisenhaus*, and Weigl turns his sensitive handling of the orchestra, remarked upon by both Weber and Hoffmann, to good effect by including an overture to open each act and by making some inventive use of motive. Some of the individual numbers are scarcely more advanced than those of the work's predecessor, but they are put to stronger dramatic use. Emmeline's cheerful mien is shown to be the unhappy pretence at which the music skilfully hints when she is left alone to mourn her lot, 'Wer hörte wohl jemals mich klagen'. The simple manner which

Weigl could command takes on a more touching quality here in its dramatic context, especially after Emmeline's first entrance in a quartet in which her agitation troubles the shape of the music, and in a duet with her father where the listener can hear that she is only assuming a happy extrovert manner. The finale builds up well through use of a motivic rhythmic figure. Paul's song opening Act II is jolly enough, but suggests a character too plain for the sensitive Emmeline; and matters seem to be on the point of resolution after Jakob turns up, playing an arpeggiated 'Swiss' melody on his flute, and touched (if secretly rather pleased) to learn from the others that she is pining for him. Paul concedes Emmeline to Jakob in broken but manly phrases, and her imminent arrival, in this *Schlussgesang*, would seem due to produce the happy ending. However, a third act was needed, so the plot is artificially extended to include some blithe Nature music and a fine *Melodramatische Scene* in which Emmeline somnambulistically approaches a hut specially built to remind her of home, only to find her dream carried over into reality as the sound of Jakob's flute issues from it with the melody they now sing in happy duet: 'Nur in dem Land, wo wir gebohren, lacht uns die Ruh, blüht uns das Glück'. Even if the context is simple and the music scarcely subtle, the interaction of dream and reality has a Romantic tinge that helped to give the work its popularity. Richard concludes matters – 'Kinder, noch lebt der alte Gott' – by appropriating the melody for purposes of a moral.

Weigl's subsequent operas include a work, *Der Bergsturz* (1813), in which further opportunity was provided for his taste for sentimental piety in natural surroundings, this time by a real-life incident (at Goldau, near Mount Rigi) in which a Swiss peasant family were overwhelmed by an avalanche on their way to their daughter's marriage. Another 'Swiss' arpeggiated melody, on clarinet with attractive woodwind writing in support, sets a scene that remains static for most of the first act, with family prayers of thanks for breakfast, a dutiful filial obeisance from the children Franz and Jette, a placid duet from the bride and bridegroom Josephine and Willer, and a homily from the old father Hatwyl on the need to cultivate the garden of marriage and weed it carefully. Only when they all reach the church does drama eventually intervene. Just as Hatwyl is blessing the happy pair, across the A major music there strikes a doomladen E♭ drum roll: 'Es wankt der Berg, die See schwillt an'. Chains of thunderous diminished sevenths as the church collapses are followed by sinister dark and silence. In Act II a Traveller comes upon the scene of destruction, and sets about moralizing upon the sudden transformation of smiling Nature in company with a passing Hermit. The two of them are bowed in lengthy prayer when a farmer points out that beneath them can be heard sounds of life. Act III opens with a highly chromatic Introduction, then a melodrama in which the entombed Hatwyl reflects that all must be dead but for him, and in his turn falls to prayer. Those on the surface begin burrowing, finding first a roof, next a balcony, finally a hole through which the voices of the entombed family emerge. Tension is built up with an insistent triplet figure, and the rescue is successfully concluded to cries of 'Gott sey gelobt! In Ewigkeit! Hallelujah!' Clearly the work's weakness lies in the undramatic sequence of pious invocations; but it comes to life with the avalanche, in which Weigl's colourful use of instruments and his chromatic harmony, well judged in its discordant onslaught on the 'normal' tonalities, succeed in giving Nature a dark underside with a genuine Romantic shudder.

If scarcely a one-work composer, Adalbert Gyrowetz never exceeded the popularity of his most famous opera, *Der Augenarzt* (1811). Of Bohemian origin, he was much encouraged by Mozart in Vienna and especially by Haydn in London before he settled in Vienna in 1793, where he pursued a busy career as Kapellmeister at the Hoftheater, required to write an opera or a ballet a year. He first made his name with a serious opera, *Agnes Sorel* (1806), to a text by Joseph Sonnleithner after Jean Nicolas Bouilly, on the conflict of love and duty between Jean Dunois, Charles VII and Agnes Sorel. After a fall from his horse, the King is taken incognito to the castle where Agnes heals him and falls in love with him. When Dunois, who also loves Agnes, discovers the situation, he tries to divide them, and eventually the need to resume fighting the English resolves the situation. However, Gyrowetz cannot manage to rise to the considerable dramatic demands of the plot, or of the characters, falling back too readily on note-for-note lines in duets, so that there is little differentiation of character, and on enervating block harmony in ensembles, with inevitably static effect.

Out of his depth with *Agnes Sorel*, Gyrowetz was clearly much impressed by the success of Weigl's two most popular works, and followed them in 1811 with his own sentimental comedy. *Der Augenarzt* is a tale of a shy army doctor, Berg, who loves Pastor Reinfeld's daughter Marie but is obstructed by his rival Igel. He takes on the cure of Reinfeld's two blind wards Philipp and Wilhelmine, who love one another. Wilhelmine turns out to be Berg's long lost sister, and Igel's machinations to claim Marie's hand are confounded. Despite a half-hearted attempt at a Vengeance Aria by Igel as he glowers into the mirror, a middle-aged man trying to reassure himself that he is still quite spry enough to woo Marie, there is little life in the characters, nor much dramatic momentum. The dénouement is the removal of the blind pair's bandages in the finale, to a fortissimo tremolo, followed by an anticlimactic 6/8 Allegro moderato, 'Seh' ich die Welt; strahlt mir das Licht?' The work's charm lies in the melodiously composed individual arias, especially when they are brought together in linked-tempo ensembles. This charm was enough to captivate Viennese audiences, though not to save the work from the lash of Hoffmann's tongue. Losing patience with the whole sentimental genre represented by Weigl and Gyrowetz, he let fly in a devastating unsigned review (*AMZ* 14 (1812), 855–64; Hoffmann, 1989, 293–6). His opening salvo was aimed to blast to pieces the fashion that gave rise to their works:

> Eine Zeit lang hatten sich die rührenden Familiengemählde unserer Bühne bemächtigt, bis sie in ihrem eignen Thränenwasser untergingen; jetzt scheinen sie von der Musik gerettet werden zu wollen, um als Opern über die Bretter zu ziehen.

> (For a time sentimental family portraits took possession of our stage, until they foundered in the flood of their own tears. Now it seems they

are hoping to be rescued by music, in order to grace the boards in the form of operas.)

However, worse was to come for the wretched Gyrowetz and his *Augenarzt*:

> . . . muss er [Hoffmann] doch dem Original insofern den Vorzug einräumen, dass es, viel weniger opernmässig bearbeitet, mehr ein rührendes Drama, worin den auftretenden Personen manchmal die besondere Lust anwandelt, ein Liedchen zu singen, und also der Maasstab der eigentlichen Oper nicht anzuwenden ist. Was soll aber aus unserer theatralischen Musik werden, wenn auch die *Oper* sich bis zu dem gemeinen Thun und Treiben des beengten bürgerlich Lebens erniedrigt, das dem Geiste, der sich in das romantische Reich, wo Gesang die Sprache ist, emporschwingen will, die Fittige lähmt, und die Phantasie erdrückt? Was für Anregungen, in die geheimnissvolle Tiefe der Musik einzugehen, und ihre, im innersten verborgenen Geister zu wecken, kann denn solch ein bürgerliches Küchenstück geben?

> (He [Hoffmann] must nevertheless give preference to the original in that, being much less operatically handled, it is more of an affecting drama in which the actors are occasionally seized by the particular desire to sing a ditty; the standards of genuine opera cannot then apply. But what is to become of music in our theatres when even *opera* lowers itself to the vulgar dealings of domestic ordinariness, which clips the spirit's wings and curbs its invention instead of letting it soar up into the Romantic realm whose language is song? What incentive to delve into the mysterious depths of music and to awaken the spirits residing at its heart can such a domestic concoction provide?)

A composer who adapted his idiom rather more successfully to both serious opera and sentimental comedy was Gottlob Bierey, whose career began before the turn of the century and who lived to admire Wagner's *Die Feen* and in return to receive a gracious pat on the head in *Mein Leben* as 'Der alte Bierey, ein erfahrener tüchtiger Musiker und seiner Zeit selbst erfolgreicher Komponist' (Wagner, 1963, 88) ('Old Bierey, an experienced, excellent musician, and in his day himself a popular opera composer'). A great admirer of Cherubini, Bierey prepared vocal scores of *Elisa*, *Faniska* and *Les Deux*

Journées and attempted to follow Cherubini's example in his serious works, of which the most successful were *Clara, Herzogin von Bretannien* (1803) and *Wladimir, Fürst von Nowgorod* (1807). In these, Cherubini's effect is felt less as formative influence than as attempted emulation, especially as this can sit rather uneasily with the lighter manner that was really Bierey's natural style. However, the *AMZ* was being rather hard on *Clara* in suggesting that it was 'zu tadeln, dass der Komponist, besonders im ersten Akt, Cherubini näher im Auge behalten hat, als ihm selbst bewusst worden' (*AMZ* 6 (1803), 207) ('to be regretted that the composer, especially in the first act, has Cherubini closer in view than he would himself have realized'). The opening scene of this somewhat Gothick opera, after a vigorous overture in varying tempos, finds Alvaro and his cowardly servant Burlerino struggling through a fearful storm towards a grim, beetling castle from which they are warned off by Federico; this is composed with an energy and a response to violent natural forces not unworthy of Cherubini, as is the first aria for Clara herself, 'Vergebens, ach!' before she loses herself in coloratura. There is also a Battle Symphony, and a Terzett in which Bierey experiments with the characters moving one by one into different time signatures. But for the most part he abandons these pretensions in favour of a more conventional mixture, with a highly sentimental (though widely praised) duet to friendship between Federico and Alvaro, a Polacca for Burlerino, some 'pathetic' arias for Clara and Federico, and a lively Presto for Trincolo in which his relish for girls impels him into a Catalogue Aria: 'Die Blonden, Brunetten, die Magen, die Fetten, die Sanften, die Blöden, die Muntern, die Spröden' etc. etc.

Bierey's talent was really better suited to the light works which occupied most of his career, including a third part of the ever-popular *Donauweibchen* and especially *Rosette, das Schweizer Hirtenmädchen* (1806). This gentle pastoral tale is little more than a succession of agreeable songs and duets (with one Trio), its popular ingredients including tuneful strophic arias, a touching Cavatina for the lovelorn Hannchen, her heart beating sadly, an effectively vigorous number for Jacob in Vengeance Aria vein, 'Ha! beim Donner des Kanonen' and a sprightly Polacca for Rosette, 'Leicht und froh entflieh des Lebens Stunden'. The work caught the public's affection, as rather more surprisingly did *Elias Rips Raps* (1810), a trivial piece for only two characters that dispenses with spoken dialogue.

Of very different significance in the emergence of Romantic opera was Friedrich Himmel. Particularly in his early years, his career was somewhat erratic, taking him from travels in Italy and the production of some Italian operas, by way of a failed attempt to stimulate a revival of German opera in Berlin with Iffland and further travels across northern Europe as far as St Petersburg, eventually back to Berlin and furious rivalry with Reichardt. Himmel's own character was also distinctly erratic. Even after his establishment in Berlin and the success of his most popular opera, *Fanchon das Leyermädchen* (1804), he was capable of trying the patience of the generally supportive Prussian royal family, on one occasion having to be removed from a rehearsal riotously drunk. Weber, introducing the work to his Dresden audience in 1817, remarked diplomatically that Himmel's 'lebenslustiger, heiterer Sinn, frohe Laune und Hang zum Lebensgenusse ließen ihm nicht Zeit, in die tiefsten Geheimnisse der Kunst zu dringen' ('pleasure-loving disposition and youthful high spirits prevented him from devoting the time needed to penetrate to music's deepest secrets'), adding that 'Versetzt in den elegantesten Zirkel des üppigen Paris, wird jedes Musikstück zum vorüberfliegenden Witz, Scherz oder zur sonstigen Betonung erhöhten Gefühles' ('The scene is laid in the most elegant and luxury-loving circles of Parisian life, and every number is a witticism caught on the wing, a joke or some other point of heightened feeling') (Weber, 1908, 283–4; Weber, 1981, 213–14).

Fanchon is the tale of a Savoyard waif who becomes rich and famous through her singing on the Paris boulevards. She sets up house with a painter, Edouard, and gives shelter to Adèle, who is fleeing from an abductor. Various complications ensue, some concerning Fanchon's attempt to bestow land in Savoy on Edouard (in the teeth of his suspicious aunt) and her arrest for the abduction of Adèle, before all is happily resolved and she can marry Edouard. The work's success was enormous: no fewer than five vocal scores were published, and it held its place in repertories for half a century. This popularity rested really on Himmel's skill as a song writer, and its forty-eight numbers (fourteen of them strophic songs) make their appeal through a pleasing tunefulness in decorating the tale or outlining the situation. It is, in fact, really a Liederspiel, and was perhaps in part an attempt to trump the ace of his bitter rival Reichardt, drawing on various popular manners including the Polacca (Edouard's lively 'Womit sich andre täuschend schmücken'), and only in the finales making any attempt to develop or sum up the dramatic situation.

Die Sylphen (1806) is another matter altogether. The plot is based on Gozzi's *La Zobeide* by the minor Berlin poet Ludwig Robert (brother of the famous actress Rahel Varnhagen). However, there is virtually no connexion between Gozzi's *tragedia fiabesca* – the bleakest of all his *fiabe* and a sinister, Bluebeard-like fantasy in which even the *commedia dell'arte* figures are dark and tormented – and Robert's mixture of rescue opera, Romantic intermingling of human and fairy, and comic Mozartian interjections. The victimized Smeraldina, Truffaldino and Brighella are replaced by Papagena, Papageno and Leporello, and Pantalone and Tartaglia by the German comic figures of Larifari and Minnewart, while the eerie, frightening improvisations indicated by Gozzi for his masks disappear in favour of robust spoken German comedy.

A vigorous, colourful overture immediately suggests aspects of *Don Giovanni* and *Die Zauberflöte* in the slow opening section, with its D minor tonality and threefold chordal exordium. Himmel is preparing the way for a twist in the plot, but also invoking the most Romantic and fantastic elements in Mozart, upon whose musical language he bases his own simpler vernacular. The music leads straight into a chorus of sylphs singing conventionally in praise of Nature – golden pastures, sparkling torrents, the blue dome of heaven – and in turn into their approach to the sleeping Sylph prince Zeleu, with whom they leave a key of understanding, a ring sent by love, and a sword. The plot turns on Zeleu's efforts to rescue Zobea, daughter of a mortal king and a Sylph princess, from the clutches of the wicked sorcerer Sinabel. Zeleu wakes to reveal his lyrical nature in an aria; Zobea also has a graceful Larghetto with some sorrowful reflections. Suddenly Papagena appears and tries to console her in a cheerful strophic song, 'Nein, nein, nichts ist betrübter'. But Sinabel is a powerful magician, and after a dark, brooding meditation he bursts into a enraged C minor aria asserting that he can call spirits from the vasty deep – 'Noch bin ich hier Meister, beherrsche die Geister' – with furious tremolos, violently stabbing chords, rushing scales and sudden off-beat emphases, in a vocal line that takes him repeatedly down to low F and E♭. In despair, Zeleu also tries to summon spirits to his aid in an excellent *Zauberformel*, or magic spell, suggesting that Himmel has learnt well from Benda and Mozart. However, who should appear but Papageno and Leporello, prattling 'Pa-pa-pa-pa-pa-geno' and (not to be outdone) 'Le-le-le-le-porello'. In a trio on Mozartian motives they agree to join forces with him in attempting Zobea's rescue. Zobea has a melodrama in which text is carefully matched to music, and moves by way of recitative into an aria and duet with Zeleu. Another invocation by a secondary character, Larifari, produces a troop of Gnomen-Cavallerie, who gallop on to end Act II. Having opened with a chromatically altered version of the overture's Andante, Act III does what it can to clear up these events. In the finale, Sinabel appears in a fountain and claims Zobea as a Sylph: 'Zobea stammet aus dem Reich der Sylphen!' In the nick of time, over the brow of the hill gallop the Gnomen-Cavallerie again, and victory is claimed by Zeleu: 'Es ist vorbei mit deinem Regimente, zum Elemente kehre, und störe nie mein Liebesglück!'

Gozzi held a fascination for German Romantic writers. His collected works were published in German in 1777–9, and attracted wide interest. Lessing and Goethe were both admirers, and in Weimar in 1802 Schiller staged an influential reworking of *Turandot* stressing the sentimental aspects above the fantastic. *Die Sylphen* looks forward almost uncannily to the Romantic operas of the following decades (Zobea's incantation anticipates Marschner's for Gertrude in *Hans Heiling*), especially in its contact between the human and the supernatural, and even further ahead. No wonder that it interested another of Gozzi's admirers, Hoffmann, fascinated as he was by the interaction of different levels of reality, and whose *Undine* was to end with a similar watery apparition. The wild absurdities with the Mozart characters not only show their continued vitality far outside their own operas, but deliberately invoke *Die Zauberflöte* and *Don Giovanni* as parent works of Romantic opera. Yet the opera did not win great success; it had to wait a year for performance, and there is some force in the complaint, when it did, that the plot is overloaded with detail (*WTz*, 8 Nov. 1806). By a coincidence this wry, brilliant Venetian fantasist would no doubt have relished, Gozzi died on the very day of the first performance of *Die Sylphen*.

Himmel's music tends to draw on various ideas and conventions that were by now becoming familiar currency, fitting them into an opera whose essential language is not very advanced. Indeed, he is most effectively himself with some of the numbers in which his melodic grace finds full expression, as with Zeleu's lyrical opening aria 'Leitet sie, ihr Himmels Wesen!', resolving to rescue Zobea, or her graceful Larghetto 'Sanft entschwand mir', later their duet, 'Ja, ich fühl' es'. Beside these, and some lively music for the Mozartian figures, the more enterprising scenes look interesting as proto-Romantic ideas set alongside a simpler, more outward manner, but the musical invention is less impressive. Even the actual juxta-position, which might be claimed as Romantic in bringing inner and outer worlds together with a stirring of comic fantasy, is incidental rather than attached to a sustained imaginative idea. Himmel's next and final opera, *Der Kobold* (1813), abandons all pretensions and settles for what is virtually a sentimental comedy in eighteen well-turned numbers that include an excellent Polacca, 'Mit dem ersten Blicke' for the lively Lisette, and finally an old-fashioned Vaudeville.

Though the operas discussed in the previous chapter were typical of many being staged at the time, none of their composers was particularly influential on the emergent generation of Romantics, except incidentally and through their successful adoption of some of the conventions that were developing. More significant, even if their operas were not so widely performed, were Georg Joseph Vogler and Franz Danzi, and their pupils and followers; and towering over the decade is the figure of Beethoven.

The Abbé Vogler remains a somewhat enigmatic figure, both admired and despised in his day, disliked by many for his arrogance and showmanship – Mozart thought him conceited and incompetent – but revered as their 'Papa' by pupils who included Danzi himself, Ritter, Winter, Weber and Meyerbeer, all of whom bore witness to the importance of his teaching for them (see Veit, 1990). Until modern times he has been largely ignored, despite the high claims made for his harmonic system and the success and influence of at least one of his operas. His first opera was the well-turned but not very remarkable *Der Kaufmann von Smyrna* (1771), written for Mannheim and responding to Mannheim conventions, with virtuoso Italianate vocalism (the characters tend to break into elaborate coloratura at the slightest provocation) being matched to virtuoso Mannheim orchestration. Works that followed included a successful melodrama in Benda fashion, *Lampedo* (1779), a Goethe Singspiel, *Erwin und Elmire* (1781), an attempt at a national opera, *Albert der Dritte von Bayern* (1781), and operas in French, Italian and Swedish. They reflect the extensive range of his travels before he achieved his major success with the important and influential *Samori* (1804).

Cast in two acts, *Samori* combines the liberal ideals of its librettist, Franz Xaver Huber, with a taste for the exotic and a mixture of comic, romantic and spectacular elements (in a manner comparable, in French opera, to the Beaumarchais and Salieri *Tarare*). The Nabob Tamburan has inherited the throne usurped by his father: only the boy Samori escaped, and has now as a young man returned secretly from exile under the name of Pando. Planning to restore him to the throne, the astrologer Rama has betrothed his own daughter Maha to Tamburan as a snare. But Maha loves Pando, whose sister Naga and Tamburan love one another. Tamburan learns of the plot, but wishes to restore the throne peacefully to the rightful heir. As Pando tries to intervene in the wedding ceremony staged between Tamburan and Maha, a violent storm breaks out (an early example of the interrupted wedding that featured in later Romantic operas). Pando tries to flee with Maha, but is deterred by an underground chorus of his murdered father and brothers (in fact, a trick of Rama's), and decides to stay and fight. Tamburan appears to be about to exact vengeance, when suddenly a curtain parts to reveal a splendid hall. The astonished Pando is crowned by Tamburan himself, and they mount the throne together.

One of Weber's student obligations was to prepare the vocal score of *Samori*, a task he came to find burdensome, but the intimate knowledge of the work he gained is reflected in his mature idiom. This includes a feeling for exoticism, but more significantly an enrichment of his orchestral vocabulary, encouraged by Vogler's emphasis in his writings on the role of instruments in 'painting' a scene or a character's mood so as to work directly on the listeners' emotions. Still more importantly, Vogler set great store by key associations and by carefully planned harmony and key relationships, particularly by thirds, to express the drama, which progresses chiefly through carefully developed musical complexes. One of his methods of making a dramatic point is shown when Pando describes his return from exile, as a stranger in his own land, to a harmonic slip from E into C. The idea is by no means unique to Vogler, but his score draws upon a systematic network of such relationships as functional to the drama. Tamburan, the benevolent despot, can express himself in vigorous rhythms but is also prone to oblique modulations and subtle chromatic harmony. 'Uneasy lies the head that wears a crown', he is, in effect, musing in his most substantial soliloquy, 'Kronen sind nur eine Bürde die das Haupt der Fürsten drükt'; and for all its rhythmic boldness the music sinks from B♭ into G♭, and later into E♭ minor – manly vigour, in fact, not excluding a sensitive nature. Like the two men, Maha has some of the eloquent accompanied recitative that also characterizes Vogler's idiom, and her sorrowful 'Wie traurig ist mein Loos' is a strong, fluent scene, shifting at one point from E♭ via G♭ into B major (really C♭ major), before returning to a different sequence of flat keys. In the Duet 'Erkläre dich!', as Maha demands to know what Rama requires of her in the plot, the music passes through a fluent sequence of movements to culminate in their confident expectation of a happy outcome in a coincidence with the theme which Beethoven conceived for his abortive opera *Vestas Feuer*, probably late in 1803, and carried over into *Leonore* in the following year (Example 21). Naga, as the second-ary lover, is rather more lightly handled, though she has a charming aria puzzling over her emotions (beginning, rather bathetically, 'Woher mag dieses kommen? Mir fehlt die Essenslust'), and wavering uncertainly between major and minor (another feature of the score). Flat keys, in particular D♭, G♭, E♭ minor, as far as C♭ major, are in general associated with grief, anxiety or foreboding, sharper keys with more positive emotions. There is even a section in the Act I finale when the chorus express their horror at the storm (notated in C minor) while the soloists reassure themselves that it is helping the successful outcome of their plot (notated in G major, the actual key of the music: this 'bitonal' notation is the work of Weber in his vocal score, and does not appear in Vogler's MS). The comic element is a little forced, though there is quite a wittily handled Trio in which Pando and Maha's duetting is constantly interrupted by interjections from the comic bass Baradra, first spoken and then in an urgently squeaked falsetto. Baradra also has a standard drinking song praising 'Essen, Trinken, Mädchen küssen', placed surprisingly close to the end; it could perhaps even have been a late sop to Viennese taste in a work far more remarkable for its choruses and ensembles than for its

(Allegro) Più Presto

Wie freu - et sich mein Herz der Won - ne

Wie freu - et sich mein Herz, mein Herz der Won - ne

(How my heart rejoices with delight)

Nie war ich so froh wie

heu - te, nie - mals fühlt' ich die - se Freu-de!

(Never was I so happy as today, never did I feel such joy!)

Allegro vivace

O na - men, na - men - lo - se Freu-de!

(Oh nameless joy!)

Example 21
(a) Vogler: *Samori* (1804), Maha and Rama
(b) Beethoven: *Vestas Feuer* (comp. 1803), Volivia and Sartagones
(c) Beethoven: *Leonore* (1805), Leonore and Florestan

Example 21

(d) Beethoven: *Fidelio* (1814), Leonore and Florestan

solo numbers. It is immediately followed by a strongly composed finale, moving forward with vigorous dramatic impetus through a series of connected movements that goes beyond most of the cumulative finales of the day and looks towards completely through-composed opera. Vogler's tendency towards uneven phrase lengths contributes to this sense of fluent prosody, and of the drama forming the music. There is also a functional use of orchestral colouring that includes powerful use of trombones and of drums, sometimes muffled. When Tamburan finally abdicates, Pando mounts the throne to the accompaniment of the kind of 'French' moralizing from the chorus with which Viennese audiences would have become familiar: 'Mehr als Zepter, mehr als Krone, zieret Edelmuth den Mann'. Weber was to be far subtler than Vogler, with a finer ear in his handling of the orchestra, and with a sharper dramatic instinct in his use of a structure of key relationships to underpin the drama, something which also enables him to make smaller harmonic points part of a work's dramatic vocabulary. But much of the stimulus came from Vogler, and much in *Samori* helped to shape the language of Romantic harmony and the structures of Romantic opera.

The most regrettable of all the losses that overtook Franz Danzi's operas is that of *Iphigenie in Aulis*, given only two performances in Munich in 1807. The review in the *AMZ* praised the work highly, especially for the unity of words and music, taking it as the text for a sermon on German serious opera with a summary history from Schütz's *Dafne* onwards, and lamenting the lack of successors to Benda, Schweitzer and Holzbauer. German composers, the article complains, have not yet raised their sights sufficiently high to true tragic opera (*AMZ* 9 (1807), 365–72). Danzi did not return to this medium. However, following the example of Weber's youthful, abandoned opera on the subject, he did produce a remarkable work, *Rübezahl der Berggeist* (1813), described on the autograph as a *romantische Oper*. Based on J. K. A. Musäus's tale of a gnome's abduction of a human girl, later also used by Spohr, the opera includes extensive ghost scenes and choruses, contrasted with the brighter arias and choruses of the human world. Particularly striking is the extended scene in Rübezahl's kingdom, bringing together melodrama, pantomime, singing and orchestral commentary, including a powerful storm graphically scored especially for wind (including piccolo) and brass, and a ghostly manifestation with speech over the orchestra. The sinister atmosphere is created largely by orchestral effect, with some use of motive, and by sombre harmony, rather than through melodic ideas. There are also signs that Danzi's interest in French opera, lightly revealed in his earlier Singspiels, now embraced Cherubini and especially Méhul: the repertory he conducted during his enlightened intendancy in Stuttgart included *Lodoiska* and *Les Deux Journées*, *Héléna* and *Uthal*, as well as works by Berton, Boieldieu, Dalayrac and Isouard. By the time the opera was written Weber had left Stuttgart for Prague, where he introduced a similar repertory of French operas, and Danzi had moved to Karlsruhe; but they kept in regular contact, and it is difficult to believe that Danzi's *Rübezahl* was unknown to the composer of *Der Freischütz*.

Of the composers born in the decade between 1776 and 1786 who were to be chiefly responsible for bringing German Romantic opera to a new maturity, Spohr had a somewhat erratic training, Weber was a pupil of Vogler and Hoffmann's education included lessons from Reichardt. The slightly younger Vogler pupil Jakob Meyer Beer was, as Giacomo Meyerbeer, to turn to Italian opera before making his splendid career in Paris.

Though Spohr's first opera, Die Prüfung (1806), is scarcely more than a single-act operetta, it indicates his ambitions not only for the furtherance of his own career in the medium that was drawing ever more interest, but for the ability of that medium to reflect new ideas. The text by Spohr's uncle Eduard Henke is lost, but is clearly one of the many plots, going as far back as the classical legend of Cephalus and Procris, in which a lover's constancy is put to the test, in this case triumphantly. It includes a striking dialogue in a duet between Natalie, attaching herself in extravagant terms to 'a maiden called Romanticism', and her father, retorting with his belief in 'a goddess called Reason'. However, this clash of the generations is scarcely reflected by the music, in a work whose most remarkable feature is the eloquent orchestration, especially for wind groups, which indicates Spohr's Romantic leanings by lending more emotional colour to the characters than the substance of their music does.

With Alruna (1808), the devotion to the supernatural in what the manuscript describes as a Romantische Oper enters Spohr's dramatic manner, to remain there in most of his following operas. Again, the text is lost, but the outlines of the plot can be discerned. In familiar operatic pairings, Herrmann loves Berta, whose lively maid Clara loves his cheerful, cowardly squire Franz. Compelled to recover some property belonging to Berta's father, Count Bruno, the men set off and in a forest encounter Alruna, the sinister Owl Queen, whose delight it is to seduce and bewitch those entering her realm: to turn, in fact, knights errant into errant knights. She attempts without success to lay her seductive spells upon Herrmann, while her companion Tio tries the same with the more responsive Franz. In Act III, Alruna and her minions pursue the escaped Herrmann in a terrifying hunt through the forest, an excellently composed scene making use of motivic recall and skilfully atmospheric orchestration. He has rejoined Franz by a grave that proves to be that of his ancestor Udo, one of Alruna's previous victims. Udo's ghost suddenly gives voice (with a little help from Mozart's Commendatore) and conveys to Herrmann a magic shield, which he uses to defeat Alruna, and matters end happily with Udo blessing the lovers' union.

For all its unevenness, *Alruna* is a considerable achievement. The awkwardnesses lie mostly in the difficulty Spohr has in reconciling his own highly chromatic harmonic idiom with his devotion to Mozart, in particular to *Die Zauberflöte* as providing the sense of sorcery and fantasy which inspired so many Romantics. So he opens his overture in E♭ minor with nine slow bars of astonishing chromatic modulations whose plunging scalic figures and mysterious melodic loops prove eventually to be the music of the ghostly Udo (an idea that may have caught the ear of the composer of another ghostly Udo, Weber's in *Euryanthe*). The major mode outcome is an imitation of *Die Zauberflöte* so blatant that Spohr defiantly declared he could think of no more admirable model, though the working out is not distinctively Mozartian, nor very individual. The obvious ill-advisedness of imitating Mozart so closely is shown in such matters as Spohr's inability to follow a strong melodic phrase with an equally good second strain. The love aria embedded in the finale of Act II opens with the rising sixth, followed by a descending scale, which characterizes some of Mozart's most sublime moments (in *Die Zauberflöte*, Tamino's 'Dies Bildnis ist bezaubernd schön' and Pamina's 'Tamino mein', in *Figaro* the Count's 'Contessa perdono'), but it then finds a lame answer (Example 22). There are other aspects of *Alruna* which reflect Spohr's operatic inexperience. To open the whole opera on a lengthy love duet is poor judgement when we have had no time to learn anything of the participants; and the succeeding numbers, a ballad-like Romanza for Herrmann 'Ein Ritter zog aus in der Wald', prettily scored, and a sprightly love duet for Clara and Franz, do little more than go through time-honoured operatic motions in an undramatic sequence. But the Act I finale is an honourable attempt at developing a dramatic progress of numbers that, despite some lapses into convention, make a genuinely cumulative end to the act. The storm opening Act II finds Spohr on surer

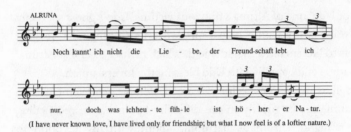

(I have never known love, I have lived only for friendship; but what I now feel is of a loftier nature.)

Example 22   Spohr: *Alruna* (1808), Alruna

ground, as he despatches Herrmann and Franz through fearful flashings and thunderings until they are brought up short by Alruna's wiles when a grotto lights up, with stage wind instruments, and her sirens sing their luring 'Willkommen, schöner Ritter' in a lilting 6/8 figure anticipating Wagner's *Parsifal* Flower Maidens. Mozart puts in another appearance, more effectively absorbed through the Vengeance Aria convention, as Alruna discharges a ferociously rocketing number taking her cue from the Queen of the Night, though here too the music fizzles out in the second strain (Example 23). Spohr provides some alternative coloratura passages in this aria taking the singer up to d′′′, suggesting that he had in mind Caroline Jagemann, mistress of the Duke of Weimar for whom the opera was given its first, unsuccessful play-through. Unnerved by that occasion, he withdrew the opera before it could come to performance.

Spohr leans, effectively enough, on other conventions, among them melodrama and, less convincingly, Polacca. Presumably his feeling that Polaccas and Cavatinas were what the public expected led him to provide a bright example of the former for the evil Tio and a tender example of the latter opening the Act II finale for Alruna, neither of whom have such dimensions to their characters. Spohr's use of motive, both for simple recall but sometimes with a suggestion of more sophisticated musical development, is adventurous. The inexperience which he himself acknowledged shows at moments, especially in the three act finales when some strong, well-related sections that grow dramatically out of one another can

(Triumph! the night flees, already day gleams)

Example 23   Spohr: *Alruna* (1808), Alruna

suddenly relapse into convention; but it is in these finales that his dramatic timing is at its most assured, and if his ambition can exceed his skill, there is much in *Alruna* to suggest more than glimpses of the course a through-composed Romantic opera might take.

It is typical of the paradoxes which E. T. A. Hoffmann liked to weave that his contribution to German opera should be of greater significance than his actual music, yet that a fair valuation of the music should have been clouded by false expectations aroused by his imaginative writings. The most important of the writings on opera belong to the period approaching his masterpiece, *Undine* (1816), when he was also emerging as an author of dazzling individuality. In his earlier years, he was more concerned with writing reviews attacking what he saw as feeble or misguided in the operas of the day, and composing operas of his own in which some of his ideas are explored. These ideas do not include the mysterious, sinister apparitions, the dark extremes of experience, the weird layerings of fantasy and reality, let alone the structural eccentricities, that were to characterize his most famous stories. At this stage of his life, however, he was already interested in the idea of music as embodying a secret imaginative world which it can communicate directly to the listener without the mediation of words.

Like all Hoffmann's early operas, his first, *Die Maske* (1799), to his own text, stands at some distance from Hiller and eighteenth-century Singspiel. It is really closer to South German or Viennese Singspiel in its reliance on broad ensembles, arias that admit some coloratura, choral scenes, and especially finales enlarging the role of the orchestra, which can effectively lead the dramatic impetus, control its pace and, within limits, communicate directly to the audience. However, his third opera, *Die lustigen Musikanten* (1805) (his second, *Scherz, List und Rache* (1801), after Goethe, is lost), represents a considerable advance. The language is still essentially that of Mozart, in whose honour Hoffmann famously changed his third name from Wilhelm to Amadeus in 1804; but as is shown by the story *Don Juan* of 1813 and by much else, he regarded Mozart's musical language as fully Romantic. Clemens Brentano's plot, if scarcely fantastic by Hoffmann's later standards, involves farcical interactions between the sibling Duke and Duchess of Famagusta, musicians including the blind old Piast and his love-lorn daughter Fabiola, a melancholy hero, Rinaldo, who arrives from Samarkand with the Minister, and a Bürgermeister and a local Nightwatchman-cum-Astronomer, the latter three being also Pantalon, Tartaglia and Truffaldin. There is no improvisation, but the use of these *commedia dell'arte* figures reflects Hoffmann's fascination with 'the magnificent Gozzi'; he was disappointed that the audience did not share this, and admiring allusions to Gozzi, whose *fiabe* he saw as a treasure-trove of operatic subjects, are scattered through his writings (with favourable comments from his Dog Berganza and his Tomcat Murr). Though vividly Mozartian in language (and closer to *Die Entführung* than to *Don Giovanni*), the music has much original invention, making some use of a rising and falling chromatic scale as a motivic idea. The orchestra itself takes on greater individuality, with some enterprising scoring, such as imaginative use of woodwind, and the setting of tremolo violins and violas against plainly bowed violins and basses at a moment of tension in the Act I finale.

With *Der Trank der Unsterblichkeit* (1808), Hoffmann for the first time used the description *Romantische Oper*, presumably having in mind the plot's fantastic events. The 'draught of immortality' is swallowed by Namarand, surrounded by wealth and luxury in Ispahan but unhappy because of life's transience, and refusing to be comforted by his beloved Mirza or by the kindly Shah's precept that to be mortal is to be free. The ensuing tangles involve him waking from a magic sleep of many years to find his house destroyed, his wives dead, and on the throne a new Shah who promptly imprisons him. He now seeks death from the guardian angel who had first given him the draught, only to find that it has all been an illusion arranged by the 'angel', in fact Mirza, and he humbly accepts his lot. The work is not only a moral tale about the certainty of death conferring meaning on life, a reflection of the miserably immortal Struldbrugs in *Gulliver's Travels* and a foreshadowing of the Karel Čapek story to which Janáček turned for *The Makropoulos Case*; it is also an example of the many plots of 'education' through a contrived illusion, such as Gluck's *L'Ivrogne corrigé*, which came to renewed popularity in Romantic times. There is little if any evidence in the music that Hoffmann was interested in the interlocking of illusion and reality that came to absorb him as a writer. Composed in a frantic thirty-six days to secure his appointment as music director in Bamberg, the music scarcely reflects the fantasy of the events, though it includes some good atmospheric moments, such as Namarand's appeal to his 'guardian angel' at the end of Act II as well as (immediately preceding it) such popular ingredients as a lively Arietta 'alla polacca' for another of his wives, Mandane (see music example 16, p. 177).

Uniquely among composers of his generation, Carl Maria von Weber was born into a family of theatre musicians and an actual travelling theatre company run by his feckless and eccentric father. He claimed, in the not wholly reliable Autobiographical Sketch he wrote for a friend in 1818, that an attraction to dramatic music began to show itself early, and that the drawbacks of the itinerant life and constant changes of teacher were offset by the need to find his own distinctive style (Weber, 1908, 3–8; Weber, 1981, 250–4). Apart from fragments of his *romantisch-komische Oper*, *Das Waldmädchen*, some of which may have been absorbed into *Silvana*, his first surviving opera is *Peter Schmoll und seine Nachbarn* (1803).

Based on a rambling novel concerning the domestic life of some émigrés who have fled the Revolution to sanctuary across the German border, *Peter Schmoll* lacks its spoken dialogue but is musically complete. It is a remarkable piece for a boy of fifteen, and goes some way towards bearing out his remarks about a struggle to assert his individuality. The musical language is basically that of the Singspiel of the day, but even the simplest numbers have a liveliness and the ability to turn familiar conventions to original effect. The plain harmonic manner is enlivened by some familiar harmonic strokes with witty dramatic relevance, as when thirds-modulations away from D to B♭ and F are attached to the lurchings and stumblings of a game of Blind Man's Buff. There is also an interest in key associations to underpin the drama (and this before he came under Vogler's influence). However, the work's most striking aspect is its emphasis on the orchestra, and its original use of the instruments. Weber admitted to being taken with the idea of using old instruments, and so recorders and basset horns make their appearance, at one point to suggest the venerability of an old man from a previous age, who is also given a striking combination of piccolos, horns, trombones and strings. Weber's love of the viola is already present, especially in a Romanza for Minette (the opera's only female role) accompanied by divided violas and lower strings, with bassoon interjections between strophes of the touching vocal melody. A section of some forty bars of the Blind Man's Buff Terzetto for Minette, Schmoll and his steward Hans Bast is for instruments alone, with a cello blundering after a nimbly evasive flute. Sometimes the young Weber asks too much of his effects, and there are ideas which he might later have executed more deftly, but there is an adventurous ear at work here.

In the years between composing *Peter Schmoll* in 1801 and *Silvana* in 1808–10, Weber had studied with the most influential of his teachers, Vogler. He had also come under the benign influence of Danzi, who re-aroused his flagging sense of vocation and encouraged him to re-work his abandoned *Das Waldmädchen*. Described as a *Romantische Oper*, *Silvana* brings together the life of the forests and the lost world of chivalry, Romantic ideals that were to mark many operas and none more thoroughly than Weber's own. Count Rudolf is unwillingly betrothed to Count Adelhart's daughter Mechthilde, who loves Albert, son of Adelhart's enemy Hanns von Cleeburg. With his other daughter Ottilie having been abducted, Adelhart is anxious for Mechthilde to make a good marriage. On a bear hunt in the woods with his bumbling squire Krips, Rudolf encounters a dumb girl, Silvana; enraptured, he carries her, sleeping, back to Adelhart's castle. When she awakes in his room, Rudolf woos her. At a tournament, Rudolf has to intervene to prevent Albert from being seized by Adelhart. Back in the forest, Ulrich is looking for his foster-daughter Silvana, and after further complications it is revealed that 'Silvana' is in fact Ottilie, exposed in the forest as a child by Adelhart as the supposed fruit of his wife's infidelity with Hanns. She is now released from the protective vow of silence enjoined upon her by Ulrich, and can marry Rudolf with Adelhart's blessing, while Mechthilde can now marry Albert; Mechthilde's maid Klärchen, who has played a minor part in the plot, can also marry Albert's squire Kurt. The opera's most striking feature is, of course, the entrusting of the part of the heroine to a performer who does not utter until the very end. The idea is not unique: coincidentally, Ferdinand Fränzl was writing his *Carlo Fioras* (1810), in which a poor dumb man saves the situation by exposing with signs the villainous Don Juan de Babastro; and there was to come the famous example of Auber's *La Muette de Portici* (1828). But Weber seems to have been first in a field that suited him well, with his rapidly unfolding gift for instrumental drama.

Singspiel elements remain in *Silvana*, but they are on the whole confined to Krips. Even here, his Arietta draws its engaging character less from the plain melody than from the deft orchestration, with an obbligato flute and bassoon two octaves apart, while the Tempo d'un Tedesco has a lively violin dancing around the cheerful drinking song. Adelhart is a more ambitious piece of character drawing. Though not yet developed as the ambivalent villain type which Weber was to portray in Lysiart, he is of this temper, for though sometimes shaken by violent fits of coloratura he does also show genuine affection for Mechthilde. Weber was still less confident with her, uncertain how to portray a sympathetic, oppressed woman who nevertheless stands in the lovers' way. There is greater assurance with Rudolf, who is more introspective by nature than the general run of operatic knights and most himself when reflecting Weber's innate tendency to think in instrumental rather than vocal lines.

The whole atmosphere of the opera tends in this direction. As soon as the characters find themselves in the open air, new invention breathes into them; and this is largely through Weber's response to nature and the world of the forest by means of the orchestra. Gently stirring figures and mysterious tremolos, cheerful huntsmen's horns, and an impressive storm, with swirling strings, booming horns and flashing piccolos, are effects Weber would have encountered in other operas, but here they are effectively connected to the drama and the characters. Their vividness, and the orchestra's ability to take the expressive lead, look forward to much that was to be realized in *Der Freischütz*. Silvana herself is an intensely Romantic conception, a child of nature, a creature of instinct and untainted simplicity, elusive and fascinating in her maimed beauty, shy but responsive to the love Rudolf offers her. She is characterized mostly by an oboe for her lively charm, a cello for the passion Rudolf stirs in her; and in the scene when she wakes in Rudolf's room, there is no need for her to speak words as Weber's instrumental skill depicts her shyness, her wonder, her slight coquettishness, then her whole-hearted response to his declarations of love. The world of *Euryanthe* as well as that of *Der Freischütz* is anticipated in this marriage of the noble emotions of mediaeval chivalry and the dwindling purity of the forests; and despite some gaucheness, it is an opera that creates and inhabits a world of its own with the touch that betokens a young opera composer embracing his vocation.

After this ambitious Romantic opera, to have written a one-act Singspiel, *Abu Hassan* (1811), based on the second half of the popular story 'The Sleeper Awakened' from *The 1,001 Nights*, might seem a surprising step backwards. However, Weber was in urgent need of money to pay off debts incurred in his Stuttgart years; and the work is in many ways a striking advance. Its very compactness – an overture and eight numbers, with two more added later – helped to concentrate his invention and to draw from him an intenser vein of lyricism and a new comic sparkle. They set each other off in this witty tale of an impoverished couple, Abu Hassan and Fatime, raising funds by blackmailing the lustful vizier Omar and then faking each other's deaths so as to claim compensation from the anxious Caliph Haroun al Rashid, who arrives in person to see what is afoot and, much amused, forgives the deception. The need for compression means that Weber is obliged to keep the action moving swiftly and to ensure that the drama guides the musical forms within very short numbers; while the pace of this brings out the lightest touch he had yet found in opera. He could take delight in neat contrapuntal strokes, as in the Terzetto when Fatime keeps the frustrated Omar shut up in a cupboard while Hassan feigns jealous rage, in slily exaggerated harmony at mentions of love and death, and in some beautifully inventive orchestration, as with a lyrical bassoon song against guitars and violas. A Polacca for Fatime uses the well-worn convention of soubrette liveliness but does so with a tender melodic line to show, in a manner typical of the opera, depths of devotion expressed with lightness and humour. Her main aria, composed later, in 1823, is a mock lament splendidly parodying the grand manner but doing so in a mere thirty-two bars. The best of the work challenges Mozart on his own ground, but in Weber's terms, and comes off honourably. *Abu Hassan* makes it the more regrettable that Weber never completed another comedy. Indeed, ten years were to go by before he wrote another opera, and that was *Der Freischütz*.

Apart from some juvenilia, Meyerbeer's German operas consist of a protracted Biblical piece, *Jephtas Gelübde* (1812), and a *Lustspiel* initially entitled *Wirth und Gast* (1813); this is based on the first half of the tale in the *1,001 Nights*, 'The Sleeper Awakened', whose second half had been set by Weber. Meyerbeer's defection to Italian opera may well have been hastened by his experiences over *Wirth und Gast*. The first performance in Stuttgart was a shambles, with the principals unsure of their music and the conductor, Conradin Kreutzer, insisting on huge cuts. The single 1814 Vienna performance of a revised version (as *Die beiden Kalifen*) failed, largely through intrigues and through problems with the singers, in its appeal to the brilliant audience gathered for the Congress (Meyerbeer, 1960, 637–40). Though regretful when his friend deserted the cause of German opera, Weber remained loyal and wrote two articles enthusiastically introducing the work, then reviewing it after his own performances first in Prague in 1815, when it was evidently a success (Weber, 1908, 262–4, 123–7; 1981, 138–40, 140–3). He staged it again, as *Alimelek*, in Dresden in 1820, when his vigorous contrasting of its qualities with Meyerbeer's Italian opera *Emma di Resburgo* (a revision of Bouilly's text for Méhul's *Héléna* relocated in 'Lanerk', near Glasgow) triggered off a spirited controversy (Weber, 1908, 305–10, 388–91; Weber, 1981, 277–89; see also a defence of Meyerbeer against Weber's attacks in *AMZ* 22 (1820), 442–4).

In the original story on which *Wirth und Gast* draws, Alimelek (as Abu Hassan is renamed to avoid confusion) gets his revenge on a group of cadgers when the Caliph Haroun al Rashid plays a trick on him by drugging his drink and installing him on the throne for a day; believing that he is now Caliph, he can set about punishing his persecutors. However, the absence of a female lead and so of any love interest led the librettist, Johann Wohlbrück, to bring to the centre of the action a new plot involving Alimelek and his beloved Irene (as she is surprisingly named). Irene proves to be Haroun's adored niece, who has disappeared and been rescued from death by Alimelek. As Caliph, Alimelek enjoys himself greatly, but after a second drug he awakes in prison, threatened with execution unless he will renounce Irene in favour of another, which he refuses to do. The same trick is played on Irene, with the same result. Assured of their mutual devotion and of Irene's happiness, the Caliph blesses their union.

A more substantial work than *Abu Hassan*, *Wirth und Gast* employs a large cast and covers two acts. Its weaknesses lie chiefly in some inexperience in dramatic pacing, so that the only three solo numbers follow the opening chorus consecutively, and several pieces tend to outstay their welcome: partly this is also, with a few striking exceptions and *pace* Weber's vigorous praise, through lack of real melodic distinction. However, much of the opera's quality lies in Meyerbeer's confident handling of the large ensembles in scene complexes and in his ability to give these dramatic life, especially through original orchestration and some skilful use of motive. If not worked symphonically, this is subtle and allusive, more than simple reminiscence motive, as when Alimelek lies in his dream and ideas from different quarters of the opera swim into his drugged mind, or when the two act finales are related by thematic means. From his teacher Vogler, Meyerbeer had acquired his ability to connect harmonic relationships, especially by thirds, to dramatic events. He can make use of these for immediately vivid colourings (as when Irene appears in the Act I finale, or for comic effect as fortunes lurch in Alimelek's drinking song), but also more subtly over a considerable range, so as to sustain dramatic momentum in both finales and in the remarkable scene of Alimelek's incarceration.

Meyerbeer's orchestration already has the grace and variety which he later developed in his great Parisian triumphs, but in this German opera there is, even at a comparatively primitive stage, the ability to use orchestral colour not only to enhance the expressiveness of the words but almost as an aspect of motive. Together with Weber, he outdoes Vogler in the handling of individual instruments, often in unfamiliar combinations, and in their use to make graphic dramatic points. He does not share Weber's love of viola tone (though there is a Weberian viola obbligato against wind and lower strings in the Terzetto, No. 11). Perhaps influenced by Méhul, and in particular *Joseph*, his preferred instrument is the cello, which he uses with great subtlety, including in a bold opening to Act II with soft three-part cellos over double bass to introduce the gentle chorus 'Ihr Schmeichellüfte, ihr Balsamsdüfte'. But the most tender side of the cello is also associated with Irene, singing with high held notes over her Andantino in the Act I finale, then moving in fluent crotchet counterpoint under Alimelek's clarinet as he reflects upon her unhappiness in 'Unglückliche Irene', and later throbbing affectingly in the opera's most striking individual number – one whose Andante section indicates the range and subtlety of Meyerbeer's orchestration – when, as defiance fails to move the Caliph, she pleads with him not to force her to renounce Alimelek (Example 24).

Bestriding this period of German opera, for a whole decade from 1804 to 1814, is one of the greatest and most problematic operas of musical history, at once of its time, a reflection of changing times,

(Oh to spare me take back your hard decree; I cannot renounce him, he is forever dear to me, I shall never renounce him.)

Example 24   Meyerbeer: *Wirth und Gast* (1813), Irene

and transcending its time. When Beethoven approached the work which he at first wanted to call *Leonore*, he was already familiar with many operas. Playing the viola in the Bonn orchestra from January 1789 to the end of 1792, he came to know, with the experience of actual performance for which there is no substitute, a good range of the local operatic fare of the day. The repertory in which he played included opera buffa, opéras-comiques by Grétry, Monsigny and Dalayrac (*Nina*), and German works by Dittersdorf (*Doktor und Apotheker*), Benda (*Ariadne* and *Romeo und Julie*) and Umlauf (*Die schöne Schusterin*), as well as Mozart's *Entführung*, *Don Giovanni* and *Figaro*. In Vienna, his opera-going may have included many Italian pieces, and German operas including Winter's *Das unterbrochene Opferfest*. Then, in 1802, he was overwhelmed by the experience of Cherubini's first Viennese productions, *Lodoiska*, followed in the same year by *Les Deux Journées*, *Médée* and *Elisa*. Other French works he admired included Le Sueur's *La Caverne* and Méhul's *Ariodant*.

There is much in the works which Beethoven encountered in these years that went into his own imagination as his opera progressed, even if it was sometimes later to be discarded. A great deal was tightened up in the revision of the 1805 original enjoined upon Beethoven in 1806, when Stephan von Breuning worked on Sonnleithner's text. If the two versions are now generally referred to by the title *Leonore*, this is a fair reflection of a work that was still closer to a French rescue opera than it remained in the final version of 1814, with G. F. Treitschke now revising the text, as *Fidelio*. There remained to the end ingredients which are identifiable in the music of recent times, sometimes strengthened and given more universal resonance as his imagination took a more powerful grip on the subject. It is noticeable, for instance, that the lovers' personal joy at release in *Leonore* turns to a universal, 'nameless' joy in *Fidelio*. As well as taking note of ideas in Gaveaux's *Leonore*, he drew upon some of his own music, especially the Cantata on the Death of Joseph II and the abandoned opera *Vestas Feuer*, whose text suggests a work filled with scenic effects – waterfalls, the Roman forum, the collapse of Vesta's Temple – of a kind with which he had grown impatient. He also responded to some of the symphonic techniques in Mozart's operas, to mixed advantage when the powerful sonata forms that drive some of the ensembles may charge the situation with unique energy but also risk acquiring a momentum beyond the drama itself. From Mozart also, perhaps, came the most impressive instance of giving the hero and heroine the arias with the largest-scale organization. The earlier, more domestic numbers in the *Leonore* of 1805 draw on Singspiel in establishing the milieu of Rocco and his home life. One of Beethoven's improvements in the final version was to drop some numbers altogether, principally 'Ein Mann ist bald genommen' and 'Um in der Ehe froh zu leben', which do nothing for the situation except to hold it up, and Pizarro's second aria, 'Auf euch nur will ich bauen', which diminishes the impact of evil made by the first. 'Um in der Ehe' is also well lost, despite the amiable nature of the music, as it reflects too closely and pointlessly the Mannheim convention of the aria with obbligato instruments (here, violin and cello) which Beethoven would have known, if only from Mozart's 'Martern aller Arten' in *Die Entführung*. Other numbers were shortened, whether in the interests of tightening up the music or of moving the action on more swiftly from the domestic scenes to the heart of the drama cannot be said, but both reasons will stand. Though the extent of cuts is always an insecure guide to the degree of improvement, it is indicative that, between 1805 and 1814, 'Jetzt Schätzchen' loses twenty-four bars, 'O wär ich schon' loses thirteen bars, 'Gut, Söhnchen, gut' loses thirty bars, and others are variously trimmed. Almost all the numbers are shortened, but the most crucial short-enings occur in the early stages, correcting Beethoven's tendency to remain dramatically static in the domestic situation before the significance of the drama had gripped him.

Other sources range wider. Ideas later abandoned include the crowd's invasion of the prison, reflecting a revolutionary fervour close to *fait historique* and the storming of the Bastille; Florestan's reflections near the end of his scena, which have not wholly detached themselves from Grétry and King Richard; and Don Fernando's lengthy moralizing, which can be laid at the door of Bouilly. The librettist of Gaveaux's *Léonore* (1798) (on which Beethoven's first *Leonore* librettist Josef Sonnleithner based his work) as well as of *Les Deux Journées*, Bouilly was a genuine liberal, but one in a French tradition of pressing home a moral across the footlights. (His remark that the Leonore subject was based on a true incident he encountered during his time as an official in Tours during the Terror comes in his autobiography, *Mes récapitulations*, as a passing reference, but the story is also likely to have been an imaginative conflation of several occurrences and in particular various characters he met in those perilous times.)

Some of these ideas lie comparatively near the surface, as do some of the suggestions from French opera. There is the immediate example of a disguised wife rescuing her husband and a dramatic trumpet call in Méhul's *Héléna* (to another text by Bouilly), but more significant was the sense of darkness composed into scenes of imprisonment, which Beethoven may have appreciated in Berton's *Les Rigueurs du cloître* and Dalayrac's *Camille*, and certainly would have done in Le Sueur's *La Caverne*, Méhul's *Ariodant* and Cherubini's *Lodoiska*. In none of these composers did he find the use of motivic recall interesting, surprisingly in one who was to take motivic development to unprecedented heights in his own instrumental music. He did, however, find further inspiration for symphonic development in the dramatic momentum of Monsigny's *Le Déserteur* but especially in the music of Cherubini. His admiration was whole-hearted, and was directly and generously expressed when Cherubini came to Vienna for *Faniska*. *Lodoiska*, with its treatment of the theme of innocence rescued and its powerful sense of the atmosphere in the depths of a sinister castle, was the prime example. Above all, it was Cherubini's tremendous sense of dramatic momentum which excited him. This charge of energy can become almost a mannerism in Cherubini, taking over a scene with a forcefulness that is more than the dramatic situation can really sustain and which can threaten to become not so much inspiring as exhausting. Beethoven's admiration sprang from the recognition of its power, and of what it held for a composer of his own temper. The inspiration for Pizarro's Vengeance Aria derives not a little from Dourlinski, but its prime source is Mozart's Queen of the Night, with additional impetus from Süssmayr's *Der Spiegel von Arkadien*, vastly popular in Vienna during Beethoven's time there. Here are the soaring and plunging arpeggios, the furious scales, the reliance on disruptive augmented seconds, the tendency to drive the metre from square four-bar phrases into something more irregular, perhaps even the common key of D minor (see music example 17, p. 181). To compare Pizarro with Dourlinski and these earlier Vengeance Arias is to recognize some sources, but also to perceive what a torrential river has flowed from them. Again, whereas the melodramas in *Les Deux Journées* have a memorable tension, the perception by a fine composer of what the technique can hold, the power of Beethoven's Dungeon Scene springs from a more profound depth of compassion.

There is also the matter of the changes in the orchestration. In a superficial sense, that of the original *Leonore* is more Romantic, in that it is softer and richer. But this is misleading. As perhaps the most striking example: the introduction to the Dungeon Scene in *Leonore* is scored as if in a cavernous spaciousness, with thick timbres and active string tremolos. In *Fidelio* everything is thinner, with the brass no longer including trumpets and trombones but resting on horns crooked in F and Eb and sounding in a harsh register against the high woodwind. Such sparer orchestration is characteristic of Beethoven's new intent. Instead of describing, he is using the violence of the sound, its sense of strain, not to depict a scene but to convey its misery. The orchestration has become a fully functional part of the expression, and in this has become in a fuller sense Romantic.

To a substantial degree, the opera's power depends upon the careful tonal organization which was increasingly becoming a structural feature of opera. In the *Leonore* versions of the opera, C major is the key of the opening and of the final resolution, a strong symmetry. But it is stronger, in *Fidelio*, to have at first a disparate series of keys for Act I and the start of Act II, with Leonore and Florestan far apart in E major and F minor/A♭ major, while Pizarro is in D minor/ major; the Prison key is B♭. Only when Leonore and Rocco have set to work digging the grave after their melodrama does the opera abandon these individual associations as the greater drama seizes hold; and in a huge circle of fifths Beethoven drops from Florestan's 'Euch werdet Lohn' (A major) through Pizarro's 'Er sterbe' (D major) and the duet between Florestan and Leonore, 'O namenlose Freude' (G major) to the triumphantly achieved finale in C major. Together with this goes the skilled preparation of a scene, and the development of its characters and relationships and its narrative power, and the acute sense of the scene's timing in the opera, by a composer with a powerful dramatic instinct. But if *Fidelio* is a thriller – and the sound of the rescuing trumpet and Rocco's outburst of thankfulness and the embrace of the long-sundered couple never fail in the theatre – it strikes deeper because Beethoven has composed them, in part through his tonal scheme, into a new condition. The Leonore and Florestan and Pizarro of *Leonore* are characters who display courage and suffering and villainy; in the opera's final form they stand as testimony to how the quality of heroism can overthrow tyranny. *Fidelio* grows from the domestic tale by way of brave endurance and a sacramental act of valour into a celebration of eternal values: the hero, or heroine, becomes the Hero and finally Heroism.

Moreover, the inconsistencies that have been laid as a reproach at Beethoven's door can, when these are his preoccupations in a unique work, be heard as an essential strength. They may be described as both external and internal. There is, for instance, an 'external' inconsistency between the domestic doings in Rocco's house and Pizarro's first appearance. On the face of it, this is just the familiar operatic contrast between good, simple folk and the villain, who must be made to seem dreadful if his defeat by the hero is to have any power. But by charging Pizarro's 'Ha! welch' ein Augenblick' with such a shocking force, Beethoven far overtakes the familiar conventions of Vengeance Aria. As well as the bounding vocal line, the jabbing off-beat accents, the sizzling string figures, there are the ferocious harmonic progressions; helped by the chorus's numbed reply, he creates a character of a completely different energy. There is an 'external' inconsistency in the placing of the sublime Quartet, which halts the drama for inward reflection, between the simple arias by Marzelline and Rocco, but an 'internal' one between music and words in the Quartet's suddenly peaceful canonic formality and the various emotions of its singers. Still more, there is an inconsistency between the exuberant words with which the Prisoners greet the light, words for which any lesser composer would find a setting of simple joyfulness, and music which, after the hushed string figures, swells from their softly intoned rapture into a hymn to the clean light of day after the stinking dungeon, to freedom after darkness and despair. By these creative means, Beethoven lifts the characters' plight beyond the particular into the universal even as the plain mechanisms of the plot proceed. To call these inconsistencies is to employ the language of those who resist *Fidelio*: they are in truth the expressive extremes which brace the drama in the mind of a great composer.

The years between the century's end and Napoleon's defeat at the Battle of the Nations in 1813 saw a profusion of opera in German lands; they were also the years in which there took place the great efflorescence of Romantic ideas embracing letters, painting, philosophy, political thought, even the sciences, and, by no means least, music. But if music was increasingly felt to be the ideal Romantic art, it was also, as so often, the slowest of all the arts to respond. Only sporadically did Romantic ideas begin to enter opera, but they were to give opera a Romantic identity with an increasing domination over Singspiel and over the continuing attempts at German grand opera. It was, indeed, the drawing together of different disciplines, and the wish to discover, in apparent opposites or irreconcilables, a new unity and wholeness and thereby to expand the range of human beings' imaginative capacities, that was to find in opera an ideal Romantic condition. Without this rich fertilization from the significant artists and thinkers of these turbulent, wonderful years, the maturing of German opera would have been still longer delayed.

It was the impact of the French Revolution which fully released the intellectual energies that were to characterize Germany in these years. When the first excitement was succeeded by dismay at the Terror, some of the greatest minds withdrew their support. Goethe became more aloof, though his mind and work continued to exercise their influence: *Wilhelm Meisters Lehrjahre* (1795–6) provided the most powerful example of the *Bildungsroman*, inspiring a whole generation as a major Romantic medium. Schiller, originally a passionate supporter of the Revolution, turned his back angrily, and while never losing his devotion to the ideals of freedom – in the *Wallenstein* trilogy (1797–9), in *Maria Stuart* (1800), in *Wilhelm Tell* (1804) – increasingly concerned himself with the fuller education of the individual free spirit. The Revolution encouraged individuality but, at a time when Germany lay under political constraint, this was turned towards things of the mind, towards the arts, sciences and philosophy, stimulating speculation and creativity and giving the artist and thinker new prominence as arbiter and guide, as inventor of the world, while the statesman, the soldier and the churchman had for different reasons little such scope.

It was by no means always the major artists who had the most influence. In a slim volume with the cumbersome title *Herzenser-giessungen eines kunstliebenden Klosterbruders* (Emotional outpourings of an art-loving monk, 1797), the young poet Wilhelm Heinrich Wackenroder gave voice to his ecstatic experience of Raphael, Michelangelo and Leonardo da Vinci, as well as his own countryman Dürer, with a passionate plea for art to be held as a form of religion, its understanding reaching the recipient through both the senses and the spirit. His most intense example is fictional, with the musician Joseph Berglinger representing the most sensitive, inward artistic nature of all, and setting an example for many musicians in Romantic fiction. Contributing to the book was Ludwig Tieck, who in 1799 introduced his friend's ideas to the Romantics gathered at Jena. Schiller was already established there, for a while; but the inner Romantic circle really comprised Friedrich Schlegel and his mistress (later wife) Dorothea Veit, August Wilhelm Schlegel and his wife Caroline, at different times the philosophers Johann Fichte, Friedrich Schelling and Georg Wilhelm Hegel, and Friedrich von Hardenberg, the subtle, evocative poet who wrote under the name Novalis. Within a short time they had established a journal, *Das Athenäum*, which in six issues from 1798 gave voice to their Romantic aspirations and included Novalis's *Hymnen an die Nacht*. August Wilhelm Schlegel added, to his own influential critical writings arguing for Romantic ideas, the translations of Shakespeare's plays that awoke a wide German readership to their Romantic nature, and which remain familiar versions to this day. His younger brother Friedrich did much to kindle new imaginative interest in Germany's literary heritage, and to stir Romantic imaginations by the use of fragments or aphorisms, as representing flashes of light in the infinite more revealing than the steadier illumination of a finite philosophical system. As contribution to the popular genre that was beginning to sweep through the German reading public, he also produced a novel, *Lucinde* (1799), scandalous in its day, describing an ardent young man who is educated to true love; it includes a pioneering Romantic discussion of the erotic appeal of night between the lovers, and of their ultimate consummation in the eternal night of death. For a few brief years, until disagreements and emotional complications began to divide them, the Jena group lived and talked and worked together in a blaze of intensity that set German Romanticism alight as an artistic beacon.

Other cities followed, notably Dresden, where Ludwig Tieck made his home and where the beauty of the buildings and the surrounding country inspired Caspar David Friedrich, with his mysterious landscapes on to which the imagination is often projected through the medium of solitary watchers; while Berlin, largest of the German cities, drew intellectuals to follow the now scattered Jena group and younger men including E. T. A. Hoffmann and Friedrich Schleiermacher, the theologian in whose anti-dogmatic Christianity 'feeling' for the infinite was supreme. But it was Heidelberg which really succeeded Jena as a centre of Romanticism. Clemens Brentano arrived in 1804, in the following year Achim von Arnim, and their publication of the collection of folk songs *Des Knaben Wunderhorn* was in the spirit of Rousseau and of Herder in giving a new force to popular art, as musicians were quick to find. It also inspired Joseph von Görres, a vivid, impulsive writer, later editor of the vigorously critical *Der rheinische Merkur*, to his collection *Die teutschen Volksbücher*. The journal founded in Heidelberg, *Die Zeitung für Einsiedler*, drew writers including Jean Paul and then the brothers Jacob and Wilhelm Grimm. Their *Kinder- und Hausmärchen* sank another well deep into German folklore; but these enduringly loved fairy tales were part of a research both scientific and imaginative into the sources of German identity, fired by Herder, that was later to find systematic expression in the Grimms' great *Deutsches Wörterbuch* which remains an imposing authority on German philology. Other centres began to spring up. The only one belonging to a musician was at Giebichstein, near Halle, where J. F. Reichardt's house, picturesquely set by a ruined castle, drew many Romantic artists for visits.

There were, in all this manifold activity, certain ideas that cast a spell on those working in very different disciplines. Reaction against frustratingly mundane, often violent political and military circumstances encouraged adventures into distant worlds of the imagination. A fictionalized view of the German Middle Ages, as flight from the present into an invented heroic past, gave new resonance to tales of mediaeval chivalry. A preoccupation with distant lands lent enchantment to the view of the cruel, colourful Orient. An absorption in the realm of night, where dreams reigned and thoughts unuttered in Enlightenment day were set free, led to the admission of the irrational into art, perhaps as fantasy interlocking with reality or suppressed horror spilling into daily life, the thrill of terror touching the thrill of beauty. As well as writing his *Hymnen an die Nacht*, Novalis placed *Heinrich von Ofterdingen*, his unfinished novel taking the example of *Wilhelm Meister* into poetic territory, in an allegorized Middle Ages as the Minnesinger of the title seeks the 'blue flower' that became a symbol of Romantic yearning. Tieck's *Franz Sternbalds Wanderungen* is set in an idyllic sixteenth century, and includes some beautiful descriptions of Nature and the painter hero's identification with it. Novalis had trained and practised as a mining geologist, and at the centre of his multifarious ideas pondered a connexion between the visible and invisible world, between the physical and the imaginative, between the turbulence of Day and 'the dwelling-place of Night'. One of the most remarkable members of the Jena circle was the physicist Johann Wilhelm Ritter, who (like his friend Novalis) took up the ideas of Luigi Galvani about 'animal electricity' with experiments involving the interaction of the animate and inanimate world. Ritter was a speculative thinker and something of a poet as well as an experimental scientist, and his faith that intuition must play a part in science was attached to a belief in matter as dynamic rather than inert, embroiled in a mysterious connexion with the living world. His idea that science might lead towards healing the division between Man and Nature found philosophical support in the theories of another friend from Jena days, Friedrich Schelling.

Although he is now little regarded, scarcely any philosopher affected his Romantic contemporaries as much as Schelling. This was above all for his so-called Nature Philosophy, in which he argued that all matter in Nature possesses a purpose suggesting a continual tendency towards a higher condition, thus linking it with the consciousness of animate life, and so being joined in a single Idea. In two brilliant youthful essays, *Ideen zu einer Philosophie der Natur* (1797) and *Von der Weltseele* (1798), Schelling used the term World Soul to describe this single condition. The arguments in the former for what he called his *große Synthesis* draw Nature and Spirit ever closer together, culminating in the phrase that kindled the Romantics' imaginations, 'Die Natur soll der sichtbare Geist, der Geist, die unsichtbare Natur seyn' (Schelling, 1797, II, 56/1706) ('Nature shall be the visible Spirit, Spirit shall be the invisible Nature'). The lyrical intensity with which Schelling described his vision was especially persuasive with artists, whose work he saw as revelatory, the infinite made finite. It had a strong appeal for a generation which was seeking ever closer contact between the arts, even hoping, with Novalis, for a union between music, painting and poetry that would form a complete, synaesthetic whole.

To a large extent, Schelling's ideas were in direct contradiction to those of Fichte, who had opposed the Ego of the mind to the Non-Ego of the world outside the mind; but Fichte was influential on a wider audience than the Romantics. Claiming that the function of the Ego was a striving towards ever greater liberation, Fichte argued that the ideal State was an organization in which all men enjoyed equal rights of freedom; and, in times when Germany was still under the control of Napoleon, this had a seductive appeal. The fourteen *Reden an die deutsche Nation* were delivered to a packed lecture hall in the Berlin Academy of Sciences in 1807–8. Arrogant and uncompromising, Fichte was a compulsive orator, browbeating his audience into following his arguments if they were to retain personal or national self-respect; and with Prussia humiliated and the French still in the city, he had little difficulty in succeeding. He appealed for a completely revised system of education, much impressing Alexander von Humboldt, who appointed him first to the chair of Philosophy at the new University of Berlin in 1810, and then as Rector. With the fourth *Rede*, Fichte insisted that men were formed by language more than language by men, claiming German as an ennobling characteristic for the nation which was best equipped to set an example and realize an ideal. He summoned Germany to a sense of identity and to confidence in nationhood. Though there were clearly dangers in this kind of patriotism (and some of Fichte's utterances were misappropriated by the Nazis a century and a quarter later), he also insisted on equal rights for minorities, resigning his Rectorship over an incident of brutality towards a Jewish student. Anti-Semitism played its ugly part among some of the more extreme nationalists, who included Achim von Arnim, Clemens Brentano and Heinrich von Kleist with their Christlich-deutsche Tischgesellschaft in 1811–13, and it was, as the boy Felix Mendelssohn miserably discovered, common for loutish Berlin students to taunt Jews in the 1819 *Judensturm* against emancipating measures. But such excrescences were not characteristic of the Romantics' aspirations for art that would not only express but actually embody the best in the German spirit.

Such brief comments on the flowering of Romantic ideas in these astonishing years can do no more than draw attention to some of the most significant figures of the time – to the originality of vision possessed by each of them, to the value in understanding something of them if the new movement of feeling that overcame music and opera in particular (and the new qualities of insight their attitudes offered for those writing about music) is to begin to be comprehended, above all to the completely novel phenomenon of each of these arts and sciences finding resonances in one another, and of this being held to be an important, if not the most important, goal towards which their practitioners strove.

Much seems to converge on the fascinating, elusive figure of E. T. A. Hoffmann, and much, though not all, does. He was himself the practitioner of at least three arts: for a large part of his career he regarded himself as primarily a composer, especially since he agreed with those who believed music was the art with the fullest access to the sublime; he was one of the most enthralling of all creative Romantic writers and critics of Romantic music, taking into new realms the links between critical and imaginative faculties; he was a gifted draughtsman whose sense of fantasy and humour was expressed most vividly in irony, caricature and self-mockery. Many of his fellow-Romantics he knew personally, and many more were familiar to him through their work; some he openly acknowledged as influences, with a readiness by no means always shown by artists aware of their heritage but anxious to conceal it so as to suggest themselves as unique vessels of a mysterious inspiration. His collection of writings *Kreisleriana* includes thoughts by the imaginary Kapellmeister Johannes Kreisler, a brilliant essay on Beethoven's instrumental music, some Novalis-inspired fragments and a satire, *Der vollkommene Maschinist*, rather in the manner of Marcello's *Il teatro alla moda*, and coheres (or rather, deliberately does not cohere) into a kind of *Bildungsroman*. Different as the two fictional musicians are, Johannes Kreisler is indebted to the inspiration of Wackenroder's Johann Berglinger, and to Wackenroder especially Hoffmann's ideas of Romantic synaesthesia are due. *Kreisleriana* also owes much to Friedrich Schlegel; and Schelling's ideas, as well as those of Ritter, found an echo in Hoffmann's intuition that music, beginning with raw, physical sound and rising into sublime experience, was the point at which the finite touched the infinite. Here, too, lie the roots of Hoffmann's absorption in the interaction of the natural and the supernatural, the real and the imaginative, outer and inner worlds: antinomies with music acting as mediating art.

Hoffmann's discontent with most of the operas of the day served to heighten his own ambitions. The most mysterious of all his musical stories is *Ritter Gluck*, which he published as his first contribution to the *AMZ* (*AMZ* 11 (1809), 305–19). We never really learn the true identity of the strange figure who takes the young man encountered in a café to hear him play Gluck's music off blank pages, finally claiming to be actually Gluck himself. The story gives no answers; it asks questions concerning the distance between the puzzlement of the young man at this phenomenon and the realm of abstract creativity in which the old man lives, between inner and outer worlds, between the mundane and the infinite. It sets Gluck in a higher sphere than run-of-the-mill life (by which Hoffmann did not only mean run-of-the-mill opera), and can serve as a preface to the review of *Iphigénie en Aulide* he wrote for the *AMZ* in the following year (*AMZ* 12 (1810), 770–3, 784–9). It is here that he first made his oft-repeated plea for true and worthy German serious opera, drawing together music and literature at the highest level. Dismayed by the contrast between the standard of the works he heard in the theatre and the noble score he saw before him on his desk, he attacked the shallowness of most operas compared to the depths and the heights he found in Gluck, and also compared to contemporary advances in symphonic music: only the month previously he had written his epoch-making review of Beethoven's Fifth Symphony. Here in *Iphigénie*, he declared, was not the incessant striving for effect by illustrating superficial or incidental matters (which he likened to the true expression of a painting being smothered beneath a riot of colours), or the constant dislocation of the drama for the sake of singers.

> So wie die mehrsten unserer neuesten Opern nur Konzerte sind, die auf der Bühne im Kostüm gegeben werden: so ist die Glucksche Oper das wahre musikalische Drama, in welchem die Handlung unaufhaltsam von Moment zu Moment fortschreitet. Alles was diesem Fortschreiten hinderlich ist, alles was des Zuhörers Spannung schwächen und seine Aufmerksamkeit auf Nebendinge – man möchte sagen, von der Gestalt auf den Schmuck – lenken kann, ist auf das sorgfältigste vermieden und eben das Ganze energisch und kraftvoll . . . Nur die höchste Erkenntniss der Kunst, nur die unumschränkte Herrschaft über die Mittel des musikalischen Ausdrucks spricht sich in der hohen Simplicität aus, mit welcher der grosse Meister die stärksten, leidenschaftlichsten Momente des Dramas behandelt.
>
> (*AMZ* 12 (1810) 784)

(Whereas the majority of our most recent operas are only concerts performed in costume on the stage, Gluck's opera is true musical drama, in which the action moves forward without stopping from one moment to the next. Whatever hinders this forward motion, whatever might reduce the listener's suspense and distract his attention to secondary matters – from the figure to its adornment, one could say – is most carefully avoided, and the extreme precision resulting from this vigorously sustains the whole . . . Only the highest artistic awareness, only an absolute mastery over the means of musical expression, can give rise to that noble simplicity with which the composer treats the most passionate moments of the drama. Hoffmann, 1989, 259)

The example chosen is Agamemnon's recitative as he wrestles with his emotions over Iphigenia's sacrifice, and Hoffmann contrasts the shrieking Furies and hissing serpents that would occupy the invention of most composers with Gluck's depiction of the unhappy father's inmost feelings. In turning to Gluck, Hoffmann was also rejecting the light French influence on Singspiel in favour of a more serious German appreciation of Méhul and Cherubini, and indeed of the elements of Gluck in Spontini.

For years, German critical writing had been filled with arguments that it was in Gluck that there was to be found the example for German grand opera, that is, for a genre rivalling French grand opera in its use of historical or mythical subjects, imposing and often historically accurate scenery, multiple soloists and a large chorus and orchestra. One of the most influential had come in Forkel's *Musikalisch-Kritische Bibliothek*, 'Ueber die Musik des Ritters Christoph von Gluck, verschiedene Schriften gesammlet [*sic*] und herausgegeben von Fried. Just. Riedel' (Forkel, 1778–9, 53–210). C. F. Cramer's widely read *Magazin der Musik* was regularly filled with praise for Gluck and admiring reports on his operas. Reichardt included in his *Berlinische musikalische Zeitung* a study of *Armide* giving the reasons for his admiration:

Gluck, zum Beobachter und Reformator geboren, war in England von Händels großen einfachen Charakter, in Gesang und Harmonie, und in Paris von Rameaus ächt tragischen Declamation und hohen Wahrheit in

Ausdruck, und von seiner Chor- und Tanzbehandlung getroffen und gerührt, und von der Idee das alles zu einem großen tragischen Ganz zu vereinigen, ganz erfüllt. *(BMZ* 28 (1805), 109–12)

(Gluck, a born observer and reformer, was impressed and moved in England by Handel's great simplicity of character in song and harmony, and in Paris by Rameau's genuinely tragic declamation and elevated truth of expression, and by his treatment of chorus and dance, and by the idea of unifying all this into a great tragic whole.)

Many more voices had joined these, especially in the *AMZ* itself. But it was Hoffmann's two pieces of writing which served to re-focus and give new intensity to them, and to inspire his own emulation.

Aurora is his own response. Composed in 1811–12, and to Germany's loss not performed in Hoffmann's lifetime, it is described as a *Grosse romantische Oper*, and represents an ambitious attempt at the serious grand opera for which he was to keep on calling for years to come. Franz von Holbein's libretto develops the earlier part of the classical legend with some twists of its own. The shepherd Cephalus falls in love with Prokris, but her father King Erechtheus's General, Polybius, once her guardian, is a rival for her hand together with the widowed King Dejoneus. In a confrontation in the temple, Cephalus is taken off to be slain by Polybius, who honourably spares his life. The dawn goddess Aurora appears to Cephalus and abducts him to her sea palace to be her lover, but she is moved by his pleas and resolves to release him and help him. In a dream scene, Philarchus reveals that years ago he disobeyed Dejoneus's wife Diomede by sparing her baby Cephalus from death. With Polybius renouncing Prokris and Dejoneus discovering Cephalus to be his son, the way would be clear for the lovers but for the need for a third act. This is provided by Aurora and Cephalus arriving magically disguised and providing further misunderstandings before all is revealed.

Hoffmann was too intelligent to challenge Gluck's genius with *Aurora*, and he did not even abandon the spoken dialogue which he deplored at the start of his *Iphigénie* review; but he saw further into the nature of Gluck's achievement than most, and he was certainly affected profoundly in what was by far the most expansive opera he had yet written. The overture manages to achieve something of a Gluckian grandeur, with a festive Allegro molto preceded by a strange Adagio that includes a foreboding figure of staccato string shudders (one he had also employed as Namarand apprehensively addresses his 'angel' in *Der Trank der Unsterblichkeit*). The ensembles and finales far outweigh the individual solo arias, which consist of a fine G minor piece for Aurora near the end (owing much to Mozart), a charming Andante amoroso for Prokris (with a surprising amount of decoration) and, impressively, a Maestoso for Polybius that successfully presents him as a strong man governed by humane concerns. The finest part of the opera comes with the Act II Quartetto and Finale, dramatically well wrought with considerable harmonic enterprise and an energy that derives, to its benefit, from Cherubini. Cephalus remains a simple shepherd, discovered on his hillside with an 'Elysian' flute solo that is touchingly recalled in the sequence of Marches that ends the whole opera as Prokris enters; and between whiles Hoffmann establishes an excellent differentiation between the three worlds of the pastoral idyll, the pomp of the court, and Aurora's mysterious, erotic realm. The orchestral sensitivity is at its height with some of the music for Aurora, who first appears to soft woodwind chords and three-part cellos; another of the final marches opens on violas, two cellos and double bass, joined by wind and trombones. There is much else to admire, including the excellently judged chromatic harmony in one of the work's best scenes, Polybius's revelation of Cephalus's survival opening Act III as he lies racked by a despairing nightmare. It is, as often with Hoffmann, the actual quality of the musical invention that betrays him. Sometimes there is little to differentiate the characters except the handling of their material, and so the drama resides chiefly in development which can be undramatically long. Nevertheless, *Aurora* is an honourable blow struck for the ideal of German grand opera.

A different voice, though also one of resonance, to speak up for Gluck and in particular for *Iphigénie en Tauride* as the exemplar for German opera, was that of Ignaz von Mosel, highly regarded in

Vienna as a conductor and composer and later as a theatre director. His *Versuch einer Aesthetik des dramatischen Tonsatzes* (1813) declared a set of well-argued principles based on Gluck's example and, as the creative origin of opera, cited Greek tragedy, with singing, instruments, inflected recitation and choruses all combining in a unified work of art. Like Hoffmann, Mosel took a stand for emotion as against depiction, and called for a proper integration of text and music:

> Die Bestimmung der dramatischen Musik ist, jene Eindrücke zu verstärken, welche der Dichter auf das Gemüth des Zuhörers zu machen, sich vorgesetzt hat. Sie soll daher – dieser ihrer wahren und ursprünglichen Bestimmung nach – bloss ein erhöhte Declamation, ein kräftiger, lebhafter, warmer Ausdruck der Gefühle seyn, welch in dem Gedichte vorkommen.   (Mosel, 1813, 30–1)

> (The purpose of dramatic music is to strengthen those impressions which the poet has set himself to make on the feelings of the listener. This will therefore – following its true and original purpose – be simply a heightened declamation, a more powerful, animated and warm expression of the feelings contained in the poem.)

He goes on to cite Algarotti with approval, and to re-emphasize the composer's task:

> Widmet er alle seine Kräfte der *Handlung*, dem *Ausdruck*, der *Wahrheit*: so wird alles, was kalte Vernunft gegen das *Wesen der Oper* einwenden könne, wegfallen, und Niemand wird es unnatürlicher finden, dass der Held der Oper singend stirbt, als dass der Held des Trauerspiels seine letzte Kräfte zur Declamation eines schönen Verses anstrengt.
>
>   (Mosel, 1813, 31)

> (He shall dedicate all his powers to *action*, to *expression*, to *truthfulness*: by this means everything that cold reason might put forward against the *nature of opera* falls away, and no-one can find it more unnatural for the hero of an opera to die singing than for the hero of a tragedy to expend his last energies on declaiming beautiful verse.)

So far from doubting the suitability of the German language for singing, Mosel suggests that 'Ihr härterer Klang den denkenden Componisten bestimmt, nicht mehr Noten anzuwenden, als Sylben in dem Verse sind' (Mosel, 1813, 11–12) ('Its harder sound encourages the thoughtful composer not to employ more notes than the verse has syllables').

Putting his precepts into practice, Mosel composed, in the same years as Hoffmann's *Aurora*, his own ambitious grand opera in Gluckian vein, *Salem*. Though the interest aroused on its Vienna première in 1813 soon waned, the work is a not inconsiderable achievement. Based on a modified version of Voltaire's *Olympie* (imminently to be set by Spontini) which renames the characters and relocates the plot in Persia, it was dismissed in the course of the *AMZ*'s review as 'mehr nachgeahmt als originell' (*AMZ* 15 (1813), 367–8) ('more imitative than original'). Cherubini rather than Gluck is cited as the main influence. There is some substance in this, especially in the music's tendency to an unremitting energy that can become its own justification, with agitated figures, pounding bass counterpoint and furious tremolos and syncopations doing duty for real melodic distinction or dramatic movement. Nevertheless, the orchestration is imaginative, and the handling of the accompanied recitatives eloquent and fluent in their movement between numbers. There is a fine example at the start of Act III for the anguished Salem, when an agitated orchestral introduction breaks its thematic material down into recitative fragments after only a page, then reassembling it with powerful effect for the aria proper (Example 25).

In 1813 the *AMZ* published Hoffmann's second great musical story, *Don Juan* (*AMZ* 15 (1813), 213–25). His other musician hero, Mozart, is here conceived as creating with music a new dimension to the Don Juan legend; for the subject of the story is not Juan himself but the opera. It is through Mozart's music, Hoffmann tells us, that Don Giovanni is turned from a simple, even rather dull, seducer and murderer into a figure of potential nobility:

Betrachtet man das Gedicht (den 'Don Juan'), ohne ihm eine tiefere Bedeutung zu geben, so daß man nur das Geschichtliche in Anspruch nimmt, so ist es kaum zu begreifen, wie Mozart eine solche Musik dazu denken und dichten konnte. (*AMZ* 15 (1813), 221)

(If one considers the text of *Don Giovanni* without attaching a deeper meaning to it, so that only the narrative aspect is taken into account, then one can scarcely comprehend how Mozart could conceive and compose such music for it.)

Hoffmann sees Giovanni as one of Nature's noblest creatures, containing within him a seed of the divine, ensnared by the Devil because of Man's Fall and tempted to seek the highest in love through an endless quest for sexual pleasure:

In Don Juans Gemüth kam durch des Erbfeindes List der Gedanke, dass durch die Liebe, durch den Genuss des Weibes, schon auf Erden das erfüllt werden könne, was bloss als himmlische Verheissung in unserer

(I see the pallid shades of the royal wives. They threaten fearfully. See, their eyes glow; see, how they gush forth flames. O Heaven, protect me!)

Example 25   Mosel: *Salem* (1813), Salem

Brust wohnt, und eben jene unendliche Sehnsucht ist, die uns mit dem
Überirdischen in unmittelbaren Rapport setzt.   (*AMZ* 15 (1813), 222)

(Through the Arch-Enemy's cunning there entered into Don Giovanni's
mind the thought that through love, through the enjoyment of Woman,
there can be attained here on earth that which dwells in our heart only as
a heavenly promise, and is that infinite longing that joins us in direct
rapport to the divine.)

In failing to rise from the physical into the ideal, Giovanni comes to
scorn human life, its morals, its institutions. In the first part of the
tale, Hoffmann brings Donna Anna, whose sexual conquest by

Giovanni he assumes to have taken place, into the narrative when the young composer in the empty theatre box (Hoffmann himself, it is implied) senses her standing by him in a gently erotic tension. She knows him and his music, and speaks softly in his ear as if she recognizes and values his understanding of her:

> So wie der glückliche Traum das Seltsamste verbindet und dann ein frommer Glaube das Übersinnliche versteht und es den sogenannten natürlichen Erscheinungen des Lebens zwanglos anreiht, so geriet ich auch in der Nähe des wunderbaren Weibes in eine Art Somnambulism, in dem ich die geheimen Beziehungen erkannte, die mich so innig mit ihr verbanden, daß sie selbst bei ihrer Erscheinung auf dem Theater nicht hatte von mir weichen können.   (*AMZ* 15 (1813), 217)

> (Just as the strangest things are brought together in a pleasant dream and devout faith comprehends things lying beyond our senses and is freely associated with the so-called natural phenomena of life, so it was that I too in the presence of this wonderful woman existed in a kind of somnambulism in which I recognized the secret ties that bound me to her so intimately that even when she appeared on the stage she could not leave my side.)

She seems to slip away, and in her next scene he is caught in an erotic synaesthesia with her and her music:

> In Donna Annas Szene fühlte ich mich von einem sanften, warmen Hauch, der über mich hinwegglitt, in trunkener Wollust erbeben; unwillkürlich schlossen sich meine Augen, und ein glühender Kuß schien auf meinen Lippen zu brennen: aber der Kuß war ein wie von ewig dürstender Sehnsucht lang ausgehaltener Ton.   (*AMZ* 15 (1813), 218)

> (In Donna Anna's scene I felt a soft, warm breath pass gently over me and transport me into an intoxicated ecstasy; involuntarily my eyes closed and an ardent kiss seemed to burn on my lips; but the kiss was a long note sustained as if from eternally thirsting desire.)

As he succumbs, he hears a distant clock striking two. In the morning, from the audience whose superficial prattlings about the performance have irritated him, he learns that the singer of Anna has died on the stroke of two. The closeness of love to death in the opera has reached out to embrace the watching composer, and the imagination of the reader. Through this extraordinary story, the concept was to shape a whole new understanding of *Don Giovanni* and to enter Romantic mythology.

In common with virtually all his contemporaries, Hoffmann did not believe that writer and musician could be united in the same person, for reasons to do with their different crafts which are comprehensively rehearsed in *Der Dichter und der Komponist* (and this celebrated dialogue takes place when the Poet and the Composer meet in the circumstances of battle, a violent outer world impelling them to discuss worlds of the imagination). With good reason, he counted himself fortunate to have secured the author of the popular tale *Undine*, Friedrich de la Motte Fouqué, as librettist for what was to prove his finest opera. Undine, in this *Romantische Zauberoper* of 1816, is a mysterious girl from the waters who was fostered by an old fisher couple when their own daughter vanished into a lake. Though warned against menfolk by the grim water spirit Kühleborn, and aware that betrayal will doom her, Undine loves and is loved by a knight, Huldbrand, and their union is blessed by the priest Heilmann. She befriends Berthalda, whom she reveals as the real daughter, not of the Duke and Duchess, but of the humble fisher folk; ashamed of her true origin, Berthalda flees, followed by the concerned Huldbrand as he is drawn away from Undine back to the human world. Huldbrand curses Undine, and now plans to marry Berthalda, but the ceremony is interrupted when Undine appears from an opened well to take Huldbrand in her arms in what Heilmann describes as a *Liebestod*.

The libretto is constructed in antitheses. The one contrast missing is the comic, for which Hoffmann, a wit in life and in prose, did not possess a musical gift; and in any case his intention for opera remained as serious as in *Aurora*. Some contrasts are conventional, such as that between the courtiers and the fisher folk, who do not, however, sing in lighthearted vein but have their own earnestness. More original to the work is the contrast between Heilmann and Kühleborn, a figure whose sinister pagan apparitions, accompanied by 'supernatural' trombones, present him as a powerful adversary to the Christian priest: there is an anticipation of Weber's Samiel and the Hermit here, and as in *Der Freischütz*, one is human, the other from the spirit world. In this there lies the opera's central tension, between Undine's spirit nature and Berthalda's humanity, with Huldbrand torn between the two. He and Undine love one another; each yearns for something lacking in their own nature, and is doomed to fail. As early as the Romanze, No. 2, the Fisherman's Wife responds to her husband's description of Undine's watery realm by asking how Huldbrand can possibly understand that : 'Er ist ja ein vernünftiger Mann' – 'He is a reasonable man', but the implication to the audience is also, 'He is a man of Reason'. The tale was already popular (as with the Donauweibchen); with *Undine* it became a central Romantic myth, as rational man and mysterious spirit, reason and instinct, vainly seek fulfilment and completion in a union that can only be consummated in annihilation.

As a composer, Hoffmann was nothing if not intelligent, and he approached this ambitious work with much perception. His idiom remains grounded in Mozart, and his models include Gluck, as with Heilmann's gravity of utterance or in the interruption of the overture by a violent storm. However, more immediate examples were to be found in Méhul, from whom he had learnt the technique of ending one number on an unfinished cadence which is resolved, after dialogue, with the next number; and Méhul gave him ideas for some use of reminiscence motive and perhaps for instrumental original-ities. These include the grave sound of a double bass underpinning Heilmann's chorale-like melody for his blessing of the bridal pair, after which a new manner enters the music. Still more powerful is the example of Cherubini, to whom Hoffmann turns chiefly for a dynamic energy to propel ensembles, especially with the use of repeated figures, restless rhythmic agitation and surging orchestral gestures. However, these can fail in real dramatic motivation and come to seem merely repetitious and mannered. Moreover, the melodic style generally lacks individuality, and though he can weave charming patterns in the more lyrical music, his feeling for counter-point does not come from deep enough in his technique or invention for it to have real creative impulse.

Yet *Undine* merits its description as a Romantic opera. Hoffmann writes music strong enough to give the waters and the forests their own power, as elements alongside the characters and working upon them. The storm breaking into the overture, with Huldbrand and the Fisherman calling into the darkness after Undine; the scene in which the waters and their spirits show their menace to Heilmann; the Act II finale as mists rise to envelop Undine, cursed by Huldbrand, and return her to her element; Undine's final appearance out of the opened well to surround Huldbrand with the deathly embrace of water: these scenes and others bring Nature into musical drama in far more than token form. The admiring Weber, already seized by the originality of Hoffmann's *Don Juan* story, appreciated the use of characteristic orchestral colour to define the course of the drama, and the linking of numbers in dramatic continuity, when he hailed the opera in famous words:

> Es versteht sich von selbst, daß ich von der Oper spreche, die der
> Deutsche will: ein in sich abgeschlossenes Kunstwerk, wo alle Teile und
> Beiträge der verwandten und benutzten Künste ineinanderschmelzend
> verschwinden und auf gewisse Weise untergehend – eine neue Welt
> bilden.   (Weber, 1908, 129)

> (Of course when I speak of opera I am speaking of the German ideal,
> namely a self-sufficient work of art in which every feature and every
> contribution by the related arts are moulded together in a certain way
> and dissolve, to form a new world. Weber, 1981, 201)

Weber was erring on the side of generosity towards a colleague whose understanding of the goals of Romantic opera was fuller than his creative realization of them. At his best, as in the choral scene in Act II with Undine's vision of Berthalda's adoption by the Duke and Duchess, and for much of the last two finales, he achieves genuine dramatic momentum articulated in musical structures and linked sequences of numbers; but the invention can fail, not only on the level of melodic and harmonic inspiration but in immediacy of response to dramatic needs. Yet generosity is earned for a pioneering work that drew upon essential Romantic ideas in a wholly original manner.

Less than a month after the first performance of *Undine*, in Berlin in 1816, Weber conducted the first performance of Spohr's *Faust* in Prague, prefacing it with an appreciative article. In its first form, this was a two-act work with spoken dialogue; much later, in 1853, and after various reworkings, Spohr turned it into a grand opera with recitatives for Covent Garden, thereby altering its form but not its essential qualities.

While Josef Bernard's libretto owes nothing to Goethe's narrative, in this first major Faust opera there is a reflection of the central element in Goethe, the hero's ceaseless striving to achieve something higher, even through the agency of evil. A crucial difference lies in the outcome, for Goethe's Faust, as the angels sing, can be redeemed if he never gives up this struggle – 'wer immer strebend sich bemüht, den können wir erlösen' – while Heaven plays no part in Spohr's opera, whose Faust, believing that through the exercise of his will he can defeat Mephistopheles, deceives himself and is finally hurled into Hell. Though there are scarcely any Nietzschean or Schopenhauerian anticipations here, it is notable that not God but the human will is proposed as the vital force with which to contend with the world, one ultimately inadequate to overcome human passions or achieve good on its own, let alone survive without divine redemption. The existence of a divine alternative is confined to an irrelevant wedding chorus from inside a church; God is, as it were, pushed off-stage, and the title page of the 1853 Peters edition of the vocal score shows Mephistopheles alone on high, smiling down sardonically at the human characters. There are, however, some echoes of the old idea of sacred and profane love, in that Faust is torn between his pure devotion to Röschen and his destructive lust for Kunigunde. Frustrated by Röschen's former lover in his wooing, he joins Kunigunde's lover Hugo in rescuing her from the wicked Sir Gulf, but, using a magic potion obtained from the witches of the Blocksberg, seduces her, then murdering Hugo. Eventually he is claimed by Mephistopheles.

Spohr approached the task of setting a text containing no lighter element by placing his emphasis on developing the various scenes of

cumulative dramatic tension. The gentler or more reflective numbers (which include Faust's charming 'Liebe ist die zarte Blüte') fall
into second place to a sequence of dramatic scenes in which there is a
serious attempt to use symphonic means to sustain tension. Cherubini was a not always felicitous model here. There is not yet the
condition of Leitmotive, but it is adumbrated in Spohr's use of
themes associated with hell, with love and with the tumult of Faust's
passionate nature, sometimes as reminiscence but also as comment
addressed to the audience across the heads of the characters. Spohr
pointed out his intentions in his preface to the libretto, and Weber
singled the technique out when he wrote how 'Glücklich und richtig
berechnet gehen einige Melodien wie leise Fäden durch das Ganze
und halten es geistig zusammen' ('A few melodies, felicitously and
aptly devised, weave like delicate threads through the whole, and
hold it together artistically') (Weber, 1908, 275; Weber, 1981, 193).
Weber himself certainly learnt from Spohr's example, constructively
with his use of motive and in his extended aria structures, but also
from where Spohr goes wrong.

For Spohr's fluent technique enables him to build up tension well
in the ensembles, but even here it can ignore the needs of the drama
with music that becomes self-perpetuating, or does not focus sharply
enough on what he is trying to convey. In part this is due to motivic
material which fails to define its subjects clearly, and compounds the
failure when even this master of chromatic harmony does not manage
to turn the material to expressive ends suggesting the drama working
in the characters' minds. Repeatedly, the self-indulgent chromatic
harmony loses contact with dramatic needs, for which Spohr had too
little human instinct. Hence there is a lack of differentiation between
the characters, even between Faust and Mephistopheles, and at times
a tendency to fall back on inappropriate convention, so that Mephistopheles's aria 'Stille noch dies Wuthverlangen', gloating over Faust's
approaching damnation, is hardly different in manner from the
drinking song near the start of the opera. Spohr's harmonic originality
yet dramatic ineptness is nowhere more sharply exposed than in the
scene when Mephistopheles summons up Sycorax to bring him the

fatal potion, in twenty bars looking straight forward to Wotan's invocation of Erda in *Siegfried*, only to be answered by her tripping on with it like some jolly barmaid (Example 26). Spohr, in fact, has with Faust chosen a great Romantic theme, striving man attempting to burst the bonds of convention and morality, in order to show that the triumphant indulgence of his senses proves his superiority, to assert that through his own efforts he can achieve good without acknowledgement of God yet disdaining the power of the Devil, and failing because he has no real moral or religious imperative. The opera never dramatizes these contending elements, partly through the text's failure to clarify the moral issues, crucially through Spohr's failure to compose to the heart of all that is involved.

Zemire und Azor (1819) is no advance on *Faust*, nor indeed was it intended to be more than a pleasant setting of the then familiar fairy tale. Spohr's chromaticisms effectively suggest the mysterious garden and its invisible spirits surrounding the unhappy Azor. For the rest, the story is told in a succession of numbers that include some ingenuities, such as a canon of 'trust' between three of the characters (at the octave and at nine bars' distance), and some conventional, agreeably turned numbers, including a long-popular aria for Zemire, 'Rose, wie bist du reizend und mild' and some sentimental or cheerful pieces in which the chromatic decorations are more or less irrelevant. If Spohr was hoping to move Singspiel and its conventions into Romantic territory, the attempt was misjudged. The most successful numbers are those that revert amiably to an earlier age.

However, the contrast between *Faust* and *Zemire und Azor* points to problems that were increasingly concerning composers. Singspiel had not lost its vitality, and was long to remain popular fare. Romantic opera had made remarkable steps, even if they were often halting, in need of crutches, and occasionally misdirected. There remained a pervading belief in some quarters that German grand opera was the true goal. Though distinctions can readily be perceived between the three traditions, or ambitions, there were overlaps, or better cross-fertilizations, that generally enriched one another rather than set them in contest, but that did also serve to emphasize dilemmas.

(Sycorax! bring in a fine goblet a draught for the joyful feast! Sycorax!
I come, I come, I bring the draught in pure and shining mica!)

Example 26   Spohr: *Faust* (1816), Mephistopheles and Sycorax

For all the praise lavished on him at the time of his greatest successes with grand opera, Johann Nepomuk von Poissl is one of the forgotten men of operatic history, remembered now only by a reputation that burned brightly for a while and then guttered into oblivion. Born into an aristocratic family in 1783, he spent his earliest years studying music quietly on his father's estate before encountering the warm encouragement of Danzi and Vogler in Munich in 1805. To his friendship with Danzi was added the enthusiastic support of Weber in 1811, and the three composers' mutual understanding and their hopes for German opera found expression in Poissl's most important work, *Athalia* (1814). His previous four operas had included two, *Antigonus* (1808) and *Ottaviano in Sicilia* (1812), based on Metastasio librettos, chosen out of his wish to bring heroic subjects into the sphere of German opera; his literary skill encouraged him to write his own texts at a time when this was virtually unknown in Germany. *Antigonus* is through-composed in an attempt, after the failure of his first opera, *Die Opernprobe* (1806), to profit from Danzi's example. For *Athalia*, he turned to the Munich actor and writer Johann Gottfried Wohlbrück, who based his text on Racine's dramatization of the Biblical story of the impious Queen of Judah who has murdered her way to the throne; however, the child Joas has been saved by Josabet, wife of the high priest Joad, and brought up secretly until, in a successful palace coup, he can be ceremonially set upon the throne and Athalia dragged off to her death. With much ingenuity, Wohlbrück turned Racine's alexandrines into German iambic pentameters.

Athalia triumphed on its performance in Munich in 1814. It was hailed locally as a major event, with the *Münchner Theater-Journal* being careful to point out its advance on Poissl's previous operas:

> Bei der Composition der Athalia hat er sich noch einen andern Zweck, ein höheres Kunstziel vorgesetzt, er hat gestrebt, uns – wie Italiener und Franzosen ihre nationale Oper haben – auch eine in bestimmtem Charakter hervorgehobene *deutsche* große Opernmusik zu geben. Er hat dieses Problem durch die Verbindung hoher Kraft mit Lieblichkeit zu lösen gesucht. Dadurch ist seine Komposition in einer neuen Art, sie ist in innigerem Einklange mit der Handlung und den Motiven des

behandelten Stücks, sie nimmt bestimmt den Charakter der Handlung in den einzelnen Scenen an, und schmiegt sich treu an dieselbe.

(MTJ 1/7 (1814), 187–8)

(In the composition of *Athalia* he has set himself another purpose, a higher artistic goal: he has striven to give us, in the way that the Italians and the French have their own national opera, emphatically *German* grand opera music of a distinctive character. He has tried to solve this problem by uniting great power with charm. In this way his music is of a new kind: it is in more intimate accord with the drama and the motive of the subject, it emphatically seizes hold of the character of the action in the individual scenes, and it remains true to them.)

The *AMZ*, in a full report from Munich (*AMZ* 16 (1814), 441–4), made a point of praising Poissl for his altruism in addressing himself to the difficult task of German grand opera when motivated not by professional need but only by his talent and his belief in the cause, and went on, in familiar tones, to praise the work as exemplary for German grand opera:

Denn da die grosse italienische Oper alles für den Gesang, wenig für richtige Declamation, noch weniger für dramatische Wahrheit leistet; das französische musik. Drama hingegen Declamation und richtige scenische Behandlung sich zur Hauptsache macht, den eigentlichen Gesang aber für sehr untergeordnet hält: so ist in diesem neuen Werke das Streben, zwischen beyden Extremen die Mittelstrasse aufzufinden, sichtbar genug. Daher kam es denn wahrscheinlich, dass der Componist in dieser seiner Arbeit nichts der Schönheit und Fasslichkeit der Melodie, nichts der Kraft der Harmonie oder der Richtigkeit der Declamation, ausser, wenn es davon für sich allein wesentlich hervortreten durfte, aufopferte, sondern jedes dieser Haupterfordernisse zu einem grossen, harmonischen Ganzen ordnete. (*AMZ* 16 (1814), 443)

(If Italian grand opera emphasizes above all singing, less accurate declamation and still less dramatic truth; if French musical drama, on the other hand, gives priority to declamation and correct staging and allots singing a secondary place; then in this new work the attempt to find a middle course between the two extremes is very evident. From this it is apparent that the composer in his work has sacrificed neither melodic beauty and clarity nor harmonic power nor accuracy of declamation, unless it is vital for him, but has brought all these prime essentials into a single, vast harmonious whole.)

Other cities hastened to take up *Athalia*, the most extreme enthusiasm being shown by the Grand Duke of Hesse, who, according to one of the few major musicians to dislike the work, Spohr, personally conducted no fewer than thirty consecutive performances (to the dismay of his orchestra). In the entry on Poissl in his Encyclopedia, Gustav Schilling declared:

> Athalia steht in Anlage und Durchführung so selbstständig und originell da, dass sich kein irgend ein Vergleichspunkt wo auffinden oder annehmen lässt. Es ist die Tatsache, dass die Oper auf mehreren der grössten Bühnen Deutschlands mit einem solchen Erfolg gegeben wurde, dass unparteiische Kenner ihr einen Platz unter den ausgezeichnetsten dramatischen Werken des Jahrhunderts zuerkennen müssen.   (Schilling, 1835–8, 491)

> (Athalia is in design and execution so individual and original that no point of comparison can be found or envisaged. The fact that the opera has been given with such success on several of the most important German stages shows that disinterested connoisseurs must allow it a place among the finest works of the century.)

Introducing it to his Prague audience in 1816, Weber observed that

> Rein eigentümlich ist ihm, nebst großer Sorgfalt und Wahrheit der Deklamation, jugendlicher, reicher Harmonienfolge und zweckdienlicher mannigfaltiger Instrumentation, eine sich sehr zu italienischer Gesanglieblichkeit hinneigende Melodieform, die neben ihrer Weichheit noch das Verdienst einer großen Singbarkeit und das gewisse Kehlgerechte hat, dessen Vernachlässigung man so oft deutschen Komponisten zum Vorwurf machen will.   (Weber, 1908, 270)

> (His music is characterized by a scrupulous attention to prosody, a youthful richness of harmony and apt, well-varied orchestration. His melodies lean strongly towards an Italian cantabile – tender, and well written for the voice – with that true regard for the vocal chords which German composers are often accused of neglecting. Weber, 1981, 185)

Weber goes on to add that many of the recitatives are models of their kind. Perhaps he was the more keen to do this as he may have had a hand in encouraging Poissl to rewrite the original version of the opera, with some spoken verse dialogue, into a through-composed work (Poissl later revised *Der Wettkampf zu Olympia* in the same way: see Waidelich, 1996, *passim*).

A strong example of the qualities singled out by Weber occurs immediately with the opera's first number, for Josabet. This consists of a sequence of recitatives, ariosos and more formal passages, with a melodic line carefully based on German prosody and sometimes accompanied by obbligato woodwind. One of Poissl's strengths lies in his ability to move the drama forward across the entire opera in such freely composed, linked movements, with set arias being the exception rather than the rule and always occurring within the framework of the music's fluent structure. It is the arioso music which dominates; recitative is always instrumentally accompanied, and essentially melodic rather than after the Italian secco model; and there is a complete absence of display coloratura. Joad is permitted a solemn, dignified prayer in Act II, where there also occurs a passage of melodrama with Joas speaking as well as singing a Romanze, while the others sing in recitative or arioso (in the original version, Joas, played at the first performances by Wohlbrück's young daughter, was predominantly a speaking role). The most striking character to emerge is Athalia herself, whose arioso flowers into some of the music's most expressive phrases and who is portrayed as violent, tense and assertive. Weber was undoubtedly referring to her when he also remarked that, 'Sinnig sind die Hauptmomente der Handlung und des Gefühles durch gewisse eindringende und herrlich wieder-kehrende Melodien zusammengehalten und bezeichnet' ('The emotional crises in the action are judiciously characterized and contained by highly charged melodies which recur at crucial points') (Weber, 1908, 270; Weber, 1981, 185). He is clearly singling out the remarkable use of motive with which Poissl characterizes the powerful Athalia and her dynamic actions throughout the work, until at its last appearance, in Act III, scene 7, a version of the idea is transferred to Joas as the throne and with it the power passes to him (Example 27).

Poissl rapidly followed this success with two more through-

Example 27   Poissl: *Athalia* (1814)
(a)   Act I, Nos. 2 and 3
(b)   Act II, start
(c)   Act III, Nos. 6 and 7

composed operas to texts of his own authorship after Metastasio. *Der Wettkampf zu Olympia* (1815) is a version of *L'Olimpiade*, and *Nittetis* (1817) sets its companion libretto: Metastasio based them both on episodes in Herodotus in which a love triangle involving two characters who are also friends is resolved when a blood relationship

(My Sammetes/ Beroe! O what happiness!)

Example 28   Poissl: *Nittetis* (1817), Beroe and Sammetes

is revealed. Introducing *Der Wettkampf* before his Dresden production in 1820, Weber was careful to associate Poissl's works with the elusive ideal of German grand opera, which he then saw as bound to be through-composed: 'eine Oper, in der die Musikstücke durch fortlaufend instrumentierte Rezitative verbunden sind, und wo demnach die Musik als Herrscherin, von allen ihren ununterbrochen in Tätigkeit gesetzten Krondienern umgeben, Hof hält' ('an opera in which the musical numbers are connected by a continuous *recitativo accompagnato*, fully orchestrated – in fact, a scene where music holds court, surrounded by her courtiers who are in perpetual activity') (Weber, 1908, 310; Weber, 1981, 290). He went on to declare that such a work must possess a grandeur drawing on classical antiquity and deriving from French classical tragedy as expressed above all by Gluck, repeating his praise for Poissl's prosody, harmony, orchestration and for the 'fließende, klar hingestellte Melodie' ('fluent and clearly defined melodies') (Weber, 1908, 311; Weber, 1981, 290). At his best, Poissl can indeed achieve melodic eloquence, as in *Nittetis* when (even if in tones borrowed from Tamino and Pamina) Sammetes and Beroe fall into one another's arms (Example 28).

Poissl's texts are expertly written to suit the kind of opera he sought, with the narrative preserved in considerable detail but entirely dispensing with the archaic Metastasian forms. There is nevertheless a stronger Italian influence on *Der Wettkampf* than on *Athalia*, with breaks between recitative and aria more marked, and some Italianate ornamentation, as when in Aristea's big tragic number, 'Liesst die Todesstunde schlagen', the introduction of a virtuoso obbligato clarinet drives her into competing coloratura. There is, moreover, a less powerful sense of cumulative dynamic movement in the finales. Though in similar vein, *Nittetis* is rather more static than either until Poissl is galvanized into action by the dramatic situation, as with Sammetes's long Act III ensemble number 'Der Geliebten theurem Willen' and can also (here, with an effective plunge from Bb into Gb as his emotions overcome him) suggest a wider harmonic awareness to underpin and express the drama.

Weber's appreciation of Poissl's orchestration may well derive from his own stimulus. Though Poissl lacks Weber's particular acuteness of ear for original instrumental combinations, he scores along similar lines, and must be given credit for anticipating some of Weber's effects. He tends to draw upon a large orchestra, with basset horns (in *Athalia*), trombones, harp and percussion sometimes including a tam-tam, but, like Weber, he can use this as a resource for some well-judged scoring almost in chamber vein. He has a fondness ahead of his time for viola tone: the second subject of the overture to *Athalia* is for violas and basses (as again in Joad's aria 'Sinai ruf'); Licidas has an aria in *Der Wettkampf* scored for solo oboe over held viola chords and violin triplets, and a penultimate March begins with violas and cellos in grave chorus punctuated by brass chords and drum rolls; the overture to *Nittetis* opens with violas over cellos and basses, and, in two later numbers, violas provide decorative figuration in the texture. There are many felicitous examples of orchestration that can lay claim to being truly Romantic in that the invention is contained at least as much in the tone colour as in the thematic material.

It is when Poissl comes to rely too heavily on orchestral decoration that his crucial weakness is exposed, namely a poverty of actual musical invention. Weber's remarks studiously avoid mention of this (though he did note in his diary, after a Munich performance of *Der Wettkampf*, 'gut und sehr schöne Musik, aber zu lang': Diary, 14 July 1815), and at their best Poissl's melodies have grace, some dignity and even eloquence. There are sensitively judged and striking dramatic situations indicating an opera composer who understands his craft; and he can produce considerable tension over the course of a movement, in particular when the drama heightens (a favourite direction impelling this is *smanioso* – frenziedly). Yet repeatedly it is the handling of the material that compels interest rather than its intrinsic appeal. Perhaps because he was aware of this, he can extend a movement by making instrumental figuration ornament the material to lend it, especially with many repetitions, the semblance of greater interest and dramatic vividness than it really possesses. His overtures can be protracted: that to *Athalia* occupies fifty-nine pages of manuscript, and in *Nittetis* there are frequent repetitions that he does not even trouble to write out in full. All his virtues – sympathetic to those around him who supported German opera while it remained a cause to be fought for, still sympathetic to posterity – cannot really conceal a certain emptiness that prevented his operas from lasting long in the repertory. His life was a struggle to establish himself, something he hoped he had achieved with *Athalia*, and, as he became impoverished, to provide for his family. His loyal admirers grew thinner in number. One was Gustav Schilling, who included a long and appreciative article in his Encylopedia (Schilling, 1835–8, 489–95). He was not successful in the posts he greatly desired and only briefly held. He died in 1865, forgotten, his operas unrevived.

Vienna offered a very different situation to that of Poissl's Munich. Theatrical life at the time of the Congress, which opened in September 1814, was at once busy and constrained. The city had suffered two occupations by the French, and as, in the wake of Napoleon's defeat, the nations gathered to redraw the map of Europe, the deliberations of the statesmen were attended by festivities of legendary exuberance, with balls, parades, firework displays, parties and receptions of all kinds and many a trip to the latest fashionable theatrical sensation. It was even alleged that these celebrations were encouraged so as to distract attention from what was really afoot, leading to the old Prince de Ligne's *mot*, 'Le congrès ne marche pas, il danse'. Having undergone various transformations, the five leading Viennese thea-tres – the Burgtheater, the Kärtnerntortheater, the Theater in der Leopoldstadt, the Theater in der Josefstadt and the Theater an der Wien – were by now providing a vast amount of entertainment for a rapidly expanding middle class. Each had its own traditions, inclina-tions, and standards, and the mixture of opera, Singspiel, plays with music, magic pieces, ballets and so on varied very much from one to the other. However, 'it was generally the custom for all five theatres to present a different work (or several shorter works) from a wide repertoire on successive evenings, rarely repeating a programme in anything like close proximity. The resulting call for fresh theatre works of all kinds was enormous, and the time given to their preparation, including writing and stage-rehearsals, was often totally inadequate' (McKay, 1991, 40–1).

Impoverished standards mattered less to the city than a ready supply of easily accessible pieces. The gentle, complacent mediocrity associated with the term Biedermeier was well served by theatrical fare that met expectations rather than disturbing them, reflecting the population's wish to be reassured in a time of post-war exhaustion. Moreover, this attitude fitted well the concerns of the Emperor Franz I, with his fears of a renewed French threat and with sharp memories of a Revolution, responsible for sending his aunt Marie Antoinette to the scaffold, that had initially been supported by the intelligentsia. At his side was his shrewd and tough Foreign Minister, Prince Metternich, determined to prevent the unification of Germany by his formation of a Deutscher Bund giving individual states autonomy in a balance of power whose scales he securely held. Fearing the nationalist spirit, which had motivated so many German artists and intellectuals, as a threat to re-established order, Metternich imposed his notorious censorship on a comparatively docile public, but one with increased access to books, journals and the theatre. Challenging ideas, reflecting the individualism of Romantic artists, were not generally welcomed and indeed firmly discouraged by Metternich's censors, who were capable of acting both ruthlessly and ridiculously in their rooting out of potential trouble. The theatre became almost entirely a place of recreation, with cosy pieces drawing reassuringly on local colour, stock figures and popular tunes. The Rousseauesque depiction of the strength and virtue of simple people softened into sentimental rural idyll; the Romantic imaginative delight in the mediaeval past became little more than colourful tales of days when knights were bold; the Romantic fascination with the contact between the real and the fantastic found its most popular outlet in stories of doltish Viennese figures of fun caught up in the fairy world. In all these circumstances, the kind of musical works which filled the theatres were generally established operas such as those by Mozart, translations of light French pieces, Italian opera at the height of the Rossini craze, travesties which emasculated German operas that included any kind of forbidden element, and a ceaseless stream of Viennese pieces for which hard-pressed composers such as the prolific Wenzel Müller turned out music often adapting numbers, in days before copyright law, taken from here, there and everywhere.

Not for the first time, Weigl seized his opportunities. Composed to a text by Treitschke some way after Bouilly's for Grétry, *Die Jugend Peter des Grossen* (1814) was an early example of many operas on the story of Tsar Peter the Great working in the shipyards of Saardam. It was clearly a gesture to Alexander I and to the impression made on those gathered for the Congress that autumn by his fascinating, unpredictable personality. Good relations with Europe's most powerful monarch were important to the assembled plenipotentiaries. Accordingly Peter enters early and indulges in a duet with his minister Lefort praising friendship, a virtue again admired in the protracted Act I finale and at the end of Act III. The remainder of the work chiefly concerns a rather lackadaisical love affair between the Tsar and Katinka, who insists that she loves him and not his position and is told by her friends that friendship is more important than love. The fear that he is leaving her produces a halting chromatic faint in the Act II finale in some contrast to the blameless diatonicism of the rest of the work, which ends in loyal celebration of everyone's friendship. However, the piece is lively indeed compared to much of the other work with which Weigl continued to beguile the public in these years, such as *Die Nachtigall und die Raabe* (1818), an insipid little pastoral after La Fontaine consisting of misunderstandings between Damon and Phillis conducted to various numbers with bird imitations.

Schubert's persistent inability to conquer the Viennese stage has remained a curiosity of musical history, one heightened when the rare experience of one of his operas in the theatre can reveal such gaps between talent, even glimpses of his genius, and its effective use. He probably embarked upon seventeen operatic works, completing three large operas and six Singspiels, but of these only *Die Zwillingsbrüder* was performed in his lifetime. He had virtually no experience of seeing his own work in the theatre, however familiar he made himself with that of others. Though his first and last completed operas were each a *Zauberoper*, *Des Teufels Lustschloss* of 1814, and a *Heroisch-romantische Oper*, *Fierrabras* of 1823, and his list includes the ambitious three-act *Alfonso und Estrella*, Schubert's characteristic form was the Singspiel. He finished six: *Der vierjährigen Posten*, *Fernando*, *Claudine von Villa Bella* (largely destroyed in 1848), *Die Freunde von Salamanka*, all composed in 1815, *Die Zwillingsbrüder* (1819), and *Die Verschworenen* (1823, whose 'conspiratorial' title was smartly changed by Metternich's censors to *Der häusliche Krieg*). They fit comfortably into Viennese expectations, and derive much of their flavour from composers familiar to Schubert in local repertories – the gentler representatives of French vaudeville and opéra-comique such as Isouard and the earlier Boieldieu and Hérold (for whose *La Clochette* he wrote two numbers), to a limited extent the lighter Rossini then entrancing the Viennese public, and among Viennese composers especially Gyrowetz and Weigl. Much else went into an idiom that, while remaining entirely Schubert's own, never developed a dramatic individuality within it. For this, blame has been laid at the door of feeble librettists, the limiting conditions of the Viennese theatre of the time, and Schubert's lack of practical experience in the opera house. All this is fair; but had he possessed dramatic genius, none of it would have mattered. The sentimental hand of Weigl lies heavily on *Der vierjährige Posten*, a mild tale of an unwitting deserter in which the inserted songs suspend the virtually non-existent action; and to this is added the influence of Gyrowetz in *Fernando*, when the pathos of a suffering child is the central feature of a slack tale of separated and reunited parents, this time in a more ambitiously Gothick atmosphere. The dialogue of *Die Freunde von Salamanka* is lost; the surviving music has much charm, and some dramatic urgency. *Die Zwillingsbrüder* is another comedy concerning twin brothers of opposing temperaments whose coincidental return after many years' absence temporarily confuses a village courtship. The most striking feature of these amiable, untheatrical pieces is the orchestration, for Schubert's ear for instruments was developing fast in these years. By the end of 1815 he had written his first four symphonies, and by 1822 the 'Unfinished', and in each of the operas there are strokes of real imagination and charm colouring the passing situations; while in *Die Verschworenen*, which has proved the most enduring of all his operas, there is some sense of the instrumentation as functional to the course of the drama, in this case a bowdlerized version of the old Aristophanes comedy of the women denying their men sex until war is called off.

However, there is no confusing the Schubert who in the year before the first of his operas had written 'Gretchen am Spinnrade', and was pouring out some of the greatest Lieder in history, with the composer of the songs in the operas. In many of his Lieder, the genius lies in the ability to discover a characteristic musical idea in the piano that can be developed across the length of the poem, illuminating it (whatever its quality) with beauty and meaning, and adding one situation to another in the course of the two great song-cycles. Though there are exceptions such as 'Erlkönig', even in Schubert's more ballad-like Lieder the tendency is for a moment of emotion to be depicted or related rather than enacted. This exploration of feeling, as opposed to the dramatization of interacting events and feelings, is essentially static, needing the art of reflection, for which there is a place in opera only as long as it is a variation of the forward movement of the drama. It is a different art from that of finding music which can instantly respond to a sudden change in the dramatic situation, to a move forward, an unexpected blow, an act of violence or treachery or revelation and so forth, music whose form is entirely conditioned by the drama yet is its principal agent of expression. So essentially different is it, indeed, that the very greatest opera composers have not been major song writers, nor the very greatest song writers major opera composers. On one side are ranged Mozart, Verdi and Wagner, whose songs would earn them little claim to musical immortality, on the other Schubert, Schumann and Wolf, with operas on the outer fringes of the repertory. It is only when there is some descent from these mightiest peaks that we encounter composers who have succeeded in both genres.

Schubert never found a satisfactory means of expressing the feelings of a character as part of a drama, and, even when the situation could reasonably be called to a halt for a song, he tended to fall back upon the conventions he knew rather than explore the new worlds of the Lied which (despite an ancestry in Reichardt, Zelter and Zumsteeg) were essentially of his own discovery. Even in the larger operas his musical gifts take him in false directions. His first completed opera, *Des Teufels Lustschloss*, composed in 1813–14 to a Kotzebue text, is on one of the plots of elaborate magical 'trials', usually to prove a lover's constancy, with an operatic ancestry in Gluck's *L'Ivrogne corrigé* and in *Die Zauberflöte* but with progeny that included Hoffmann's *Der Trank der Unsterblichkeit*, Meyerbeer's *Wirth und Gast* and the boy Liszt's solitary opera, *Don Sancho*. The excuse is to bring as many weird and sensational happenings as possible on to the stage until such time as the presiding figure, priestly, avuncular or paternal, can pronounce himself satisfied that the hero has learnt his lesson or proved his virtue and resolve. To alert the audience, the term *natürliche Zauberoper* is sometimes found (and was used for Schubert's second version). Not surprisingly, the young Schubert is soon floundering well out of his depth, conventional in his resources, which were quite effective with numbers for which there were good models (including an occasional helping hand from the Mozart of *Don Giovanni*), but melodically bland and quite unable to cope with a farrago which would have defeated a better man, who in any case probably would not have touched it with a barge-pole. His two most ambitious operas, *Alfonso und Estrella* and *Fierrabras*, belong to the 1820s and a new phase of German grand opera.

For the great majority of Germans in the first years after the Congress, daily life continued much as it had for centuries. Some three quarters of the population lived on the land, and an agrarian economy and outlook dominated in times when there were as yet virtually no manufacturing industries. Towns were far separated, effectively the further when roads were often hardly better than dusty, rutted carriage tracks that in winter turned to mud and ice. Apart from a token four-mile link between Nuremberg and Fürth in 1835, it was not until 1839 that the first railway was laid, the seventy-mile Leipzig–Dresden line (one of the first to work as an engine-driver on it, and to commit his career to the development of the German railway network, was Weber's son and biographer Max Maria). The isolation and habits of rural life were reinforced by a patriarchal system in which noble or princely landowner stood at the head of a chain of responsibility descending by way of administrator or gamekeeper, through farmer or forester, to peasant. Away to the East, the peasants' condition might be little better than serfdom; nearer to Central or Western Germany, there was on the whole a more liberal interaction between classes, and an acceptance of the order of society as generally just and at least providing stability and security. The traditions of rural life were reflected in the country-man's almost mystic attachment to beast and field and forest, in a fascination with legend and folk tale, and in the rituals and conventions that have always surrounded country sports, for instance such matters as which game fell into the categories of 'hohe Jagd', 'mittlere Jagd' or 'niedere Jagd' and hence was available to prince, squire or peasant.

These aspects of German life continued to attract deep devotion, in some ways one more conscious – sentimental rather than naive –

from those who were no longer such a natural part of it: a growing middle class gravitating to the towns but retaining links with their origins or even, with prosperity, returning to become first-time land-owners; philosophers and artists with heightened appreciation of Rousseauesque values, as well as of Nature's mysterious, awesome, irrational, threatening aspects; students and intellectuals for whom there was to be found in all the diversity of the far-flung countryside and forest a manifestation of what served to join Germans in a common experience. For Metternich, however, striving to preserve the newly organized thirty-nine states of Germany in the precarious Deutscher Bund, such unity was as dangerous as progress, and he reacted with a despot's touchiness to the formation of the *Burschenschaften*. These student associations, originating in Jena in 1815, combined idealism and a sense of democratic brotherhood jumbled up with some silly but fairly harmless Teutonic pseudo-ritual and some far from harmless xenophobia and anti-Semitism. When in 1819 one of their number murdered the dramatist Kotzebue as a Russian spy, Metternich put through the so-called *Karlsbader Beschlüsse* dissolving them and imposing restraint on the universities. The *Burschenschaften*, with their attachment to an idealized past and their vague aspirations for a pan-German future, their love of forest and country and of tavern and folk songs, also embraced ominous elements that were to weave a dark thread into the fabric of German history, but their origins and nature lay in a response to the cherished substance of German country life.

There is much here upon which the phenomenal success of Weber's *Der Freischütz* rested. Performed within weeks of the Berlin version of Spontini's *Olimpie* in 1821, it had the effect of polarizing loyalties to composers who actually held each other in mutual respect, since it was easy to identify, only weeks after Napoleon's death, this noble Parisian grand opera with the grandeur associated with his van-quished imperial venture. *Der Freischütz* was the product of German life and lore, ancient but refreshed with new awareness and given new artistic maturity. The rural setting of its story of Max, who contracts an alliance with a fellow-huntsman Kaspar in league with the devil Samiel and forges seven magic bullets in the midnight horrors of the Wolf's Glen, so as to recover his lost marksmanship and thereby earn his bride Agathe, spoke instantly to German communality of feeling. The social order on which the work's conventions rest was not that of the *ancien régime*, lingering on from an essentially French pre-Revolutionary example, but one of familiar experience, princely landowner in touch with head forester, huntsman and peasant, and deferring only to the man of God living in Romantic isolation. When the huntsman Max's marksmanship fails him, he is taunted by his lowly peasant victor with the pseudo-French insult 'Mosje!', but the reassurance to the shocked head forester that the villagers' mockery should be taken in good part rings true. At the conclusion, the Prince doffs his hat to the hermit, and gladly accepts his judgement. If the hermit's timely intervention is little distinguishable from that of the *deus ex machina* of opera seria, the new context is all-important. This is a community whose nature is whole.

The opera's melodies, Weber had no hesitation in admitting, arose from his careful study of folksong (and from a youth cheerfully spent singing to his guitar in taverns). Yet these are never quoted, nor identified with their original words, nor indeed are they all German: the Huntsmen's Chorus, soon joyfully co-opted into German popular song books, is little different in manner from the other folk choruses but actually derives from part of the eighteenth-century French street song 'Malbrouk s'en va t'en guerre'. It is not quotation or association which is the point, but the successful integration of vernacular material into a work of art. In the vivid atmosphere which Weber creates, the presence of potent French influence can be overlooked, especially as this was an acceptable musical alliance in the face of the Italian enemy. Probably few at the time would have realized the extent to which Max's melodic style depends on Méhul, though this and much else in the work is due to Weber's careful absorption into his style of the many French works in his repertories during his ten-year operatic silence while conducting in Prague and Dresden.

From Méhul and Dalayrac, too, came the association of a brief musical idea, perhaps even a single gesture, with an essential dramatic ingredient in the opera. Here, it is the attachment of the diminished seventh chord to the powers of evil, conferring on its dislocation of normal tonality the shock of Romantic horror corrupting a fresh and ordered world. The subtlety of the key associations, including the organization of the entire Wolf's Glen scene on a diminished seventh tonal pattern, was Weber's own. From deep in his German heritage came the emphasis on instruments, here making orchestration more than ever a functional part of the invention and hence the orchestra the most important expressive agent of the drama. The strong example of Méhul's *Ariodant* had also provided the idea of orchestral colour as reflection of a dark drama: in the case of *Der Freischütz* (again, Weber made no secret of his intentions) it is a descent from light into darkness and back into light. The nature and detail of Weber's scoring is a direct consequence of his dramatic needs. It depends principally upon his pioneering ability to use primary colours, often novel (such as low flute thirds or shrieking piccolos, clarinets in their deepest register, unmuted viola tone singled out against the remaining muted strings) but always kept simple and making use of an instrument's tonal individuality. By such means there is composed into orchestral sound the image of a pure world, one then tainted with evil before recovering its pristine condition. The clarinet which sings blithely of Max's lost woodland happiness is the same instrument whose sinister low thirds introduce the Wolf's Glen; the horns softly intoning woodland purity at the start of the overture or chorusing the huntsmen's joy in the chase are the same instruments that, with cunning choice of crook and register, blaspheme this innocence with their vicious blare in the demoniacal Wild Hunt. As with the vile ritual in a Wolf's Glen adjacent to the sunlit forest clearing, darkness is close to the serenest tone on one and the same instrument.

The characters themselves stay very close to long-established Singspiel type: pure heroine, lively soubrette, well-meaning but misled hero, grim villain, benign prince, holy hermit. If they are scarcely subtle, they possess memorability, and their very simplicity helps them to take their place as part of the fabric of their simple world. Familiar musical elements converge – Polacca, cavatina, Vengeance Aria, melodrama, village marches and dances – to give the first audiences a sense of being in an old landscape newly discovered. Though Weber's is by no means the first overture to use elements of its parent opera, it distils the drama into a sonata structure with unprecedented virtuosity. The Wolf's Glen scene is a central finale such as had never before been written, embracing melodrama, song, aria, chorus, all eventually overwhelmed by raging orchestral description. If the sun and warmth, the fresh delight in forest life had an immediate appeal, the impact of the darkness into which Weber plunges the drama was still greater as the physical manifestation of evil now becomes a subject for opera. The work is set in the beautiful surroundings of the Böhmer Wald, the range of wooded heights between Bavaria and Bohemia that long remained one of the remotest and least frequented regions of Germany; it takes place shortly after the Thirty Years War, in which Samiel's agent Kaspar reveals he has fought, even taking part in the foulest of its massacres, the so-called Magdeburger Tanz, the sack and burning of the peaceful old city of Magdeburg. The memory was notorious enough for this to have stirred horrifying associations even in 1821, and to have spoken with a shudder to Romantics becoming familiar with the idea of the ghastly thrill of the irrational and sinister suddenly distorting the even course of life.

The immediate success of *Der Freischütz* in opera houses of all sizes across the length and breadth of Europe was one of the sensations of operatic history. The appeal of its sheer tunefulness, its orchestral virtuosity, its beguiling woodland tale and shocking diabolism set it on an enduring career in German-speaking lands. This was in fact initially very uneven both in performance and reception: Berliners remained loyal; a number of smaller theatres staged performances on the crest of the fashionable wave but with slender resources and erratic outcome; in Vienna, to Weber's wrath, censorship removed both Samiel and the hermit and the bullets were replaced by little arrows, while a row of parodies not only reflected the work's wild popularity but tamed it to Viennese taste. However, the skilful use of a folk tale, folk-inspired music and characters deriving from national life proved an inspiration to composers of other heritages seeking their own national emancipation. Naturally its influence on the secure traditions of Italy and France was negligible, but Verstovsky in Russia, Moniuszko in Poland, Smetana in Bohemia, even a small handful of English composers struggling with the formation of a national tradition, turned to *Der Freischütz* as an example of what might be achieved with national legend, atmosphere and music in the hands of a patriotic composer. However, Weber himself had no wish to repeat a success which quickly came to irk him. Having brought Singspiel into a new condition, he now turned aside from his half-finished comedy *Die drei Pintos* to set his sights on the still elusive ideal of German grand opera.

Euryanthe remains notoriously a problem work. The goal it seeks, with music of greater scope and power than that of *Der Freischütz* or of any German opera of its time, is never quite achieved through crucial failures in dramatic judgement. Helmina von Chezy's libretto has drawn much reproach, with some cause. Set in twelfth-century France, its knightly plot concerns the innocent Euryanthe, whom the jealous Lysiart wagers her lover Adolar he can seduce. Though troubled by scruples, Lysiart commits himself to an alliance with Euryanthe's evil friend, the sorceress Eglantine, who has persuaded Euryanthe to betray a dark family secret. When Lysiart publicly claims that Euryanthe has been false, she misunderstands and does not defend herself. Adolar takes her into the desert to kill her. After she has saved him from a huge snake, he relents to the extent of abandoning her instead. She is rescued by the King on a hunt, and the truth is revealed; Lysiart kills Eglantine and is led away, Adolar and Euryanthe are reunited.

The plot is riddled with absurdities and improbabilities, but these are all too closely connected with the failure to set at the centre a hero and heroine of human proportions. Weber cannot be absolved from blame for accepting all this in the interests of his novel intention, which was to bring German grand opera, Romantic opera and elements of Singspiel into a new synthesis. By the second decade of the century most German operas could be thus categorized, or at least recognized; and in spite of much overlapping of genres, at which points some of the most interesting ideas can be found, the distinctions existed in practice as well as in description. Weber's admiration for Poissl's operas sprang in good part from recognition of their nature and intent, and in introducing *Der Wettkampf zu Olympia* to Dresden audiences he had attempted to set out some definitions (see p. 293). The emphasis on continuous recitative is vital to his purpose, and it is in such passages that *Euryanthe* achieves its most distinctive and impressive character. Weber's injunction to Chezy to give him uneven lines of verse that would challenge his melodic invention, and hence liberate him from the enervating cadential regularities of much German libretto writing, is of no less importance in ensuring that it is music which holds court in the set numbers. He went on to identify the subjects for grand opera as likely to be taken from classical antiquity, in a context of French classical tragedy, and to regret that, with the advance of Romantic opera, further examples of German grand opera were improbable. This clearly points to an ideal different from grand operas such as those by Mosel and Poissl.

Though Weber never defined his aims precisely, what emerges from the lengthy wranglings about the libretto described by Helmina von Chezy, even with partiality and with the hindsight of nearly twenty years (Chezy, 1840), and from the evidence of letters, underlines his determination to bring all the contemporary elements of German opera into a new expressive whole. *Euryanthe* differs from earlier examples of German grand opera in this attempted assimilation. Among its ingredients are lighter 'Singspiel' pieces and examples of local colour such as the May Song with chorus and the Hunting Chorus, the latter absorbed from *Freischütz* simplicity into novel and more fluent surroundings as the huntsmen now become agents of the plot. Other elements include Euryanthe's Cavatinas and a powerfully original use of Vengeance Aria in Lysiart's appearance at the start of Act II, the greatest scene in the opera. It is too simple to attach these directly to Italian example, since much had by now been amalgamated into German opera, especially in the fire of Mozart's genius. Moreover, the force of the orchestra in Lysiart's Act II scene drives the aria from its powerful exemplars in Mozart and Cherubini forward to a new expressive condition. Weber sets at the core of his opera the moral division between a 'light' pair (Euryanthe and Adolar) and a 'dark' pair (Eglantine and Lysiart); in this, he further puts into operatic currency the concept of the anti-hero, the bass Lysiart, divided against himself, driven by dark emotional forces but anguished by moral scruple. Much else in the work, however, continues to derive from French example: this includes the *Prière* of French opera (for Euryanthe), and most skilfully of all the reconciliation of Adolar's French-influenced serenade with the stanzaic structure of *Meistergesang* and the fuller participation of the orchestra. Nevertheless, the serenade expresses no more than troubadourish platitudes, and while these are required by the conventions of the court in which he utters them, he never breaks free from them. Lysiart, in the Andante section of his great Act II scene, reveals a warmth and depth of emotion that set him far beyond Adolar in humanity, and make his inability to surmount his jealousy and commitment to evil genuinely tragic.

Weber has also derived from French opera the use of reminiscence motive, in particular as he had experienced it in the works of Dalayrac and Méhul. The adroit variety of its use in *Euryanthe* to characterize the nature and actions of the evil Eglantine shows that within self-imposed limits he was developing a new mastery of motivic transformation, in a manner perhaps influenced by Poissl (Example 29). The various orchestrations and harmonizations of the ghost music, finally achieving the major key as they are laid to rest, are also those of a dramatic composer ahead of his time. Weber's failure to develop this further into the condition of motive leading the drama symphonically has also caused puzzlement. But this was not yet his intention. Introducing himself and his ideas to 'the art-loving citizens of Dresden' in 1817, he turned Reichardt's despairing

comment about the Germans being in the arts only imitators (*nur Nachahmer*) to positive account, while at the same time implying that the German tradition was now long and secure enough to be capable of genuine creative development of its own.

> Die Kunstformen aller übrigen Nationen haben sich von jeher bestimmter ausgesprochen als die der Deutschen. In gewisser Hinsicht nämlich. – Der Italiener und Franzose haben sich eine Operngestalt geformt, in der sie sich befriedigt hin und her bewegen. Nicht so der Deutsche. Ihm ist es rein eigentümlich, das Vorzügliche aller übrigen wißbegierig und nach stetem Weiterschreiten verlangend an sich zu ziehen: aber er greift alles tiefer. Wo bei den andern es meist auf die Sinnenlust einzelner Momente abgesehen ist, will er ein in sich abgeschlossenes Kunstwerk, wo alle Teile sich zum schönen Ganzen runden und einen. (Weber, 1908, 276–7)

Example 29   Weber: *Euryanthe* (1823)
(a) Act I, sc. 3
(b) Act I, sc. 3
(c) Act I, sc. 4
(d) Act I, sc. 4
(e) Act II, sc. 5

(No people has been so slow and uncertain as the German in
determining its own specific art forms. Both the Italians and the French
have evolved a form of opera in which they move freely and naturally.
This is not true of the Germans, whose peculiarity it has been to adopt
what seems best in other schools, after much study and steady
development; but the matter goes deeper with them. Whereas other
nations concern themselves chiefly with the sensuous satisfaction of
isolated moments, the German demands a self-sufficient work of art, in
which all the parts make up a beautiful and unified whole. Weber, 1981,
206–7)

Though this was written ostensibly as a demand for a well-balanced
ensemble in his new opera house, there lies not very far behind it the
familiar call for the unified work of art. But at this stage, he was
concerned to bring all the elements he knew so well in German
opera into a coherently related whole, not to fuse them into a
Gesamtkunstwerk. The symphonic technique for that did not yet exist,

nor perhaps could have lain within his idiom. Throughout his maimed, fragmented English opera *Oberon* there is ample evidence of new skills in the use of a single motive, the three-note rising figure associated with Oberon's magic horn, to guide and characterize the drama. His intention, had he lived, was to rewrite *Oberon* as a German opera, and though it is impossible to envisage how that might have been brought about, there can be little doubt that a still more continuous texture than that of *Euryanthe* would have been sought, and that motive would have played a significant part in its realization. But for all its flaws, in its inventive range, its originality and its dramatic power *Euryanthe* is superior to all other German grand operas of the 1820s.

By not quite three months in 1823, Spohr's grand opera *Jessonda* (28 July) preceded *Euryanthe* (25 October). Despite Weber's championship of *Faust*, Spohr had been equivocal about him, and was made the more so by the success of *Der Freischütz*, indeed may have been spurred to new efforts by its popularity. When he wrote in a prefatory article to *Jessonda* that 'we should no longer speculate on mere theatrical effects, as several of the modern composers do . . . but compose music of a true dramatic character', it seems likely that he had in mind the vast popular appeal of *Der Freischütz* (which he admitted his own music lacked). A tinge of jealousy can be excused, and he cannot be blamed for setting his sights on what he regarded as something higher than the sensationalism of the Wolf's Glen.

If, apart from a divinely aimed thunderbolt, *Jessonda* eschews the supernatural, it incorporates the appeal of the exotic at the centre of the plot, though Spohr, with his gift for colourful orchestration and his delight in expressive harmony, is curiously reluctant to exploit this. Jessonda, widow of the Rajah of Goa, must commit suttee, the immolation rite insisted on by the High Priest Dandau even though her true love has always been the Portuguese General, Tristan d'Acunha. The young priest Nadori, sent to bear this message, is transfixed by the beauty of her sister Amazili. The Portuguese advance, but when Tristan discovers Jessonda, Dandau holds him to the terms of a truce not to interfere with the ceremony. It is only when Dandau's men attack the Portuguese fleet that Tristan feels absolved from his word, and storms the city in time to rescue Jessonda and unite Amazili with Nadori.

Like Weber in *Euryanthe*, but with very different means and outcome, Spohr gathers different ingredients into his concept of German grand opera as a genre absorbing and transcending outside influences. His awareness of French grand opera in general, and Spontini in particular, is reflected in the statuesque opening scene of mourning over the body of the dead Rajah, in some of the characters' rather formal emotional stances, in the superfluous ballet opening Act II, and in the nocturnal scene when a vast statue of Brahma is struck by lightning. He is not afraid to draw on an Italianate melodic line, as in the Act I Trio, and when he comes to the Jessonda–Amazili duet to blend this into a more Germanic lyrical manner. His German heritage is acknowledged in the concentration on orchestral expression, where his skills with chromatic harmony can prove a liability as well as an asset. At times, as with the officers' trio before they rush off into battle, a fairly conventional vocal line over repetitive string figuration is not redeemed by the meandering chromatic wind figures which intrude themselves everywhere. Yet there are some superb inventions, among them Jessonda's narration of her journey to India, and none better than when Nadori, the Brahmin novice as innocent of women as Shakespeare's Ferdinand, comes to announce Jessonda's fate and is struck silent by Amazili's beauty, leaving the orchestra to articulate his 'spirits, as in a dream, all bound up' (Example 30). The eloquence of this annunciation of death was not lost on Wagner, one of the work's admirers. Spohr's skill with orchestral recitative can overtake Weber's, building up large-scale scene complexes in each act, and making use of a fluent movement between conversational recitative and more formal declamation or arioso, even if he can sometimes crank up recitative for another stretch of narration with a conventional interrupted cadence. His longer-term timing is not so secure, allowing him to give Tristan and Nadori in quick succession two arias in Polacca rhythm. But there is a searching instinct for stage effect and an ability to seize

(As the next morning rises from the waters of the sea, in the heat of the fire you must . . . .)

Example 30   Spohr: *Jessonda* (1823), Nadori

and hold the listener's attention as the drama moves towards its climax.

Neither of Schubert's two completed grand operas can match these qualities in Weber or Spohr, despite their wealth of beautiful and characteristic music. For *Alfonso und Estrella* (1822), his only through-composed opera, Schubert recruited his friend Franz von Schober as librettist, and the two of them spent a contented autumn working side by side in a castle near Vienna. Perhaps the friendship was too comfortable, without a critical edge: Schober, no operatic craftsman, was happy to provide a sequence of verses he knew would suit his friend's lyrical gift, while Schubert, with slack dramatic instincts, seems to have accepted all that was set before him. The outcome is chaotic. Schober's text is a bland but complicated tale of Estrella, daughter of the usurped King Froila, and her love for Alfonso, son of the usurper Mauregato, whose general, Adolfo, frustrated in his designs on Estrella, is eventually imprisoned until Froila, his troops under Alfonso victorious in battle, dispenses forgiveness to everyone in need of it. As a theatrical dilettante, Schober eagerly gathered up plenty of models, among them rescue opera, an historical setting, and some Romantic trappings such as descriptions of nature and chivalric attitudes (though not a supernatural element). Schubert in turn rummaged into his own experience of the Viennese stage, and came up with the pastoral placidity of Weigl for atmosphere, touches of Gluck to show gravity of purpose, and the ever-popular Rossini to enliven ensembles. Rather than this being a serious attempt by composer and librettist to find fruitful stimuli for German grand opera, there is more the sense of a pair of magpies at work. Schubert's qualities are best shown in the duets to which the pairings at the centre of the story (lovers, enemies, rivals, father–child, in various combinations) make the text prone. So prone is it, indeed, and so innocent of dramatic sense were the collaborators, that much of the work consists of strings of duets during which little or nothing occurs. It takes six numbers covering half an hour's music at the start of the opera before the characters find the energy to do much more than praise their happy valley, while Act II opens with a request for a ballad, immediately granted, which is absurdly misplaced and has nothing much to do with the plot. Throughout these two acts Schubert filled the numbers with some charming music that never once (not even in Adolfo's Vengeance Aria) produces a dramatic thrust, indeed whose pastoral tranquillity saps any half-hearted resolves for action which the characters make. By Act III it is too late, even though after Alfonso's victory Schubert suddenly galvanizes himself into action and, with numbers following one another compactly, fluently and irregularly, gives a glimpse of his operatic potential.

Fierrabras, a *Heroisch-romantische Oper* written for the Kärntnertortheater in 1823 when *Alfonso und Estrella* was rejected, was itself rejected in the wake of the failure of *Euryanthe*. Setting its grand opera sights higher, it is based on a much more complicated plot. This concerns couples on opposing sides in the wars between the Franks and the Moors, with Charlemagne's daughter Emma in love with Eginhard, while the Moorish Fierrabras also loves her but is loved by his compatriot Florinda, in turn loved by the Frankish Roland. The complexities involve battles, sieges, imprisonments, the near-execution of Roland and a great deal of unmotivated behaviour by pasteboard figures whose chivalric attitudes avail them little. It would have taken a composer better experienced in operatic intricacies to have clarified all this musically, and Schubert does not make much distinction between any of the characters. There are some good numbers when he feels himself on home ground, as with the opening spinning chorus and when Eginhard, serenading Emma in a forlorn A minor, is answered by her A major consolation. Some of the most effective music is in the melodramas, though it is asking a lot of a singer, in one of them, to report on events invisible to cast or audience by this means. Yet the whole of the finale to Act I finds Schubert, as with the *Alfonso und Estrella* Act III sequence, suddenly in dramatic command, which makes his other miscalculations the more regrettable. Choruses and marches which perhaps intend the grandeur of Spontini outstay such welcome as they have, some events are allowed to sprawl where conciseness is demanded while others are over before there is time to grasp their import, farewells under the threat of danger are protracted beyond any dramatic reality. It is this erratic sense of progress, intermittently charged with some fine music, which makes *Fierrabras* a frustrating work.

In his operas, Schubert never manages to harness his genius as a composer of Lied and of symphony to musical drama, and so it tends actually to work against him. Often he seems to come into his own when telling a tale rather than enacting one, while the length of stride with which he can build long symphonic movements out of a few musical ideas is still more unsuitable for opera unless the ideas are motives animating the characters and their feelings. Schubert's sense of motive, in both *Alfonso und Estrella* and *Fierrabras*, is confined to a rather similar phrase attached to the two heroes without much idea of what then to do with it: in *Fierrabras*, the motive is principally concerned with contributing a generalized sense of the heroic. Repeatedly, he composes happily on in symphonic mode while his characters are kept waiting for him to finish so that they can get on with the plot. The true opera composer will be ready to interrupt and redirect his music for the sake of the drama; the great opera composer will make new musical forms that have their existence and strength entirely because of such dramatic imperatives.

Nevertheless, *Fierrabras* earns an honourable place as an ambitious attempt at German grand opera by one of the greatest composers of these years to approach the task. Few by the various lesser composers to try their hands at the genre could approach it in quality. One of the most ambitious is Heinrich Marschner's *Lucretia*, produced in 1827. As far as can be judged by the first act, the only one of the two to survive, this work on the rape of Lucretia owes almost everything to Spontini in general and to *La Vestale* in particular. Through-composed, it is dominated by ensemble scenes with an almost omnipresent chorus, and the static plot (most of the action comes in the second act) and conventional stances of the characters fail to be enlivened by the insistent flourishes of coloratura. Marschner, who had tried out various operatic manners before this, his sixth work, was on the brink of finding his true vein with Romantic opera, but still appears to be some way from it.

Some of the problems that troubled Schubert's operatic career also afflicted Mendelssohn. He was, as in all matters, precocious, and by the time he had achieved the first public production of one of his operas, with *Die Hochzeit des Camacho* in 1827, he had completed four Singspiels and reached the age of only eighteen. There are other attempts in his sketchbooks, among them the beginnings of quite an amusing little domestic drama about his banker relations that includes a lively chorus of bank clerks. *Die Soldatenliebschaft* (1820) is a nimble piece based on a French vaudeville, conventional in manner but touched with the sense of pace, contrapuntal skill used to witty ends and the subtle ear for instruments that early marked him. More assurance is shown in *Die beiden Pädagogen* (1821), a deft skit on rival methods of education all too familiar to the young genius – the liberal Pestalozzi versus the traditional Basedow – built into a plot of lovers and impersonations which uses Singspiel figures with even greater flexibility and wit. *Die wandernden Komödianten* (1822) is musically more extended, and shows greater subtlety of characterization, but though ambitiously constructed it is awkwardly proportioned and lacks the sharpness of its predecessors. The fourth and last of these early pieces, all to texts by a young doctor friend, Johann Ludwig Casper, was *Der Onkel aus Boston* (1824). The libretto is incomplete, but shows signs of continuous music developing situations whose complexity is set out in too much dialogue and resolved rather too early in the work. Mendelssohn had clearly absorbed some of the lessons of Mozart's finales to more profound effect, and he had experienced the Berlin sensation of 1821, *Der Freischütz*. However, for all their skill and charm, and their amusing and affecting touches, these pieces inhabit a classical world preserved into Romantic times. None of them had been exposed to any audience wider than his loyal domestic circle.

The failure of *Die Hochzeit des Camacho* at the Berlin Schauspielhaus in 1827 consequently came as a shock. Based on an episode in *Don Quixote*, the twist in whose plot had already done duty for Schenk's *Der Dorfbarbier*, this version has Quiteria forced by her rich father Carrasco to abandon her lover Basilio in favour of the rich Camacho. The secondary lovers Vivaldo and Lucinda have their own romance to sustain. Basilio wastes away, his morbid pallor leading everyone to expect his imminent demise. When evidently on the point of expiry, he is permitted to go through a deathbed form of marriage; whereat he leaps up hale and hearty. There are various incidental complications, including a ballet of Love and Wealth. Don Quixote, easily muddled by the confusions into worsening them, and Sancho Panza play largely peripheral roles. Some of the uncertainties which bedevilled Schubert in *Fierrabras* repeat themselves

here. In the wake of *Der Freischütz*, Mendelssohn had a growing
awareness of how Singspiel characters could be given a somewhat
richer Romantic dimension. *Euryanthe* helped him to add to this and,
together with the forms of Spohr's *Jessonda*, to make his own semi-
continuous form in which dialogue is dispensed with in the ensemble scenes and some use of motive (especially for the watching
figure of Don Quixote) broods over the proceedings. There is a
further sense that, like Schubert, this immensely gifted composer
had not yet found his feet securely on the stage. When Basilio and
Quiteria are parted, a Septet with Chorus (No. 7) and the succeeding
chorus build up a multiple movement with ingenuity and show an
interest in letting dramatic contrasts of tempo and texture respond
to the implications of the text. Yet Mendelssohn's instinct for
regularity constantly asserts itself, so that dramatic movement can
halt for the music to continue energetically enough but with bland
harmonies and well-proportioned choral entries, while in the orchestra there is a tendency to suggest busy activity on the stage with
passages of the fugato he had mastered while still a child. His ear for
instruments, together with the sylvan beauty of his *Midsummer
Night's Dream* score, show as Basilio moves sadly away from Quiteria
and soft woodwind phrases swell and grow richer to surround him
like the woods into which his voice slowly vanishes. Quiteria, too,
has her moment in which despair leads her simple village nature to
take on a new dimension. When she is distracted by grief at Basilio's
loss, Mendelssohn calls upon further Shakespearian memories of
Ophelia to write her a touching Mad Aria in which she first poses
and answers her own questions, and is then precipitated into fast
sections portraying her disintegrating reason and final pathetic
disarray.

Mendelssohn spent the rest of his short life bewailing the lack of a
suitable libretto, but for his only remaining opera he reverted to
Liederspiel with *Die Heimkehr aus der Fremde*. This was to prove the
most successful of all his operas, a charming, inventive work, beautifully scored, which alone of them has had a modest career on the
stage. Mendelssohn's only other operatic music came in 1847 with

some material for *Die Loreley*, which includes Rhinemaidens but lacks atmosphere. By then, his natural operatic manner had grown outdated, and it is difficult to envisage him moving into the world of Romantic opera by building upon the very real merits of *Die Hochzeit des Camacho*.

The immense public success of *Der Freischütz* naturally provided an impetus for composers with either serious ambitions for Romantic opera or simply anxieties about missing a bandwagon. In the case of the prolific Conradin Kreutzer, probably both these considerations, and several others, applied. His forty-odd stage works include Singspiels, Romantic and magic operas, even a tragedy. The years he spent as Kapellmeister at different Viennese theatres were in many ways a case of the right man in the right place at the right time, for the stage pieces that poured from his pen more or less annually met Viennese taste effortlessly; yet their fluency does not exclude some attractive and imaginative music, and it may be that in a theatrical milieu with fewer demands and less volatile taste he might have been able to develop the lyrical vein that shows in his best work. By the time he left Vienna in 1840, his manner had worn thin, and the cities which traded on his reputation to stage his new operas did not choose to invite him back.

Kreutzer's *Libussa*, which won him his position in Vienna in 1822, is one of the better of many contemporary operas making an immediate response to Weber's effects. Based on Brentano's *Historisch-romantisches Drama, Die Gründung Prags*, this is no national epic such as Smetana later composed, but an adventurous love story concerning the founding families of the Bohemian nation. The opera gets down to *Freischütz* business straight away with a Huntsmen's Chorus into which there is inserted a Cavatina for Wladislaw, declaring the joys of the open air and the chase. These are promptly exchanged for other joys as, with cries of 'Welche Jungfrau!', he rescues Libussa from a bear and they fall into one another's arms for two love duets (the second ending 'Allegro à la chasse'). The complexities of the plot concern Libussa withholding her true identity as heir to the throne from Wladislaw, who eventually turns out to be Premysl, her destined dynastic husband and co-founder of the Bohemian nation. One of the most touching characters is Libussa's maid Dobra, charged with pretending to be Libussa but then herself falling in love with Wladislaw: in Act II she has the opera's finest aria, 'Fest verschlossen still im Herzen'. *Libussa* is an uneven work (Schubert, bored, left at the end of the first act, even though he had heard that Act II was better, as he told Joseph Spaun: letter of 7 December 1822). It is filled with familiar ingredients such as a Polacca for Wladislaw, a good Vengeance Aria for the wicked Domoslaw and a Romanze with dream narration for the retainer Botak (which Schubert might have liked), as well as a Trio for three Priests and some light, folk-like pieces, mixed with larger dramatic arias of which the best comes near the end for Libussa. In the earlier numbers she is rather a blank character who does little more than declaim nobly affirmative arpeggios, and the opening duets have the instant lovers singing in heroic lines that scarcely differentiate them. Only belatedly does Libussa, revealing her true identity, manage to join womanly warmth to dynastic assertions. There are some skilfully written arias, and Kreutzer's quick instinct for the stage keeps matters moving well.

The success of *Libussa* won Kreutzer his post as Director of the Kärntnertortheater, and he also revived for Stuttgart an earlier Romantic opera of 1813, *Der Taucher*, in 1823. This also opens with a Huntsmen's Chorus, and includes some attractive nature music as well as an impressive Melodrama and Ballet in which Fata Morgana puts the hero Ivo to sleep; but everything really leads towards the long finale based on Schiller's ballad about a diver plunging into a whirlpool to retrieve a golden cup hurled in as a challenge by the King. This is a well-composed sequence of movements bringing the work to an exciting conclusion, with arias and narrations, a Fishermen's Chorus, dances for sailors and knights, and some vivid orchestral description of swirling mists and churning seas as the hero Ivo plunges into the whirlpool. The opera makes some attempt at use of motivic, or at any rate characteristic, arpeggios, but these scarcely hold together a work with such a broken-backed plot.

However, more significant responses to ideas that Weber had brought to a head were not long in following, especially to the *Schauerromantik* of *Der Freischütz* and to the depiction of the simple tenor hero as being of less substance than the ambivalent baritone villain in *Euryanthe*. Hoffmann's *Undine*, even though it was better known by repute than in performance, also contributed to the continuing Romantic interest in the interaction of the human and the spirit worlds. Fascination with these ideas combined to arouse interest in the subject of vampires, an ancient superstition given new interest when John Polidori published his story *The Vampyre* in 1819, allowing the publishers to pass it off as the work of his former employer Byron. Though Byron had begun such a tale in 1816, in imitation of Mary Shelley's *Frankenstein*, it is difficult to see how his writing even at its worst could have been confused with Polidori's ridiculously mannered style. However, it was the subject matter, especially when the prose was veiled in translation, which appealed to various composers. Polidori tells how the sinister nobleman Ruthven accepts young Aubrey as his travelling companion, though rumours about Ruthven's vices cause them to part. In Greece, Aubrey falls in love with Ianthe, but seeking shelter from a storm in a dark hut he happens upon a violent struggle; rescuers discover Ianthe dead, with fang marks on her neck, her mysterious assailant vanished. Later, Aubrey is reconciled to Ruthven, who is then mortally wounded by robbers and, dying, swears Aubrey to secrecy about his crimes for a year and a day. Ruthven's recovery when his corpse is placed in moonlight leads Aubrey to realize that his friend is a vampire, and the one who murdered Ianthe. Back in England, Aubrey finds that his sister is to marry Ruthven, but the term of his oath expires too late, and she also falls victim to the vampire. The two composers who produced vampire operas in 1828, Lindpaintner and Marschner, both set librettos based largely on a play by Heinrich Ritter, *Ein Uhr!*, in turn based on Polidori. Marschner's opera was produced in Leipzig in March 1828, Lindpaintner's in Stuttgart that September. To the annoyance of both composers, the two works got in one another's way, different though their treatments are.

After some success with his two previous operas, *Sulmona* and *Der Bergkönig*, Peter Lindpaintner clearly felt that he had a touch with the *Schauerromantik*. *Der Bergkönig* (1825), like earlier operas by Weber and by Danzi (see p. 245), is loosely based on J. K. A. Musäus's Rübezahl tale in his *Volksmärchen der Deutschen* (1782–6). It settles for separate numbers with none of the sense of structural growth Spohr was to bring to it, and with a more conventional disposition of characters. Its strongest scene is that opening Act II, as the central figure, Luchsius, invokes 'Dunkle Mächte' with powerful chords and shuddering tremolos showing that the example of *Euryanthe* was still potent; and he concludes the act with a dramatic disappearance into the abyss in a scene that includes dance and melodrama. For the rest, there is plenty of freshly conceived music celebrating the world of light and air, some attractive lyrical numbers for the hero and heroine, Hugo and Johanna, and some well-judged lighter ones for the secondary lovers, Kunz and Bertha. But Lindpaintner set much greater store by *Der Vampyr*. Cäsar Heigel's libretto confusingly gives the name Aubry to the baritone vampire. He has been promised Isolde by her father, Port d'Amour, from whom he has then exacted a vow of secrecy about his true nature. Hippolyt is her tenor lover, to whom she has become betrothed. Festive preparations are interrupted by a sudden cry from Isolde's maid Balbine announcing that Isolde has disappeared while hunting, at which Etienne, the castle gardener, suggests that she must have fallen victim to a vampire, and sings a ballad to illustrate his point. When Isolde reappears, she recounts how a strange man appeared to her in a dream; her emotions are torn between him and Hippolyt, especially when before her there now stands the figure of her dream, Aubry, 'ein junger Mann ganz leichenblass'. He seems to be supplanting Hippolyt in her affections, but she begs for time, during which Aubry lures another young girl, Etienne's lover Lorette, into the garden. Felled by Hippolyt, Aubry exacts an oath of silence from him until midnight, and is revived by the moon's rays. Only belatedly does Isolde realize in a vision that Aubry is a vampire. Finally, Aubry's renewed attempt to seize Isolde is frustrated by Port d'Amour deciding that a father's holy right is stronger than the forces of Hell and revealing the truth. Aubry's castle collapses and he is dragged down to Hell.

Lindpaintner's original version was with spoken dialogue; later, in 1850, he turned the work into a grand opera with recitatives, in the process considerably tightening up the rather loosely assembled final scene (including dropping an intrusive Prayer for Isolde). He did nothing to clear up other loose ends such as the rather casual appearances and disappearances of some of the minor characters, and the lack of a reconciliation between Isolde and Hippolyt. In both versions the opera is more remarkable for some effectively handled ingredients than for its overall dramatic strength. A place is found for many features that had proved reliable in the hands of previous Romantic composers, notably Spohr and Weber, and for ideas and imports, especially fashionable in Paris in these years, such as the interrupted betrothal and the collapsing castle. More specifically popular musical ideas include the ballad for Etienne, Polaccas, Vengeance Arias that owe much to Mozart's Queen of the Night (see White, 1987, 42–4), a choral prayer, a three-part canon and conventionally shaped Cavatinas and Romanzas, while Act II, as Aubry is born away in a storm before reviving in the moonlight, draws heavily on the vocabulary of the Wolf's Glen. However, though some of the numbers outstay their welcome and hold up the drama, Lindpaintner has an excellent sense of how to handle the cumulative scene complex that was increasingly a feature of German opera, and both the opening scene and the finales to his first two acts have real dramatic impetus and vitality. Harmonically he is to an extent beholden to Spohr, but he can judge well the dramatic balance between diatonic simplicity for the human world and the creepy chromaticism that invades this from the supernatural realm of the vampire, a point established early on in Etienne's ballad and brought into the emotional heart of the work as Isolde finds herself pulled between Hippolyt and the sinister appeal of the vampire. Her swoon is to the harmonized descending chromatic scale that was coming to stand for the mysterious, in Wagner's hands to represent

Example 31

(a) Lindpaintner: *Der Vampyr* (1828), Isolde's swoon

(b) Wagner: *Die Walküre* (1870), Brünnhilde's magic sleep

Brünnhilde's lowering into magic sleep, here the supernatural lover's dangerous lure into darkness (Example 31).

Marschner's librettist Wilhelm Wohlbrück, with whom he was to have several successful collaborations, makes a number of crucial improvements on Ritter by including consideration of other versions, as well as taking account of Polidori's original. Surrounded by witches and evil spirits, the vampire Ruthven obtains another year on earth provided he can sacrifice three young brides before the following midnight. He takes Janthe into a cave and murders her, but is stabbed by her father. Finding him almost lifeless, Aubry agrees to carry him into the moonlight to revive. Ruthven's vampire nature is thus revealed, but Aubry is sworn to secrecy, on pain of becoming a vampire himself, in return for having once had his life saved by Ruthven. Aubry is now welcomed by his lover Malwina, who is, however, promised by her father to the Earl of Marsden that day. The Earl proves to be none other than Ruthven. Emmy, a peasant girl due to marry George, sings a ballad about vampires, at which Ruthven appears and soon seduces and murders her, too; he is then shot by her betrothed, George. Once more revived, Ruthven prepares to marry Malwina, but Aubry is now willing to sacrifice himself and reveals the truth. Ruthven is dragged down to Hell, and Aubry is after all free to marry Malwina.

Wohlbrück's text is superior to Heigel's in several significant respects. The vampire's need to provide three victims heightens the tension, a stronger imperative for silence is laid upon Aubry, and the plot moves forward more steadily to its dénouement. Even the elements of light relief prove unnervingly relevant. Emmy's vampire ballad concludes with the sudden appearance of Ruthven himself (a point not lost on Wagner with Senta's Flying Dutchman ballad), and the cheerful drinking quartet is to words (for instance, the men sing of drinking the blood of the grape) which prove to be paralleled in Emmy's off-stage murder at that exact moment. The opera is permeated by this paralleling of the innocent and the diabolical. Before we have encountered any of the characters, the overture (in its original position: Pfitzner's edition places it after the first scene) gives us a version of the descending chromatic scale figure familiar from the opening of the Wolf's Glen scene and used thematically by Spohr three years previously in *Der Berggeist* (see below, p. 332): here, it will be associated with Ruthven's 'Ha! welche Lust' (Example 32). Transformation of this into Malwina's theme is achieved in the course of the overture by gradually widening the sinister semitone intervals into diatonic arpeggios until the theme becomes that of her 'O lass, Geliebter' (Example 33). In Ruthven's 'Ha! welche Lust' the conventional Vengeance Aria arpeggios are joined to his own descending chromatic scale, but also suggest a distinctly ambivalent relationship to Malwina (Example 34). Though there is never any suggestion that Malwina has a redemptive role to play, innocence and evil are joined, which is not the case in the *Freischütz* overture upon which the piece is otherwise generally modelled, or indeed in *Der Freischütz* at all. Ruthven's vengeance aria may begin by invoking comparisons with the uncompromising villainy of Beethoven's Pizarro, but changes to sadness as he muses on the compassion for his victims which his condition has forfeited, before he has to rouse himself to renewed blood lust. In turn, compassion is invited for the vampire's own suffering.

Allegro con fuoco

Example 32   Marschner: *Der Vampyr* (1828), Overture

MALVINA

O   lass, Ge-liebter, dich be-schwö - ren,   er - stik - ke nicht den frohen

Mut, noch lebt   ein   Gott,   noch lebt ein Gott.

(O beloved, promise yourself not to suppress your cheerful spirit, there still lives a God)

Example 33   Marschner: *Der Vampyr* (1828), Malwina

RUTHVEN

Ha!   wel-che Lust, in   lie - ben-den Ko - sen mit lüs - ter-nem Muth

(Ha! what delight, in loving caresses with lustful spirit . . .)

Ach,   einst fühlt' ____ ich   selbst ____ die   Schmer-zen
ih - rer Angst ____ im   war - men Her - zen.

(Ah! once I myself felt the pains of her anguish in a warm heart)

Example 34   Marschner: *Der Vampyr* (1828), Ruthven

Marschner has learnt from Weber's Lysiart, and here takes the opportunities presented by his librettist, but he does not explore the idea further. There is, for instance, no return of compassion for the vampire's condition even as he causes unspeakable suffering, or at his damnation. Though Marschner has the motivic technique for exploring depths or subtleties of character well within his grasp, he lacks the understanding or resolve to apply it in an opera which soon becomes no more than a thriller. It is, however, an excellently written thriller. Marschner is at his strongest with the eerie or the tense. The orchestral description of the vampire's revival in the moonlight has the authentic Romantic shudder, and in building up suspense and excitement over a long scene he is in his element, especially in the finale to Act I responding to the text with tonal and harmonic procedures, and by the use of characteristic figures, that together develop the dramatic situation in masterly fashion. Though he allots a simple Lied to Janthe, and gives Emmy a fetching oddity with a song in shifting metres, his melodic manner is not up to characterizing Malwina strongly, so that her linking with the vampire's theme remains no more than a piece of thematic transformation without dramatic force. Nevertheless, Wagner's interest – he conducted the work and composed extra music for Aubry – was by no means misplaced.

Several opera composers, apart from Lindpaintner, had had their eye caught by the legend of the earth spirit Rübezahl, related as the first of five tales in the second part of Musäus's *Volksmärchen der Deutschen*, among them Vogler, Weber and Danzi. In Musäus's version, this is an engagingly told story of Emma, daughter of the ruler of the Riesengebirge, whose beauty captivates a gnome one day as she is bathing in a forest pool. He bears her off to his underground palace, but all his blandishments fail to win her, pining as she is for the upper air and for her lover Ratibor, and her languishing is unconsoled by the arrival of her companion Brinhilde. Eventually she deludes the lovesick gnome into making proof of his devotion by counting the plants growing in his domain, and while he is so engaged she uses his magic to conjure up a fine horse and fly on its back up to her own realm and the arms of Ratibor. From his foolish cabbage-counting the gnome acquires the name Rübezahl.

The most important operatic treatment of the story came in 1825 from Spohr (who had also considered the subject in 1813) as *Der Berggeist*. Learning of the joys of human love from Troll, a man become gnome, the Berggeist steps in before the wedding of Alma and Oskar, rooting the bridegroom to the earth and bearing the bride off through a storm to his subterranean kingdom. Here, Troll flirts in vain with Alma's companion Ludmilla, who in her spirit manifestation is incapable of love, while the Berggeist prepares for marriage to Alma. Having distracted the Berggeist's attention into counting flowers, Ludmilla, Alma and Troll make their escape. He overtakes them, but, persuaded that human love is not for him, returns underground with Troll.

Musäus's puckishly contradictory spirit ('mit sich selbst in stetem Widerspruch') is here developed into the ambivalent Berggeist, riven between his supernatural being and his longing for human love, while the bright and charming Emma becomes the emotionally complex Alma. She is, moreover, abducted by the Berggeist in a familiar Romantic contest between human innocence, on the brink of marriage, and menacing powers of darkness. Don Giovanni's near-seduction of Zerlina, peasant bride who is confused to discover in her simple nature an urgent sexual force, casts a long shadow over Romantic opera. Spohr's own Kunigunde is spellbound into yielding to Faust on the night of her wedding to Hugo; Weber's Agathe, whose bridal wreath has been confused with a funeral wreath and who arrives for the shooting trial in her wedding dress, seems at first to have fallen to her bridegroom's devilishly directed bullet; Marschner's Vampire is required to seduce no fewer than three brides before killing them. As Alma awaits Oskar, her expressions of love for him are gradually overwhelmed by the approach of the Berggeist, while in his kingdom she seems to be on the brink of union with him. Here and in other operas, there is more than the suggestion of a vengeful Dionysus wreaking havoc on human order.

The expansion of the characters from Musäus's lighthearted fairy tale puts some strain upon them and upon the details of the plot, in particular making an absurdity of the plant-counting device, but it does give Spohr the material for the kind of opera he was seeking to write. *Der Berggeist* far overtakes both *Jessonda* and *Euryanthe* in fluency and in the construction of large scene complexes as the main structural device. The opera's principal weakness lies in its lack of melodic distinction in the arias and other numbers absorbed within these scenes, as with the Berggeist's declaration of love to Alma in Act II or her Act III apostrophe to hope. Spohr is not alone in finding it easier to discover a simple tunefulness for the secondary characters, and there is a touching note in Troll's attempted wooing of Ludmilla, who in her spirit form cannot respond except in dance. But the whole of the Introduction in the underworld, as the earth spirits puzzle over the nature of human love and the Berggeist sets off in search of it, is well integrated, and with the last two scenes of Act I new strength and cohesion begin to bind the music. Left alone at her own request, Alma finds herself apprehensive even as she keeps protesting her love for Oskar. As she moves from recitative into her aria, 'Holde Stätte', spirit voices cut tritonally across her placid E♭ with abrupt A major interjections. The steadily tensing orchestral interventions and darkening chromatic harmony seem to reflect not only the approach of the earth spirits but her troubled state of mind, and her reiterations of love for Oskar repeatedly fail to calm her though they succeed in further arousing the earth spirits. Finally the Berggeist himself appears and carries her off through a climactic storm. It is a scene of considerable psychological complexity, and one developed with masterly control of orchestral and harmonic re-sources, the chromatic tensions here functional and never lapsing into the self-indulgence that is always in danger of invading Spohr's style. It also enables him to make sophisticated use of motive, especially as the descending chromatic scale associated with the Berggeist steadily comes to dominate the music. The theme declares itself immediately in the overture, and is used with much subtlety throughout the work. Though he first appears as a menacing figure, and his capture of Alma in Act I, scene 7 is violent, he produces a more powerful impression than Oskar. His final acknowledgement of defeat in Act III, scene 7 is made with dignity, as he renounces love and turns to descend to his own realm (Example 35).

A further opera reflecting the continuing interest in the central idea while considerably altering Musäus's plot is Poissl's *Der Unters-berg*. This also finds its most secure touch in an Act II Melodrama, in the depths of the mountain, which owes something to the Wolf's Glen. The work again includes a lively Huntsmen's Chorus, with eight horns on stage: as often with Poissl, the instrumental effects are

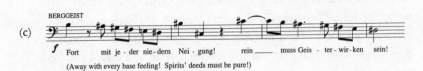

(c)

BERGGEIST

f Fort mit je - der nie - dern Nei - gung! rein ___ muss Geis - ter - wir - ken sein!

(Away with every base feeling! Spirits' deeds must be pure!)

Example 35   Spohr: *Der Berggeist* (1825)
(a) Overture
(b) Act I, sc. 7
(c) Act III, sc. 7, Berggeist

always well devised to underline the drama, and the importance of this is signalled in an overture which includes a mysterious passage for muted violins with double bass, followed by clarinets in their lowest register. The actual musical material can be thin, and the sense of dramatic momentum that informs Poissl's major works has here somewhat deserted him.

The most important of the operas after *Undine* treating the union of earth spirit and mortal woman, and much the most successful, was Marschner's *Hans Heiling* (1833). Combining various sources, Eduard Devrient's libretto concerns the doomed romance between Heiling, who resolves to leave his disapproving Earth Queen mother's subterranean kingdom for the sake of Anna, a village girl who has been persuaded by her mother to accept him largely for his riches. Though Anna has a somewhat awed respect for him, his morose and jealous nature soon antagonizes her, and when she defies him by dancing at a festival he turns away in despair, even as she is drawn back to her former lover Conrad. In a forest, the Earth Queen confronts her with the truth about Heiling's nature; shocked, she is taken home by Conrad. When Heiling appears with jewels for her, she recoils, and Heiling lunges at Conrad with a dagger. Alone in the mountains, he resolves to return to his own realm. At Conrad's wedding to Anna, he makes one last attempt on his rival, but his sword shatters, and he yields to the Queen's pleas for him to forgive the mortals and return to her, leaving Conrad and Anna in one another's arms.

The work's strengths lie in the through-composed scenes, which Marschner evolved further than in *Der Vampyr*. The opening scene in the Earth Queen's kingdom is powerfully integrated, not only setting out a strong atmosphere but establishing it as Heiling's true realm. When he emerges into the light of human day, he can only seem in the wrong element. This becomes apparent when it transpires that he has nothing to offer Anna, no longer even a compulsive fascination, apart from wealth. Marschner ineffectively delays a declaration of love for her until the 12/8 middle section of 'An jenem Tag' ('Ich liebe dich mit tausend Schmerzen, mit Höllenquälen lieb' ich dich'). She answers this by simply telling him to cheer up, and by now has no inclination to leave the safety of Conrad's arms. 'As well as being a *Rheingold* in which Alberich renounces gold for love, this is a *Fliegende Holländer* in which the Dutchman loses out to Erik' (Hughes, 1998, 196). However, these prefigurations do not lie in depth or subtlety of character so much as in ideas and sounds which caught Wagner's ear, as with the blithe descending trumpet arpeggio which accompanies the Queen's final plea for forgiveness, and, most famously, her earlier appearance threatening Anna with vengeance in lines that anticipate Brünnhilde's appearance to Siegmund in the *Todesverkündigung* (Example 36). The finest individual scene discovers Anna's mother Gertrude waiting fearfully in her storm-bound hut for

Grandioso

(You have also fallen prey to the avenging fury of the mighty spirits)

(You have seen the Valkyrie's searing gaze: now you must go with her!)

Example 36
(a) Marschner: *Hans Heiling* (1833), The Queen of the Earth Spirits
(b) Wagner: *Die Walküre* (1870), Brünnhilde

Anna to return: she begins in melodrama, speaking her fears over the orchestra and then moving by way of a hummed melody into a ballad. This is Marschner's capacity for sinister effect at its most inventive. The scene opening Act III as Heiling ponders his predicament alone in the mountains, before deciding to return to his element, comes too late to win understanding, and is in any case stronger on atmosphere than on psychological subtlety. He is, nevertheless, a striking figure in the line of Marschner's divided souls, the most interesting of whom together with him and the Vampire is Bois-Guilbert in the *Ivanhoe* opera *Der Templer und die Jüdin* of 1829. Bois-Guilbert is another villain with a conscience who completely dominates the work, in his great scena 'Mich zu verschmähen!' showing himself as torn by guilt as Lysiart and, like Lysiart, contributing ideas to Wagner's Telramund.

The only foreign composer of any distinction to contribute to German opera during these years was no less a figure than Spontini. However, though features of his style had proved an influence on German composers, his own German works were less successful. To mark the visit of the Grand Duke Nicholas of Russia to Berlin in 1821 with his wife Charlotte, daughter of Friedrich Wilhelm III, he was obliged to cobble together hastily a 'Festspiel mit Tänzen und Märschen', *Lalla Rûkh*. This was a set of eight tableaux based on extracts from the four narrative poems inserted in Thomas Moore's story, published in 1817 and immediately popular in Germany. Framed by an introductory march and a long closing sequence of dances, it consists of five Romances and – the most interesting number – a chorus of three sopranos and tenor as genies vocalizing while sylphs dance, all in decorative figuration over fairly static harmony. When the Grand Duchess, who had much enjoyed taking the part of Lalla Rûkh, expressed regret that it all had to be over and done with so soon, the King arranged for the designer, Wilhelm Hensel, to make paintings of the scenes (it was at their exhibition in his studio that Hensel met his future wife, Mendelssohn's sister Fanny). Furthermore, Spontini was encouraged to turn this ephemeral piece into a *Lyrisches Drama* in two acts. This he did in the following year as *Nurmahal*, drawing on earlier music as well as on *Lalla Rûkh* (and including an effective reworking of the genies and sylphs scene as a dream sequence). Its most remarkable number is the opening scene, in which the people stream on to the stage from all sides with cries interrupting some freely composed recitative (in which Spontini was no doubt helped by his experienced librettist, Carl Herklots). There is also a striking climax, when the quarrelling lovers Nurmahal and Dscheangir confront one another across the chorus and dancers, their anger and misery bringing the action to a halt. For the rest, the static nature of the numbers betrays their origin, and too often (as with an aria for Nurmahal's rival Zelia) they revert to Italian opera seria with interminable coloratura and woodwind decoration, or to French opera with dance and chorus halting rather than furthering the action.

There is little that is German in these pieces. With *Alcidor* (1825) Spontini attempted *Zauberoper*, in response to the current interest in operas of magic and mystery. The subject derives ultimately from a tale in the *1,001 Nights*, set out in a complicated plot concerning the love of Alcidor and Selaide triumphing in the teeth of the wicked magician Ismenor. Once more, it was written in a hurry, this time for a royal wedding; and once more, Spontini seems ill at ease with the genre, producing a work that is really closer to French *féerie*, with touches of Parisian grand opera, than to German Romantic opera, and whose ceremonial occasion is further reflected in the elaborate, static stage effects of Karl Schinkel. He builds up some quite effective if ponderous musical complexes as the finale to Act II and in a so-called *Wüstenbild* in Act III after the collapse of a fairy palace; and he contributes his own interest in novel orchestral effects with a set of three tuned anvils in the introduction. Finally, he gathered himself together to compose his last work, a *Grosse historisch-romantische Oper* which he came to believe his masterpiece, *Agnes von Hohenstaufen*.

This time, he was not to be hurried. Indeed, only the first act was ready by the time of the scheduled première in May 1827; the complete work was performed two years later, and an extensively revised version followed in 1837. With it, Spontini hoped to crown his life's work by marrying Parisian grand opera, to which he had contributed so much, with the achievements of German grand opera. The plot, in its final version, concerns the appearance in Mainz of Heinrich, son of Henry the Lion, despite banishment by the Emperor Heinrich VI von Hohenstaufen, so as to win Agnes von Hohenstaufen. Discovered and imprisoned, he escapes and succeeds in winning Agnes over the head of his rival King Philip of France and marrying her. Only the intervention of the Imperial Knights, and of his brother Philip and Agnes's mother Irmengard, overcome the Emperor's resistance. To this array of royalty and aristocracy is added a huge cast of German princes, French troubadours, priests, nuns and people, together with a ballet that includes Venus, the Spirits of the Seine and the Rhine and of German heroism, and a vast orchestra to match. There is, further, a large stage band whose most significant function is to imitate an organ accompanying the nuns' chorale in the church scene in Act II, something in which Spontini took pride but which some of his critics thought an unnecessary substitution for the actual organs which by now were a familiar theatrical adjunct. The work's real problems arise from Spontini's attempts to make the best of both French and German worlds, by trying to integrate the Parisian grand opera tradition of individual emotions caught up in dynastic clashes with the dynamic scenic complexes that were increasingly marking German opera as a formal principle. The outcome is a work that proceeds, at a cumbersome pace, by means of enormous tableaux in which multiple choruses oppose one another, sometimes with dramatic interruptions, to the virtual exclusion of the characters' emotional lives. Agnes, buffeted by political events, plays no real part in the action and has little identifiable character. Though there is no shortage of harangues from the many principals, the trio 'Noch glänzt der erste Morgen unsers Bundes' for Agnes, Irmengard and Heinrich in the first scene of Act III is exceptional in giving the characters' emotions an opportunity to interact. It is difficult not to conclude that the grandeur of Spontini's finest operas has here inflated into windy grandiosity, and that his touch has finally failed him.

Once again, it was from revolutions in France that a new impulse came to events in Germany. Though the rising against Charles X in July 1830 and the consequent violence at the barricades in Paris bore no comparison to the convulsion of 1789, shock waves were sent deep into Europe; but now their passage was across a Germany of a wholly different political and social order, and one whose cultural, artistic and theatrical life had undergone a complete transformation. Moreover, these strands in German life were more closely interwoven than before. The customs union, or *Zollverein*, of 1834 which looms so large in nineteenth-century German history was crucial not only for creating a single national market. One of its consequences was an immediate acceleration of the development of the railways, so that from the tentative beginnings there were some 1,250 miles of track by the mid-forties, and ten years later 5,000 miles. Improved communications in turn stimulated banking, commerce and industry, leading to an ever-enlarging middle class, one urban, prosperous, ambitious and with cultural and social interests in which the theatre played a central part. Yet the notorious political stagnation of times that were, as in most countries of Europe, confused rather than merely apathetic, was not conducive to artistic adventure. In opera, the Romantic enthusiasm had slackened, its gestures remaining but with only spasmodic reinvigoration giving continued lease of life; while ambitions for grand opera had unclear motivation, with the best works produced almost in spite of themselves. The mild romantic idealism of Friedrich Wilhelm IV, who succeeded in 1840, gave Prussia little in the way of a lead, and responses to it were ineffectual. Then in 1848 France's overthrow of another king, Louis-Philippe, stimulated renewed and much more powerful agitation across a Europe seized with revived revolutionary ideas and hopes for national identities. In Germany and Austria, the upheavals brought the fall of Metternich and the call for unification at the National Assembly summoned in Frankfurt. Wagner was but one of the artists and intellectuals who fought in the troubles following its failure, then fleeing to Switzerland.

Operatic production in the years leading up to the middle of the century, then, was marked more by hopeful profusion than by quality or a sense of identity, by haphazard diversity rather than by steadiness of aim. A still-divided Germany supported different traditions and repertories, often for fortuitous reasons. A Duke, Elector, Prince and even King controlling his Hoftheater could find considerable cachet in being able to boast a successful composer, who in turn would be eager for this secure base. Weber had been summoned to the royal Saxon court in 1817 as director of the German department of the Dresden Hoftheater alongside the Italians, to be assisted until his death in 1826 by Marschner for two years and succeeded by Reissiger in various positions until his death in 1859 (with Wagner as second Kapellmeister from 1843 to 1849). Hummel was at the ducal court of Weimar from 1819 to 1837, and Liszt from 1848 until 1861. Lindpaintner was at the ducal court of Stuttgart from 1819 until his death in 1856, Spohr at the electoral court of Kassel from 1822 until his own death in 1859. The willingness of these distinguished men to serve a Hoftheater, sometimes over decades and for life, is sufficient indication of the mutual importance of the post to ruler and composer. Other Hoftheaters had more irregular arrangements, dictated by political or economic considerations, but could often count on periods of service from major musicians. Though the numbers were dwindling fast, around the middle of the century there were Hoftheaters (of very different natures) in cities including Berlin, Dresden, Stuttgart, Munich, Hanover, Karlsruhe, Brunswick, Weimar, Darmstadt, Kassel, Schwerin and Oldenburg, with Vienna occupying a category of its own. Conditions were attractive not only for material reasons: the resources were generally encouraging to the production of Romantic opera.

However, the comparative social exclusiveness of the Hoftheater limited the possibility of the exchange of ideas with a wider and often more forward-looking public. Establishing a Stadttheater was usually a more hazardous undertaking, with artistic enterprise on the part of a town council or a business consortium having to be balanced with the need to make money to meet the sometimes exorbitant rents. Repertories were mixed, standards even more so; and the enthusiastic welcome given to a new work was no guarantee of its survival in the local repertory or of its wider dissemination. Nevertheless, also in mid-century there were Stadttheaters in cities including Aachen, Augsburg, Berlin, Bremen, Breslau, Cologne, Danzig, Düsseldorf, Frankfurt am Main, Hamburg, Königsberg, Leipzig, Magdeburg, Mannheim, Nuremberg, Prague, Riga, Vienna, Wiesbaden and Würzburg. In many of these, and not necessarily in the largest towns, work of considerable enterprise was done, with encouragement given by audiences that included students, intellectuals and artists nurturing ideals for German opera that had their origins in the precept and practice of Mosel, Hoffmann and Weber. Some of the most significant composers of the day often put in valuable years in a Stadttheater before, in some cases, finding a more permanent and comfortable home in a Hoftheater. Among them had been Weber, Hoffmann, Lindpaintner and Spohr in the first two decades of the century, later Lachner, Kreutzer, Mendelssohn, Lortzing and Wagner.

There was, moreover, little in the way of critical or journalistic support, certainly nothing to match that given in the early years of the century by the *AMZ*. With Rochlitz's resignation in 1819, the *AMZ* itself had entered a slack period which the appointment of Gottfried Wilhelm Fink in 1827 did nothing to redress. Neither *Cäcilia*, under Gottfried Weber from 1824 to 1839 and Siegfried Dehn from 1842 to 1848, nor the Berlin *Iris*, under Ludwig Rellstab for its twelve-year career from 1830 to 1842, nor the Viennese *Der allgemeine musikalische Anzeiger*, under I. F. Castelli from 1829 to 1840, made such a point of championing opera, or indeed of breaking lances on behalf of any cause except that of their parent publishing houses. It was largely this timidity that drove the group of musicians around Schumann to found what they at first called the *Neue Leipziger Zeitschrift für Musik* (later simply the *Neue Zeitschrift für Musik*). Fink, knocked head over heels as 'Knif', was a particular target for Schumann's scorn, and the *NZM* did much to enliven critical dialogue and then to speak up for new voices (notably that of Chopin, who had been dismissively treated by Rellstab). But though the *NZM* was in a surprising number of ways modelled on the *AMZ*, it concerned itself more with instrumental music than with opera, especially in the early days and before it expanded its format from four to eight pages. Only later did a series of reports from operatic centres become an established feature, and even then they lacked the enthusiasm and the sheer volume of coverage that had marked the *AMZ* in its heyday. A frequent complaint was the difficulty of getting a new opera performed outside its parent city, but there were seldom essays of sufficient quality to lend weight to this urging. A striking and understandable exception was the series of articles by Karl Franz Brendel, editor of the *NZM* from 1845 until his death in 1868, on Schumann's *Genoveva* (*NZM* 33 (1850), 1–4, 17–18, 49–50). For the rest, the opera composer who found most favour was Lortzing.

Another crucial problem for German opera was the lack of singers to contest the all-powerful Italians. Julius Cornet, a versatile Austrian man of the theatre who had begun his career as a lyric tenor, identified this among other problems in a searching study of the German stage (Cornet, 1849). There were few German teachers of any distinction to foster a native school, a distinguished exception being Johann Miksch in Dresden, and those who did teach had little idea of dramatic style or of how to foster one. Cornet claims that in the years 1816–24 there were over sixty Austrian singers spread across Europe, finding little in the way of training or employment, though matters improved in the following decade with artists of the stature of Henriette Sontag, Caroline Seidler, Wilhelmine Schröder-Devrient, Anna Milder-Hauptmann, Therese Grünbaum, Anton Haizinger, Franz Anton Forti and Franz Wild, of the generation born in the years around the turn of the century. Repertory was another problem for those with ambitions for a national tradition, since though the

Italian influence declined during the thirties and forties, Italian operas
still tended to outnumber German ones, with French operas reaching
about double the number. Cornet does not regard the situation as
disastrous, claiming that a German singer could learn bel canto from
the ever-popular Rossini, declamation and an elevated style from
Spontini, acting and how to speak from opéra-comique, and taste
from Mozart. He puts his finger on another problem when he calls
for greater centralization and above all a major conservatory that
could provide training in all branches of opera, with greater security,
including pensions, for artists. All the arguments and the evidence he
amasses in his book, informative if somewhat tendentiously written
as it is, converge on his re-formulation of the long expressed German
desire for a fully unified work of art:

> **Oper** nennen wir jenes Bühnenschauspiel, welches durch Vereinigung
> der Poesie und Musik in ein Ganzes nicht nur den Gefühlsausdruck der
> Charactere handelnder Personen erhöbt, die Situationen anschaulicher
> ausmalt, den Wortbegriff ergänzt, sondern auch als selbstständiges
> musikalisches Drama Empfindungen erregen, das Gefühl erheben muß.
> Besondere Ausschmückung durch Dekorationspracht, Tanz usw. ist
> nicht Bedingung, sondern Accessorium der Oper.   (Cornet, 1849, 10)

> (We term **opera** a staged play which through the unification of poetry
> and music in a single entity not only heightens the performers'
> expression of the characters' feeling, depicts the situations more vividly
> and fills out the ideas in the words, but also as a self-sufficient musical
> drama must stir up emotions and enhance sensations. Special
> embellishments by means of splendid décor, dances etc. are not of the
> essence of opera but are its accessories.)

Cornet's book was published in the same year in which Wagner was
beginning to address himself to the matter in his most important
writings on opera. Hoping that a young German genius would take
note of his words, Cornet reports that many musicians regarded the
times as transitional, crying out for a new lead artistically as well as
politically. As symptomatic of the times, he finds the new works
coming from German composers as generally of poor quality.

Surveying the years between around 1830 and the establishment of

Wagner as the dominant figure in German opera, it is difficult to disagree. After two Romantic operas, *Pietro von Abano* (1827) and *Der Alchymist* (1830), both well below his best, Spohr had fallen silent, only returning to the stage with a grand opera, *Der Kreuzfahrer* (1845), an attempt at a genre that scarcely suited him. Much the same was the case with Marschner, who lost his touch with Romantic opera after *Hans Heiling* and failed to find it in grand opera with *Kaiser Adolf von Nassau* (1845) (as Wagner, who conducted the première, entertainingly describes in *Mein Leben*: Wagner, 1963, 343–6; 1983, 291–4). Some Romantic conventions were now sufficiently well established for most Kapellmeisters to be able to turn out works that met a demand in their theatres, often rather too easily and, as Schumann pointed out, spurred on by Weber: 'Der ungeheure Succeß des "Freischütz", scheint es, hat die deutschen Componisten zu Aufforderungen an Beifallsbezeugungen verleitet, die nun einmal nicht durch Absicht herausgefordert werden können' (Schumann, 1854, IV, 169) ('It seems that the enormous success of *Der Freischütz* has misled German composers into attempts to excite demonstrations of applause which cannot be achieved just by design'). Even a comparatively obscure figure such as Joseph Wolfram, who pursued a career as a lawyer and civil servant despite being offered the Dresden post as Weber's successor in 1826, could handle the genre competently. His *Der Bergmönch* (1830) leans heavily on Weber for a drama of a wicked superintendent of mines, Wolf, allying himself to sinister underground powers and trying to kill the hero Michael, who manages to climb out of the abyss and revive the fainting Franciska, to general rejoicing. When unsure of his next move, Wolf tends to break into a Vengeance Aria, one of them ('Noch bin ich Herr!') interrupting a Trio in some need of enlivening. The rest of the cast are not slow to fall upon their knees in a Preghiera. *Der Freischütz* provides the model for hero, heroine and villain, as well as for miners and villagers. However, Wolfram can find some original touches. Even in some of the simpler numbers, he shows an ability to lend his characters interest with well-judged chromatic harmony and in particular a fluency with uneven metres, and some excellent choruses include one for the underground Salamanders ('Finstre Gnomen, hellflammende Geister sind wir'). Eventually the Spirit of the Harz appears to pronounce reconciliation. Wolfram was more at home here, with a model on which he could build, than when he attempted a *Heroisch-romantisch* opera, *Das Schloss Candra* (1832), a kind of Spontinian grand opera of French besieging Spaniards, filled with ballets and pompous choruses, together with some attractive instrumental effects (the score includes an expressive solo for the rare keyed trumpet) and ending in a last-minute rescue and pardon from a Field-Marshal.

Weber's actual successor in Dresden, Karl Reissiger, was one of many Kapellmeisters of the day who took their duties to include the provision of new operas. Having developed an excellent ensemble in Dresden, and conducted the triumphant première of *Rienzi*, he was then portrayed as idle and reactionary by Wagner, who clearly felt that this was the only possible explanation for anyone declining a libretto by Wagner himself, *Die hohe Braut*. Reissiger's most successful opera, *Die Felsenmühle zu Etalières* (1831), a drama of a group of Germans fighting in French territory, supports at any rate some of Wagner's case. It is scarcely more than an old-fashioned rescue opera, not very well paced, with its numbers (which reveal a mixture of French, German and Italian influences) reaching their climax in an escape from a burning mill followed by a grateful return to the Vaterland. A cumbersome grand opera, *Adèle de Foix* (1841), on the subject of one of Francis I's disreputable amorous exploits, was rather generously praised as a courageous effort by Schumann in what he admitted were lean times for German opera, though he deplored its fashionable eclecticism and tendency to pander to public taste (*NZM* 17 (1842), 79–81).

Franz Gläser flowered as a composer only on his arrival as Kapellmeister in Berlin in 1830, having spent over twenty years in Vienna working for the Leopoldstadt and Josefstadt theatres. For them, he had turned out dozens of stage pieces (his full list of works runs to over a hundred) that were intended to provide no more than passing amusement, and were usually smartly despatched on their way by the press for their feebleness or 'trivialer Witz' (*AMZ* 23 (1821),

9, of *Die drei Zeitungen*). His best known work, *Des Adlers Horst* (1832), is another matter, and was one of the few works of the 1830s to keep its hold on the repertory, which it did for almost half a century. Based on a story by Schopenhauer's mother Johanna, to a text by Karl von Holtei intended for Meyerbeer, it tells of Rose and Richard, a married couple separated by misunderstandings. When Richard arrives in a village and encounters Rose, whom he has believed dead, she refuses to see him. But when she dances with Rennert at the haytime celebrations, the peasants blame her for the separation and turn their backs on her. She decides to leave so as not to cause further trouble, but at the crucial moment an eagle seizes her baby and flies off with it. Rose climbs a peak of the Riesengebirge looking for the baby, but finds herself on the wrong peak, separated from the eagle's eyrie by a vast chasm. In her despair, she calls Richard's name; he is by now on the other peak, but does not dare to shoot the eagle until divine guidance intervenes in the form of a thunderbolt that fells a tree so as to bridge the two peaks. He shoots and kills the eagle. The baby is saved, and so is the couple's marriage.

This ludicrous tale is the basis of an opera of some quality. The debts and the failings are easy enough to identify. The debts are mostly to Weber, with Richard's first aria, 'O daß der Felsen starren Kluft', invoking memories of Max, while the village scenes recall much else in *Der Freischütz* without the melodic sharpness or the sense of dramatic timing. Gläser's Viennese background is reflected in a good deal of French influence, also occasionally some Italianisms. Too many of the choruses and dances outstay their welcome, suggesting that part of their function is to fill out the slender action, especially when they become bogged down in the over-regular metres and predictable rhyme-schemes from which Weber had been seeking to escape after *Der Freischütz*. One of the liveliest numbers, in the old Catalogue Aria convention, has a trio of drinkers rattling their way through a list of wines from all countries before settling for Hungarian wine, an import so improbable in a Riesengebirge village as to reinforce the feeling that this is of Viennese inspiration, perhaps even a recycling from an earlier theatre piece.

However, much of it is done with considerable spirit; and the opera takes a different turn with the third act, which is through-composed. Early audiences reacted uneasily to this change from a Singspiel manner, and indeed Gläser can find himself out of his depth (or perhaps, in the circumstances, with his feet off the ground). Act II ends with furious tremolos and urgent, panicky figures as the eagle captures the child, and the confused villagers fall to a conventional Preghiera. With Act III, Richard scales the peak, clouds surrounding him and his life; Rose, on her peak, hears the Act II Preghiera from far below. The continuous texture is not very successfully handled by a composer who must have had little experience of it, and a good deal of the Act is uncomfortably close to melodrama with recitative replacing speech, in that there are short bursts of music coupled with some undistinguished melodic interventions and a few longer snatches of music. However, the work caught the ear of Wagner, who not only conducted it but took note of at least one of its ideas, Rose's apostrophe to the sun which had been a feature of other Romantic operas (notably Weber's *Oberon*) but which certainly played a part in the conception of Brünnhilde's awakening in Act III of *Siegfried*.

Attempting to mix the genres of Romantic and grand opera, Johann Christian Lobe had his one real success with *Die Fürstin von Granada* (1833), a so-called *Große Zauberoper mit Tanz, Pantomime und Tableaux* in five acts that achieved a respectable number of productions following its Weimar première. The piece is a sorry jumble of effects, packed around the attempt of the wicked fairy Solabella (in fact, the Princess of the title) to obtain a magic girdle by bewitching its owner Harita into abandoning his lover Nadire for her. She is ultimately frustrated by the timely intervention of the good fairy Zofira. This naive, not to say simplistic, tale is encumbered over five acts with mime scenes, tableaux, static choruses and a plethora of ballets for giants and dwarves, together with fairies, elves and other supernaturals. Only occasionally does Lobe's invention (which includes a feeling for colourful orchestration) rise to the many different occasions that present themselves in the plot. It is no surprise to find a long review in the *NZM* complaining of the work's confused attempts at originality, and concluding that 'Der Text ist ohne Poesie, die Musik ohne Romantik' (*NZM* 3 (1835), 25–6, 33–5, 37–9) ('The libretto lacks poetry, the music lacks Romanticism'). Though Lobe contributed to the libretto, he failed to use his considerable powers as a writer and critic on his own work, or to see that the times were abandoning this kind of conception. He was by no means alone among the composers of these years who deluded themselves into thinking that some kind of German grand opera might emerge from a combination of the ingredients of Romantic opera with others that had been learnt from Spontini and were now being re-learnt from Meyerbeer, whose credentials were all the stronger for being a German expatriate successfully established in Paris, at first impressively with *Robert le Diable* in 1831 and then conclusively with the triumph of *Les Huguenots* in 1836.

Karl Krebs, an expert Kapellmeister who worked in Hamburg from 1827 to 1850, was another who first won and then forfeited Wagner's approval, perhaps because his tastes were more inclined to remain attached to the grand opera manner of *Rienzi* than to embrace the new subtleties of *Lohengrin*. His *Agnes Bernauer* (1833, revised in Dresden as *Agnes, der Engel von Augsburg*, 1838) is a four-act grand opera amply furnished with Parisian effects that include a castle, a tournament ground, imposing distances glimpsed through mighty edifices or bridges, processions, dances (one a Waffentanz with brandished weapons), an opening chorus of smiths clanging anvils and a final dramatic plunge from blazing battlements, as well as careful details of costumes that include authentic Tyrolean dress. The plot is a new treatment of the popular story of Agnes Bernauer (popular enough to have been satirized for its Romantic sentimentality in Weber's *romantisch-vaterländisches Tonspiel* skit in his novel *Tonkünstlers Leben*). Historically, the beautiful Agnes was secretly married to Duke Albrecht III of Bavaria, her humble estate arousing the dynastic wrath of Albrecht's father, who in 1435 had her drowned in the Danube. The opera makes her the daughter of an old smith, who has rejected the apprentice Ottmar for a mysterious young man named Antonio. On his arrival at the head of his retinue, 'Antonio' turns out to be Duke Ernst's son Albrecht, and bears her off to his castle. The jealous Ottmar makes common cause with the Reichs-kanzler, Percival, who, affronted by this 'bad' marriage, infiltrates Albrecht's castle with a group of conspirators disguised as pilgrims, including Ottmar. Receiving news of this during his absence, Albrecht (pausing only for a Preghiera) sets off to the rescue. In the teeth of threats and demands from Percival and Ottmar, who tries to reclaim her, Agnes holds fast to her love for Albrecht. As it is stormed, the castle catches fire. Ottmar seizes Agnes, and hurls her from the battlements into the river (in an alternative ending, Albrecht reaches her in time, and it is Ottmar who is hurled to his death).

The work is a well-wrought attempt at Parisian grand opera in German terms, one of the most successful of the time. It is fluently composed, and there is a genuine sense of forward movement, with inserted numbers for the most part finding a suitable incidental role within the progress of the drama. Krebs contrives an effective opening chorus for the smiths, with Agnes languishing at an upper window; a succeeding Abendlied led by old Bernauer as Agnes grieves for 'Antonio' moves towards an impressive multi-sectional aria for her before the dramatic processional finale to Act I and the arrival of 'Antonio' as young Duke Albrecht. The lyrical, quasi-Italianate manner which his pseudonym suggests is ingeniously married to a more plebeian rustic German style for the peasant Agnes. The second act falls back on a more conventional mixture of standard ingredients (such as a Vengeance Aria for Ottmar who, though a high bass rather than a tenor rival to Albrecht, is scarcely of the villainous stature to justify it) and a tournament scene that culminates in Albrecht being disowned by his father. A well-handled third act includes a strong aria for Agnes, and the arrival and seizure of the castle by the conspirators are managed with real tension. The dénouement needs scarcely more than plenty of noisy action music of the kind already adumbrated. The problem with the opera is that it goes through well-judged motions without a sufficient charge of invention. Too often Spohr-like chromatics do duty for real emotional intensity; or an effective if conventional stage circumstance delivers rather empty music to fill it; or, more damagingly, the arias and ensembles lack the melodic distinction needed to validate them. Krebs's opera reflects the problem common to the operas of these years. A framework is in place, one skilfully crafted. What is missing is the judgement of such a framework's enduring worth, and the realization that a new vision was necessary; or, simply, sufficient inventive charge to fill it.

For the moment, it was lacking, and the example of French grand opera in the early 1840s seemed too strong to ignore. Lachner's *Catharina Cornaro* (1841), Wagner's *Rienzi* (1842), Lindpaintner's *Die sicilianische Vesper* (1843), Marschner's *Kaiser Adolf von Nassau* (1845) and Lindpaintner's *Lichtenstein* (1846) formed part of a procession of grand operas attempting, with greatly varied success, to import the genre to Germany. Franz Lachner, who had conducted a censored version of *Les Huguenots* as *Die Anglikaner und die Puritaner* in Munich in 1838, turned not only to Meyerbeer but to the tried if not now always trusty models of Cherubini and Spontini. Based on a translation of Vernoy de St-Georges's libretto for Halévy's *La Reine de Chypre*, *Catharina Cornaro* tells of the Venetian noblewoman betrothed against her will to Jakob von Lusignan, King of Cyprus. When her lover Marco Venero is attacked by assassins hired by Onofrio, a member of the Council of Ten, his mysterious saviour turns out to be the magnanimous King, who then dies defending his kingdom against the Venetians. Warmly received in the *NZM* (17 (1842), 71–3), the work had a considerable success, and held a place in German repertories for some forty years. Its effects include a chorus of approaching gondoliers (surprisingly, in 2/4) to open Act II, and a much-admired Finale to Act III in which across a solemn organ accompanying a church service comes the sound of revellers dancing a tarantella, in two 6/8 bars to each of the organ's 4/4 bars. There are several strongly written arias, one for old Andrea Cornaro that includes a certain amount of energetic coloratura, several for the heroine, of which the most striking comes in Act II, 'Ach, all' mein Hoffen ist dahin', a multi-sectioned number that includes a letter-reading passage and builds to a powerful climax: the example of Weber's Reiza was not lost on Lachner. His finales can flag, and he can seem to attempt reanimation with arbitrary tempo changes; but that to Act II expertly develops its effects, which include a Preghiera for Catharina, an effective scene with Marco's voice approaching from afar and a strong duet between the lovers. The original ending to Act IV showed a catastrophic lapse of judgement, for a grand opera audience, by allowing the king to die quietly surrounded by prayers. A later revision produced a more celebratory conclusion. Yet for all its awareness of effective example in its models, the work cannot conceal a lack of characterization, perhaps partly through uncertainty about the emotional depth that the three central figures could be allowed in the dynastic plot.

This creative indecision was, to a greater or lesser degree, to bedevil composers of the mid-century decades. Even the most expert could find themselves imprisoned by routine, though the routines had changed; and indeed expertise could then be a two-edged sword, enabling a composer to provide a new work in the usual theatrical hurry, but exposing inventive weakness with more ambitious genres especially in times when the language of music was developing in new directions. In these circumstances, apparently reliable precedents could prove a hazard. The success of *Der Freischütz* was still casting far too long a shadow over any opera with a pastoral setting and a touch of villainy or the supernatural, while the subtler implications of *Euryanthe* were fully understood by few. Spohr offered all-too-beguiling temptations to composers trying to come to terms with chromatic harmony, and moments of extreme chromaticism for sensational effect were often ill-judged, or simply irrelevant. Despite a greatly increased interest in orchestration for colourful or impressive effect, no composer came remotely near to grasping the orchestral possibilities of motive for much more than reminiscence. Meyerbeer was a dangerous example for those with ambitions for grand opera but less than his inventive elegance and sophisticated sense of effect; moreover, he could call upon a librettist, Scribe, who understood the Parisian audience perfectly and was a craftsman of outstanding skill. The lack of a comparable audience in any German operatic centre, one with a sense of style, literary acuity and clear expectations, can only be partly blamed for what remained the most serious constraint of all, the poor standard of German librettos. Even those composers who appealed for more inventive texts (they included Weber, Spohr and Marschner) showed flawed judgement in what they actually accepted. The librettos of the time repeatedly deal in cliché as far as subject and handling are concerned, and by sticking to routine German verse forms, both in metre and in rhyme scheme, tie their composers' hands.

In these circumstances, it is not surprising that a more modest aim could be better assured of hitting a target, and that the tradition of Singspiel could provide a familiarity within which there might be ease of manoeuvre. One of the most successful works to bring Romantic elements into the genre came from the experienced and widely travelled Conradin Kreutzer, with his *Das Nachtlager in Granada* (1834). Based on a play by Weber's *Freischütz* librettist Friedrich Kind, it tells of how a lost huntsman strays into a Spanish valley, where he is immediately overwhelmed by the charms of Gabriele. She gently rejects him, for she is secretly in love with Gomez, while also being pursued by Vasco. The huntsman is provided with the night's shelter of the title in an old Moorish castle, where his musings on her charms are interrupted first by her arrival to warn him of treachery and then by the jealous Vasco and some shepherds, intent on murder. He foils them, and when a retinue of other huntsmen arrives he reveals himself as the benevolent Prince Regent and blesses the lovers' union. Kreutzer makes some attempt to absorb the numbers into a continuous texture, hard though he finds it to break away from recitative cadential conventions. Given his fresh melodic gift, many of the individual numbers are excellent, among them the huntsman's introductory song, 'Ein Schütz bin ich', and bolero rhythms play their part in the local colour. His emotional touch is less certain. He cannot find the resources for the duet when the huntsman declares his love to Gabriele ardently while she tries to lighten the situation with womanly kindness, and the music settles for an empty mutual jollity; Kreutzer is happier with the succeeding scene as the huntsman acknowledges that he is not for her, and she wonders whether she can trust his promises of help. More than a little Biedermeier sentimentality coats scenes of some human subtlety. Kreutzer's orchestral touch is at its surest as evening falls and the Angelus calls the shepherds to prayer, and is more seriously engaged in the freely composed scena as the huntsman lies in the ruined castle reflecting on the beauty of the night and of Gabriele, wondering at his emotions, while a violin solo weaves a golden thread through his thoughts. The treacherous attack on him reveals an altogether larger operatic talent, and a strong sense of cumulative drama expressed principally through arioso linking more formal numbers; and there is a touching conclusion as the Prince Regent, now revealed, gives his willing but rueful blessing to Gabriele and takes leave of his glimpse of pastoral bliss. The times have changed, if not that much: rustic true love survives threat, but the kindly aristocrat must now renounce his own hopes of a Rousseauesque idyll for it to be assured.

Other efforts were not so felicitous. Carl Loewe did not succeed in making a transition to the stage from the dramatic ballad at which he excelled, and not even Spontini's recommendation could secure performance of his *Rudolf, der deutsche Herr* in Berlin in 1825. His comic Singspiel *Die drei Wünsche* (1834) fared better, though its treatment of the tale of the 'philosopher' Bathmendi bringing three wishes to Hassan (who makes a mess of them) is very thin, no more than a succession of light songs without the dramatic tension of his ballads and with finales in a *Liedertafel* manner lacking any dramatic development. Josef Dessauer had some success with *Ein Besuch in St Cyr* (1838), a mild, unpretentiously tuneful Singspiel nearer to opéra-comique in manner, as its setting and lightly sentimental subject suggest (Dessauer had been popular in Paris, and hoped in vain for a French libretto). Despite its Romantic and grand opera pretensions, *Johanna d'Arc* (1840) by 'J. Hoven' (the pseudonym adopted by Johann Vesque von Püttlingen) is really no more than a weak number opera in which Joan never shows much character after making a touching farewell to her home (with a pastoral cor anglais solo). The scene of her recognition of the Dauphin at Chinon is muffed, and eventually she dies to a sentimental angel chorus. This inability to make much of number opera afflicted many more who tried their hand at the genre. Heinrich Esser, Kapellmeister at Mainz from 1841 to 1847, had some success with *Thomas Riquiqui* (1843), set in a French village in the aftermath of the Revolution, and another of the many pieces which continued to turn to French originals in the poverty-stricken situation of German librettos. This one is a simple tale of a fugitive aristocrat, Amalie von Montfort, who has taken refuge with the cobbler Riquiqui; he has promised to marry her, but eventually renounces her on discovering that she really loves the Chevalier von Beauval, and instead marries the devoted Jacqueline. It is fairly flimsy stuff, a stylistic mixture of German, Italian and especially French influences and making some simple use of reminiscence motive with Riquiqui's entrance aria, 'Arbeit und Frohsinn'. Esser's *Die zwei Prinzen* (1845) is set in the time of the English Wars of the Roses, though also based on a French original. It is really the story of the love between Käthchen and Lambert Simnel, the pretender to the throne whom Richard Simon tries to promote as Graf Warwick. The ensembles never really find any dramatic momentum, and the music is simple and repetitive, with the best of it residing in naive numbers such as a Romanze for Simnel in D♭, the increasingly popular key for Romantic intensity, 'Lebt wohl, des Lebens schönste Träume', and a cheerful Arie for Käthchen's father, a cook and innkeeper named John Bred.

The two composers whose careers, each of over two decades and overlapping one another, contributed most to German opera during the middle years of the century were Lindpaintner and Lortzing; but the contrast between their actual achievements is significant. In Lindpaintner's case, the promise of much talent and a sympathetic musical nature was never fully realized, in part through his constant changes of direction. By the time he settled in Stuttgart for life in 1819, he had already written nearly half his work, winning some success with Romantic opera and Singspiel, and earning himself by the 1830s a fine reputation as a conductor, 'der beste Orchesterdirigent in Deutschland', considered Mendelssohn (letter to Zelter, 15 Feb. 1832). After the Romantic operas *Der Vampyr* and *Der Bergkönig* of the 1820s he turned increasingly towards grand opera, perhaps in an attempt to match Meyerbeer's huge local popularity. *Die Genueserin* (1839) is in fact a comparatively brief work, consisting of fifteen numbers in two acts, but in between some song-like arias and block harmony choruses it packs into its Venice Carnival setting a farrago of colourful entertainment: Russians march on (in 3/4); Tyroleans stamp Ländler; dervishes whirl. The first act finale generates some momentum, but events are otherwise fairly static. He followed this with *Die sicilianische Vesper* (1843), whose four-act handling of the thirteenth-century massacre gives him much better room and a stronger drama. An impressive overture, modulating widely (at one point from A♭ via E, C and F to D♭ in the space of eight bars), develops considerable strength through use of a repeated motivic figure. The actual opera is more conventional, for much of the time hardly more advanced than *Euryanthe* but taking its opportunities with a good deal of enthusiasm, and including not only set pieces handled colourfully but some telling dramatic interventions, as when the Sicilians point to the arrogant French rulers with withering chromatic scorn for their effete nature. Yet Lindpaintner cannot sustain the impetus his opera sorely needs, and he is no more than tentative in his recourse to motive. The massacre itself occupies as few as thirty-six bars of chromatic figures, first descending and then ascending. The work's successor, *Lichtenstein* (1846), expands into five acts, taking a sixteenth-century Swabian subject designed to please Lindpaintner's Stuttgart patron, King Wilhelm I of Württemberg, and is really a kind of Singspiel-cum-pageant masquerading in pretentious clothes. Apart from including an excellent scene for the heroine, Marie, wandering alone in a dark cave, it is clogged with static choruses, prayers and interrupting arias, and concludes with a *Festliches Zwischenspiel* that is really a tableau of Württemberg's future. This includes a set of five *Traumbilder*, with poems spoken over music, one of them hailing Württemberg's greatest poetic son: 'Der deutsche Dichter für das Ideal – Ja, Schiller ist's!'

Lindpaintner would have been wiser to stick to the manner of the Singspiel he wrote in 1836, *Die Macht des Liedes*. This is a charming comedy in the manner of the old 'Turkish' opera, telling a light-hearted tale of two friends, Selim and Nadir, rescuing Selim's lover Delia. She has fallen into the hands of the slave-master Harun, who intends selling her to Olkar, the Nabob of Lahore. Presenting himself to her captor as a musician, Selim is asked what instrument he plays, and replies with a lively Catalogue Aria: 'Harfe, Leier, Violine, / Flöte, Horn und Mandoline, / Oboe und Clarinette, / Trommel, Pauke und Trompete, / alle spiel ich gut und schön'. He proves much of his point in a witty aria with neatly characterized obbligatos from flute, oboe, horn and bassoon, to general delight, and throws in a charming French Romance for good measure. However, it is a Nightingale Song – the bird cannot sing unless it is free – which impresses the amiable Nabob and wins Delia her freedom, at which the three friends decide to remain at his liberal and cultured court. It is a pity that Lindpaintner did not more often stay within the bounds of the talent he demonstrates in this most agreeable work.

Though they were both accomplished men of the theatre, it was Lortzing's wider experience of practical considerations and much harder and more versatile theatrical life that enabled him to develop his gifts to the utmost. He grew up as an actor and singer, also turning out the music that was called for, learning the trade of a theatre musician from the inside and under the pressure of regular theatrical life at a commercial level. Lacking Lindpaintner's conducting gifts and dogged by bad luck, he was forced from pillar to post in search of employment and died while under notice of dismissal from one of the humblest of all the appointments he managed to obtain, unable to pay his doctor's bill.

He began his composing career with an effective but imitative rescue opera, *Ali Pascha von Janina* (comp. 1824, prod. 1828), which owes much to *Die Entführung*, and four pasticcios which draw on Mozart's actual music (one of them exclusively). Then, *Die beiden*

Schützen (1835) set the tone for his greatest early success, *Zar und Zimmermann* (1837). Based on the much-used story of Peter the Great working disguised as a carpenter in the shipyards of Saardam (with added comic and amorous misunderstandings), it is a skilful mixture of Singspiel and opéra-comique, laid out in numbers separated by spoken dialogue in a formulation from which he seldom departed far. This consisted normally of an opening chorus to set the scene, followed by a series of short numbers with finales of considerable dramatic agility. Bred in the conventions of the small-town German theatre, he took more from the singer-types encountered there than from subtler characterization. The Burgomaster Van Bett's 'O sancta justitia' is in a long line of introductory arias, but its comic fluency (which includes the theatre joke of a singer failing to manage a low F, supplied by a helpful bassoon) sets the tone for much that lay ahead in Lortzing's work. Similarly, Marie's tender arias, and Peter Ivanov's elegant ones, are in a familiar vein which Lortzing shows to possess rich yields still to be mined. He also has the theatrical experience to make much of the contrast between the lyrical and the comic, and at the start of Act III the wit to compose the scene in which Van Bett tries to rehearse a hapless chorus who fail to understand him, commit all manner of wrong entries, and then fall to abusing one another. For this, as for virtually all his operas, he wrote his own text, and was one of the first German composers consistently to do so.

A similar approach marks *Caramo* (1839), *Hans Sachs* (1840), *Casanova* (1841) and the immensely successful *Der Wildschütz* (1842), though Lortzing was constantly modifying and rethinking the proportions and introducing new methods, for instance with some indications of Leitmotive in *Casanova*. The confidence won with these popular works encouraged him to take a step in the direction of Romantic opera with *Undine* (1845), a rehandling of the Fouqué story which had once served Hoffmann. Nevertheless, Lortzing's familiar framework is still in place, with the introduction of a comic squire and cellarer and a rather awkward happy ending. The subject did free his invention from some of his over-used gestures and encourage a richer harmonic palette and an orchestral fluency that includes more enterprising use of motive. *Der Waffenschmied* (1846) and *Zum Gross-admiral* (1847) mark his return to a more familiar vein, from which an ill-advised attempt at revolutionary opera to catch the mood of the moment was made with *Regina*. Though it was composed in 1848, the turbulent political situation kept it off the stage until 1899; but artistically it was also ill-advised, since the lack of light relief removed the possibility of the contrasts upon which much of Lortzing's dramatic timing depended, and the almost continuous music placed too many demands on a technique insufficiently prepared for them. With *Rolands Knappen* (1849) the circumstances of magic opera once more encouraged an enlargement of means, including orchestral, together with greater rhythmic and metrical fluency and a greater use of chromatic harmony. He was by no means alone in using chromaticism to add expressive tension when making the conventional progression from dominant to tonic to introduce what turns out to be a simple aria. There are many examples in this vein from other composers, of which perhaps the most extreme (three years after *Tristan*) is the introduction to a simple Morning Song for Helge near the start of Franz von Holstein's blamelessly rustic *Der Haideschacht* (1868) (Example 37).

However, Lortzing's use of chromatic harmony reflects something more fundamental than the spicing up of plain ideas, as practised by Holstein and others. His theatrical grounding gave him a strong practical sense of what worked with the audiences of the day, and this he saw as his craft, but he also brought to it creative skills that enlarged the idiom out of recognition – or rather, to the point at which audiences were delighted by new recognition of the familiar forms of song given an artistic quality not easily to be found in the space left between the twin ambitions of Romantic and grand opera. Lortzing knew all the conventions, which comic devices came off, which dramatic situations could be relied upon for effect, which character-types belonged to another age and which were enduring, and he was well versed not only in the opera buffa, opéra-comique and Singspiel encountered in an itinerant theatrical youth but also in the farces, comedies and sentimental plays of different repertories.

Example 37   Holstein: *Der Haideschacht* (1868)

Later, he was to express a dislike for the classics, to the point of satire in mocking Mendelssohn's *Antigone* music and the contemporary Sophocles vogue in *Der Wildschütz*, whose source in an obscure Kotzebue play was the kind of basic theatrical fare upon which he felt he could more readily build.

Much of his skill lay in concentrating on the popular elements with which his audience would have been comfortable, but also in reconstituting an opera's proportions so that they gained freshness from their novel handling and, especially, were charged with new invention. Though he could draw upon motive, and melodrama, and substantial orchestral description, his main emphasis was on song and song-like ensemble. The songs are almost never routine insertions, such as introductory songs or drinking songs, but play a functional role which he was able to ensure the better through acting as his own librettist. They might advance the action, or clarify a character's psychology, or even shed ironic light on the proceedings. Their occurrence would be dramatically well timed, but in a familiar context draw on unfamiliar elements, in particular on expressively chromatic harmony and, no less, upon irregular phrase lengths, which could tense the music expressively alongside the words with five- or six- or seven-bar melodies overriding the regular four or eight stressed lines. Furthermore, without losing his claim on the audience's sense of familiarity, he could by such means integrate his songs into ensembles.

Lortzing's inheritance of course goes back deep into eighteenth-century Singspiel, though he was careful to discard almost all the slighter and trivial elements and knew precisely how to distinguish between populist and popular. His integration of song, as he developed it (and distinguished it crucially from the concert Lied and the operatic aria) into structures which it could animate, lay close to the centre of his achievement. This can be readily perceived and (importantly to Lortzing) instantly enjoyed in the most popular of his operas, above all *Die beiden Schützen*, *Zar und Zimmermann* and *Der Wildschütz*, to which was later added *Der Waffenschmied*. It suffuses *Undine*, as well as the unsatisfactory *Regina* and the remarkable achievement of *Rolands Knappen*. There is nothing to indicate that, had his life not been cut short in 1851 at the age of forty-nine, he would have sought to break these creative bounds. Nor is it enough to suggest that he was a classical composer operating in Romantic times. Though the latent regularity of his music, from his melodies to his more extended structures, proposes expectations such as the classical composer will creatively deny or fulfil, he composed in a full understanding of his own times. His rejection of the aspirations of Romantic or grand opera was made in honest admission that his talents did not lie in those realms, and though there was a forgivable tinge of bitterness in a man whose life had been a struggle to earn a living, he composed in the belief that he was honouring the tradition of Singspiel and serving an audience. Perhaps he was fortunate not to live to see the genius of Wagner overwhelm German opera.

In 1840, the name of Richard Wagner would have meant little in Germany. His first opera, *Die Feen*, composed in 1833–4, had failed to reach the stage, and was not to do so until 1888, after his death. *Das Liebesverbot* was given its first performance at Magdeburg in 1836, but the second performance had to be cancelled when only six people turned up for it. Not until the Dresden première of *Rienzi* in 1842 did Wagner experience a triumph, one soon to be muted when Berlin failed to take to the work in 1847 and other theatres proved reluctant to invest in an expensive enterprise. Two and a half months after *Rienzi*, *Der fliegende Holländer* disappointed the Dresdeners, who had been expecting something on similar lines; it was dropped after four performances, though the same year saw productions in Riga (under Heinrich Dorn) and Kassel (under Spohr), and Wagner himself conducted one in Berlin in 1844. Thereafter it was also slow to find homes. With the Dresden première of *Tannhäuser* in 1845, there appeared the rift between Wagner's supporters and enemies in controversy that was never thereafter to leave him. Even then, Liszt's advocacy with his Weimar performance in 1849 was needed to confirm the work's importance. It was Liszt, again, who staged *Lohengrin* in 1850 when Dresden failed to support Wagner after his flight in the wake of the political upheavals of 1849. By the 1850s, he was known throughout Europe, as a writer as well as a composer, clinching his controversial fame in 1861 with the scandal over the revised *Tannhäuser* in the Paris that had once rejected *Rienzi*. Enraged by the disruptions when he refused to comply with the ballet conventions of the Opéra, he was confident enough to withdraw the work after three performances. He was by now the most famous composer north of the Alps, one attracting violent hostility and equally violent partisanship, but rarely indifference. As his stature grew, so his shadow fell increasingly heavily across other composers seeking to find a way forward for German opera.

The 1840s saw the last two 'pre-Wagnerian' German operas, apart from those of Lortzing, to achieve and retain wide popularity in and beyond Germany, Friedrich von Flotow's *Martha* (1847) and Otto Nicolai's *Die lustigen Weiber von Windsor* (1849). Whereas Lortzing's style is, for all the outside influences, rooted in German Singspiel, a stronger awareness of French opéra-comique and Italian opera buffa respectively infuses the work of Flotow and Nicolai. In Flotow's case, his first ten operas to be performed were written and staged in Paris, where he studied with Reicha and Pixis. Some of these were collaborative works, others were to be revised, enlarged, translated into German or otherwise refashioned and equipped with new titles and altered plots, to the point at which it can be fairly said that 'a comprehensive survey of Flotow's works today presents almost unsurmountable difficulties' (Peter Cohen, article on Flotow in *The New Grove Dictionary of Opera*). The cross-fertilization between French and German opera, however, indicates how close the two traditions could lie, especially at a fairly light level. This was especially so in the hands of a composer with a melodic grace (including a love of dance forms) and a sense of elegant theatrical effect which had been brought out in his Paris training and experience, coupled with an ability to score resourcefully and to allow motive to guide the invention which reflects more Germanic inclinations.

Apart from two youthful pieces which appear to be lost, Flotow's first German work, and his only opera to challenge the popularity of *Martha*, was *Alessandro Stradella* (1844). Loosely based on an episode in Stradella's adventurous life by 'W. Friedrich' (F. W. Riese), the plot centres on his abduction of old Bassi's ward Leonore, which he achieves by gondola in the confusion of Carnival. At his house near Rome, he is returning from their wedding when he is confronted by Malvolino and Barnarino, bandits disguised as pilgrims and hired by Bassi to murder him and recover Leonore. When he responds by welcoming them and singing a Romance about the generous nature of robbers who help the poor and shelter the wandering minstrel, the softhearted bandits abandon their plan, until an increased fee from the enraged Bassi rekindles their resolve. Piety now overcomes them when they overhear Stradella practising his hymn to the Virgin Mary for her coming festival, and falling to their knees, they join in. With Bassi also mollified, Stradella is ceremonially borne on a litter to the picture of the Virgin which all expect will confer divine grace upon them.

The work is a very successful instance of Flotow's disposition towards both French and German opera, and indeed of his ready recycling of material, in this case from a one-act *pièce lyrique* with dialogue of 1837. Despite his description of the later work as *romantische Oper*, and the absence of dialogue, it is really closer to opéra-comique and especially French grand opera. Though this in no way hampered its success in Germany, Karl Franz Brendel had a point in regarding it a somewhat distracting compromise (*NZM* 22 (1845), 201–3, 209–10). The musical atmosphere is light, the lovers sentimental, with the greatest tension building up in the Scène und Nocturno (*sic*) of Leonore's escape and the succeeding Carnival. This gives Flotow the opportunity for extended choral and ballet sequences in the French manner, though the scene is somewhat protracted and, through exigencies of the plot, comes rather early in the work as the finale to Act I, rather than in such a scene's natural place ending Act II (where Flotow then feels obliged to insert another ballet). Acts II and III are chiefly marked by some scenes of local colour and enlivened by the comic bandits, who arrive separately, reading their instructions as to how to find Stradella's house, and team up together. Flotow's model here is the bandit pair Giacomo and Beppo in Auber's *Fra Diavolo*, with their lightly repeated notes and flippant exchange of short phrases (they may in turn have coloured Verdi's Samuel and Tom in *Un Ballo in maschera*). The score is also remarkable for Flotow's preparation of the theme of Stradella's 'Jungfrau Maria' hymn, which opens the overture and the Act III introduction on sonorous bassoons, horns and trombones, and recurs at various points in allusions or half-allusions colouring the invention (for

(Virgin Mary, in Heavenly light, Madonna on high, Mother of the Lord!)

Example 38   Flotow: *Alessandro Stradella* (1844), Stradella

instance, by the incursion of triplet figures into the melodic lines). By these means, the hymn's eventual appearance comes to seem a realisation of much that has gone before, and indeed to have been all along the virtuous centre of Stradella's raffish nature which earns him Leonore's love, the bandits' reform and Bassi's blessing. Even if the final scene's pieties are sentimental, they are arrived at with theatrical and musical cunning (Example 38).

Flotow's greatest success, *Martha* (1847), has a similarly tangled origin. In its first manifestation, it was a ballet-pantomime, *Lady Harriette*, hastily thrown together in 1844 for the Opéra's ballerina Adèle Dumilâtre when the Director, Léon Pillet, had his artistic scruples about her talents overcome by a mysterious gentleman placing on his desk 100,000 francs to finance the piece. The composers were Frédéric Burgmüller and Edouard Deldevez, with Flotow contributing the first act. When the Viennese success of *Alessandro Stradella* led to a commission, he revived the ballet's music for a four-act opera on a similar plot. Tired of court life and of her suitor, Sir Tristan Mickleford, Lady Harriet persuades him to join her maid Nancy and herself at the Richmond hiring fair, the three of them disguised as Martha, Julia and Bob. The girls then find themselves contracted to the farmers Lyonel and Plumkett. They manage to escape from the farmhouse, though not before 'Martha' has won Lyonel's heart, especially with her singing of 'The Last Rose of Summer'. At a royal hunt, Harriet rejects Tristan again, now herself thinking tenderly of Lyonel, though she publicly rejects him for fear of scandal. Arrested, he is revealed to be really the Earl of Derby, but he now angrily refuses Harriet's apologies and offer of marriage. When she and Nancy stage a re-enactment of the Richmond Fair and offer themselves again to Lyonel and Plumkett as 'Martha' and 'Julia', they are lovingly accepted.

If *Alessandro Stradella* owes much to the example of Parisian grand opera, here it is opéra-comique which provides the inspiration for a work that also includes German and Italian elements with remarkably little stylistic incongruity. Plumkett's Porterlied, praising John Bull's ability to keep out the damp with strong beer, is a drinking song clearly aimed at Viennese taste; Lyonel's love song 'Ach! so fromm' is virtually an Italian aria (and won its greatest popularity as 'M'appari'); Nancy's 'Jägerin, schlau im Sinn', about Cupid as hunter, has a French cut and elegance. Other elements are more subtly intertwined, with Lyonel's music being marked by the French qualities that helped to form Weber's Max; and the Act III finale benefits from both the techniques of the Italian stretto and a more symphonic harmonic and orchestral resourcefulness that suggest German means of searching out emotional depth. Most strikingly, more than in *Alessandro Stradella* Flotow holds the work together by a melodic individuality that coheres further through his highly original use of motive. Whereas in *Stradella* the outcome in the climactic hymn 'Jungfrau Maria' was subtly prepared by two full orchestral quotations and by elements occurring earlier at significant moments, in *Martha* it is the song 'The Last Rose of Summer' which unifies the opera, recurring no fewer than five times. However, its significance is greater than that of a 'theme song'. Thomas Moore's words, with their forlorn imagery, were well matched to a folksong he declared was an altered version of *The Groves of Blarney*, but the melody is so apt that it might almost have been composed by Flotow. So much is this so that, as well as bringing the melody back repeatedly, he can allow its features, in particular the rising and falling three notes that open and close its thrice repeated main phrase, to tinge other music of emotional significance. Its first appearance is prepared by Lyonel's 'Mein ich doch' and then answered orchestrally. Harriet's lovelorn 'Hier in stillen Schattengründen', Nancy's amorous hunting song 'Jägerin, schlau im Sinn', and the serving girls' chirpy 'Ich kann nähen' offering their services at the start and the close of the opera, all begin with the song's first phrase and include the falling three notes, while the Quintet 'Mag der Himmel Euch vergeben', as Harriet accepts reproaches for what has turned out to be a cruel jest, significantly opens with an inversion of the song's first three notes. There are many other less obvious reminiscences as, with a unique and beautifully judged application of motive, the simple charm of the 'Last Rose' folksong seems to suffuse the opera's invention with its scent. It is by no means impossible that Wagner, prepared to turn a good idea from any origin to his own creative advantage, remembered this unprecedented technique when with incomparably greater wealth of resource he caused the invention of *Die Meistersinger* to be permeated with a phrase from an old song (Example 39).

Though he went on to write several more German works before returning to French opera, Flotow never came near to repeating these successes. His next opera, *Sophia Catharina* (1850), is in four acts divided into two parts, with a ballet, and in some ways marks a return to the manner of *Alessandro Stradella*, while lacking that work's fluency and charm; and its successor, *Rübezahl* (1852), has little in common with earlier operas on the tale and is really a fairly simple romantic comedy set in the Riesengebirge. It shares with its predecessors the fine ear for orchestral sound, particularly for woodwind, that distinguishes Flotow's style, as when Veronika's aria begins on unaccompanied oboe and clarinet and includes a charming imitation of church bells in the orchestra.

Nicolai's operas, unlike Flotow's, owe virtually nothing to French example but take much in their manner from Italy. This was the country to which he moved after studies in Berlin, and for which his first four operas were written. Attempts to naturalize two of them, *Il templario* (1840) and *Il proscritto* (1841), by means of German translations in 1845 and 1844 respectively did not persuade the Viennese, but after much searching for a subject, and after settling in Berlin as Kapellmeister, he eventually triumphed with *Die lustigen Weiber von*

(a)

MARTHA

Letz-te Ro - se wie magst du so ein - sam hier blühn? Kei -ne
Dei - ne freund-li - chen Schwes-ter sind längst schon da - hin.

Blü - te hauchst Bal - sam mit lieb - li - chem, lieb - li -chem Duft, kei - ne

Blätt - chen mehr flat - tern in stür - mi - scher Luft.

('Tis the last rose of summer, Left blooming alone; All her lovely companions Are faded and gone;
No flower of her kindred, No rosebud is nigh, To reflect back her blushes,
Or give sigh for sigh!—Thomas Moore)

(b)

MOLLY PITT

Ich kann näh-en, ich kann mäh-en, ich kann sä-en Fä-dern dre-hen, ich kann

bü-geln, ich kann strie-geln und ver-se-hen Hof und Haus.

(I can sow, I can mow, I can sew and stitch, I can iron, I can comb,
and oversee the household)

(c)

LYONEL

Mein' ich's dich so treu und ehr - lich, lau - ter ist mein Herz und rein

(I love so truly and honourably, my heart is pure and clean)

(d)

NANCY

Jä - ge-rin, schlau im Sinn zie-let mit den Bli - cken

weiss in Eil' Pfeil auf Pfeil aus dem Aug' zu schi - cken

(The huntress, crafty-witted, aims with a glance, knows at speed
how to send arrow upon arrow from the eyes)

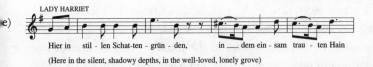

LADY HARRIET

Hier in stil - len Schat-ten - grün - den, in __ dem ein - sam trau - ten Hain

(Here in the silent, shadowy depths, in the well-loved, lonely grove)

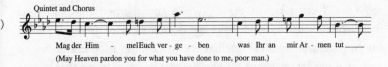

Quintet and Chorus

Mag der Him - mel Euch ver - ge - ben was Ihr an mir Ar - men tut __

(May Heaven pardon you for what you have done to me, poor man.)

Example 39   Flotow: *Martha* (1847)
(a) Act II, Martha
(b) Act I, Molly Pitt
(c) Act I, Lyonel
(d) Act III, Nancy
(e) Act III, Lady Harriet
(f) Act III, Quintet and Chorus

Windsor (1849). By cruel misfortune, he died from a stroke only two months later, at the age of thirty-eight.

Even here, the Italian influence is marked, especially in the aria for Frau Fluth (Mistress Ford), 'Nun eilt herbei', a full-scale coloratura showpiece, for all its human perceptions, and in Fenton's Romance 'Horch, die Lerche' and the succeeding Duettino between him and Anna (Anne Page). By contrast, the most obviously German number is the drinking song 'Als Büblein klein', which Nicolai's librettist, Samuel Mosenthal, adapted from the song 'When that I was and a little tiny boy' that closes *Twelfth Night*. Though a little lumpish, it is more inventive than many such songs, and care is taken to integrate it into the plot. However, the self-critical Nicolai was perceptive enough to see that his real model for this speeding comedy should indeed be Italian opera buffa, but the opera buffa of Mozart, and in particular *Le nozze di Figaro*. He was not so foolish as to try to emulate Mozart, but the real quality of *Die lustigen Weiber* lies in his skill in reconciling his own melodic warmth and rich feeling for the orchestra to Mozart's genius with symphonic finales. The whole of the opera's Act I finale, from Falstaff's arrival at Mistress Ford's house by way of Ford's furious search and Falstaff's eventual removal in the laundry basket to the muddy Thames, derives from the *Figaro* example, as two clever and lively women outwit a jealous husband so as to dispose of an imagined seducer (there is even a reference from later in *Figaro*, when the shamed husband begs forgiveness of his wife). Nicolai steers well clear of imitation, using his considerable musical intelligence to develop momentum in his own manner by means of well-contrasted lyrical sections that evolve within themselves and in turn project the next movement. This well-judged absorption of Mozartian influence into his own Romanticism, which includes the atmospheric orchestral description that lends enchantment to the moonlit finale in Windsor Forest, well earned the work a following that has never quite died away.

Not the faintest shadow of Wagner falls across these works, entering German opera as they do from different national directions. For Schumann, standing at the centre of German Romanticism as one of its greatest artists, resistance to foreign domination was an article of faith, but he was able to resist Wagner's well-meaning interference, if not wholly his influence. Though the diaries he shared with his wife Clara, and various other accounts, record dismissive remarks about Italian opera, he generally avoided such attacks in his critical writing, and a rare full-scale confrontation with French opera came with his celebrated demolition of Meyerbeer's *Les Huguenots*. After seeing several performances he drew his sword (as he put it) and rode into action against what he regarded as 'höchste Nicht-Originalität und Styllosigkeit' (*NZM* 7 (1837), 74), something highly perilous for German opera. From about 1840, his interest in dramatic music heightened steeply, and, for instance when reviewing Reissiger's *Adèle de Foix*, he urged his compatriots not to try to please but to trust in their originality (*NZM* 17 (1842), 79–81). So having accepted criticism of *Tannhäuser* by Schumann, regarding it as perceptive, Wagner was astonished to find that when in a genuine wish to return a favour he offered advice, this 'sonderbarer Mensch' was undisposed to listen to criticisms of the *Genoveva* text, which

Wagner thought old-fashioned and muddled (Wagner, 1963, 376; 1983, 319–20).

Whether or not Wagner could have helped, he was undoubtedly right. By the late 1840s, Schumann had considered numerous subjects, including Christopher Columbus, Till Eulenspiegel, Faust, Héloïse and Abélard, *The Odyssey*, subjects from Hans Andersen, Calderón, Chateaubriand, Goethe, Hoffmann, Kalidasa, Mörike, Byron (*The Corsair*, for which he wrote a couple of numbers), Shakespeare (*Romeo and Juliet*), and three 'Wagnerian' subjects: *Der Wartburgkrieg, Die Nibelungen* and *Tristan und Isolde*. The wild disparity of this range suggests, to say the least, operatic uncertainty. Eventually Schumann settled on Tieck's *Leben und Tod der heiligen Genoveva* of 1799, a *romantische Dichtung* set in the eighth century. The example of the innocent bride, falsely accused and finally justified, clearly impressed him from *Euryanthe*, a work he greatly admired, and his friend Robert Reinick was set to work on Tieck's sentimental tale. However, he then came upon Friedrich Hebbel's drama *Genoveva* of 1843, a much stronger, darker work in which the emphasis shifts to the self-torment of Golo, who is in love with Genoveva but, when he is rejected, becomes the jealous compasser of her downfall. Doubtless struck by the increased similarity with *Euryanthe* and the character of Lysiart, Schumann asked for Hebbel's approach to be taken into consideration, and when Reinick failed in the attempt, wrote the text himself. The outcome only served to underline the fact that a highly intelligent and literate composer-critic is not necessarily the same thing as a good librettist.

In the text's final form (which Reinick disowned), Siegfried answers the summons of Hidulphus, Bishop of Trier, to lead his armies against the Moorish invasion of France from Spain. He entrusts his new bride Genoveva to the care of Golo, secretly in love with her. Golo kisses her as she sleeps, but his tenderness turns to hatred when he is then repulsed. He tricks the old steward Drago into hiding in Genoveva's room, and then, with his evil sorceress foster-mother Margarethe, bursts in and kills Drago; Genoveva is imprisoned as an adulteress. On his way home from the wars,

Siegfried is shown scenes of Genoveva and Drago together in Margarethe's magic mirror, and orders her death. Golo leads her into the desert, and when she still refuses him, leaves her to her fate. At the last minute, she is saved by a mute youth, Angelo. Siegfried, learning the truth when Drago's ghost forces it out of Margarethe, arrives in time to be reconciled to her.

Even Liszt, who championed an opera he claimed to prefer above all others of the last fifty years apart from Wagner's, was obliged to confess its lack of dramatic vitality despite the excellence of much of the music (letter to Anton Rubinstein, 3 Apr. 1855). It was a bold concept to cast Golo as a lyric tenor, Siegfried as a baritone, and to introduce Golo musically before anyone except the Bishop and the chorus: the stage is well set for a drama of a man destroying himself through his inability to control his passion. Golo's pain is declared in an anguished recitative, ending with a reminiscence of Lysiart in his words, 'Konnt' ich flüchten, verbergen mich', immediately before the much more conventional love duet between Siegfried and Genoveva. Yet for all his understanding of divided natures, Schumann cannot manage to develop a full portrait of Golo. Having presented himself with a marvellous opportunity as Golo bends over the sleeping Genoveva for his stolen kiss, he then provides no music for this tantalizingly complicated moment, only resuming composition after a moment's silence with the stealthy arrival of Margarethe. When Genoveva, still unaware of Golo's emotions, asks him to join her in her song about loving hearts sundered by distance, Schumann, master of irony in his Heine songs and especially in *Dichterliebe*, makes little of this invitation or of Golo's gnawing despair. The action moves forward to Golo's attempted embrace and rejection as 'Ehrloser Bastard!' Thereafter, Golo's portrayal too often falls back on fairly simple villainous gestures; and though Genoveva is scarcely any more vivid a character than Euryanthe, comparable situations – such as the evil pair swearing a sinister supernatural pact, or the abandoned heroine wandering in the desert – can only draw attention to Schumann's lack of dramatic invention. Even Drago's ghost, providing quite a well-imagined scene, lacks the weirdness of his *Euryanthe* counterparts.

Schumann is perhaps trying too hard to build upon a distinguished, if flawed, model to fashion a large-scale, four-act grand opera whose sprawl he cannot control. His finales lack momentum, and, as with Schubert, too often the development of a musical idea is given primacy over dramatic considerations. The choral writing is as plain as that of his *Das Paradies und die Peri*, and the sinister figure of Margarethe remains colourless. There is also a curious incoherence in his use of motive. First proposed in the third bar of the overture, the only important motive possesses a distinctive physiognomy, and seems to be associated chiefly with Golo, but returns in such a bewildering variety of situations as to rob it of any central meaning. The supposition must be that Schumann is intending it to represent a general concept, perhaps villainy, or chivalry both upheld and betrayed.

Wagner, with *Tannhäuser* composed and with *Lohengrin* filling his mind, would have been sure to regard *Genoveva* as belonging to a world of Romantic opera left behind by some two or three decades; and one of the paradoxes of *Genoveva* is the contrast between Schumann's inventive talent and his failure to advance the genre into new expressive regions. By the 1850s, *Tannhäuser* and *Lohengrin* had set new standards, which composers of lesser talent but greater theatrical skill than Schumann found it difficult to ignore. Those who did tended to find themselves similarly outmoded. The Darmstadt Kapellmeister Carl Mangold had actually written a *Tanhauser*, unaware of Wagner's work, and achieved a modest success when it was performed in 1846; it omits the song contest and contrives a happy ending, with the Paris-style collapse of the Venusberg, and Tanhauser's marriage. However, Mangold's talent was scarcely up to the subject, or to a four-act grand opera on another old German saga, *Gudrun* (1851), which proceeds at a halting pace, with the dutiful inclusion of minstrel ballads, a Kriegers Morgenlied (suggesting nothing so much as a *Liedertafel*) and other pieces of local colour doing little to enliven a sluggish piece of work. Franz von Holstein fared little better with *Der Erbe von Morley* (1852). Though it has some basis in Scott's *Guy Mannering* and *The Monastery*, the opera suggests that his model was a much more successful Scott opera of similar inspiration, Boieldieu's *La Dame blanche* of 1825, and that his musical influences were Weber and Marschner. He can include such numbers as a hornpipe and (after the judge Blackstone, hearing a drone, has exclaimed, 'Ich hör' den Pibrok klingen') a Scottish folk dance, but the manner, as well as the nature of his fascination with Scott, is that of an earlier generation.

In the case of Heinrich Dorn, the ignoring of Wagner was deliberate, and complicated. Dorn had begun his career as a disciple of Weber, and had championed Wagner before falling out with him. In Berlin from 1849 to 1869 as co-conductor (with Wilhelm Taubert) of the Hofoper, where he conducted *Tannhäuser*, he became friends with Liszt, who drew him back to an interest in Wagner, especially in Wagner's use of motive in *Tannhäuser* and *Lohengrin*. In December 1852, Wagner completed the text of *The Ring*, beginning work on the music of *Das Rheingold* in September 1853 and finishing the full score on 26 September 1854. Deciding that he would write his own opera on the subject, Dorn seems to have begun composing *Die Nibelungen* also in the autumn of 1853, having it ready to go into rehearsal by 20 December for its première under Liszt on 20 January 1854. He managed to publish his text in 1853 a month before the private printing of Wagner's *Ring* text.

The version of the *Nibelungenlied* prepared for Dorn by Emil Gerber provided thirty-three numbers, linked by freely composed passages of arioso, divided into five acts. So as to win Brunhild, Queen of Iceland, in the single combat with her that is her price for her hand, Günther, King of Burgundy, enlists Siegfried, Prince of the Nibelungen, to fight in his stead, disguised by the Tarnhelm he has won from the dragon Fafner as part of the Nibelung hoard. For this deception, which overrules the angry objections of Günther's kinsman Hagen, Siegfried's reward is the hand of Günther's sister Chriemhild. In Burgundy two years later, Brunhild discovers the deception from Chriemhild, and persuades Hagen to act as her avenger. In Act III, Hagen stabs Siegfried in the back as they are out hunting in the Odenwald. Chriemhild's laments go unanswered until the arrival of Etzel. Ten years later, at her marriage to Etzel, she unavailingly demands the Nibelung hoard and the handing over of Hagen. In the last act, Chriemhild causes Günther and Brunhild to be executed, then striking down Hagen and killing herself.

In its basic structure, *Die Nibelungen* is a number opera, though it is in the formal numbers that Dorn shows himself most conventional. A Sailors' Chorus, 'Ahoi! ahoi!', and another, 'Vom Rhein, vom deutschen Rhein', recall his mastery of popular *Liedertafel* choruses, and another actually uses music he wrote for a *Deutsche National-hymne*. Many of the solo numbers are little more than bland cavatinas, and Chriemhild's plaint turns to *bel canto* for its example; while the dramatic confrontations between the characters are often conducted in parallel thirds that rob them of any adversarial tension. For all his wish to distance himself from Wagner, it is when he moves into freer composition that Dorn can show greater individuality, as with the opening arrival of Siegfried, Günther and Hagen sailing their ship through stormy seas. But the score's most striking feature is its use of motive. In some cases, this hardly moves beyond the reminiscence motive with which Dorn was familiar from *Euryanthe* and no doubt much French opera, as with the love themes attached to the two couples, Günther and Brunhild, Siegfried and Chriemhild. But many more occur, and some are certainly 'transformed along specifically Lisztian lines', arousing suspicions that Liszt may have played more than a tokenly supportive hand (Leverett, 1990, 130). Though Dorn cannot begin to approach Wagner's mastery at the stage it had reached in *Das Rheingold*, let alone later in *The Ring*, a few of the musical ideas and developments are along similar lines, in that the return of a motive can be used not simply as reminiscence but ironically, or modified to shed a changed dramatic light on a situation, or to make contact with a different motive in a new expressive context. Such devices are bound to seem rather artificial when the material is of modest quality, and especially when it is worked without the dramatic instinct motivating Wagner's work.

However interesting to observe, in the historical and especially the Wagnerian context, they do not seem the natural evolutionary product of Dorn's otherwise plain invention and conventional dramatic stances.

Dorn's Berlin colleague Wilhelm Taubert also resisted Wagner, while not remaining wholly immune to his influence. Of his two Shakespeare works, *Macbeth* (1857) is stronger than his *Twelfth Night* opera *Cesario* (1874). The text keeps quite effectively close to Shakespeare until near the end, apart from a few nods to German opera convention such as a jolly song for the Porter and a ballad for Macduff in the banquet scene. At Dunsinane, Lady Macbeth gives a running commentary on Macbeth's battle with Macduff, then joining a long line of operatic sopranos by throwing herself off the battlements, whereat the Witches reappear and claim Macbeth before vanishing. Apparent anticipations of Wagner, as with the rising chromatic figure before Duncan's murder, are really no more than the chromatic language of the day for mysterious or sinister events (Example 40). Nor is the motivic technique much more advanced than that of *Euryanthe*, consisting almost entirely of a figure for the Witches and another, an impassioned rising arpeggio, apparently representing Lady Macbeth's evil ambition (it virtually disappears once Duncan is dead). Not surprisingly, it is Lady (as Taubert, like Verdi, calls her) who dominates the opera. Her invocation of the spirits, 'Kommt jetzt hervor, Ihr Morddämonen alle, wo Ihr auch harrt in unsichtbarer Kraft' ('Come, you spirits / That tend on mortal thoughts!') takes the example of the *Euryanthe* invocation, especially when it comes to the shuddering tremolos and sudden violent outbreaks that accompany 'Komm, finstre Nacht, und hülle jede Spur in schwarzen Höllendampf' ('Come, thick night, / And pall thee in the dunnest smoke of hell'). After this, the comparative timidity of the Sleepwalking Scene comes as a disappointment.

Apart from light pieces deriving from French originals and attaching themselves to French example, German comic opera of the 1830s and 1840s had been above all in the hands of Lortzing, whom Peter Cornelius implicitly dismissed when on Christmas Day 1849, the day

Example 40 Taubert: *Macbeth* (1857)

after his 25th birthday, he wrote a long and touching letter to his friend Carl Hestermann modestly taking stock of his own achievements and expectations. In the course of it, he suggested that, 'Ein Weg ist für uns Komponisten noch offen; unsere drei großen Tragiker haben wir in der Musik gehabt, aber (und lachen Sie nur getrost über den Idealisten Peter) der Aristophanes ist noch nicht dagewesen' ('One path remains open to us composers: we've had our three great tragedians in music, but (and you may well laugh at the idealist Peter) the Aristophanes has not yet appeared') (letter of 25 December 1849). He had already contemplated writing a comedy, and with his most successful work he clearly hoped to emancipate German comic opera from Singspiel.

Der Barbier von Bagdad (1858) is a curious amalgam of past, present and even future. For his plot, Cornelius (his own librettist) turned to the once popular source of the *1,001 Nights*, and the tale of the lovelorn Nureddin who pines for Margiana. Old Bostana brings word of a rendezvous arranged when Margiana's father, the Cadi, is at the mosque, but first Nureddin must be shaved and prepared by the garrulous old barber Abul Hassan, who then most unwelcomely stands guard outside the Cadi's house as the lovers meet. Various complications and misunderstandings ensue: eventually Nureddin is obliged to hide from the returning Cadi in a chest and almost stifles, but Abul Hassan manages to revive him and all ends happily. Though there is no spoken dialogue, this return to the Oriental opera of previous generations is also marked by the renovation of various Singspiel devices, such as the patter song in which Abul Hassan declares his skills, 'Bin Akademiker / Doktor und Chemiker / Bin Mathematiker / Und Arithmetiker / Bin auch Grammatiker / So wie

Ästhetiker . . .' and so on in a dazzling verbal tour de force which the music matches no less brilliantly. Here Cornelius's model was above all Dittersdorf (*Doktor und Apotheker*), also the opera buffa convention of the Catalogue Aria picked up for expert use by, among others, Jakob Haibel (*Der Tyroler Wastel*). Although he was not yet part of the Bayreuth circle, Cornelius would have had the opportunity to read the poem of *The Ring* with Liszt in Weimar, where he settled in 1852, and he is clearly satirizing its *Stabreim* when the Barber and the Cadi exchange such lines as 'Ruchloser Richter, der sich ungerecht rächt'. If so, Wagner's sense of humour held good in the face of this heroic audacity, for his affection remained steady even when Cornelius later declined to follow him to Munich until *Der Cid* was finished. The music shows virtually no Wagnerian influence, from which, indeed, Cornelius was trying to distance himself (at the time he knew no Wagner later than *Lohengrin*). He does, however, accept French influence in the figure of Berlioz, whose *Benvenuto Cellini* he had translated for Liszt's second set of Weimar performances in 1856; and this shows above all in the canonic duet between Bostana and Nureddin 'Wenn zum Gebet', which could not have taken the shape it does without the example of the Trio 'Demain soir mardi gras' in *Cellini*. There are suggestions of Berlioz's harmonic originality; and it is from Cornelius's turning of this to his own ends, especially in Margiana's music, that a potent example came for one of his admirers, Richard Strauss, whose comedies (in particular *Intermezzo*) owe much to Cornelius.

However, if Cornelius nursed hopes that he might play Aristophanes in the history of German opera, he was deceiving himself. For all the work's lyrical warmth and charm, and the gentle humour and intelligence with which the music can enliven the situations, it lacks not only Aristophanic sharpness but the true comic sense of pace and timing. Perhaps in the wish to tap a deeper vein of comedy by banishing spoken dialogue in favour of a continuous texture and a richer orchestral contribution, Cornelius dwells too long on situations without moving the plot along. The opera is slow off the mark, with Nureddin's sighings occupying too much time and the barber delaying the action with his self-congratulations, while Margiana does not appear at all until Act II. The patter-songs, in which verbal and musical dexterity are brilliantly matched, stand out rather than setting an example for the more fluent pace which the dénouement demands. It is this which has denied the work a steady place in repertories, though not one in the affection of musicians.

The only performance of *Der Barbier von Bagdad* given in Cornelius's lifetime was the notorious Weimar première at which long-simmering local resentments against Liszt boiled over, leading to his abrupt departure from the town. Still hoping for a popular success, Cornelius turned to tragedy with *Der Cid*, this time achieving two performances in Weimar in 1865. Since then, the work has largely languished. The reasons are not far to seek, and rest chiefly upon the lack of action and upon the influence of Wagner. Yet the work's static qualities, less damaging than in a comedy, allow Cornelius to explore the tensions in the relationship between Ruy Diaz (the Cid) and Chimene, torn between hatred for his killing of her father in a family feud and a love she can scarcely bear to acknowledge. After he has declared his own love, his departure at the head of the armies of Castile against the Moors plunges her into ever deeper self-conflict, exacerbated by a rival, Alvar Fanez, offering to kill him during the battle and then by rumours of his death. His triumphant return leads to complete reconciliation and the blessing of their union.

The shadow of *Lohengrin* falls over the work to some extent, especially in the courtly formalities of the first act, and elsewhere in musical gestures such as the opening of the Introduction, and the high, poised string textures accompanying Chimene's dream of Ruy Diaz's death in battle and restoration to life by Heaven. The similarities do not extend much further. The plot is of a very different order, and apart from the closeness of Cornelius's Fernando to Wagner's Henry the Fowler, two kings sounding like many others in chivalric operas, the characters have nothing significant in common. The whole of the nocturnal second act, from the beautiful female chorus invoking peace upon Chimene to her eventual farewell to

Ruy Diaz as he departs for battle, is a superb study in the confusion between two people falling ever more passionately in love as they struggle against their emotions. Chimene, in particular, is portrayed with great subtlety, the chromatic harmony skilfully suggesting her ambivalence yet also supporting melodic lines that can move from the lyrical to the heroically powerful, sometimes in a manner subtly at odds with the accompaniment as her torment deepens and resolves. Left alone by her women, she wrestles with her conflicting emotions until driven to prayer; but the allusions to the Lord's Prayer (the pious Cornelius avoids the actual words of Luther's Bible, perhaps feeling such use of them to be blasphemous), and to forgiveness for those who have trespassed against us, spur her to renewed rage and the rejection of prayer. The arrival of the Bishop (with similar allusions to the Beatitudes) does nothing to ease her anguish. It is Ruy Diaz's secret appearance at her side which drives them together on a 'dark voyage' whose outcome they fear, but which, as he is summoned to battle, forces from her the blessing which he craves. Cornelius was consciously trying to write independently of Wagner, but not in ignorance of him, and it seems at least possible that he was able to repay a part of the debt if a theme of Ruy Diaz's valour caught in the ear of Wagner when it came to a transformation of Parsifal's theme (Example 41).

Cornelius knew well that he had to distance himself from Wagner if he was ever to achieve anything: 'Das kann ich nicht in Wagners Nähe leisten. Er konsumiert mich . . . *Wagners Atmosphäre hat eine große Schwüle, er verbrennt und nimmt mir die Luft*' ('I can't manage it in Wagner's proximity. He consumes me . . . *Wagner's atmosphere is stifling; he burns, and robs me of air*') (letter to his brother Carl, 26 Nov. 1864). His resolve to act independently took an extreme form when in 1866 he began work on a third opera, *Gunlöd*, making use of some of the *Edda* material drawn upon by Wagner for *The Ring* but composing it into something closer to song opera than music drama. The effort proved too much: at the time of his death in 1874 he had managed to write only a little more than an act, and to orchestrate none of it.

Example 41

(a) Cornelius: *Der Cid* (1865)

(b) Wagner: *Parsifal* (1882)

Nevertheless, *Der Cid* stands head and shoulders above other attempts at serious opera written in the 1860s and the years in which Wagner's stature had become impossible to ignore. Some composers did attempt to perpetuate older ideas and methods. Louis Schindelmeisser's *Melusine* (1861) is a not ineffective work developing, with some motivic working, the idea of the struggle between sacred and profane love; there is even some anticipation of Kundry in Melusine's position as an enchantress longing for redemption and rescue from the evil sorcerer Albergo by Raymund, who is torn between her and the virtuous Bertha. The use of such devices as an opening Huntsmen's Chorus seems by now to be not so much imitating *Der Freischütz* and *Euryanthe* as invoking something constant in the national consciousness, and the excellent scoring of the supernatural sequences owes more to Mendelssohn than to Weber. Mendelssohn himself had begun work on *Die Loreley*, leaving only two not very effective choruses on his death in 1847, and the subject was taken up by Max Bruch. His *Die Loreley* (1863) is another attempt at dramatizing the contest between sacred and profane love, with the peasant girl Lenore selling her soul to the Rhine Spirits in exchange for an irresistible beauty that duly enslaves Count Otto and eventually compels him to hurl himself into the Rhine after her. Composed in numbers separated by recitative, the work includes some attractive arias and choruses, and a powerful Invocation of the Rhine spirits that derives from the Wolf's Glen but also owes something to Wagner in its scoring: this did not save Bruch from finding his opera used by the Press as a stick with which to beat Wagner. Sacred and profane come into full conflict with *Die Katakomben* (1862), Ferdinand Hiller's attempt at a grand opera in Meyerbeer vein set in ancient Rome. The personal drama and eventual death of the Roman noble Lavinia is acted out against the conflict between Christianity and paganism, with Act II set entirely in the depths of the catacombs. Hiller's gift for expressive orchestration comes to his aid here, and is much needed since the work is unenterprising harmonically and, though Lavinia's part is quite strongly written, lacks melodic distinction.

But by then, Wagner's inexorable advance in the consciousness of musicians and public had made such enterprises all but untenable, with even *Der Cid* forced into a weaker position than it might have found without his presence on the scene. Awareness of *The Ring* was emerging: excerpts from *Das Rheingold* and *Die Walküre* had been played in Vienna on 26 December 1862, and vocal scores published in 1861 and 1865, though the two operas were not staged until 1869 and 1870.

Wagner had recently finished his first opera, *Die Feen*, when in June 1834 he also published the first of his writings on music, *Die deutsche Oper*. The essay appeared anonymously in the newly founded *Zeitung für die elegante Welt* which (despite its title) reflected the radical views of its editor, Heinrich Laube. Though there is still a possible doubt as to the essay's authenticity, it sets out many of the ideas that in these years were absorbing Wagner, ones which find renewed expression in *Über deutsches Musikwesen* (1840) and again in the early part of *Oper und Drama* (1852). The pedantry of German music, and German opera's failure beside the song of Italian opera (especially Bellini, for whom Wagner's admiration never wavered) and beside the drama of French opera (especially Gluck and Auber), are equally deplored, with the social and political conditions of eighteenth-century German courts held largely responsible in *Über deutsches Musikwesen*. Here, Mozart is singled out as incarnating the history of German art and artists, and *Die Zauberflöte* claimed as the first great German opera: 'Bis dahin hat die deutsche Oper so gut wie gar nicht existiert; mit diesem Werke war sie erschaffen' (Wagner, *GS*, 1, 162) ('Until then German opera was as good as completely non-existent; with this work it was created'). Weigl and Winter are mildly commended, but Weber is reproved for having over-reached himself with *Euryanthe*, Spohr for lack of drama and Marschner for imitating Weber in the interests of quick popularity. The essay ends with praise for Boieldieu and especially for Auber's *La Muette de Portici*, and with a vision of German and French opera linked in a supreme brotherhood.

Über deutsches Musikwesen was published on 12 July 1840, almost ten months after Wagner's arrival in Paris, in the *Revue et Gazette musicale*. The first of his Paris writings, it is clearly designed to flatter

French sensibilities while at the same time drawing attention to the presence in Paris of a German composer with ambitions. Notoriously, Wagner often wrote inconsistently, self-contradictingly, selectively, with different ends in mind, sometimes arguing a case and sometimes trying out a theory which his creativity might then swiftly overtake, describing events as he felt they ought to have happened rather than as they did (even when not writing actual fiction), veering in his political views and unleashing ideas that could be brilliantly original and far-sighted, sometimes merely foolish, or driven by prejudices that could descend to the repulsive anti-Semitic utterances. The Old Bayreuth fidelities that confused his musical genius with a steady system of ideas have long since fallen away; keys to 'secrets' of his formal principles are no longer found operative; Jungian or Freudian or Marxist responses have taken their place as only part of the history of Wagner reception; but it is still possible to encounter interpretations of his work that rest upon the untenable assumption that he was consistent throughout a creative career that combined the most extraordinary single-mindedness with many changes of stance. In touching here – no more than that – on some of the ways in which he is an heir musically to what had gone before him in German opera, it is still important to remember the length of his career, the gradual development of some works that lay dormant for much of that length, and the changing contexts in which he wrote and composed.

Die Feen rests to some extent upon the example of German Romantic opera in Weber's *Der Freischütz*, but more upon the Marschner of *Der Vampyr* (as Wagner was willing to admit) and particularly *Hans Heiling* (as, joining a long line of composers trying to cover their real tracks, he was less willing to admit). There is also a touch of Papageno and Papagena in the buffo pair of lovers; and, especially in the vocal writing, Wagner is even more dependent upon French and Italian example than is often accepted. However, the Romantic tradition of water-spirits or mountain-spirits or other supernatural beings attempting union with mortals was by now an ageing genre, familiar from various operas of earlier decades but for

Wagner needing transformation into subtler expression. This is only one of many instances in his career where, especially in a composer with such an acute response to so much in previous German musical history, it is not only the significant detail which catches his ear, but the gathering weight of historically influential ideas which guides his mind. Though Wagner cannot have known Hoffmann's *Undine*, the importance of such a work by a man whose writings he greatly admired would have lent force to his acknowledgement of the idea, and Hoffmann's Romantic enthusiasm for Gozzi must have played a part in the selection of *La donna serpente* as his subject material. *Die Feen* draws the substance of its plot from Gozzi, with its tale of the half-fairy Ada and the human Arindal surviving trials to achieve union and immortality in her magic realm; there are also anticipations of later Wagnerian ideas, acknowledged when the opera was described in *Eine Mittheilung an meine Freunde* (1851). The most striking of these, as well as the union of human and supernatural, are the forbidden question and, above all, redemption through love into some eternal, mystical condition. It was also a characteristic of the German Romantic operas of the first three decades of the century, with so many new stimuli working upon them, to have included more original musical ideas than the talents of their composers were able to develop thoroughly. The most significant feature in this opera is the tendency to pursue the interest shown by many of Wagner's predecessors in extending a continuous musical growth across whole scenes. He does not yet possess the technique to restrain this from a certain prolixity, but *Die Feen* is remarkable in many ways, in its own right as well as when set beside the generally sorry operatic fare of the 1830s, and also for its adumbrations of much that was to come.

Wagner's impatience with German opera soon began to show after *Die Feen*. The June in which he published *Die deutsche Oper* found him spending an enjoyable holiday in Bohemia with Theodor Apel, and by his own account responding with enthusiasm to the work of Laube and the writers who had been labelled Junges Deutschland. With their embracing of liberal politics in the wake of the July Revolution of 1830, and their rejection of dogmatic Christianity, of the unrealities in Romanticism and of what they saw as bourgeois constraints on sexual morality, the Young Germans had an immediate appeal for Wagner. He shared their admiration for Wilhelm Heinse's strange novel *Ardinghello* (1787), which, though originally something of a pioneering Romantic *Künstlerroman*, had won new appeal through its delight in Italian art and its celebration of a communistic society in the Greek islands where the hero eventually settles, surrounded by lovers. Such ideas, coupled with the impression made by Wilhelmine Schröder-Devrient in Bellini's *Romeo and Juliet*, helped to turn Wagner away from German models. For *Das Liebesverbot*, he relocated *Measure for Measure* from Vienna to Palermo, making Shakespeare's Angelo into a hypocritical German pedant, Friedrich, and the outcome of the plot into a carnival in which the vitality of the people triumphs over a repressive – and repressed – ruler, overthrows bourgeois morality and ushers in a new era of emotional freedom. The work is, however, not Italian in the sense that Wagner's predecessor of the previous two decades, Meyerbeer, had composed actual Italian operas. Though the music has a brightness almost totally lacking in *Die Feen*, such Italian gestures as there are lie on the surface of German craftsmanship, which includes some skilful use of reminiscence motive owing more to *Euryanthe* than Wagner cared to admit. Moreover, Bellini is a less striking model than Auber, to whose *La Muette de Portici*, as Wagner did admit, the music (in particular the revolutionary tone of the concluding carnival) owes much.

Rienzi, written partly in 1838–9 in Riga and resumed after a gap in Paris in 1840, was Wagner's attempt to win the success which Meyerbeer had shown was possible at the Opéra. However, Hans von Bülow's mordant witticism about *Rienzi* being Meyerbeer's best opera misses the mark, for the work leans more directly on *La Muette de Portici* and all that Wagner was to praise in his obituary article *Erinnerungen an Auber* of 1871, especially the absorption of arias and ensembles into a larger structure and the pace and urgency of the narrative recitative. There also stands behind the work the stately example of Spontini, as Wagner described him in *Erinnerungen an Spontini* in 1851:

> das letzte Glied einer Reihe von Komponisten, deren erstes Glied in
> Gluck zu finden ist; was Gluck wollte, und zuerst grundsätzlich
> unternahm, die möglichst vollständige Dramatisirung der Opernkantate,
> das führte Spontini – so weit es in der musikalischen Opernform zu
> erreichen war – aus. (Wagner, *GS*, v, 86)

> (the last link in a chain of composers whose first is to be found in Gluck;
> what Gluck wanted, and first undertook so fundamentally, the most
> thorough dramatization possible of the operatic cantata, was carried
> through – in so far as it could be achieved in musical operatic form – by
> Spontini.)

Wagner's wholehearted embracing of the eighteenth- and early nineteenth-century German faith in Gluck as an example for German
grand opera also took practical form in his work arranging *Iphigénie
en Aulide*. His resentment of Meyerbeer for failing to help him during
his painful two and a half years in Paris still shows in this article, but
the issue of Meyerbeer's influence is different: Wagner took more
from Auber and Spontini, even from another composer he admired,
Halévy, than from Meyerbeer's brilliant handling of Parisian grand
opera. Above all, this shows in his careful formal structures, which
were designed to draw form and expression closer together
(especially in the last three of the work's five acts: see Deathridge,
1977, 40–1). For all its faults, *Rienzi* is a serious attempt, in so far as
the conditions of Parisian opera and Wagner's technique in handling
them permitted, at a synthesis of music and drama more radical than
mere simultaneity of different theatrical means.

It did not take Wagner long to insist that his first three operas were
of a different order from all that followed, that with *Der fliegende
Holländer* 'schlug ich eine neue Bahn ein' (Wagner, *GS*, IV, 316) ('I
struck off on a new path'). In considering some of the directions
which this path took, leading Wagner on from what had gone before
in German opera, it is important to distinguish between different
kinds of influence. It should also be borne in mind that though the

greatness of his achievement sets him in a dominating position in the history of the genre, the attitude to him of some German historians (especially those closer to his own time), as the culmination of a long series of attempts at realizing the true condition of German opera, both misrepresents him and does very much less than justice to what had been previously achieved in a rich history. This temptation was the greater because the opening of Bayreuth in 1876 with the first complete performance of *Der Ring des Nibelungen* came as the first major artistic event in a Germany so recently, at last, politically unified.

Wagner's capacity to remember and absorb any musical idea that might nourish his creativity is famous. Sometimes these *trouvailles* are no more than coincidental, or the common property of Romantic music. Sometimes the effectiveness of a gesture caught in his mind, whether consciously or not, to emerge in a similar guise. The closeness of the Mountain Queen's warning appearance in *Hans Heiling* to the *Todesverkündigung* in *Die Walküre* is a familiar example (see p. 334), and many others are to be found in the operas, often quite minor pieces, which he knew from his work as a conductor or in other ways. Sometimes particular stylistic traits, such as Spohr's harmony or Weber's orchestration, fostered ideas and formed re-sources that were to mark his style. These were a simple influence on a good many other composers as well, and certainly Wagner's idiom would hardly have been the same without them, but it is useful to make a distinction between them and larger dramatic or musical ideas that were more profoundly influential on his work. For all his equivocal relationship to Weber, the opposition of a 'dark' and a 'light' pair in *Lohengrin* owed much to *Euryanthe*, and the idea of Tannhäuser's divided soul to that opera's Lysiart and to Marschner's Ruthven, Heiling and Bois-Guilbert. Wagner's contact with Parisian grand opera left an ineradicable mark upon his dramaturgy. Some of its theatrical devices, such as the mechanics for transformations and the consequent musical gestures, are scarcely an influence so much as ideas taken over and put to new and original use. Other features which affected him more significantly can be observed in scenes from the interrupted wedding of *Lohengrin* to the *Festwiese* in *Die Meister-singer*, the conflagration of Valhalla in *Götterdämmerung* and the collapse of Klingsor's castle in *Parsifal*. Schopenhauer's impact upon him in 1854, overtaking that of Feuerbach (and actually leading to a rewriting of the end of *Siegfrieds Tod*), changed, or more accurately confirmed, his art at the deepest level, leaving its mark upon everything he wrote from that moment; and this was but the most important of a range of influences coming from outside music on a composer the breadth of whose reading astonished not only Nietzsche among his friends. Though it is, by the nature of the manner in which a composer absorbs such different kinds of influence, mistaken to try to draw a dividing line between them, they should be recognised as operating on different expressive levels.

There has never been serious disagreement that the greatest single musical influence on Wagner was Beethoven. He himself, though he changed his mind and shifted his ground here as in most matters, always acknowledged this. His admiration ranged from his youthful copying and transcription of the Ninth Symphony for piano, by way of performances of the Ninth with which he always impressed his audiences, to writings that include the story *Eine Pilgerfahrt zu Beethoven* (1840) and essays, above all the centenary tribute *Beethoven* (1870) in which the importance of Beethoven to him is repeatedly expounded. His copying of the Ninth sprang from his immediate fascination with the haunting sound of the bare fifths that open the symphony, and in this case we need not doubt the testimony of *Mein Leben* when the evidence is plain in the opening of the Allegro con brio of his own youthful C major symphony and especially with the ghostly effect, which he found in these bars, transferred to the opening of *Der fliegende Holländer*. There are plenty of examples of other gestures, taken from Beethoven, which find their way into his early instrumental works, where of course one would expect to find them before they had been fully absorbed (see Kropfinger, 1974); but the influence of the Ninth ran far deeper.

Wagner was by no means alone in this. It is not too much to say that the whole of nineteenth-century music was set on a new course with the astonishing moment in Vienna on the night of 7 May 1824 when a man rose to his feet among the instruments and sang, 'O Freunde, nicht diese Töne!' Beethoven's Ninth served to confirm Hector Berlioz's growing conviction that the concept of symphony must be extended to include dramatically inspired forms, and he went so far as to compare Beethoven's opening up of a new world of music to him with Shakespeare's revelation of a new universe of poetry. Though Wagner liked to claim that it was a rehearsal of Beethoven's Ninth soon after his arrival in Paris which inspired his *Faust-Ouvertüre* as the intended first movement of a Faust symphony, it seems more likely that the true stimulus was the experience of hearing what could be achieved with dramatic symphony in Berlioz's *Roméo et Juliette*. Moreover, the thematic transformations in the finale of the Ninth were probably the single most important influence on Liszt's *Faust Symphony* and Piano Sonata, and on his whole technique of handling thematic material. Liszt and Berlioz exchanged dedications of their *Faust Symphony* and *Damnation of Faust*; Wagner sent the score of *Tristan* to Berlioz with an admiring inscription to him as the author of *Roméo et Juliette*.

Wagner's own admiration for Beethoven was lifelong. His youthful devotion to the Ninth found expression in *Eine Pilgerfahrt zu Beethoven*, as the deaf composer outlines to his young visitor where the future might lie: 'Warum sollte aber die Vokalmusik nicht ebenso gut als die Instrumentalmusik einen großen, ernsten Genre bilden können?' (Wagner, *GS*, I, 110) ('But why should vocal music not form a great, serious genre as good as instrumental music?'). *Eine Pilgerfahrt zu Beethoven* is no vainglorious attempt to claim a mantle of greatness, but an affecting account of an imagined meeting between the deaf master and the young composer 'R . . .', who comes to understand that from the Ninth Symphony there must now proceed a unification of words and music on a new, dramatic plane. 'Beethoven' goes on to look for a synthesis of the 'elemental' music of instruments and the 'individual' music of song in his new choral symphony. Speaking in his own voice, Wagner pursues the idea in *Das Kunstwerk der Zukunft* (1850), *Oper und Drama* (1851), *Zukunftsmusik*

(1861), *Beethoven* (1870) (in which his ground has shifted under the impact of reading Schopenhauer), *Über die Anwendung der Musik auf das Drama* (1879), and elsewhere in his writings. Yet from his unfeigned admiration for Beethoven and the Ninth, a good deal of misunderstanding has flowed. Even his last years, in 1880, at a time when he was contemplating writing symphonies after *Parsifal*, he was obliged to correct misapprehensions:

> Wie neulich auch davon die Rede war, daß R. die Beethoven'sche Melodie fortgesetzt habe, verneint er das entschieden und sagt, das sei etwas ganz Abgeschlossenes; 'ich hätte nicht komponieren können, wie ich es getan habe, wenn Beethoven nicht gewesen wäre, aber was ich verwendet und erweitert habe, sind vereinzelte geniale Züge bei dramatischen Vorgängern wie selbst Auber, indem ich an etwas andrem mich hielt als die Oper'.   (Cosima Wagner, 1976–7, II, 635)

> (Recently, too, when it was suggested that R. had carried on the Beethoven type of melody, he denied it emphatically, saying that had been something complete in itself: 'I could not have composed in the way I have done if Beethoven had never existed, but what I have used and developed are isolated strokes of genius in my dramatic predecessors, including even Auber, allowing myself to be led by something other than opera'. Cosima Wagner, 1978–80, II, 572)

There have been many attempts to pin down the nature of Beethoven's influence on Wagner. Similarities of gesture, based on his thorough knowledge of Beethoven, do not account for enough. The gently throbbing chords in the Adagio of Beethoven's E♭ Quartet (Op. 127) possibly stayed in Wagner's mind when he came to the section in the *Tristan* love duet beginning 'O sink hernieder' (Kropfinger, 1975, 209–13), but if so it is an atmospheric influence rather than one of idiom. His admiration for the C♯ minor Quartet (Op. 131) was enormous, but as selective as a composer's will usually tend to be:

> Alles liegt in den 4 ersten Noten des Anfanges, dann übergibt er sich der Fugen-Arbeit, die selbst – für Musiker – nicht sehr interessant ist . . . es gehörte zum Ehrenpunkt eines Musikers, eine Fuge zu schreiben. Aber bei Roheiten, Ungeschicktheiten kommt es hier zu einer Stimmung, von der ich verstehe, daß er sie hatte.   (Cosima Wagner, 1976–7, II, 636–7)

(Everything lies in the first 4 notes at the beginning, then he busies himself with some fugal writing, which is not very interesting – even for musicians . . . it was a point of honour with a musician to write a fugue. But through the roughnesses and awkwardnesses there emerges a mood such as I can well imagine him to have had. Cosima Wagner, 1978–80, II, 573)

Writing of the movement in *Beethoven*, as part of an imaginative account of a day in the composer's life, Wagner suggests that nothing more melancholy had ever been expressed in music. If he had been interested in technical influence more than mood, he might have remarked (unless he was deliberately drawing attention away from it) that this slow fugue, one as far distant as it is possible to imagine from musicianly obligations of honour, proceeds through a wonderfully judged key progression of rising thirds from C♯ until its goal is reached with the D that is to be the satisfying key of the second movement. It is a technique Wagner himself matches with the descending progression of keys in the Wahn-Monolog in *Die Meistersinger* that brings him down in a chain of thirds from the F♯ of Wahn to the warming C major dawn of 'Johannistag'. Furthermore, Wagner takes little account of the Quartet's Andante variations. In this movement of genius, it is not the outline of the theme which is decorated, after eighteenth-century fashion; rather, the few notes embodying its melodic and harmonic essence, which themselves are subject to rearrangement during the movement, evolve into widely differing melodic and rhythmic forms – variation, in fact, from a theme's innermost nature outwards, something that might have held creative interest for Wagner and his handling of motive. Though the Diabelli Variations were regular fare in Wahnfried evenings, Wagner responded with enjoyment but little personal involvement, as he admitted to Cosima in connexion with the variations in the E major sonata (Op. 109): 'Auf die Variationen der e moll [*recte* dur] Sonate zurückkommend, sagt er, Beeth. habe diese Form geliebt und sich ein Gütchen getan in den 33 V.; er, R., könne es nicht' (Cosima Wagner, 1976–7, 226) ('Returning to the variations in the E major Sonata, R. says that Beeth. loved this form and gave himself a treat in the 33 V.; he, R., cannot do it.' Cosima Wagner, 1978–80, 197).

Wagner was, clearly, less concerned as a composer with the thematic contemplation inherent in variation and fugue, which increasingly absorbed Beethoven in his last years, than with the dynamic processes of sonata that especially marked the symphonies he conducted most, the Third, Fifth, Seventh and Ninth. The remark recorded by Cosima rings completely true: he was led by strokes of genius in his dramatic predecessors, but would not have composed as he did if Beethoven had never existed. German opera had never really proceeded beyond the use of reminiscence motive for purposes of dramatic illustration and a limited range of development, and it is difficult to see where a new move could have originated: it did not come from Spohr or Marschner, who lived until 1859 and 1861, and even had he survived beyond 1826 it could scarcely have come from Weber, whose sonata-form movements generally reflect a lack of commitment to the process. It did not at first come from Wagner, whose increasingly subtle handling of motive for the different creative purposes of *Der fliegende Holländer*, *Tannhäuser* and *Lohengrin* does not essentially bring about a transformation from reminiscence motive into Leitmotive. In drawing sonata and drama together into what was to be the condition of Leitmotive with *The Ring*, Wagner was not 'carrying on the Beethoven melody' or imitating his processes, but from Beethoven's example searching out new techniques of his own to serve what he conceived to be the dramatic needs of tragedy. In this sense, Beethoven was indeed an inspiration, one that influenced the whole of Wagner's thinking about musical drama. The moment was ripe. For all the hesitations and the tentativeness, German opera, especially since the influx of French operas in the wake of the French Revolution, had increasingly been looking to the symphonic means that were its national heritage, and therefore to the role of the orchestra and to developmental techniques; yet it had never been able to find a way of outgrowing the limitations of reminiscence motive while it still lacked the major creative imagination that could justify new techniques by their development in theory and then in successful practice.

Wagner's 1849 flight from the revolution in Dresden to Switzerland gave him the opportunity to take stock in the wake of the gains made with *Tannhäuser* and *Lohengrin*. The most important of his writings from this time, *Das Kunstwerk der Zukunft* (1849), *Oper und Drama* (1850–1) and *Eine Mittheilung an meine Freunde* (1851), argue a new operatic aesthetic, *Oper und Drama* in particular exploring some technical ideas on poetry and its setting that were soon to be overtaken by his own creative achievement. It is a work in the line of earlier theoretical writings, which to an extent it reflects in its argument for a *Gesamtkunstwerk* based on the example of ancient Greece. In setting off on his own course, with his somewhat specious arguments about the severance of the arts of Greece in its decline and their coming together in an artwork of the future, Wagner is really trying to think out and defend his own creative future. The ideal of a *Gesamtkunstwerk* (if not by this name) had a long history in Germany, from Harsdörffer in the seventeenth century with *Seelewig* and the eighteenth-century Hamburg controversialists, by way of philosophers including Leibniz and Schelling, writers of the stature of Lessing and Herder, aestheticians of whom Sulzer was the most important, the contributors to the *AMZ*, and composer-critics led by Hoffmann, Weber and Mosel. What tended to distinguish the German writings from those of other nations was the ideal of a genuine fusion of the arts, rather than their simultaneous stage presence; and the general German acknowledgement of Algarotti and admiration for Gluck only served to emphasize this. Wagner's ideas included some not very lucid responses to the socialist aspirations of the years in which he was writing, as well as what must have seemed to many of the 'friends' he addressed the impossible ambition of a festival theatre dedicated to his works. On a technical level, he argues the case for *Stabreim* (even if he later much modified his original argument), this archaic ligament of oral Teutonic epic constituting a genuinely new contribution to the debate. It was one that led to a crucial breakthrough in that the periodicity of end-rhyme, with its cadential implications, could yield to the fluency of what he called *unendliche Melodie* and the freedom of melodic utterance, guided by words and meaning, that even the earliest

German opera composers sought (later, of course, he brought back rhyme when it suited him). With this, he found his own way through the problems that had beset generations. The significance of motive, under the inspiration of Beethoven, in creating a new kind of musical order was part of this discovery of direction.

The labelling of motives (initiated by the assiduous and well-meaning Hans von Wolzogen for the first Bayreuth *Ring*) has long been found misleading, though some use of it is inescapable if only as verbal shorthand. The fundamental problem with labelling motives is that it ignores both the motives' wide variety of nature and purpose and the fact that this variety is essential to Wagner's musical language. For instance, the motive associated with the Giants, a musical analogue of their lumbering gait, is no more than the kind of reminiscence motive Wagner would have met many times in the operas of 'dramatic predecessors' such as Méhul, Weber and Spohr, and its principal transformation, turning the perfect fourths into augmented fourths when Fafner becomes a dragon, is less sophisticated than much in the 'predecessors'. On the other hand, as Wagner himself points out in *Über die Anwendung der Musik auf das Drama*, a simple nature motive can merge with the motive associated with Valhalla and 'mehr als Wotan's Worte uns ein Bild der furchtbar verdüsterten Seele des leidenden Gottes gewahren lassen sollte' (Wagner, *GS*, X, 188) ('more than Wotan's words gives us an image of the dreadfully darkened soul of the suffering god'). He goes on to draw attention to the Rhinemaidens' motive 'mit welchem diese in kindlicher Freude das glänzende Gold umjauchzen' (Wagner, *GS*, X, 189) ('with which they exult over the shining gold in childlike joy'), and to point out that the later, violent transformations of this would be unthinkably sensational in a symphony when there was no dramatic motivation. This follows on from a discussion in which he attempts to dispose of the term *Leitmotiv* (he accepted *Motiv*) and refers to *Grundthemen*, or 'basic themes', directing attention on to the musical processes in which they live dramatically. Examples of many different kinds could be multiplied almost indefinitely, for it is not too much to say that everything in *The Ring* which can be identified as a motive has its own individual nature and operation in the drama.

It is, then, in the development of motives that the drama resides; and the crucial move from even the most sophisticated use of reminiscence motive into symphonic use of *Leitmotiv* – the influence of the 'dramatic predecessors' merging into that of Beethoven – takes place as the music comes to shape and embody the drama. In the wake of the two of his operas most deeply infused with Schopenhauer, *Tristan und Isolde* and *Die Meistersinger von Nürnberg* (the one newly conceived, the other long-meditated and now transformed), Wagner's resumption of work on *The Ring* brought him quickly to Act III of *Siegfried*. The Schopenhauerian first scene of this act can count among his greatest achievements. Wotan, torn between his need to stop the young hero who will climb the mountain and pass through the fire to wake Brünnhilde, and his longing for these events to come about and to resign himself to the end, summons up Erda for her counsel. In an orchestral prelude lasting fifty-four bars before the curtain rises, and another dozen before Wotan enters, the turmoil in the god's mind is portrayed. Motives are brought in and combined. Erda's rising figure, its falling inversion for the end of the gods she once prophesied and the Valkyries' galloping arpeggios combine, especially, with the powerful descending scale that was, back in *Das Rheingold*, first associated with Wotan's spear but has moved through representing the agreements engraved upon it and his infraction of them, all now merged into the descent into darkness that is its consequence. Not even the most assiduous motive-spotter can possibly now listen by ticking these off by name: they have evolved into a symphonic process in which (leaving aside the violent energy and the dark scoring of the music) associations accrued over the length of the cycle, not referentially to things or persons but progressively as their meaning has evolved with the drama, work directly upon the mind of the listener. That Wagner set his greatest store by the musical procedures being of prime dramatic significance is confirmed by his sketches for this prelude, which show him struggling (and at first failing) to get the sequentially ascending entries of the descending scale on the right notes for the musical structure, and having to work out his harmonic pattern in shorthand at the bottom of the page. There is no narrative content in this music: it is pure symphonic dramatic writing.

However, 'influence' is little better than plagiaristic if its beneficiary does not put it to a use beyond anything that its originator could have envisaged. There are crucial differences between Beethoven's symphonic procedures and Wagner's. The only area of a sonata form movement relevant to Wagner is the development section. The first hearing of any of his motives is a statement but not a symphonic exposition, and they go through nothing comparable to the summation of experience in a symphonic recapitulation: a final new motive (once briefly adumbrated) is to be heard at the very last moment of *Götterdämmerung*. Wagner confronted this problem in a key passage of *Über die Anwendung der Musik auf das Drama*.

> Dennoch muß die neue Form der dramatischen Musik, um wiederum als Musik ein Kunstwerk zu bilden, die Einheit des Symphoniesatzes aufweisen, und dieß erreicht sie, wenn sie, im innigsten Zusammenhange mit demselben, über das ganze Drama sich erstreckt, nicht nur über einzelne kleinere, willkürlich herausgehobene Theile desselben. Diese Einheit giebt sich dann in einem das ganze Kunstwerk durchziehenden Gewebe von Grundthemen, welche sich, ähnlich wie im Symphoniesatze, gegenüber stehen, ergänzen, neu gestalten, trennen und verbinden: nur daß hier die ausgeführte und aufgeführte dramatische Handlung die Gesetze der Scheidungen und Verbindungen giebt, welche dort allerursprünglichst den Bewegungen des Tanzes entnommen waren. (Wagner, *GS*, x, 185)

(However, the new form of dramatic music must, in order to become a work of art as music, demonstrate the unity of the symphonic movement, and this it achieves when, in the most intimate inner cohesion, it extends over the whole drama, not merely over a few smaller, arbitrarily emphasized parts. This unity consists of, pervading the entire work of art, a web of basic themes which as in a symphonic movement contrast, complete, re-form, separate and combine; except that here the construction and execution of the dramatic action gives the laws of the separations and combinings, which were there originally taken from the movement of the dance.)

Wagner's metaphor of a 'web' (or 'fabric') recalls Weber's, in connexion with Spohr's *Faust*, of a few melodies which like 'leise Fäden' (delicate threads) run through the whole work and hold it together (Weber, 1908, 275; Weber, 1981, 193). However, there is as great a difference between threads and a whole web as there is between Spohr's methods (or Weber's own) and Wagner's. In Wagner's case, it is the evolution of the motives and of their meaning which forms the drama, so that in a passage such as the opening scene of Act III of *Siegfried* all that has gone before comes together in a new dramatic condition.

This scene, containing Wotan's defeat by Siegfried and his departure to await the end in Valhalla, demands nothing less than the richness of expressive technique which, after *Tristan* and *Die Meistersinger*, Wagner could now command; and there is some evidence that he had earlier felt the need to break off work on *Siegfried*. On 1 October 1878 Cosima recorded, in connexion with *Tristan*, 'R. kommt darauf zurück, wie es ihm Bedürfnis gewesen, sich auszurasen musikalisch, weil er in den Nibelungen durch das Drama gezwungen gewesen war, sehr oft den musikalischen Ausdruck einzuengen' (Cosima Wagner, 1976–7, 188) ('R. talks again of his need at that time to push himself to the limit musically, since in the *Nibelungen* the requirements of the drama frequently forced him to restrict the musical expression': Cosima Wagner, 1978–80, 161). He also declared that it was the urge to express himself symphonically for once that led to *Tristan*.

Tristan can indeed be felt as symphonic in nature, but the many attempts that have been made to pin this down are inevitably bound to do so by reference to previous symphonic example. Wagner's originality, and his characteristic Romantic necessity to find new forms for each new creative task, meant that each of his remaining three individual operas, *Tristan*, *Meistersinger* and *Parsifal*, demanded a rethinking of what might still be experienced as symphonic. In the case of *Tristan*, the heightened role of the orchestra involves the development of ideas with much greater freedom of movement, as inner states rather than outer actions are explored; and this is achieved not only by means of the chromatic harmony that was, famously, brought to a new intensity as a consistent element of the work, but in the movement between sections that are tonally comparatively secure (as at the most intense inwardness of the centre of the Act II love duet) and those which are chromatically and modulatorily more active.

With *Die Meistersinger*, the symphonic techniques are, in the nature of the subject, entirely different. In an opera whose polarities are order (both supportive and constricting) and disorder (both threatening and challenging), tonal polarities are as remote as possible: that is, a C major representing the work's most secure and self-confident aspect and an F♯ that stands for a Schopenhauerian *Wahn*, the distorting illusion which Sachs must turn to positive account. The language of the opera is, again in the nature of the subject, primarily melodic (rather than more emphatically harmonic as in *Tristan*), the most important elements of it deriving from an actual *Meisterton*. This gives Wagner the opening phrase for his overture, for the succeeding chorale, for Walther's Spring Song and later Prize Song, for Eva's despairing outburst to Sachs and for much else suffusing the invention of the whole opera (Example 42). Especially, there is in the Quintet both the reconciliation of the phrase and its inversion simultaneously, and also the transfiguration of F♯ (written as G♭) as a positive tonality. It is the multivalent handling of the melodic kernel of a song that lies at the centre of an opera about song as a metaphor of order and renewal (see Warrack, 1994).

Though it is the summation of his career, *Parsifal* is of Wagner's mature works the least readily heard in symphonic terms. However different, the opposition of chromaticism and diatonicism derives from both *Tristan* and *Meistersinger*; there is also greater subtlety of harmonic practice than in *Tristan* and of melodic practice than in *Meistersinger*. It also has, set at its heart, the strangest of all Wagner's

(a)

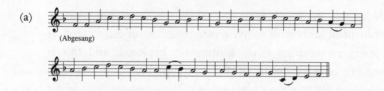

(Abgesang)

(b)

etc.

(c)

(d)

(e)

(f)

(g)

Example 42   Wagner: *Die Meistersinger von Nürnberg* (1868)
(a) Original Meisterton
(b) Overture
(c) Act I, Chorale
(d) Act I, Walther's Spring Song
(e) Act III, Walther's Prize Song
(f) Act III, David's song
(g) Eva's outburst to Sachs
(h) Act III, Quintet

"Durch Mit-leid wis-send, der rei- ne Tor, har- re sein, den ich er - kor."

(Through compassion made understanding, the pure fool. Wait for him, the one I chose.)

Example 43   Wagner: *Parsifal* (1882), Gurnemanz

motives and the most mysterious in operation, that of Parsifal
himself (Example 43).

In its full version, this is heard only twice in the entire opera. Its
first appearance, near the start, is as a three-bar orchestral allusion
when Gurnemanz speaks of Amfortas's suffering, 'Toren sind wir,
auf Lind'rung zu hoffen, wo einzig Heilung lindert' ('We are fools to
hope for his relief when only a cure will relieve him'), followed by a
briefer allusion several bars later under Gurnemanz's words, 'Ihm
hilft nur eines, nur der Eine!' ('Only one thing can help him, only the
One himself!'). Soon after the wounded Amfortas is borne in on his

litter, his unknown redeemer is identified with the words that go with the first half of the motive, 'Durch Mitleid wissend, der reine Thor', though these are also allusive as they are broken up by an exchange with Gurnemanz, 'und war's nicht so?' 'uns sagtest du es so' ('was that not it?' 'you told us so'). Only at the end of Gurnemanz's narration, and then in the Hall of the Grail, is the motive given in full, with its words. Its later occurrences are fragmented, as with Kundry's naming of Parsifal, in the violent distortions of the Act III prelude and at the very end of the work combined with the motive that 'signifies no more and no less than the ambivalent core of the work; the suffering of Amfortas before the means of salvation he has forfeited' (Beckett, 1981, 35). The 'anticipations' of the motive are not really, as has sometimes been suggested, a belated use of the technique proposed by Wagner in *Oper und Drama* as 'Ahnung' but not put into practice. Rather, they are citations of something known to Amfortas and Gurnemanz (and perhaps Kundry), but not to the others on the stage, or to us in the audience. Unlike Wagner's other motives, some of the most important of which form the Prelude, it already 'exists' before the work begins, giving it a unique condition in time; and only when it has been fully stated does it recede, as variation of part of it can begin. It is the subtlest example of a characteristic of other *Parsifal* motives, which infiltrate the musical action in a manner that, if we are still to refer to Beethoven, at last suggest a distant and transmuted response to the meditations upon melodic essence in his last sonatas and quartets.

The distorting effect that the very greatest creative figures have on our perception of the long history of one art form in one national tradition is almost impossible to avoid. This is particularly true of those artists whose late works take them beyond a maturity which still has at least a coherence with the tradition the artist has developed. No one follows, except chronologically, Michelangelo's last sculptures, or *The Tempest*, or Beethoven's last quartets, or *Parsifal*. The chance that Mozart wrote only a single German operatic masterpiece, and the further chance of his early death, only add to the impression, unjust to the integrity and achievement of many earlier German operas, that the whole tradition reaches, in the works of Wagner's maturity, a consummation that makes a particular sense of all that preceded them. To give the composers and works that preceded Wagner's masterpieces their proper due, to see them clear in their times and places as they would have been seen if Wagner had died after writing *Rienzi*, has been one of the purposes of this book. To contribute to giving Wagner his proper due has been another.

APPENDIX

LIST OF OPERAS

This is intended as a checklist of the German works discussed or mentioned in the text. Under genre, what seems to be the composer's preferred appellation is first given, though this often varies from MS to published scores to catalogues, playbills and other references; the description Singspiel (Spl) covers a very wide range, from plays with song insertions to large-scale operas, but here indicates that a work has spoken dialogue. Account is not generally taken of different versions.

Composer	Title	Text Composer	Genre	Acts	First produced
André	Der Töpfer		Komische Oper (Spl)	1	Hanau, 1773
	Erwin und Elmire	Johann Wolfgang von Goethe	Schauspiel mit Gesang (Spl)	2	Frankfurt, 1775
	Das wütende Heer	Christoph Friedrich Bretzner	Operette (Spl)	3	Berlin, 1780
	Belmont und Constanze	Christoph Friedrich Bretzner	Operette (Spl)	3	Berlin, 1781
Asplmayr	Die Kinder der Natur	Johann Joseph Felix von Kurz	Singspiel	2	Vienna, 1778
Beethoven	Vestas Feuer	Emanuel Schikaneder	(Grosse Oper)	unf.	(comp. 1803)
	Leonore 1 (Fidelio 1)	Joseph Sonnleithner	Oper (Spl)	3	Vienna, 1805
	Leonore 2 (Fidelio 2)	Sonnleithner, rev. Stefan von Breuning	Oper (Spl)	2	Vienna, 1806

	Fidelio (3)	Sonnleithner, rev. Georg Friedrich Treitschke	Oper (Spl)	2	Vienna, 1814
Benda	*Ariadne auf Naxos*	Johann Christian Brandes	Duodram	1	Gotha, 1775
	Der Jahrmarkt	Friedrich Wilhelm Gotter	Komische Oper (Spl)	1	Gotha, 1775
	Medea	Friedrich Wilhelm Gotter	Melodram	1	Leipzig, 1775
	Walder	Friedrich Wilhelm Gotter	Ernsthafte Operette (Spl)	1	Gotha, 1776
	Romeo und Julie	Friedrich Wilhelm Gotter	Ernsthafte Oper (Spl)	3	Gotha, 1776
Bergt	*List gegen List*	Christoph Friedrich Bretzner	Operette (Spl)	1	Leipzig, 1797
	Das Ständchen	C. Schulz	Intermezzo (Spl)	1	Leipzig, 1802
Bierey	*Clara, Herzogin von Bretannien*	Christoph Friedrich Bretzner	Opera seria	3	Leipzig, 1803
	Rosette	Christoph Friedrich Bretzner	Singspiel	2	Leipzig, 1806
	Wladimir, Fürst v. Nowgorod	Matthäus Stegmayer	Opera seria	3	Vienna, 1807
Brandl	*Elias Rips Raps*	Wilhelm Häser	Intermezzo (Spl)	1	Breslau, 1810
Bruch	*Germania*	?Schott	Singspiel	3	(comp. 1800)
	Die Loreley	Emanuel Geibel	Grosse romantische Oper	4	Mannheim, 1863
Cannabich	*Elektra*	Wolfgang Heribert von Dalberg	Musikalische Deklamation	1	Mannheim, 1781
Clasing	*Mischelli und sein Sohn*	Anton Kirchner	Singspiel	3	Hamburg, 1806
Conradi	*Die schöne und getreue Ariadne*	Christian Heinrich Postel	–	3	Hamburg, 1691
Cornelius	*Der Barbier von Bagdad*	Composer	Komische Oper	2	Weimar, 1858
	Der Cid	Composer	Lyrisches Drama	3	Weimar, 1865

Composer	Title	Librettist	Genre	Acts	Place, Date
	Martha	'W. Friedrich' (Friedrich Riese)	Romantisch-komische Oper (Spl)	4	Vienna, 1847
	Sophia Catharina	Charlotte Birch-Pfeiffer	Romantisch-komische Oper (Spl)	4	Berlin, 1850
	Rübezahl	Gustav Heinrich Gans zu Putlitz	Romantische Oper (Spl)	3	Retzien, 1852
Franck	*Die drei Töchter des Cecrops*	Maria Aurora von Königsmark	Sing-Spiel	5	Hamburg, 1680
	Cara Mustapha	Wilhelm Vogel	Singspiel	3	Hamburg, 1686
Gläser	*Des Adlers Horst*	Karl von Holtei	Romantisch-komische Oper (Spl)	3	Berlin, 1832
Gyrowetz	*Agnes Sorel*	Joseph Sonnleithner	Grosse Oper (Spl)	3	Vienna, 1806
	Der Augenarzt	Johann Emanuel Veith	Oper (Spl)	2	Vienna, 1811
Haibel	*Der Tyroler Wastel*	Emanuel Schikaneder	Komische Oper (Spl)	3	Vienna, 1796
Handel	*Almira*	Friedrich Christian Feustking	Singspiel	3	Hamburg, 1705
? Haydn	*Die Feuersbrunst*	?	Singspiel	2	Eszterháza, ?1778
Hiller, Ferdinand	*Die Katakomben*	Moritz Hartmann	Ernste Oper	3	Wiesbaden, 1862
Hiller, J. A.	*Lottchen am Hofe*	Christian Friedrich Weisse	Comische Oper (Spl)	3	Leipzig, 1777
	Die Liebe auf dem Lande	Christian Friedrich Weisse	Comische Oper (Spl)	3	Leipzig, 1768
	Die Jagd	Christian Friedrich Weisse	Comische Oper (Spl)	3	Leipzig, 1770
Himmel	*Fanchon das Leyermädchen*	August von Kotzebue	Singspiel	3	Berlin, 1804

Composer	Title	Text	Genre	Acts	First produced
	Die Sylphen	Ludwig Robert	Zauberoper (Spl)	3	Berlin, 1806
	Der Kobold	after Friedrich Wilhelm Gotter	Komische Oper (Spl)	4	Vienna, 1813
Hoffmann	Die Maske	Composer	Singspiel	3	(comp. 1799)
	Die lustigen Musikanten	Clemens Brentano	Singspiel	2	Warsaw, 1805
	Der Trank der Unsterblichkeit	Julius von Soden	Romantische Oper (Spl)	4	(comp. 1808)
	Aurora	Franz Ignaz von Holbein	Grosse romantische Oper (Spl)	3	(comp. 1811–12)
Holstein	Undine	Friedrich de la Motte Fouqué	Zauberoper (Spl)	3	Berlin, 1816
	Der Haideschacht	Composer	Oper (Spl)	3	Dresden, 1868
	Der Erbe von Morley	Composer	Oper (Spl)	3	Leipzig, 1872
Holzbauer	Günther von Schwarzburg	Anton Klein	Singspiel	3	Mannheim, 1777
Hoven	Johanna d'Arc	Otto Prechtler	Romantische Oper (Spl)	5	Vienna, 1840
Kauer	Das Donauweibchen	Karl Friedrich Hensler	Romantisch-komisches Volksmärchen mit Gesang (Spl)	3	Vienna, 1798
Keiser	Orpheus	Friedrich Christian Bressand	Singspiel	5	Hamburg, 1698
	Octavia	Barthold Feind	Singspiel	3	Hamburg, 1705
	Masagniello	Barthold Feind	Drama musicale (Spl)	3	Hamburg, 1706
	Croesus	Lucas von Bostel	Singspiel	3	Hamburg, 1711

Composer	Title	Librettist	Genre		Place, year
Krebs	*Agnes Bernauer*	August Lewald	Grosse Oper (Spl)	4	Hamburg, 1833
Kreutzer	*Der Taucher*	Samuel Bürde	Romantische Oper (Spl)	2	Vienna, 1813
	Libussa	Joseph Karl Bernard	Romantische Oper (Spl)	3	Vienna, 1822
	Das Nachtlager in Granada	Carl von Braun	Romantische Oper (Spl)	2	Vienna, 1834
Lachner	*Catharina Cornaro*	Vernoy de St. Georges, trans. Alois Büssel	Grosse tragische Oper (Spl)	4	Munich, 1841
Lindpaintner	*Der Bergkönig*	Carl Hanisch	Romantische Oper (Spl)	3	Stuttgart, 1825
	Der Vampyr	Cäsar Max Heigel	Romantische Oper (Spl)	3	Stuttgart, 1828
	Die Macht des Liedes	Ignaz Franz Castelli	Komische Oper (Spl)	3	Stuttgart, 1836
	Die Genueserin	Carl Philipp Berger	Grosse romantische Oper (Spl)	2	Vienna, 1839
	Die sicilianische Vesper	Heribert Rau	Grosse romantische Oper (Spl)	4	Vienna, 1839
Lobe	*Lichtenstein*	Franz Dingelstedt	Festoper – Grosse Oper (Spl)	5	Stuttgart, 1846
	Die Fürstin von Granada	Composer and Philipp Sondershausen	Grosse Zauberoper (Spl)	5	Weimar, 1833
Loewe	*Rudolf, der deutsche Herr*	Composer	Grosse Oper (Spl)	3	(comp. 1825)
Lortzing	*Die drei Wünsche*	Ernst Raupach	Komisches Singspiel (Spl)	3	Berlin, 1834
	Ali Pascha von Janina	Composer	Singspiel	1	Münster, 1828
	Die beiden Schützen	Composer	Komische Oper (Spl)	3	Leipzig, 1837
	Zar und Zimmermann	Composer	Komische Oper (Spl)	3	Leipzig, 1837

Composer	Title	Text	Genre	Acts	First produced
	Caramo	Composer	Grosse komische Oper (Spl)	3	Leipzig, 1839
	Hans Sachs	Philipp Reger, Composer, Philipp Düringer	Komische Oper (Spl)	3	Leipzig, 1840
	Casanova	Composer	Komische Oper (Spl)	3	Leipzig, 1841
	Der Wildschütz	Composer	Komische Oper (Spl)	3	Leipzig, 1842
	Undine	Friedrich de la Motte Fouqué	Romantische Zauberoper (Spl)	4	Magdeburg, 1845
	Der Waffenschmied	Composer	Komische Oper (Spl)	3	Vienna, 1846
	Zum Grossadmiral	Composer	Komische Oper (Spl)	3	Leipzig, 1847
	Regina	Composer	Romantische Oper (Spl)	3	(comp. 1848)
	Rolands Knappen	Composer, Georg Meisinger, Carl Haffner	Komisch-romantische Oper (Spl)	3	Leipzig, 1849
Mangold	Tanhauser	Eduard Duller	Oper	4	Darmstadt, 1846
	Gudrun	?Composer	Grosse Oper	4	Darmstadt, 1851
Marschner	Der Vampyr	Wilhelm August Wohlbrück	Grosse romantische Oper	2	Leipzig, 1828
	Der Templer und die Jüdin	Wilhelm August Wohlbrück	Grosse romantische Oper (Spl)	3	Leipzig, 1829
	Hans Heiling	Eduard Devrient	Grosse romantische Oper (Spl)	3	Berlin, 1833
	Kaiser Adolf von Nassau	Karl Gollmick	Grosse Oper	4	Dresden, 1845

Composer	Title	Librettist	Genre	No.	Place, Year
Mattheson	*Cleopatra*	Friedrich Christian Feustking	Drama per musica (Spl)	3	Hamburg, 1704
Mendelssohn	*Die Soldatenliebschaft*	Johann Ludwig Casper	Singspiel	1	Berlin, 1820
	Die beiden Pädagogen	Johann Ludwig Casper	Singspiel	1	Berlin, 1821
	Die wandernden Komödianten	Johann Ludwig Casper	Singspiel	1	Berlin, 1822
	Der Onkel aus Boston	Johann Ludwig Casper	Singspiel	3	Berlin, 1824
	Die Hochzeit des Camacho	Friedrich Voigt	Singspiel	2	Berlin, 1827
	Die Heimkehr aus der Fremde	Karl Klingemann	Liederspiel (Spl)	1	Berlin, 1829
Meyerbeer	*Jephtas Gelübde*	Aloys Schreiber	Ernsthafte Oper (Spl)	3	Munich, 1812
	Wirth und Gast (Alimelek)	Johann Gottfried Wohlbrück	Lustspiel (Spl)	2	Stuttgart, 1813
Mosel	*Salem*	Ignaz Franz Castelli	Lyrische Tragödie (Spl)	3	Vienna, 1813
Mozart	*Bastien und Bastienne*	F. Weiskern, J. Müller, J. A. Schachtner	Singspiel	1	Vienna, 1768
	Zaide	Johann Andreas Schachtner	Singspiel	2	(comp. 1780) (unf.)
	Die Entführung aus dem Serail	Christoph Friedrich Bretzner	Singspiel	3	Vienna, 1782
	Der Schauspieldirektor	Gottlieb Stephanie	Singspiel	1	Vienna, 1786
	Die Zauberflöte	Emanuel Schikaneder	Singspiel	2	Vienna, 1791

Composer	Title	Text	Genre	Acts	First produced
Müller	Das Neusonntagskind	Joachim Perinet	Singspiel	2	Vienna, 1793
	Die Schwestern von Prag	Joachim Perinet	Singspiel	2	Vienna, 1794
	Der Sturm	Karl Friedrich Hensler	Heroisch-komische Oper (Spl)	2	Vienna, 1798
Neefe	Die Apotheke	Christian Friedrich Weisse	Comische Oper (Spl)	2	Berlin, 1771
	Amors Guckkasten	Johann Baptist Michaelis	Operette (Spl)	1	Leipzig, 1772
	Der Einspruch	Johann Baptist Michaelis	Comische Oper (Spl)	1	Leipzig, 1772
	Sophonisbe	August Gottlieb Meissner	Musikalisches Drama	1	Leipzig, 1776
Nicolai	Die lustigen Weiber von Windsor	Salomon Hermann Mosenthal	Komische-fantastische Oper (Spl)	3	Berlin, 1849
Poissl	Athalia	Composer	Grosse Oper (Spl)	3	Munich, 1814
	Der Wettkampf zu Olympia	Composer	Grosse Oper (Spl)	3	Munich, 1815
	Nittetis	Composer	Grosse Oper (Spl)	3	Darmstadt, 1817
	Der Untersberg	Composer	Romantische Oper (Spl)	3	Munich, 1829
Reichardt	Cephalus und Prokris	Karl Ramler	Melodrama	1	Berlin, 1777
	Die Geisterinsel	Friedrich Wilhelm Gotter	Singspiel	3	Berlin, 1798
Reissiger	Die Felsenmühle zu Etalières	Karl Borromäus von Miltitz	Romantische Oper (Spl)	2	Dresden, 1831
	Adèle de Foix	Robert Blum	Grosse Oper (Spl)	4	Dresden, 1841

Composer	Title	Librettist	Genre		Place, year
Ritter	*Die lustigen Weiber von Windsor*	Georg Römer	Singspiel	3	Mannheim, 1790
Schenk	*Der Zitherschläger*	Carl Ludwig Seidel	Singspiel	1	Stuttgart, 1810
	Der Dorfbarbier	Paul and Joseph Weidmann	Singspiel	1	Vienna, 1796
Schindelmeisser	*Melusine*	Ernst Pasqué	Romantische Oper (Spl)	4	Darmstadt, 1861
Schubaur	*Die Dorfdeputierten*	Gottlob Ephraim Heermann	Singspiel	3	Munich, 1783
Schubert	*Des Teufels Lustschloss*	August von Kotzebue	Zauberoper (Spl)	3	(comp. 1814)
	Der vierjährige Posten	Theodor Körner	Singspiel	1	(comp. 1815)
	Fernando	Albert Stadler	Singspiel	1	(comp. 1815)
	Claudine von Villa Bella	Johann Wolfgang von Goethe	Singspiel	3	(comp. 1815)
	Die Freunde von Salamanka	Johann Mayrhofer	Komisches Singspiel	2	(comp. 1815)
	Die Zwillingsbrüder	Georg Ernst von Hofmann	Posse (Spl)	1	Vienna, 1820
	Alfonso und Estrella	Franz von Schober	Oper	3	(comp. 1822)
	Die Verschworenen	Ignaz Franz Castelli	Singspiel	1	(comp. 1823)
	Fierrabras	Josef Kupelwieser	Heroisch-romantische Oper (Spl)	3	(comp. 1823)
Schumann	*Genoveva*	Composer	Oper	4	Leipzig, 1850
Schürmann	*Ludovicus Pius*	Christian Ernst Simonetti	Singspiel	3	Brunswick, 1726
Schuster	*Der Alchymist*	August Gottlieb Meissner	Comische Oper (Spl)	1	Dresden, 1778
Schütz	*Dafne*	Martin Opitz	Pastorale tragicomoedia (Spl)	1	Torgau, 1627
Schweitzer	*Die Dorfgala*	Friedrich Wilhelm Gotter	Komische Operette (Spl)	3	Weimar, 1772

Composer	Title	Text	Genre	Acts	First produced
	Alceste	Christoph Martin Wieland	Singspiel	5	Weimar, 1773
	Rosamunde	Christoph Martin Wieland	Singspiel	3	Mannheim, 1780
Spohr	*Die Prüfung*	Eduard Henke	Operette (Spl)	1	Gotha, 1806
	Alruna	?	Grosse romantische Oper (Spl)	3	(comp. 1808)
	Faust	Joseph Karl Bernard	Romantische Oper (Spl)	2	Prague, 1816
	Zemire und Azor	Eduard Gehe	Romantische Oper (Spl)	2	Frankfurt, 1819
	Jessonda	Eduard Gehe	Grosse Oper	3	Kassel, 1823
	Der Berggeist	Georg Döring	Romantische Oper	3	Kassel, 1825
	Pietro von Abano	Karl Pfeiffer	Romantische Oper (Spl)	3	Kassel, 1830
	Der Alchymist	F. G. Schmidt (Karl Pfeiffer)	Romantische Oper (Spl)	3	Kassel, 1830
	Der Kreuzfahrer	Composer and Marianne Spohr	Grosse Oper	3	Kassel, 1845
Spontini	*Nurmahal*	Carl Alexander Herklots	Lyrisches Drama (Spl)	2	Berlin, 1822
	Alcidor	Emmanuel Théaulon de Lambert	Zauberoper mit Ballet (Spl)	3	Berlin, 1825
	Agnes von Hohenstaufen	Ernst Raupach	Grosse Historisch-romantische Oper	3	Berlin, 1829
Staden	*Seelewig*	Georg Philipp Harsdörffer	Geistliche Waldgedicht (Spl)	3	Nuremberg, 1644
Standfuss	*Der Teufel ist los*	Christian Friedrich Weisse	Singspiel	2	Leipzig, 1752
	Der lustige Schuster	Christian Friedrich Weisse	Singspiel	3	Lübeck, 1759
Süssmayr	*Der Spiegel von Arkadien*	Emanuel Schikaneder	Heroisch-komische Oper (Spl)	2	Vienna, 1794

Composer	Title	Librettist	Genre	Place, date	No.
Taubert	*Macbeth*	Friedrich Eggers	Oper	Berlin, 1857	5
Telemann	*Der geduldige Socrates*	Johann Ulrich König	Komisches Singspiel	Hamburg, 1721	3
	Pimpinone	Johann Philipp Praetorius	Intermezzo (Spl)	Hamburg, 1725	3 sc.
	Adelheid	?Johann Philipp Praetorius	Singspiel	Bayreuth, 1725	3
Theile	*Adam und Eva* (lost)	Christian Richter	Singspiel	Hamburg, 1678	5
Umlauf	*Die Bergknappen*	Paul Weidmann	Original-Singspiel (Spl)	Vienna, 1778	1
	Die schöne Schusterinn	Gottlieb Stephanie	Singspiel	Vienna, 1779	2
	Das Irrlicht	Gottlieb Stephanie	Singspiel	Vienna, 1782	3
Vogler	*Der Kaufmann von Smyrna*	Christian Friedrich Schwann	Singspiel	Mannheim, 1771	1
	Lampedo	C. F. Lichtenberg	Melodram	Darmstadt, 1779	1
	Erwin und Elmire	Johann Wolfgang von Goethe	Singspiel	Darmstadt, 1781	1
	Albert der Dritte von Bayern	Karl von Traitteur	Singspiel	Stuttgart, 1781	5
	Samori	Franz Xaver Huber	Heroisch-komische Oper (Spl)	Vienna, 1804	2
Wagner	*Die Feen*	Composer	Grosse romantische Oper	(comp. 1834)	3
	Das Liebesverbot	Composer	Grosse komische Oper	Magdeburg, 1836	2
	Rienzi	Composer	Grosse tragische Oper	Dresden, 1842	5
	Der fliegende Holländer	Composer	Romantische Oper	Dresden, 1843	3
	Tannhäuser	Composer	Grosse romantische Oper	Dresden, 1845	3
	Lohengrin	Composer	Romantische Oper	Weimar, 1850	3

Composer	Title	Text	Genre	Acts	First produced
	Tristan und Isolde	Composer	Handlung	3	Munich, 1865
	Die Meistersinger von Nürnberg	Composer	(No description on score)	3	Munich, 1868
	Das Rheingold	Composer	Vorabend (of Ring)	1	Munich, 1869
	Die Walküre	Composer	Erster Tag (of Ring)	3	Munich, 1870
	Siegfried	Composer	Zweiter Tag (of Ring)	3	Bayreuth, 1876
	Götterdämmerung	Composer	Dritter Tag (of Ring)	3	Bayreuth, 1876
	Der Ring des Nibelungen (as cycle)	Composer	Bühnenfestspiel		Bayreuth, 1876
	Parsifal	Composer	Bühnenweihfestspiel	3	Bayreuth, 1882
Weber	Das Waldmädchen	Carl von Steinsberg	Romantische Oper (Spl)	2	Freiberg, 1800
	Peter Schmoll	Joseph Türk	Singspiel	2	Augsburg, 1803
	Rübezahl	J. G. Rhode	Singspiel	2	(comp. 1804–5)
	Silvana	Franz Carl Hiemer	Romantische Oper (Spl)	3	Frankfurt, 1810
	Abu Hassan	Franz Carl Hiemer	Singspiel	1	Munich, 1811
	Der Freischütz	Johann Friedrich Kind	Romantische Oper (Spl)	3	Berlin, 1821
	Euryanthe	Helmina von Chezy	Grosse Heroisch-romantische Oper	3	Vienna, 1823
Weigl	Das Waisenhaus	Georg Friedrich Treitschke	Singspiel	2	Vienna, 1808
	Die Schweizerfamilie	Ignaz Franz Castelli	Lyrische Oper (Spl)	3	Vienna, 1809
	Der Bergsturz	Johann Anton Friedrich Reil	Singspiel	3	Vienna, 1813

	Title	Librettist	Genre	No.	Place, Date
	Die Jugend Peters des Grossen	Georg Friedrich Treitschke	Singspiel	3	Vienna, 1814
	Die Nachtigall und die Raabe	Georg Friedrich Treitschke	Singspiel	1	Vienna, 1818
Winter	*Cora und Alonzo*	Franz Joseph Maria von Babo	Melodrama	4	Munich, 1778
	Lenardo und Blandine	Josef Franz von Götz	Melodrama	2	Munich, 1779
	Reinhold und Armida	Franz Joseph Maria von Babo	Melodrama	3	Munich, 1780
	Das unterbrochene Opferfest	Franz Xaver Huber	Heroisch-komische Oper (Spl)	2	Vienna, 1796
	Das Labyrinth	Emanuel Schikaneder	Heroisch-komische Oper (Spl)	2	Vienna, 1798
Wolfram	*Der Bergmönch*	Karl Borromäus von Miltitz	Romantische Oper (Spl)	3	Dresden, 1830
	Das Schloss Candra	Eduard Gehe	Heroisch-romantische Oper (Spl)	3	Dresden, 1832
Zumsteeg	*Tamira*	J. L. Huber	Melodrama	1	Stuttgart, 1788
	Die Geisterinsel	Friedrich Wilhelm Gotter	Singspiel	3	Leipzig, 1799
	Das Pfauenfest	F. A. C. Werthes	Singspiel	2	Stuttgart, 1801
	Elbondocani	J. C. F. Haug	Singspiel	1	Leipzig, 1803

BIBLIOGRAPHY

The following bibliography consists of works which have been cited in the text, together with some which provide a useful background to particular topics. Given the scale of the subject, it has not been possible to cite general histories or studies of individual composers or of cities and other operatic centres. Many of these can be found in the bibliographies attached to the relevant entries in *The New Grove Dictionary of Opera* and *Die Musik in Geschichte und Gegenwart*.

Algarotti, Francesco, 1755. *Saggio sopra l'opera in musica* (Livorno; reprinted in Raffaele Mattioti, Pietro Pancrazi and Alfredo Schiaffini, eds.: La letteratura italiana, storia e testi, 46, II, *Illuministi italiani*, 433–80).

Allroggen, Gerhard, 1969. 'Die Opern-Ästhetik E. T. A. Hoffmanns', in Heinz Becker, ed., *Studien zur Musikgeschichte des 19. Jahrhunderts*, xv, Beiträge zur Geschichte der Oper (Regensburg), 25–33.

Baesecke, Anna, 1935. *Das Schauspiel der englischen Komödianten in Deutschland, seine dramatische Form und seine Entwicklung*, in Lorenz Morsbach and Hans Hecht, eds., *Studien zur Englischen Philologie* (Halle).

Batley, E. M., 1965–6. 'The Inception of "Singspiel" in Eighteenth-Century Southern Germany', *German Life and Letters* 19, 167–77.

1969. *A Preface to The Magic Flute* (London).

Baumann, Thomas, 1985. *North German Opera in the Age of Goethe* (Cambridge).

1987. *W. A. Mozart: Die Entführung aus dem Serail* (Cambridge).

Beckett, Lucy, 1981. *Richard Wagner: Parsifal* (Cambridge).

Benedix, Roderich, 1847. *Bilder aus dem Schauspielerleben* (2 vols., Leipzig).

Berlin, Isaiah, 1992. *Vico and Herder* (London).

1993. *The Magus of the North. J. G. Hamann and the Origins of Modern Irrationalism* (London).

Berlioz, Hector, 1852. *Les Soirées de l'orchestre* (Paris; trans. Jacques Barzun, *Evenings with the Orchestra*, New York, 1956, 2/1973).

Bertuch, Georg, 1693. *Disputatio juridica de eo quod justum est, circa ludos scenicos operasque modernas, dictas vulgò 'Operen'* (Kiel).

Biedenfeld, Friedrich von, 1848. *Die komische Oper* (Leipzig).

Bigenwald, Marta, 1934. *Die Anfänge der Leipziger Allgemeinen Musikalischen Zeitung* (Diss., Univ. of Freiburg-im-Breisgau; publ. Sibiu-Hermannstadt, 1938).

Bolte, Johannes, 1893. *Die Singspiele der englischen Komödianten und ihre Nachfolger in Deutschland, Holland und Skandinavien*, Theatergeschichtliche Forschungen, VII (Hamburg and Leipzig).

Bostel, Lucas von, 1686. *Der Glückliche Gross-Vezier Cara Mustapha* (Hamburg).

Bouilly, Jean-Nicolas, 1836–7. *Mes récapitulations* (2 vols., Paris).

Branscombe, Peter, 1966. '*Die Zauberflöte*: Some Textual and Interpretative Problems', *PRMA* 92, 45–63.

1971. 'Music in the Viennese Popular Theatre of the Eighteenth and Nineteenth Centuries', *PRMA* 98, 101–12.

1991. *W. A. Mozart: Die Zauberflöte* (Cambridge).

Braunbehrens, Volkmar, 1986. *Mozart in Wien* (Munich; trans. Timothy Bell, *Mozart in Vienna*, Oxford, 1991).

Brauneck, Manfred, ed., 1970–2. *Spieltexte der Wanderbühne* (4 vols., Berlin).

Brockpähler, Renate, 1964. *Handbuch zur Geschichte der Barockoper in Deutschland*, Die Schaubühne. Quellen und Forschungen zur Theatergeschichte, LXII (Emsdetten).

Buelow, George J., 1970. 'An Evaluation of Johann Mattheson's Opera, *Cleopatra* (Hamburg, 1704)', in H. C. Robbins Landon, ed., *Studies in Eighteenth-Century Music: a Tribute to Karl Geiringer on his Seventieth Birthday* (London), 92–107.

1972. '*Die schöne und getreue Ariadne* (Hamburg 1691): A Lost Opera by J. G. Conradi Rediscovered', *AcM* 44 (1972), 108–21.

1983. With Hans Joachim Marx, eds., *New Mattheson Studies* (Cambridge).

Calmus, Georg, 1908. 'Die ersten deutschen Singspiele von Standfuss und Hiller', *Publikationen der Internationalen Musikgesellschaft*, Supplement, 2nd series, VI (Leipzig).

Castelli, Ignaz, 1861. *Memoiren meines Lebens* (Vienna and Prague).

Charlton, David, 1976. 'Motive and Motif: Méhul before 1791', *ML* 57/4.

1978. 'Motif and Recollection in Four Operas of Dalayrac', *Soundings* 7 (June).

1992. 'On Redefinitions of "Rescue Opera"', in David Galliver, ed., *Music and the French Revolution* (Cambridge), 169–88.

1996. 'The French Theatrical Origins of *Fidelio*', in Paul Robinson, *Ludwig van Beethoven: Fidelio* (Cambridge), 51–67.

Chezy, Helmina von, 1840. 'Carl Maria von Webers Euryanthe. Ein Beitrag zur Geschichte der deutschen Oper', *NZM* 13, Nos. 1–6, 9–11.

Cohn, Albert, 1865. *Shakespeare in Germany* (London and Berlin).

Corneilson, Paul Edward, 1992. *Opera at Mannheim, 1770–1778* (Ph.D. Diss., Chapel Hill, N.C.).

Cornelius, Peter, 1904–5. Carl Maria Cornelius, Edgar Istel and A. Stern, eds., *Peter Cornelius: Literarische Werke* (3 vols., Leipzig).

Cornet, Julius, 1849. *Die Oper in Deutschland und das Theater der Neuzeit* (Hamburg).

Costenoble, Carl Ludwig, 1912. Alexander von Weilen, ed., *Carl Ludwig Costenobles Tagebücher von seiner Jugend bis zur Übersiedlung nach Wien* [1818] (Berlin).

Creizenach, Wilhelm, [1888]. *Die Schauspiele der englischen Komödianten* (Berlin and Stuttgart, n.d.), in Joseph Kürschner, ed., Deutsche National-Litteratur, XXIII.

Dahlhaus, Carl, 1974. 'Romantik und Biedermeier. Zur musikgeschichtlichen Charakteristik der Restaurationszeit', in *AMw*, 22–42.

Dahlhaus, Carl and Norbert Miller, 1999. *Europäische Romantik in der Musik* (2 vols., Stuttgart and Weimar).

Dean, Winton, 1971. 'Beethoven and Opera', in Denis Arnold and Nigel Fortune, eds., *The Beethoven Companion* (London), 331–86.

1982. 'German Opera', in Gerald Abraham, ed., *NOHM*, VIII, *The Age of Beethoven, 1790–1830* (London), 452–522.

Dean, Winton and John Merrill Knapp, 1989. *Handel's Operas, 1704–26* (Oxford).

Deathridge, John, 1977. *Wagner's Rienzi: A Reappraisal Based on a Study of the Sketches and Drafts* (Oxford).

Dent, Edward J., 1976. Winton Dean, ed., *The Rise of Romantic Opera* (Cambridge).

Devrient, Hans, 1895. *Johann Friedrich Schönemann und seine Schauspielergesellschaft: ein Beitrag zur Theatergeschichte des 18. Jahrhunderts*, Theatergeschichtliche Forschungen, XI (Hamburg and Leipzig).

Dittersdorf, Karl von, 1798–9. 'Korrespondenze des Herrn v. Dittersdorf mit einem Freunde über Musik. Gegenstände', *AMZ* I, 138–41, 201–5.

1801. Karl Spazier, ed., *Karl von Dittersdorf's Lebensbeschreibung, seinem Sohne in die Feder diktiert* (Leipzig).

Doerry, Hans, 1926. *Das Rollenfach im deutschen Theaterbetrieb des 18. Jahrhunderts* (Diss., Berlin).

Dyer, D. G., ed. and trans., 1975. *Jacob Bidermann: Cenodoxus*, Edinburgh Bilingual Library, 9 (Edinburgh).

Ehinger, Hans, 1929. *Friedrich Rochlitz als Musikschriftsteller* (Leipzig).

Eisenberg, Ludwig, 1903. *Grosses Biographisches Lexicon der Deutschen Bühne im XIX Jahrhundert* (Leipzig).

Elmenhorst, Hinrich, [1688]. *Dramatologia Antiqvo-Hodierna, Das ist: Bericht von denen Oper-Spielen* (Hamburg, n.d.).

Engländer, Richard, 1945. 'The Struggle between German and Italian Opera at the Time of Weber', *MQ* 31/4, 479–91.

Fend, Michael, 1997. 'Die Opéra comique und ihr Einfluß auf das europäische Musiktheater im 19. Jahrhundert', in Herbert Schneider and Nicole Wild, eds., *Bericht über den Internationalen Kongreß Frankfurt 1994*, 299–322.

Flaherty, Gloria, 1978. *Opera in the Development of German Critical Thought* (Princeton, N.J.).

    1983. 'Mattheson and the Aesthetics of Theater', in George J. Buelow and Hans Joachim Marx, eds., *New Mattheson Studies* (Cambridge), 75–99.

Flemming, Willi, 1923. *Geschichte des Jesuitentheaters in den Landen deutscher Zunge* (Berlin).

    1930. *Das Ordensdrama* (Leipzig).

    1931. *Das Schauspiel der Wanderbühne* (Leipzig).

Forkel, Johann Nicolaus, 1778–9. *Musikalisch-Kritische Bibliothek* (Gotha; R/1964).

Frederick [Frederick II, the Great], 1780. *De la littérature allemande; des défauts qu'on peut lui reprocher; quelles en sont les causes; et par quels moyens on peut les corriger* (Berlin).

Garlington, Aubrey S., 1977. 'German Romantic Opera and the Problem of Origins', *MQ* 63, 242–60.

Genast, Eduard, 1862. *Aus dem Tagebuche eines alten Schauspielers* (Leipzig).

Gerber, Ernst Ludwig, 1790–2. *Historisch-Biographisches Lexicon der Tonkünstler* (2 vols., Leipzig).

    Neues Historisch-Biographisches Lexicon der Tonkünstler (4 vols., Leipzig).

Goethe, Johann Wolfgang von, 1824. *Wilhelm Meisters Lehrjahre* (trans. Thomas Carlyle, London).

    1949–54, 1960–4. Ernst Butler, ed., *Johann Wolfgang von Goethe. Gedenkausgabe der Werke, Briefe und Gespräche* (24 vols., Zurich; 2 supp. vols., Zurich).

Göpfert, Bernd, 1877. *Stimmtypen und Rollencharaktere in der deutschen Oper von 1815–1848* (Wiesbaden).

Goslich, Siegfried, 1937. *Beiträge zur Geschichte der deutschen romantischen Oper* (Leipzig; rev. 1975 as *Die deutsche romantische Oper*).

Gottsched, Johann Christoph, 1730. *Versuch einer critischen Dichtkunst* (Leipzig).

Haas, Robert, 1911. Introduction to DTÖ, xxxvi (Vienna).

Haase, Rudolf, 1963. *Leibniz und die Musik: ein Beitrag zur Geschichte der harmonikalen Symbolik* (Hommerich).

Hadamovsky, Franz, 1966. *Die Wiener Hoftheater (Staatstheater) 1776–1966* (Vienna).

Hanslick, Eduard, 1875–1900. *Die moderne Oper* (9 vols., Berlin).

Harsdörffer, Georg Philipp, 1641–9. *Frauenzimmer Gesprächspiele* (8 vols., Nuremberg; reprint, ed. Irmgard Böttcher, 1968–9).

Helmrich, Elsie Winifred, 1912. *The History of the Chorus in the German Drama* (New York).

Herder, Johann Gottfried, 1877–1913. Bernhard Suphan, ed., *J. G. Herders Sämmtliche Werke* (33 vols., Berlin).

Herz, E., 1903. *Englische Schauspieler und englische Schauspiele zur Zeit Shakespeares in Deutschland*, in Berthold Litzmann, ed., Theatergeschichtliche Forschungen, xviii (Hamburg and Leipzig).

Hey, Julius, 1886. *Deutsche Gesangs-Unterricht: Lehrbuch des sprachlichen und gesanglichen Vortrags* (Mainz).

Hiller, Ferdinand, 1880. *Künstlerleben* (Cologne).

Hiller, Johann Adam, 1773. *Anweisung zur Singekunst in der deutschen und italienischen Sprache* (Frankfurt and Leipzig).

　　1784. *Lebensbeschreibungen berühmter Musikgelehrten und Tonkünstler neuerer Zeit* (Leipzig).

Hoffmann, E. T. A., 1963. Friedrich Schnapp, ed., *E. T. A. Hoffmann. Nachlese. Dichtungen, Schriften, Aufzeichnungen und Fragmente* (Munich, 2/1978).

　　1967–9. Hans von Müller and Friedrich Schnapp, eds., *E. T. A. Hoffmanns Briefwechsel* (3 vols., Munich).

　　1989. David Charlton, ed., *E. T. A. Hoffmann's Musical Writings*, trans. Martyn Clarke (Cambridge).

Hövel, Ernst, 1912. *Der Kampf der Geistlichkeit gegen das Theater in Deutschland im 17. Jahrhundert* (Münster).

Hughes, Derek, 1998. '"Wie die Hans Heilings": Weber, Marschner, and Thomas Mann's *Doktor Faustus*', *COJ* 10, 179–204.

Hunold, Christian Friedrich (pseud. Menantes), 1706. *Theatralische/Galante und Geistliche Gedichte* (Hamburg).

Kirby, F. E., 1962. 'Herder and Opera', *JAMS* 15, 316–29.

Koch, Hans-Albrecht, 1974. *Das deutsche Singspiel* (Stuttgart).

Koszyk, Kurt, 1966. *Deutsche Presse im 19. Jahrhundert* (Berlin).

Kretzschmar, Hermann, 1901–2. 'Das erste Jahrhundert der deutschen Oper', *SIMG* 3, 270–93.

Kropfinger, Klaus, 1974. *Wagner und Beethoven* (Regensburg; rev., trans. Peter Palmer, Cambridge, 1991).

Kruse, Georg Richard, 1918–19. 'Meyerbeers Jugendopern', *ZMw* 1, 399–413.

Küstner, Karl Theodor von, 1857. *Taschen- und Handbuch für Theaterstatistik* (Leipzig).

Le Bar, Ann Catherine, 1993. *Musical Culture and the Origins of the Enlightenment in Hamburg* (Ph.D. Diss., Washington).

Leibniz, Gottfried Wilhelm, 1938. Preussische Akademie der Wissenschaften, ed., *Sämtliche Schriften und Briefe*, III (Leipzig).

Lessing, Gotthold Ephraim, 1925–35. C. G. Lessing, J. T. Eschenburg and C. F. Nicolai, eds., *Gotthold Ephraim Lessing: sämmtliche Schriften* (31 vols., Berlin).

  1965. Dorothy Reich, ed., *Laokoon* (Oxford).

Leverett, Adelyn Peck, 1990. 'Liszt, Wagner and Heinrich Dorn's *Die Nibelungen*', *COJ* 2, 121–44.

Liliencron, Rochus von, 1890. 'Die Chorgesänge des lateinischen Schuldramas im 16. Jahrhundert', *VMw* 6, 309ff.

Lindberg, J. E., 1967. 'Gottsched gegen die Oper', *German Quarterly* 40, 673–83.

Lindner, Ernst Otto, 1855. *Die erste stehende Deutsche Oper* (Berlin).

Lobe, Johann Christian, 1859. *Aus dem Leben eines Musikers* (Leipzig).

  1869. *Consonanzen und Dissonanzen* (Leipzig).

Löwen, J. F., 1766. *Geschichte des deutschen Theaters* (Hamburg; ed. H. Stümke, Berlin, 1903).

Loewenberg, Alfred, 1978. *Annals of Opera*, 3rd edn (London).

Luther, Martin, 1883–. *Kritische Gesamtausgabe* (Weimar).

McKay, Elizabeth Norman, 1991. *Franz Schubert's Music for the Theatre* (Tutzing).

Marpurg, Friedrich Wilhelm, 1749–50. *Der critische Musicus an der Spree* (Berlin).

  1754–78. *Historisch-kritische Beyträge zur Aufnahme der Musik* (Berlin).

  1760–4. *Kritische Briefe über die Tonkunst* (Berlin).

Marx, Hans Joachim, 1982. *Johann Mattheson: Lebensbeschreibung des Hamburger Musikers, Schriftstellers und Diplomaten* (Hamburg).

Mattheson, Johann, 1713. *Das neu-eröffnete Orchestre* (Hamburg).

1728. *Der musicalische Patriot* (Hamburg).

1739. *Der vollkommene Capellmeister* (Hamburg).

1744. *Die neueste Untersuchung der Singspiele, nebst beygefügter musicalischen Geschmacksprobe* (Hamburg).

Meinardus, Ludwig, 1878. *Rückblicke auf die Anfänge der deutschen Oper in Hamburg* (Hamburg).

Meyer, Reinhard, ed., 1980. *Die Hamburger Oper: eine Sammlung von Texten der Hamburger Oper aus der Zeit 1678–1830* (Munich).

Meyerbeer, Giacomo, 1960–. Heinz and Gudrun Becker, eds., *Giacomo Meyerbeer: Briefwechsel und Tagebücher* (Berlin).

Michtner, Otto, 1970. *Das alte Burgtheater als Opernbühne von der Einführung des deutschen Singspiels (1778) bis zum Tod Leopolds II (1792)* (Vienna).

Mizler von Koloff, Lorenz, ed., 1739–1754. *Neu-Eröffnete Musikalische Bibliothek, oder Gründliche Nachricht nebst unpartheyischem Urtheil von musikalischen Schriften und Büchern* (4 vols., Leipzig; R/Hilversum, 1966).

Morhof, Daniel Georg, 1682. *Unterricht von der Teutschen Sprache und Poesie* (Kiel; rev. and enlarged Lübeck and Frankfurt, 1700, R/1969).

Mosel, Ignaz von, 1813. *Versuch einer Aesthetik des dramatischen Tonsatzes* (Vienna).

Mozart, W. A. 1962–75. Wilhelm A. Bauer, Otto Erich Deutsch and Joseph Heinz Eibl, eds., *Mozart: Briefe und Aufzeichnungen* (Kassel).

Müller, Ulrich and Peter Wapnewski, 1986. *Richard-Wagner-Handbuch* (Stuttgart; trans. as *Wagner Handbook*, London, 1992).

Nadler, Josef, 1912–18. *Literaturgeschichte der deutschen Stämme und Landschaften* (Regensburg).

Oliver, A. R., 1947. *The Encyclopedists as Critics of Music* (New York).

Paldamus, F. C., 1857. *Das deutsche Theater der Gegenwart* (Mainz).

Price, Lawrence Marsden, 1953. *English Literature in Germany* (Berkeley and Los Angeles).

Rauch, Christoph, 1682. *Theatrophania, Entgegen gesetzt Der so genanten Schrifft Theatromania. Zur Werthädigung der Christlichen vornemlich aber deren Musicalischen Operen und Verwerffung aller Heidnischen und von den Alten Kirchen-Vättern allen Verdamnteten Schauspielen* (Hanover).

Reden-Esbeck, F. J. von, 1881. *Caroline Neuber und ihre Zeitgenossen: ein Beitrag zur deutschen Kultur- und Theatergeschichte* (Leipzig).

Reichardt, Johann Friedrich, 1774. *Über die deutsche comische Oper* (Hamburg). 1782/91. *Musikalisches Kunstmagazin* (2 vols., Berlin).

1804. *Vertraute Briefe aus Paris geschrieben in den Jahren 1802 und 1803* (3 parts, Hamburg).

Reipschläger, Erich, 1911. *Schubaur, Danzi und Poissl als Opernkomponisten* (Diss., Rostock, 1911; historical and biographical part only, Berlin).

Reiser, Anton, 1681. *Theatromania, oder Die Werke der Finsternis in den öffentlichen Schau-Spielen, von den alten Kirchen-Lehrern und etlichen heidnischen Scribenten verdammet* (Ratzeburg).

Rice, John A., 1995. 'Leopold II, Mozart, and the Return to a Golden Age', in Thomas Baumann and Marita Petzoldt McClymonds, eds., *Opera and the Enlightenment* (Cambridge), 271–96.

Riedinger, Lothar, 1914. 'Karl von Dittersdorf als Opernkomponist. Eine stilkritische Untersuchung', *SMw* 2, 212–349.

Robinson, Paul, 1996. *Ludwig van Beethoven: Fidelio* (Cambridge).

Rusak, Hedwig, 1930. *Gozzi in Germany: A Survey of the Rise and Fall of the Gozzi Vogue in Germany and Austria* (New York).

Scheibe, Johann Adolf, 1737–40. *Der critische Musikus* (4 parts, Hamburg; 2/1745, R/Hildesheim, 1970).

Schelling, Friedrich von, 1927. Karl Schelling, ed., *Friedrich von Schelling: Sämmtliche Werke* (14 vols., Stuttgart and Augsburg, 1856–61; reprint in new arrangement of original edition, ed. Manfred Schröter, Munich).

Schenk, H. G., 1966. *The Mind of the German Romantics* (London).

Schiedermair, Ludwig, 1930. *Die Deutsche Oper: Grundzüge ihres Werdens und Wesens* (Leipzig).

Schilling, Gustav, 1835–8. *Encyclopädie der gesammten musikalischen Wissenschaften, oder Universal-Lexicon der Tonkunst* (Stuttgart; R/1973).

Schletterer, Hans Michel, 1863. *Das deutsche Singspiel von seinen ersten Anfängen bis auf die neueste Zeit*, Zur Geschichte dramatischer Musik und Poesie in Deutschland, 1 (Augsburg).

Schmidt, Gustav Friedrich, 1933–4. *Die frühdeutsche Oper und die musikdramatische Kunst Georg Caspar Schürmanns* (2 vols., Regensburg).

Schmitt, Friedrich, 1874. *System zur Erlernung der deutschen Aussprache* (Munich).

Schneider, Herbert, 1997. 'Die deutschen Übersetzungen französischer Opern zwischen 1780 und 1820. Verlauf und Probleme eines Transfer-Zyklus', in Hans-Jürgen Lüsebrink and Rolf Reichardt, eds., *Kulturtransfer im Epochenumbruch Frankreich-Deutschland 1770 bis 1815* (Leipzig).

Schnyder von Wartensee, Xaver, 1887. *Lebenserinnerungen* (Zurich).

Schulz, Friedrich, 1790. *Geschichte der grossen Revolution in Frankreich* (Berlin).

Schulze, W., 1936. *Die Quellen der Hamburger Oper 1678–1738* (Hamburg-Oldenburg).

Schumann, Robert, 1854. *Gesammelte Schriften über Musik und Musiker* (4 vols., Leipzig; 4/1891, R/1968, 5/1914).

Schusky, Renate, ed., 1980. *Das deutsche Singspiel im 18. Jahrhundert: Quellen und Zeugnisse zu Ästhetik und Rezeption* (Bonn).

Schütz, Heinrich, 1931. Erich Müller, ed., *Heinrich Schütz, Gesammelte Briefe und Schriften* (Regensburg; R/1976).

Schütze, Johann Friedrich, 1794. *Hamburgische Theatergeschichte* (Hamburg; R/1975).

Spitz, Lewis W., 1957. *Conrad Celtis* (Cambridge, Mass.).

Spohr, Louis, 1860–1. *Selbstbiographie* (Kassel and Göttingen; anon. trans., London, 1865).

Staël, Germaine de, 1958. Jean de Pange and Simone Balayé, eds.: *Mme de Staël: De l'Allemagne* (Paris).

Stephanie, Gottlieb, 1792. *Sämmtliche Singspiele* (Liegnitz).

Subotnik, Rose Rosengard, 1976. 'Lortzing and the German Romantics: a Dialectical Assessment', *MQ* 62, 241–64.

Sulzer, Johann Georg, 1771–4. *Allgemeine Theorie der Schönen Künste* (4 vols., Leipzig; supp. 1792–9; R/1967–9).

Szarota, Elida Maria, 1978–87. *Das Jesuitendrama im deutschen Sprachgebiet* (4 parts in 7 vols., Munich).

Träger, Claus, ed., 1975. *Die französische Revolution im Spiegel der deutschen Literatur* (Leipzig).

Tusa, Michael C., 1991. *Euryanthe and Carl Maria von Weber's Dramaturgy of German Opera* (Oxford).

Tyler, Linda L., 1991. '"Zaide" in the Development of Mozart's Operatic Language', *ML* 72, 214–33.

Uffenbach, Johann Friedrich von, 1747. 'Von der Würde derer Singgedichte, oder Vertheidigung der Opern' (Hamburg); reprinted in Lorenz Christoph Mizler von Kolof, *Neu-Eröffnete Musikalische Bibliothek* 3 (Leipzig), 377–408.

Valentin, Jean-Marie, 1978. *Le théâtre des Jésuites dans les pays de langue allemande (1554–1680)* (Bern).

Veit, Joachim, 1990. *Der junge Carl Maria von Weber: Untersuchungen zum Einfluß Franz Danzis und Abbé Georg Joseph Voglers* (Mainz).

1991. 'Abuhassan, Der Admiral und Alimelek – Opern aus der Vogler-ischen Schule', in Hans John und Günther Stephan, eds.: 'Giacomo Meyerbeer (1791–1864), Große Oper – Deutsche Oper', Schriftenreihe der Hochschule für Musik 'Carl Maria von Weber' Dresden, xxiv (Dresden), 48–69.

Wagner, Cosima, 1976–7. Gregor-Dellin, Martin, and Dietrich Mack, eds., *Cosima Wagner: Die Tagebücher 1869–1883* (2 vols., Munich).

1978–80. *Diaries 1869–1883*, trans. Geoffrey Skelton (2 vols., London).

Wagner, Richard, 1871. *Gesammelte Schriften und Dichtungen* (10 vols., Leipzig) [*GS*].

1963. Martin Gregor-Dellin, ed., *Richard Wagner: Mein Leben* (Munich; trans. Andrew Gray, Cambridge, 1983).

Waidelich, Gerrit, 1996. '"Weder *Italienisch* noch *Französisch*, sondern rein *Deutsch*". Johann Nepomuk von Poißls *Athalia* als Oper "ohngefehr im Genre der Gluck'schen"', in Joachim Veit and Frank Ziegler, eds., *Weber-Studien*, iii (Mainz), 318–46.

Warrack, John, 1987a. 'Französische Elemente in Webers Opern', in Günther Stephan and Hans John, eds., *Carl Maria von Weber und der Gedanke der Nationaloper*, Schriftenreihe der Hochschule für Musik 'Carl Maria von Weber' Dresden, x (Dresden), 277–90.

1987b. 'Mendelssohn's Operas', in Nigel Fortune, ed., *Essays in Honour of Winton Dean* (Cambridge), 263–97.

1994. *Richard Wagner: Die Meistersinger von Nürnberg* (Cambridge).

Weber, Carl Maria von, 1908. Georg Kaiser, ed.: *Sämtliche Schriften von Carl Maria von Weber* (Berlin and Leipzig).

1981. John Warrack, ed.: *Carl Maria von Weber: Writings on Music*, trans. Martin Cooper (Cambridge).

Weisse, Christian Felix, 1806. Christian Ernst Weisse and Samuel Gottlob Frisch, eds., *Selbstbiographie* (Leipzig).

Westernhagen, Curt von, 1973. *Die Entstehung des 'Ring'* (Zurich; trans. Arnold and Mary Whittall, *The Forging of 'The Ring'*, Cambridge, 1976).

White, Pamela C., 1987. 'Two Vampires of 1828', *OQ* 5 (1987), 22–57.

Wichner, Josef, 1897. *Stundenrufe und Lieder der deutschen Nachtwächter* (Regensburg).

Wieland, C. M. von, 1775. 'Versuch über das teutsche Singspiel und einige dahin einschlagende Gegenstände', in *Der teutsche Merkur* 3–4; reprinted in Wilhelm Kurrelmeyer, ed., *Wielands Gesammelte Schriften*, xiv (Berlin, 1928), 74–99.

1818. *Geschichte der Abderiten* (Vienna).

Winckelmann, Johann, 1825–9. *Johann Winckelmanns sämtliche Werke* (12 vols., Donaueschingen; reprint ed. Joseph Eiselein, Osnabrück, 1965).

Winter, Peter von, 1824. *Vollständige Gesangschule* (Mainz).

Wolff, Hellmuth Christian, 1957. *Die Barockoper in Hamburg (1678–1738)* (2 vols., Wolfenbüttel).

Zelm, Klaus, 1981. 'Reinhard Keiser und Georg Philipp Telemann: zum Stilwandel an der frühdeutschen Oper in Hamburg', in *Die Bedeutung Georg Philipp Telemanns für die Entwicklung der europäischen Musikkultur im 18. Jahrhundert: 8. Magdeburger Telemann Festtage*, 1 (Magdeburg), 104–13.

German operas are listed in the alphabetical register, but cross-referred to their composer, where page references will be found.